At a Crossroads

DIRECTIONS IN DEVELOPMENT
Human Development

At a Crossroads

Higher Education in Latin America and the Caribbean

María Marta Ferreyra, Ciro Avitabile, Javier Botero Álvarez, Francisco Haimovich Paz, and Sergio Urzúa

1 2 3 4 20 19 18 17

ISBN (paper): 978-1-4648-1014-5
ISBN (electronic): 978-1-4648-1015-2
DOI: 10.1596/978-1-4648-1014-5

Cover photo: © EFE. Used with the permission of EFE. Further permission required for reuse.
Cover design: Debra Naylor, Naylor Design, Inc.

Library of Congress Cataloging-in-Publication Data has been requested.

Contents

Boxes

Figures

Tables

Acknowledgments

This book was prepared by María Marta Ferreyra (task team leader), Javier Botero Álvarez (co-task team leader), Ciro Avitabile, Francisco Haimovich Paz, and Sergio Urzúa. Important additional contributions were made by Paola Bordón, Juan Esteban Carranza, Jesse Cunha, Ricardo Espinoza, Chao Fu, Carlos Garriga, Ana Gazmuri, Jean-Francois Houde, Rodolfo Manuelli, Christopher Neilson, and Miguel Székely. The team was ably assisted by Angélica Sánchez Díaz, Uriel Kejsefman, Alonso Bucarey, Nathalie González Prieto, Silvia Guallar Artal, Amanda Loyola, Octavio Medina, and Emmanuel Vazquez. The work was conducted under the general guidance of Augusto de la Torre, chief economist for the Latin America and the Caribbean Region of the World Bank, with substantial inputs from Daniel Lederman, deputy regional chief economist, and Reema Nayar, practice manager, Education Global Practice.

The team was fortunate to receive advice and guidance from three distinguished peer reviewers: Eric Bettinger, Francisco Marmolejo, and Hugo Ñopo. While the team is very grateful for the guidance received, these reviewers are not responsible for any remaining errors, omissions, or interpretations. Additional insights from Karthik Athreya, María Paula Gerardino, Clement Joubert, Soo Lee, Mario Macis, Julián Messina, Francisco Pérez Arce, Krzysztof Wozniak, and other participants in a workshop that took place on November 12 and 13, 2015, are gratefully acknowledged. We wish to thank Rita Almeida, Sandra Baum, Vinicius Botelho, Jose Joaquín Brunner, Barbara Bruns, Stephanie Cellini, Matthew Chingos, Laura Chioda, David Deming, Elizabeth Fordham, Ana García de Fanelli, Alieto Guadagni, Ítalo Gutiérrez, Jesko Hentzel, Kevin James, Carlos Medina, Ángel Melguizo, Tatiana Melguizo, Paulo Meyer Nascimento, Renato Pedrosa, Samuel Pienknagura, Christian Posso, Alberto Rodríguez, Jamele Rigolini, Joana Silva, and Juan Vázquez Mora for valuable conversations, comments, and information. We are grateful to Enrique Alasino, Ana Balsa, Marcelo Becerra, Leandro Costa, Michael Drabble, Alexandra Escobar, Tabaré Fernandez, Fernando Landa, Pablo Landoni, André Loureiro, Erick Meave, Harriet Nanyonjo, Tatiana Velasco, and Hongyu Yang for assisting us in our search of country-level information.

The team is grateful to Joseph Coohill for editing the manuscript. Book design, editing, and production were coordinated by the World Bank's formal publishing unit under the supervision of Rumit Pancholi. Last, but not least, the team thanks Ruth Delgado and Jacqueline Larrabure for unfailing administrative support.

July 2016

About the Authors

María Marta Ferreyra is a senior economist in the Office of the Chief Economist for Latin America and the Caribbean of the World Bank. Her research specializes in the economics of education, with special emphasis on the effects of large-scale reforms. Her research has been published in journals such as the *American Economic Review*, the *Journal of Public Economics*, and the *American Economic Journal–Economic Policy*. Before joining the World Bank, she served as a faculty member at the Tepper School of Business at Carnegie Mellon University. She holds a PhD in economics from the University of Wisconsin–Madison.

Ciro Avitabile is a senior economist in the Education Global Practice of the World Bank and a senior lecturer at the University of Surrey in the United Kingdom. He holds a bachelor's degree from Bocconi University and a PhD in economics from University College London. Before joining the World Bank, Dr. Avitabile worked at the Inter-American Development Bank and at the University of Naples. His research focuses on nutrition, cash transfers, and education choices in developing countries. He has published in the *American Economic Journal, Applied Economics*, the *Journal of Human Resources*, and the *Journal of Law and Economics*.

Javier Botero Álvarez is a lead education specialist at the World Bank. He earned a PhD in physics from Louisiana State University in 1986. Before joining the World Bank, he served in several leadership positions in education in Colombia. He started the Research and Special Studies Center at the Escuela Colombiana de Ingeniería, where he served as provost and president. He was the viceminister of education in 2002. He was also the country's first viceminister for higher education, a position in which he served during 2002–07 and 2010–12. Before his public policy service, he held several academic and research positions, including at the University of Freiburg in Germany, Escuela Colombiana de Ingeniería in Bogotá, the Oak Ridge National Laboratory (University of Tennesee) in the United States, the Atomic and Molecular Data Unit at the International Atomic Energy Agency in Vienna, and the University of Ulm in Germany. His physics research has been published in journals such as *Physical Review Letters*, *Physical Review A*, *Journal of Physics B*, and *Zeitschrift fur Physik D*, as well as in several proceedings.

Francisco Haimovich Paz has been an economist in the World Bank Group's Education Global Practice since 2015. Before joining the Education Global Practice, he worked at the Poverty Reduction and Equity Unit and the Human Development Sector Unit in Europe and Central Asia at the World Bank, and for the Inter-American Development Bank. He has also worked as a researcher at the Center for Distributive, Labor and Social Studies at the Universidad Nacional de La Plata in Argentina. He specializes in applied microeconomics, with a particular focus on education, labor markets, and income distribution. His research has been published in the *Journal of Applied Economics* and the *Journal of International Development*. He holds a PhD in economics from the University of California at Los Angeles.

Sergio Urzúa is an associate professor of economics at the University of Maryland. He is also a research associate at the National Bureau of Economic Research, a research fellow at the Institute for the Study of Labor, and an international research fellow at Clapes-UC (Chile). His research focuses on the role of abilities, skills, and uncertainty as determinants of schooling decisions, labor market outcomes, and social behavior. His research in econometrics analyzes selection models with unobserved heterogeneity. His research agenda includes the evaluation of social programs and educational systems in developing economies.

Abbreviations

ACR	access rate
AHELO	Assessment of Higher Education Learning Outcomes
ARWU	Academic Ranking of World Universities
CAE	Credito con Garantía Estatal (State Guaranted Credit, Chile)
CAPE	Caribbean Advanced Proficiency Exam (OECS countries)
CARICOM	Caribbean Community and Common Market
CEDLAS	Centro de Estudios Distributivos Laborales y Sociales (Center for Distributive, Labor and Social Studies, Argentina)
CENEVAL	Centro Nacional de Evaluación para la Educación Superior (National Center for Evaluation of Higher Education, Mexico)
CERES	Centros Regionales para Educación Superior (Regional Centers of Higher Education, Colombia)
CFTs	Centros de formación técnica (Technical training centers, Chile)
CINDA	Centro Interuniversitario de Desarrollo (Inter-University Center of Development)
CLA	College Learning Assessment (United States)
CNA	Comisión Nacional de Acreditación (National Accreditation Commission, Chile)
CNED	Consejo Nacional de Educación (National Education Council, Chile)
CONAPE	Comisión Nacional de Préstamos para Educación (National Comission for Student Loans, Costa Rica)
CONOCER	Consejo Nacional de Normalización y Certificación de Competencias Laborales (National Council for the Normalization and Certification of Competences, Mexico)
CRUCH	Consejo de Rectores de Universidades Chilenas (Council of Chancellors of Chilean Universities, Chile)
DEED	Diretoria de Estatísticas Educacionais (Brazil)
DHS	Demographic and Health Surveys

DiNIECE	Dirección Nacional de Información y Evaluación de la Calidad Educativa (National Council of Information and Evaluation of Education Quality, Argentina)
ENADE	Exame Nacional de Desempenho de Estudantes (National Assessment of Student Achievement, Brazil)
ENAHO	Encuesta Nacional de Hogares (National Household Survey, Peru)
ENEM	Examen Nacional de Ensino Medio (National Assessment of Secondary Education, Brazil)
ENES	Examen Nacional para la Educacion Superior (National Assessment for Higher Education, Ecuador)
EXANI-II	Examenes Nacionales de Ingreso (Entry National Tests, Mexico)
FIES	Fundo de Financiamento Estudantil (Student Financial Fund, Brazil)
FONABE	Fondo Nacional de Becas (National Scholarship Fund, Costa Rica)
FSCU	Fondo Solidario de Credito Universitario (Fund for University Student Loans, Chile)
GDP	gross domestic product
GSA	Graduate Skills Assessment (United States)
HEI	higher education institution
ICETEX	Instituto Colombiano de Crédito Educativo y Estudios Técnicos en el Exterior (Colombian Institute for Student Loans and Study Abroad, Colombia)
IESs	institutos de educación superior (higher education institutes, Peru)
IESTs	instituciones de educación superior tecnológica (higher education technological institutes, Peru)
IPs	Institutos profesionales (professional institutes, Chile)
ISCED	International Standard Classification of Education
ISCED-F	International Standard Classification of Education: Fields of Education and Training
MCESCA	Marco de Cualificaciones para la Educación Superior Centroamericana (Qualifications Framework for Higher Education in Central America)
MIDE	Modelo de Indicadores del Desempeño de la Educación (Model of Indicators of Education Performance, Colombia)
NQF	national qualifications framework
OECD	Organisation for Economic Co-operation and Development
OECS	Organization of Eastern Caribbean States

OPSU	Oficina de Planificación del Sector Universitario (Planning Office for the University Sector, República Bolivariana de Venezuela)
PAA	Prueba de Aptitud Académica (Costa Rica)
PIAAC	Programme for the International Assessment of Adult Competencies
PNBB	Programa Nacional de Becas Bicentenario (Bicentennial Scholarship National Programme, Argentina)
PNBU	Programa Nacional de Becas Universitarias (University Scholarship National Programme, Argentina)
POMA	Prueba de Selección y Orientación Academica (University Selection and Academic Orientation Test, Dominican Republic)
PRONABEC	Programa Nacional de Becas y Crédito Educativo (National Programme for Scholarships and Student Loans, Peru)
PPP	purchasing power parity
ProUni	Programa Universidade para Todos (University For All Programme, Brazil)
PSU	Prueba de Selección Universitaria (University Selection Test, Chile)
QAS	quality assurance system
QS	quality system
SABER	Systems Approach for Better Education Results
SCR	secondary completion rate
SEDLAC	Socio-Economic Database for Latin America and the Caribbean
SENA	Servicio Nacional de Aprendizaje (National Learning Service, Colombia)
SES	socioeconomic status
SIES	Servicio de Información de Educación Superior (Higher Education Information Service, Chile)
SNC	Sistema Nacional de Competencias (National System of Competences, Mexico)
SNGCH	Sistema Nacional de Gestión del Capital Humano (National System for the Management of Human Capital, Colombia)
SNIES	Sistema Nacional de Información de la Educación Superior (National Tertiary Education Information System, Colombia)
SPADIES	Sistema para la Prevención de la Deserción de la Educación (Superior System for the Prevention and Analysis of Dropouts in Tertiary Education Institutions, Colombia)
STEM	science, technology, engineering, and mathematics
ST&I	science, technology, and innovation

SUNEDU	Superintendencia Nacional de Educación Superior Universitaria (University Higher Education National Superintendence, Peru)
TTD	time-to-degree
TVET	technical vocational and education training
UIS	UNESCO Institute for Statistics
UNAM	Universidad Autónoma de Mexico (Mexico)
UNESCO	United Nations Educational, Scientific and Cultural Organization
UWI	University of the West Indies
WAP	working-age population
WVS	World Values Survey

Overview

In the pursuit of growth and equity, no country can afford to ignore higher education. Through higher education, a country forms skilled labor and builds the capacity to generate knowledge and innovation, which boosts productivity and economic growth. Since acquiring greater skills raises a person's productivity and her expected earnings, a good education system is also the basis for achieving greater equity and shared prosperity on a societal level. Particularly in societies mired with persistent and profound inequality, high-quality education can act as "the great equalizer": the ultimate channel of equal opportunities, and the ultimate hope for parents who long for a better future for their children.

In this study, we investigate three important aspects of higher education in Latin America and the Caribbean: *quality*, *variety*, and *equity*. A good higher education system offers quality, variety, and equity to maximize students' potential given their innate ability, interests, motivation, and academic readiness at the end of high school. Since people differ in these aspects, and the economy needs various types of skills, a *variety* of offerings allows students to find their best match. A good higher education system trains engineers as well as technicians—economists as well as administrative assistants. In addition, a good higher education system offers *quality* programs that maximize students' potential, given their best match. Because the mere availability of variety and quality does not guarantee students' access to or success in them, a higher education system displays *equity* when students have access to equal opportunities.

Societies vary in how they determine equity in higher education, since they differ in what they consider "fair." For instance, some societies consider it fair to give students of the same academic readiness access to the same opportunities, whereas others consider it fair to give all students access to the same opportunities, despite differences in their academic readiness or other characteristics. Regardless of their view of equity, higher education systems face the fact that quality, variety, and equity are interdependent. For instance, providing higher education access to disadvantaged students may improve equity, but possibly at the cost of quality if those students are limited to low-quality higher education options.

Hence, equity is best served by giving students access to high-quality programs at which they can succeed, an outcome that is more likely when a variety of programs are offered.

Higher education in the region has expanded dramatically in the last 15 years as the average gross enrollment rate (defined as the ratio between higher education enrollment and the population ages 18–24 years)[1] has grown from 21 percent to 43 percent between 2000 and 2013. Currently, the system includes approximately 20 million students, 10,000 institutions, and 60,000 programs. The higher education system has a rich history that dates back to the early 1500s, with the founding of the University of Santo Domingo, followed by the (then) Pontifical University of San Marcos (Lima) and the Royal and Pontifical University of Mexico (Brunner 1990).

Today, higher education is at a crossroads. The large expansion experienced since the early 2000s has given rise to a new, complex landscape. Concerned with access and social mobility, policy makers expanded the system at a time of economic growth, fiscal abundance, and a rising middle class. As a result, access grew for all students, but particularly those from the low- and middle-income segments. These "new" students, who were previously underrepresented in higher education, constitute a critical piece of the new landscape, as are the higher education institutions (HEIs) and programs serving them.

Concerns about quality loom over the large equity gains experienced by higher education systems in the region. The rapid expansion of the systems, the characteristics of the "new" students, and perhaps the lax regulation of some HEIs have led many to question the quality of their programs and, thus, the equity of a system in which not every student gains access to a high-quality option.

At this crossroads, Latin America and the Caribbean faces an opportunity not to be missed. The policy decisions made 10 or 15 years ago have had profound consequences on today's environment. Today's decisions will have long-lasting, far-reaching consequences on the region's future as well.

The remainder of this overview is organized as follows. We begin by characterizing the role and capabilities of each agent in the higher education system (students, institutions, and the policy maker) as well as the distinctive characteristics of the higher education sector from an economic perspective. Then we present the main facts documented in the report, and discuss the main lessons learned through the report's analytical work. We conclude with policy considerations.

It is important to note that the study focuses on one role of the higher education system: the instruction of undergraduate students. While higher education systems have other roles (for example, the production and dissemination of research, the formation of graduate students and new researchers, and extension programs geared toward the community at large), not all HEIs take up these roles to the same extent, and there are scant data on these other roles. Furthermore, the instruction of undergraduate students is arguably the main role of HEIs in Latin America and the Caribbean. In addition, this study focuses mostly on the private returns to higher education. Although higher education yields returns to society as a whole, for data-related and technical reasons we restrict the scope to private returns. Although higher education finance is an important aspect of higher education systems, a detailed study of this issue is beyond the scope of the current report.

Students, Institutions, and the Policy Maker

Because higher education is at a crossroads, it is important to recall what the agents in higher education (students and their families, HEIs, and the policy maker) can and cannot do, as well as their motives to engage in higher education.

The final outcome reached by a *student* in higher education (for example, employment, final GPA, or admission to graduate school) results from the contribution of multiple inputs. These include her effort, innate ability, and academic readiness. They also include inputs provided by the HEI, such as professors, peers, labs, and facilities. The important point is that individual academic readiness and effort are indeed inputs, and policies that merely give access to higher education without being mindful of students' academic readiness—or without providing incentives for student effort—will fall short of their potential benefits.

The possibility that students might not graduate brings us to another important point, namely that higher education is a risky investment. This risk affects some students more than others, since some students are less academically ready for higher education and more likely to drop out than others.

When making decisions, students and their families view higher education programs as "bundles" consisting of such elements as the program, peer students, student effort requirements, expected returns in the labor market, expected social and labor market connections, and distance to desirable locations. As this report documents, not all students care about these elements equally. For instance, high-ability students tend to care more about their peers' ability than their lower ability counterparts.[2] In addition, a distinctive regional feature is students' strong preference for attending an HEI close to home.[3] These two elements have important consequences on market structure.

While some students pursue higher education to improve their economic prospects, others seek the opportunity to learn a subject of their interest and are less concerned about economic payoffs. Still others seek the "college experience," roughly defined as immersion in a new environment, with new peers, exposed to new ideas and perspectives. The multiplicity of goals is a challenge for the policy maker seeking to regulate the sector (Deming and Figlio 2016). Yet regardless of their goals, many students conduct a cost-benefit analysis when deciding whether to pursue higher education and what option to choose. If they attend college, they will incur the cost of tuition and other expenses, such as books and transportation, and will receive a college graduate's salary upon graduation. If they do not attend college, they will likely earn a high school graduate salary. The ability to design efficient, responsible, and equitable funding systems is perhaps the most obvious way for the policy maker to affect students' decisions, although it is not the only one.

Regardless of how the policy maker intervenes, the fact remains that her intervention is necessary because left to its own devices, the market will not achieve the social optimum of maximizing each person's potential and meeting the economy's skill needs. Several reasons contribute to this outcome. First, higher education provides a benefit not only to the person who receives it but also to society at large. Even when the market rewards a higher education graduate for her output, society also enjoys the contributions from her innovations, knowledge production, and research findings. Moreover, society benefits from the presence of higher education graduates in ways not fully rewarded by the market. For instance, these graduates might be more involved citizens and raise healthier children. In the presence of such *externalities*, students contemplating higher education will not internalize the full social benefits and will invest less in it than the social optimum.

Second, students with the greatest potential to benefit from a particular program may not be able to afford it. These *liquidity constraints* for talented individuals detract not only from equity but also from efficiency, since the economy fails to realize its full productive potential. A cautionary note: while liquidity constraints may be an obstacle to access, another may be the lack of academic readiness for higher education work. As documented in this report, students from lower income families tend to be less academically ready than those from higher income families, which may be evidence of an inequitable primary and secondary education system.

While the credit market could, in principle, mitigate short-term liquidity constraints, this market is imperfect. Higher education loans typically lack the collateral or guarantee required by financial institutions, since students borrow to finance an investment embodied in themselves. Moreover, a higher education loan is risky for a bank, since the bank only has noisy information on the loan's profitability. Similarly, the student may be uncertain over her graduation probability or the long-term returns of her higher education program. As a result, left to its own devices the credit market will play a smaller role, if any, in financing higher education than in the social optimum.

Third, higher education is a complex "product" characterized by strong *information asymmetries*, and it is difficult for students and parents to assess the quality and variety of offerings. Consider, for instance, a student interested in biology who is trying to choose a program suited for work in industry. She might not know what specific programs would train her better for industry than for research. She might see similar programs and not know how to differentiate among them, perhaps because the HEIs themselves choose not to reveal the relevant information. Or she might know that graduates from a particular program obtain high-paying jobs after graduation, yet not know whether this is due to the program's ability to select high-performing students, or to the rigor of its training and instruction. The ensuing lack of information leads some students to make suboptimal choices, such as enrolling in low-quality programs while also taking on heavy college loans.

To further complicate matters, some students and parents are better than others at "information processing," namely at assessing the quality and variety of higher education programs, and at comparing long-term costs and benefits of alternative career paths and financing options. Such disparities, associated with parental background and education (Castleman 2013; Horn et al. 2003; Tornatzky et al. 2002), only exacerbate the inequities. Cognitive biases, too, prevent students from making sound decisions, by making them overestimate the returns from some programs or be overconfident about their chances of success.[4] In Latin America and the Caribbean, where transferring across programs is rather difficult, the cost of making the wrong decision can be quite high. This raises the stakes on a decision in which there is no opportunity at "learning by doing," since most individuals make this decision only once (or just a few times) over their lifetime.

Information asymmetries, information-processing difficulties, cognitive biases, and decision-making costs can interfere with the higher education system's ability to form the skills required in the labor market. For instance, an economy may suffer a shortage of computer programmers yet have a surplus of journalists. Even though market wages should act as indicators of relative scarcity to future graduates (that is, computer programmers should earn more, on average, than journalists), students may not use this information when making choices, or may not realize they lack the academic readiness necessary to pursue the higher paying program.

Fourth, higher education markets feature *imperfect competition*. Setting up and running an HEI is costly, a force that would naturally concentrate the system around relatively few providers and give them market power. The actual degree of concentration largely depends on legal and regulatory barriers to the entry of HEIs; if barriers are low, the system might experience considerable entry of new providers and relatively low concentration. Yet even if entry is plentiful, the fact that each HEI offers a *differentiated product* (for example, geographic location, program type, student peer ability, curriculum focus, academic rigor, and expectations) allows HEIs to compete along multiple dimensions, and gives each HEI a certain degree of market power over the students that choose it.

For instance, most students in the region attend an HEI close to home. This gives HEIs a considerable market power in their geographic areas. Similarly, higher education markets in the United States were quite localized a few decades ago and, as they became geographically more integrated, they became more competitive (Hoxby 2009). Hence, while bringing higher education to additional locales can raise access for students in those places, special care is needed to prevent those HEIs from exploiting their natural market power by offering low-quality services.

Another instance of imperfect competition arises through tuition subsidies for students enrolled in public HEIs, a practice common to all countries in the region, some of which go as far as offering tuition-free public HEIs. When policy makers subsidize public HEIs but do not provide financial aid for private HEIs, they contribute to creating a captive demand for public HEIs, composed of students who have no other choice. While making education available to such students might be desirable, the ensuing market power for public HEIs deserves the policy maker's close attention.

Of much concern, too, is the market segment formed by students who are poorly informed about higher education programs and returns, are financially illiterate, and are academically unprepared for higher education. These students may be drawing from their families' meager savings or from student loans to finance their higher education. This segment naturally invites the entry of low-quality, high-price HEIs, and deserves the policy maker's close attention.

Furthermore, in typical competitive markets, firm exit disciplines the market by forcing low-demand products (which, presumably, have the lowest quality) out of the market. Yet a crucial difference between such markets and the higher education market is that the exit of an HEI can be quite costly for students, particularly those enrolled in the HEI. Societies, then, cannot afford frequent HEI exits.

Because students vary in income, ability, place of residence, gender, parental education, preferences, and goals pursued in higher education, there is room for the system to offer a wide range of higher education options. As a result, students *sort* across HEIs and programs. Sorting has three important consequences. The first is that not every student has access to the same options. Low-ability students, for instance, cannot gain access to selective programs, although this does not necessarily mean that their programs will be of low quality. Because high-ability students prefer attending higher education with other high-ability students, forcing some selective programs to admit lower ability students will lead some high-ability students to switch to other programs.

The second consequence of sorting is that the market becomes segmented by HEI type, and not every segment expands during an expansion. Since the selective segment expands mostly to admit high-ability students, it falls on the nonselective segment to admit lower ability students. Because there are many lower ability students, nonselective programs and HEIs will compete for them, sometimes fiercely.

The third consequence of sorting is that analytical or policy-related efforts on higher education must be mindful of the sector's vast heterogeneity and avoid one-size-fits all approaches. Heterogeneity among students, institutions, and programs is a theme of our study.

Some Stylized Facts

At the current crossroads, it is useful to describe some stylized facts from the recent expansion. These facts show a complex landscape with bright spots yet also cautionary notes.

The Region Has Experienced a Large, Rapid Expansion in Higher Education Since the Early 2000s

On average, the higher education gross enrollment rate in Latin America and the Caribbean rose from 17 percent in 1991 to 21 percent in 2000 and to 40 percent in 2010. Since the 2000s, the expansion has been large and rapid

Figure O.1 International Benchmarking of Gross Enrollment Rates, 2000, 2005, and 2010

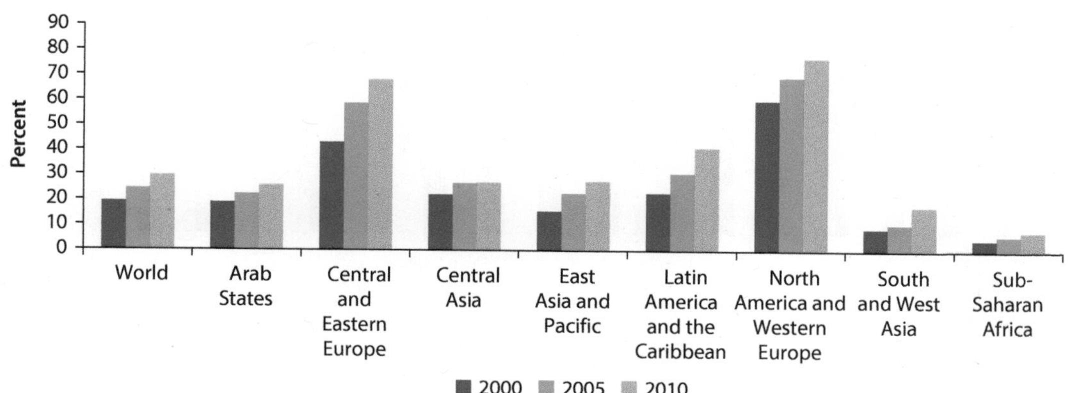

Source: United Nations Educational, Scientific and Cultural Organization (UNESCO), http://data.uis.unesco.org/?queryid=142.
Note: Total enrollment in tertiary education (ISCED 5–8), regardless of age, expressed as a percentage of the total population of the five-year age group following the theoretical age of secondary school graduation. For each region, the figure shows the weighted average over the corresponding countries.

by international standards (figure O.1). For example, although Central Asia had a similar gross enrollment rate as Latin America and the Caribbean in 2000, it had reached only 27 percent in 2010. The enrollment growth in Latin America and the Caribbean has been accompanied by a large supply-side expansion. Since the early 2000s, approximately 2,300 new HEIs have opened and 30,000 new programs have been created. Hence, approximately one-quarter of the current HEIs and half of the current programs have been created since the early 2000s.

While enrollment rates measure the number of students *currently* enrolled, in much of the study we focus on another indicator: the access rate. This captures the fraction of individuals ages 18–24 years who have *ever* had higher education access. While some of those individuals might be currently enrolled, others might have already finished their course of study or might have dropped out.[5] Access grew dramatically as well, from 18 percent to 28 percent between 2000 and 2013. We can decompose the access rate growth into a portion resulting from greater high school graduation rates and a portion resulting from greater college entry rates on the part of high school graduates. The decomposition indicates that, on average, 78 percent of the increased access rates can be attributed to greater high school graduation, although with large variation across countries (figure O.2).

Indeed, the increase in college entry rates explains most of the growth in the very countries where access grew the most, such as Chile, Colombia, Ecuador, and Peru. In these countries, policy makers implemented aggressive policies aimed at expanding access. In addition, the private sector played an important role, and policies such as student loans and scholarships facilitated access to private HEIs.

Figure O.2 Decomposition of Changes in the Access Rate between 2000 and 2013

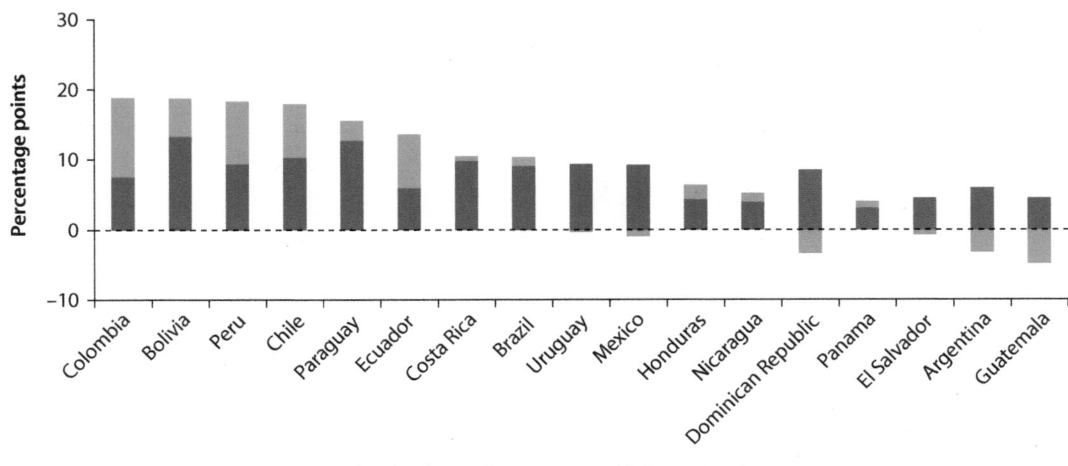

Source: World Bank calculations based on SEDLAC.
Note: The vertical bars show the change in access rate, in percentage points. Change is computed as the difference between circa 2013 and circa 2000. In each bar, the orange portion corresponds to the change explained by changes in the higher education entry rate, and the blue portion corresponds to the change explained by changes in the secondary school completion rate.

Higher Education Access Became More Equal, Although Access Is Still More Prevalent at Higher Income Levels

Although higher education is the educational level with the most unequal access in the region (figure O.3, panel a), there has been substantial progress over the last 15 years, with increasing higher education participation among low- and particularly middle-income groups (figure O.3, panel b). While the poorest 50 percent of the population (B50) represented only 16 percent of higher education students in 2000, this group constituted approximately 24 percent of higher education students in 2012. Based on our estimates, an additional 3 million students from B50 are now enrolled in higher education relative to that in 2000. Overall, B50 students account for about 45 percent of the enrollment growth. Thus, the average student whose representation has grown in higher education (the "new" student) comes from low-income families, and is less academically ready than her more advantaged peers.

Despite the more equal access, youth from the top income quintile are still 45 percentage points more likely to gain higher education access than youths in the bottom quintile. Nonetheless, 56 percent of this gap can be explained by the poorer youths' lower high school graduation rates (figure O.4). In other words, those youths are less likely to gain access to higher education mostly because they do not graduate from high school. Furthermore, a similar picture emerges for the access gap between the top income quintile and the second, third, and fourth quintiles.

Closing the high school graduation gap, however, will not eliminate the higher education access gap because of the remaining gap in college entry (or enrollment)

Figure O.3 Inequality in Access in Latin America and the Caribbean, by Education Level, circa 2000 and 2012

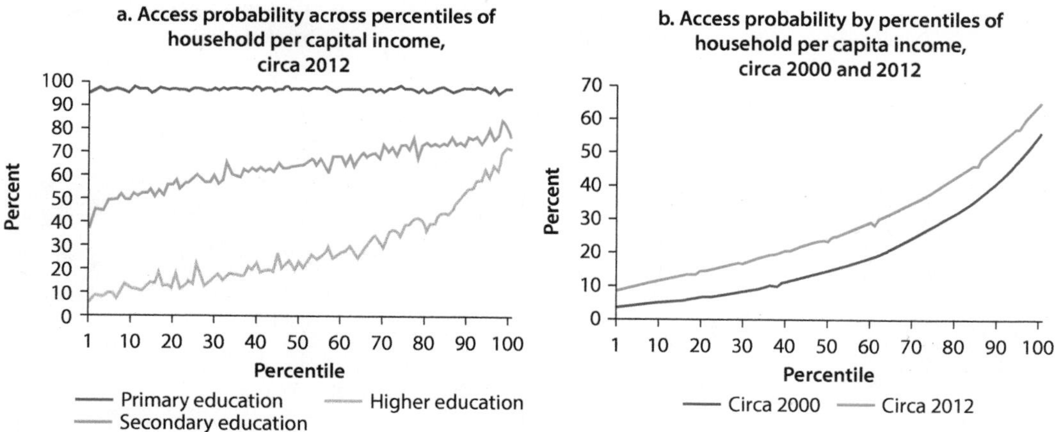

Source: World Bank calculations using SEDLAC.
Note: The probability of access to higher education is the share of individuals ages 18–24 years who have ever had access to higher education. The probability of enrollment in secondary education is the share of individuals ages 12–18 years who have ever had access to secondary education. The probability of enrollment in primary education is the share of individuals ages 6–12 years who have ever had access to primary education. The figure reports simple averages over the countries' indicators.

Figure O.4 Decomposition of Access Gaps in Higher Education among Youths Ages 18–24 Years, Latin America and the Caribbean, circa 2013

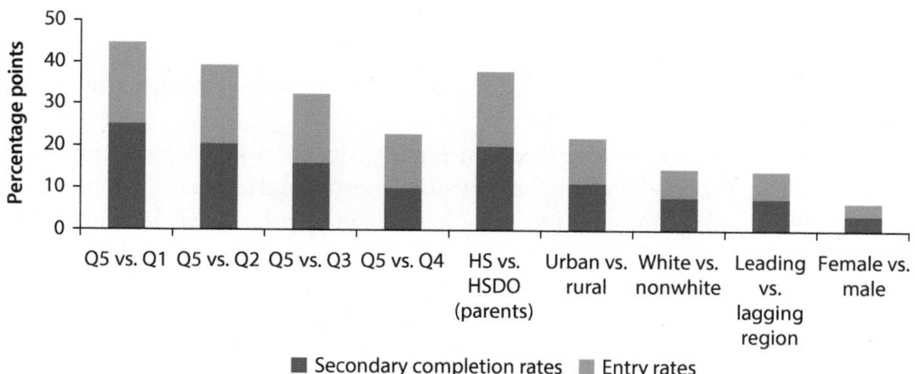

Source: World Bank calculations using SEDLAC.
Note: Each vertical bar depicts the access gap between youths of two different groups. For instance, the first bar indicates that youths from the top quintile are 45 percentage points more likely to gain access to higher education than youths from the bottom quintile. In each bar, the blue portion indicates the gap due to secondary completion rates; the orange portion indicates the gap resulting from higher education entry rates. Each bar depicts the simple average across countries.
HS = high school (completed); HSDO = high school dropout; Q = quintile (Q5 is the richest; Q1 is the poorest). Leading (lagging) region refers to regions where higher education access is above (below) the national access median.

rates *among high school graduates*. Data from Colombia show that differences in academic readiness explain 41 percent of the entry gap between the top and bottom income bracket among high school graduates, and differences in academic readiness and maternal education explain 71 percent of the gap (figure O.5, panel a). In other words, not all high school graduates are equally ready for college.

Figure O.5 Higher Education Entry Rate Gaps and Academic Readiness, Colombia, 2009

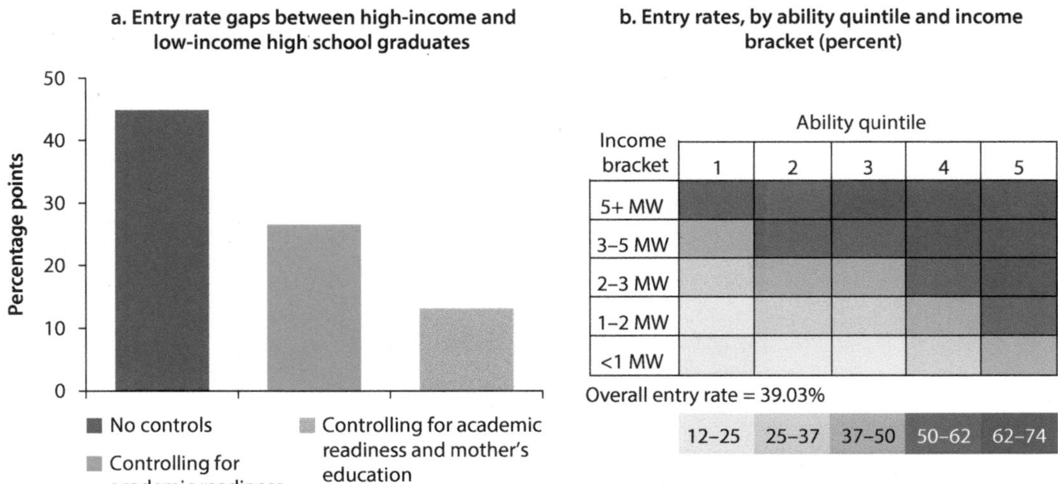

Source: World Bank calculations using Saber 11 and SPADIES, and Carranza and Ferreyra 2017.
Note: The entry rate is the percent of high school graduates taking Saber 11 in 2009 who enter college within five years of finishing high school. Panel a shows the gap in entry rates between students from high-income families (family income is 5 or more times the minimum wage) and from low-income families (family income is below the minimum wage). We report the unconditional gap (blue bar), the gap conditional on Saber 11 (orange bar), and the gap conditional on Saber 11 and mother's education (green bar). Academic readiness is proxied by the Saber 11 score, standardized by semester year. Panel b shows college entry rates by ability quintile (based on Saber 11 score) and family income bracket of high school graduates. MW = minimum wage.

As a result, college entry rates are lower for lower ability students, regardless of their income (figure O.5, panel b).

Contrary to popular perception that higher education spending is regressive because higher income students benefit disproportionately from it, we find that current higher education spending is (at least slightly) progressive because of the increased presence of low- and middle-income students. Furthermore, a back-of-the-envelope calculation indicates that the expenditures associated with *expanding* higher education coverage are four times more progressive than the *average* higher education spending.

The Private Sector Played a Critical Role in the Higher Education Expansion

On average, the market share of private HEIs rose from 43 percent to 50 percent between the early 2000s and 2013. Most of the new HEIs and programs have been opened by the private sector (figures O.6 and O.7). To serve more students, HEIs can either expand their existing programs or open new ones. In countries with available data, we observe that while public HEIs have been more likely to expand existing programs than open new ones, the opposite has been true for private HEIs.

Private HEIs open new programs for multiple reasons. Sometimes they open a nonselective version of a selective program offered by another institution (as is the case of nonselective law programs for students who would not be admitted to selective law programs). Other times they offer a more appealing, but also

Figure O.6 Change in the Number of Public and Private HEIs, Latin America and the Caribbean, circa 2000–13

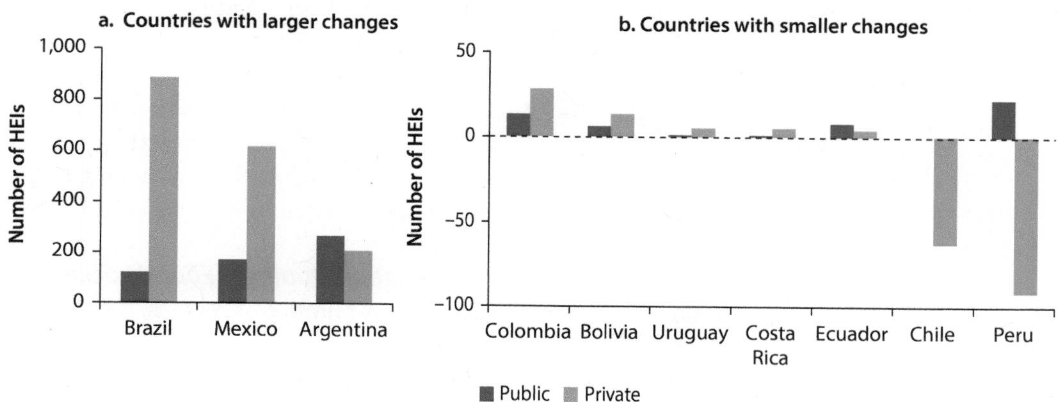

Source: Countries' administrative information; see annex 5A for detailed information.
Note: The figure depicts the change between circa 2000 and circa 2013 of the number of public and private HEIs. The large decrease in the number of private HEIs in Chile is mostly explained by the closing of technological institutes. In Peru, it is explained by the closing of teacher education institutions. Country-specific notes on the counting of HEIs: Chile: new branches of existing HEIs are not counted as new HEIs for consistency with other countries. Colombia: Servicio Nacional de Aprendizaje (SENA) and institutions specialized in graduate education are not included; HEIs are identified by Sistema Nacional de Información de la Educación Superior (SNIES) code rather than by name. Mexico: institutions specialized in graduate programs are included; exclusively online institutions are not. Bolivia and Ecuador: only universities are included. Costa Rica: five international HEIs are not included because of a lack of enrollment data. HEI = higher education institution.

Figure O.7 Change in the Number of Programs in Public and Private HEIs, Latin America and the Caribbean, circa 2000–13

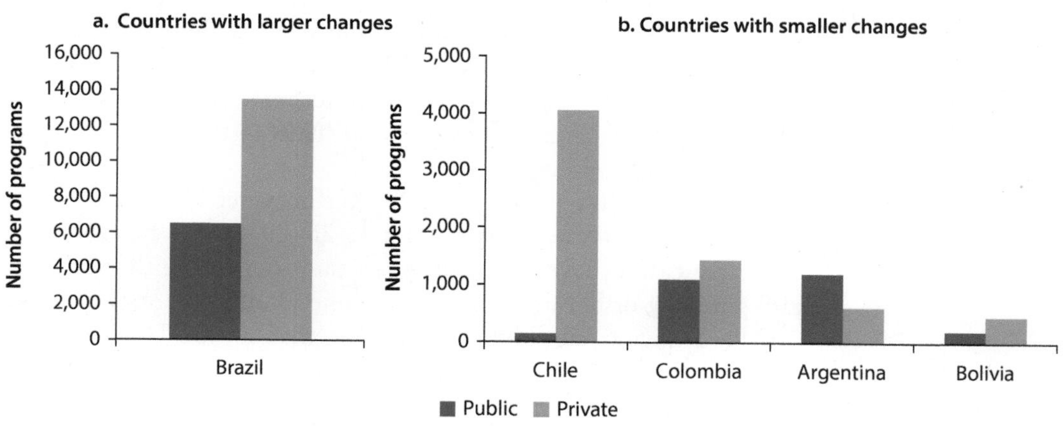

Source: Countries' administrative information; see annex 5A for detailed information.
Note: Data pertain to the following years: Argentina (2005, 2013), Bolivia (2000, 2011), Brazil (2001, 2013), Chile (2005, 2015), and Colombia (2000, 2013).

narrower, version of a program already offered by another institution (for example, when opening sports journalism even though a social communication program offered by a competing HEI provides some of the same skills). Yet in other cases they offer a structured, predictable environment that suits some students better than that of public HEIs, or that make both the student and the HEI more accountable for their actions.[6]

Whereas private HEIs draw higher income students than public HEIs, on average both public and private HEIs now serve a higher share of low-income students than in the early 2000s. Furthermore, both public and private HEIs now serve a higher share of students residing outside urban areas.

Despite their relatively low income, these "new" students have been able to afford private higher education because of the student loans and scholarships implemented in some countries and because of the recent growth in family incomes. Indeed, the greater ability to afford higher education has been another manifestation of the rise of the middle class documented by Ferreira et al. (2013).

When Measured by Outcomes, Higher Education Quality Is Found Lacking

Measuring education quality is challenging for a number of reasons. One reason is a lack of agreement over the expected outcomes of education. While standard datasets often measure outcomes such as higher education completion and earnings after graduation, they rarely measure other outcomes. Hence, choices of quality measures are largely dictated by data availability.

Another critical challenge when measuring education's quality is disentangling the contribution of the different inputs, which is necessary to quantify the distinct contribution of HEIs. For instance, if we measure higher education's output for a particular student as her score in an end-of-college competence exam, then inputs consist of (a) the student's ability, effort, and academic readiness for higher education work; (b) the ability and effort of her peers; and (c) the HEI's *value added* through teaching, training, and provision of materials such as lab equipment. It would be informative to measure the value added of HEIs to outcomes such as end-of-college competence exams and graduates' wages. The necessary data are generally not available; even when available, the resulting value added measures are highly sensitive to estimation techniques and sample selection (Melguizo et al. 2017; Shavelson et al. 2016). Thus, in this report we focus on the system's outcomes and inputs.

Judging from its outcomes, the system's performance is disappointing. On average, about half of the population ages 25–29 years who have ever started higher education have not completed their degree—either because they are still studying or because they have dropped out (figure O.8). Only Mexico and Peru have a completion rate near that of the United States (equal to 65 percent). Furthermore, the completion rate has declined over time, as individuals ages 60–65 years had an average completion rate equal to 73 percent (Szekely 2016).

Using administrative data from Colombia, we have estimated that about 37 percent of the students starting a bachelor's program drop out of the higher education system.[7,8] The fraction rises to about 53 percent among students who start short-cycle programs, a finding that has strong implications for variety.[9] Perhaps not surprisingly, lower income and lower ability students are more likely to drop out than their more advantaged peers.

Moreover, about 36 percent of all dropouts in Colombia leave the system at the end of their first year (figure O.9), in contrast to approximately 15 percent

Figure O.8 Completion Rates for Youths Ages 25–29 Years, Latin America and the Caribbean, circa 2013

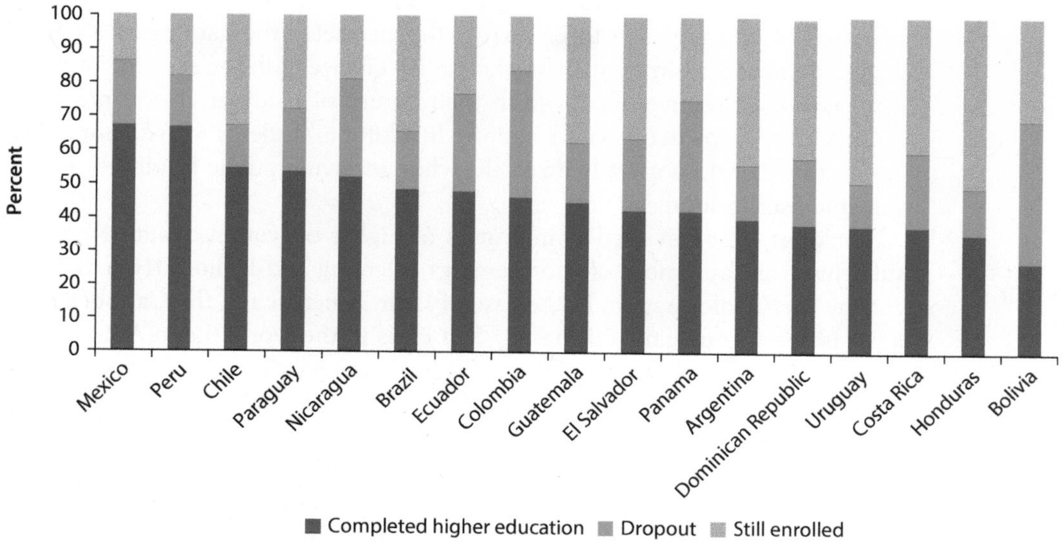

Source: World Bank calculations based on SEDLAC.
Note: For each country, individuals ages 25–29 years who have ever started higher education are classified into three groups: those who completed their program, those who dropped out, and those who are still enrolled. Completion rates are estimated as the ratio between youths ages 25–29 years who completed a higher education program and the number of people ages 25–29 years who ever started a higher education program.

Figure O.9 Percent of Students Who Drop Out of the Higher Education System in Each Year, Relative to All Dropouts, Colombia, 2006

Source: World Bank calculations based on SPADIES.
Note: The figure shows the percentage of students who drop out of the system in each year of college, relative to all students who drop out. For example, 35.5 percent of all students who drop out do so during their first year. Data corresponds to the cohort of students who started their first program in the first semester of 2006.

in the United States. Despite the concentration of dropouts at the beginning of their college career, almost 30 percent of all dropouts leave the system after spending four years in it.

For the countries with available data, time-to-degree (TTD) is high (on average, 36 percent longer than the stipulated time); in some countries, students take twice as long to graduate as they are supposed to. Although average TTD is comparable to that in the United States, the fact that the statutory duration of Latin American and Caribbean programs is typically longer than that of U.S.

programs means that students spend more years in higher education in the former region, thus facing a higher opportunity cost in terms of foregone salaries. When they take too long to graduate, students delay the earning of a college graduate salary and imperil their graduation chances (although some students may have an incentive not to finish their course of study given the prevailing returns to incomplete higher education). In addition, students who do not graduate on time (or do not graduate at all) while receiving public funding consume valuable fiscal resources.

Rankings are often used as indicators of higher education quality. Although suffering from a number of shortcomings (Deming and Figlio 2016), they still convey useful information. In the case of Latin America and the Caribbean, the news is not encouraging. Of the top 500 HEIs in the world, Latin America and the Caribbean has about 10; Africa is the only region with fewer HEIs in the top 500 (figure O.10).

When Measured by Inputs, the Higher Education Quality Picture Is Mixed

A critical input in higher education (and, indeed, in education in general) is student ability. In this report we define a student's ability broadly to include not only her innate talent but also her academic readiness for higher education, as measured by her performance in high school exit or higher education entry exams. Based on this definition, a "low-ability" student might be one who is innately talented but received low-quality elementary and secondary education and is thus poorly prepared for college. Since family income and student ability are positively correlated, low-income students are, on average, low-ability students. Thus, higher education systems in Latin America and the Caribbean have absorbed a large number of students with poor academic preparation for higher education work. Any conclusions about possible output deterioration must take this "input deterioration" into account as well.

Professors are another critical input. As figure O.11 shows, on average the student-faculty ratio in the region is in line with that of developed countries and comparator countries in Eastern and Central Europe and in East Asia and

Figure O.10 Universities in the ARWU Top 500 Ranking, by Region, 2014

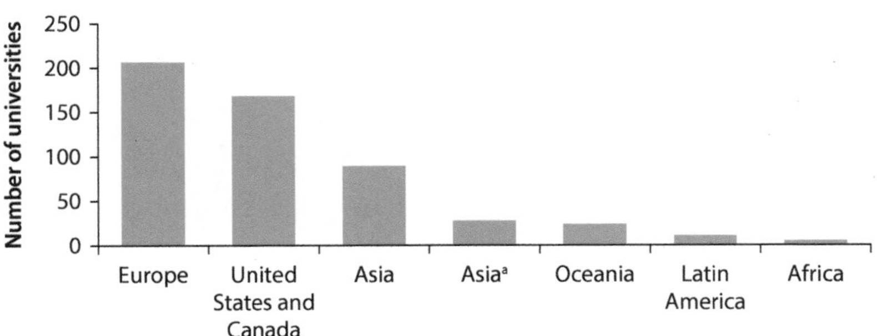

Source: Academic Ranking of World Universities 2014. Shanghai Ranking Consultancy, http://www.shanghairanking.com/.
a. Minus Japan and China.

Figure O.11 Student-Faculty Ratio, circa 2013

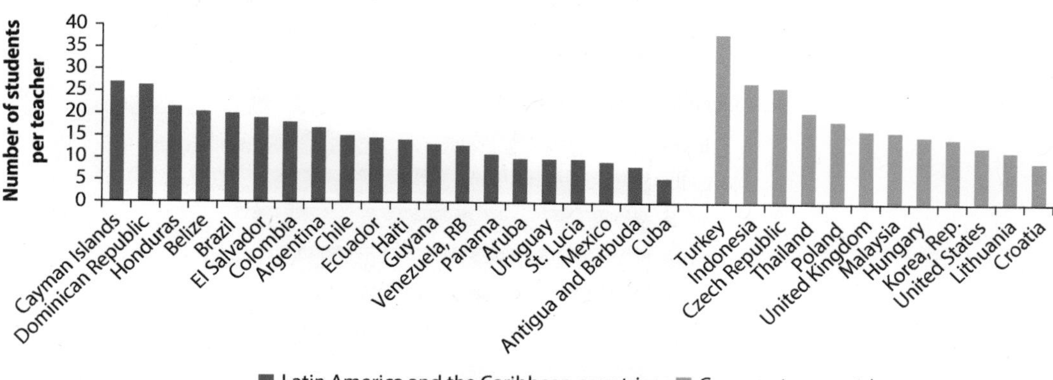

Source: United Nations Educational, Scientific and Cultural Organization (UNESCO), http://data.uis.unesco.org/index.aspx?queryid=180.

the Pacific. But unlike countries in the developed world, the Latin America and the Caribbean region spends a larger share of its higher education spending in faculty and staff salaries (as opposed to facilities, materials, and equipment). Relative to other professionals who graduated from HEIs in Latin America and the Caribbean, graduates who become professors fare better, on average, in salaries, and work fewer hours. They are more likely to be unionized and enjoy pension and health-care benefits through their job (figures O.12 and O.13). This, coupled with the large share of higher education spending devoted to salaries, suggests that unionized faculty and staff may have high bargaining power in several countries.

Average per-student spending is lower, in absolute terms, than in the developed world or comparator East Asia and Pacific countries, although it is in line with comparator Central and Eastern European countries (figure O.14, panel a). To the extent that high-quality faculty, labs, and equipment are costly, they are largely out of reach for the Latin American and Caribbean region. At the same time, when measured against gross domestic product (GDP) per capita, per-student spending in higher education is in line with that in the developed world. This indicates that the region is making a similar effort (relative to income) as the developed world even though it is poorer (figure O.14, panel b). Furthermore, in many countries in the region, per-student spending relative to income is only slightly below the East Asia and Pacific's average, but is well above that in North America, Western Europe, and Central and Eastern Europe.

In recent years, most countries in the region have implemented quality assurance processes and established accreditation agencies. Although the evidence on their impact is mixed, perhaps indicating the importance of design issues, these agencies have been able to establish and enforce minimum input requirements on faculty, curricula, and infrastructure. Based on such requirements, the agencies

Figure O.12 Income Percentile of the Median Higher Education Professor and Graduate, 2012

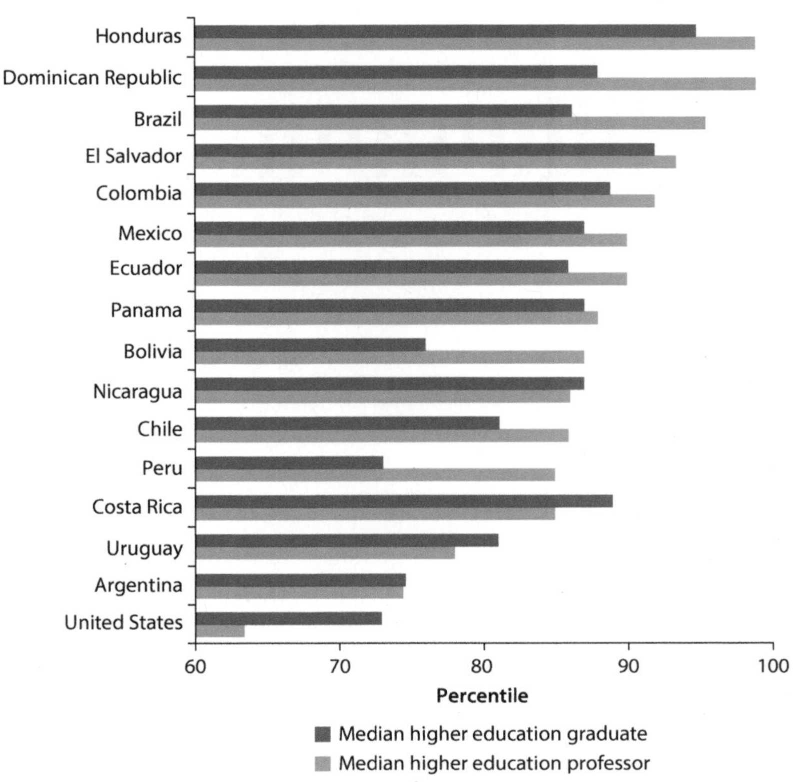

Source: World Bank calculations using SEDLAC (Latin America and the Caribbean) and IPUMS (Integrated Public Use Microdata Series; United States).
Note: To identify professors in the household surveys, we combine information on main economic activity, sector of employment, and level of education. Specifically, we consider an individual to be a professor if (a) she or he reports being employed as a higher education professor; or (b) she or he reports being employed in higher education and has graduated from a higher education program.

have closed some existing low-quality programs and prevented the opening of additional low-quality programs.

Thus, judging quality based on inputs depicts a region that (a) spends (relative to income) and staffs its classrooms in line with the developed world and even better than some of its comparators, although perhaps less efficiently; (b) has incorporated a large amount of students with poor academic preparation for higher education work; and (c) has implemented quality assurance and accreditation processes.

There Is More Variety of Institutions and Programs, But Still Little Variety of Fields of Study

During the expansion, the system has acquired greater variety in multiple dimensions. The market share of private and nonuniversity HEIs has risen in most

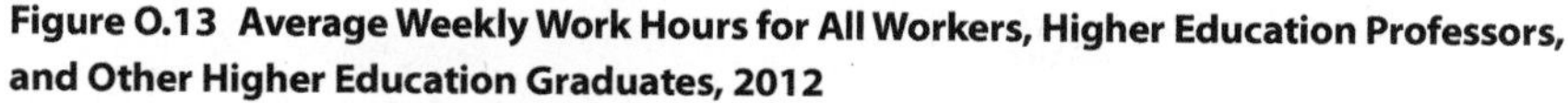

Figure O.13 Average Weekly Work Hours for All Workers, Higher Education Professors, and Other Higher Education Graduates, 2012

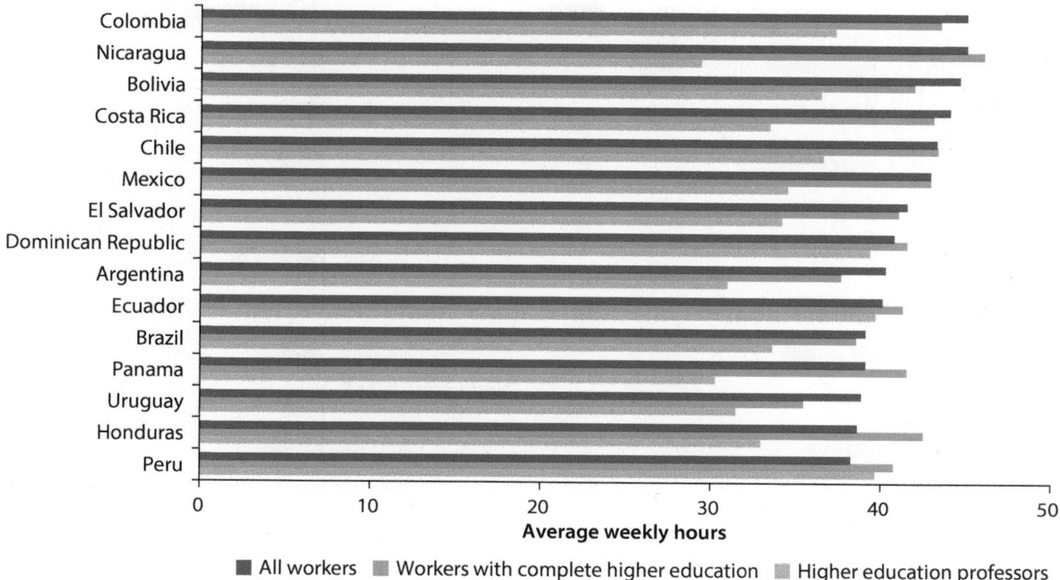

Source: World Bank calculations based on SEDLAC.

countries (figures O.15 and O.16), as has the market share of short-cycle programs. The greater number of programs has expanded the set of options for all students, but more so for the "new" students. Furthermore, higher education has expanded to new locales. This increase in variety has stimulated the entry of many students into the system.

At the same time, variety is lacking in one important dimension: across fields (table O.1). On average, Latin America and the Caribbean graduates a lower share of scientists, and a higher share of teachers, than the United States, the United Kingdom, and comparator countries. It graduates a lower share of engineers than comparator countries, and a higher share of individuals with a business, law, or social science degree than the United States or the United Kingdom. Some of these trends may have become stronger over time, since most new programs have opened in business, law, and social sciences.

As Lederman et al. (2014) point out, historically, students in the region have had a greater tendency to focus on social sciences than students in places such as the United States or the United Kingdom. But they also point out that Latin America and the Caribbean's deficit of scientists and engineers may be related to the region's low innovation relative to the developed world.[10] Given the low flow of graduates from these fields into the region's workforce, this deficit may persist for a while.[11]

Figure O.14 Higher Education Spending, 2009

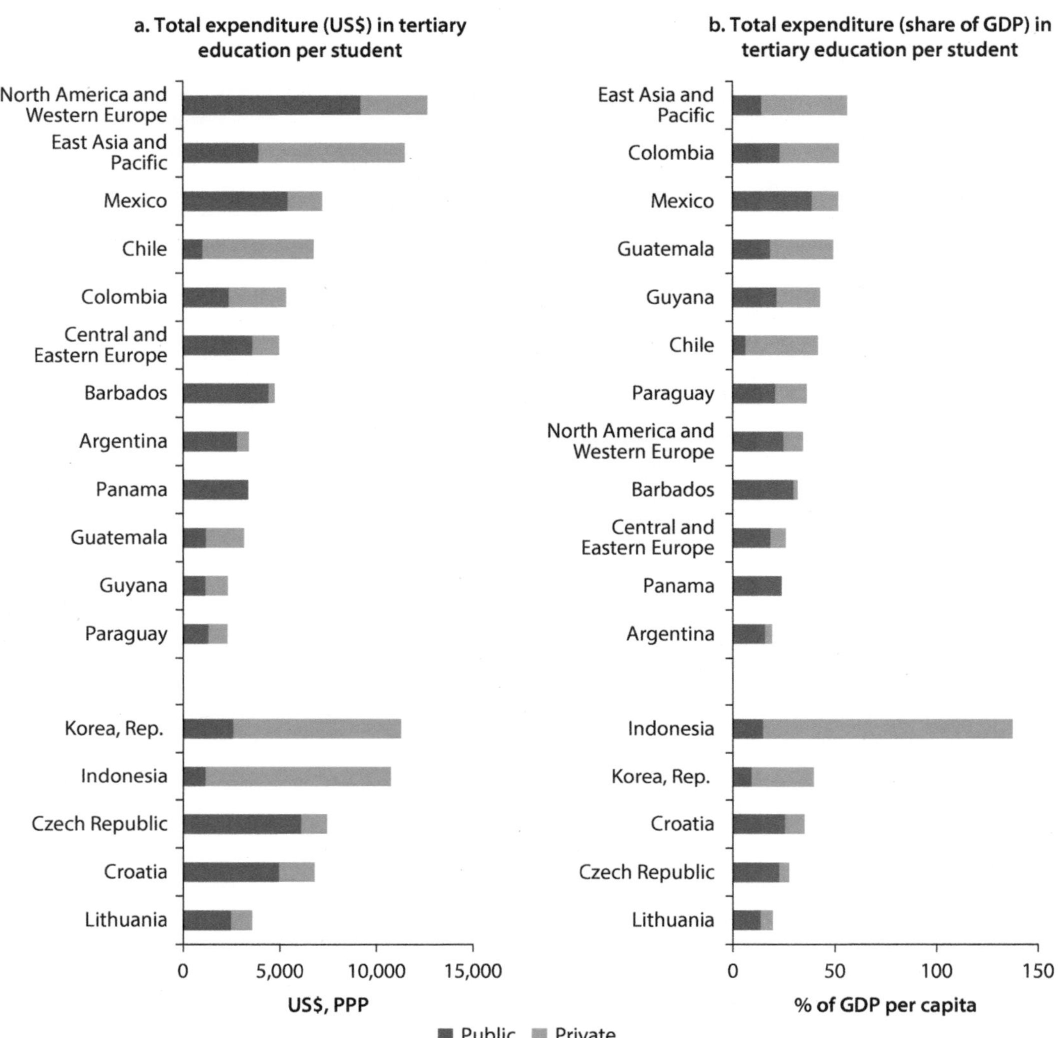

Source: World Bank calculations based on UNESCO Global Education Digest 2011 and World Development Indicators.
Note: Mexico is not included in the group of North American and Western Europe countries. East Asia and Pacific includes Australia, Indonesia, Japan, New Zealand and the Republic of Korea. For regional indicators, the figure reports simple averages over the corresponding countries' indicators. "Public" refers to government funding; "private" refers to nongovernment funding. PPP = purchasing power parity.

Although the region already has a large share of graduates in the business, law, and social science fields, in some countries these fields have higher returns, on average, than other fields. On these grounds, then, students appear to be making rational decisions. Yet returns in these fields show wide variation.

Figure O.15 Enrollment Share of Public and Private HEIs, Latin America and the Caribbean, circa 2000 and 2013

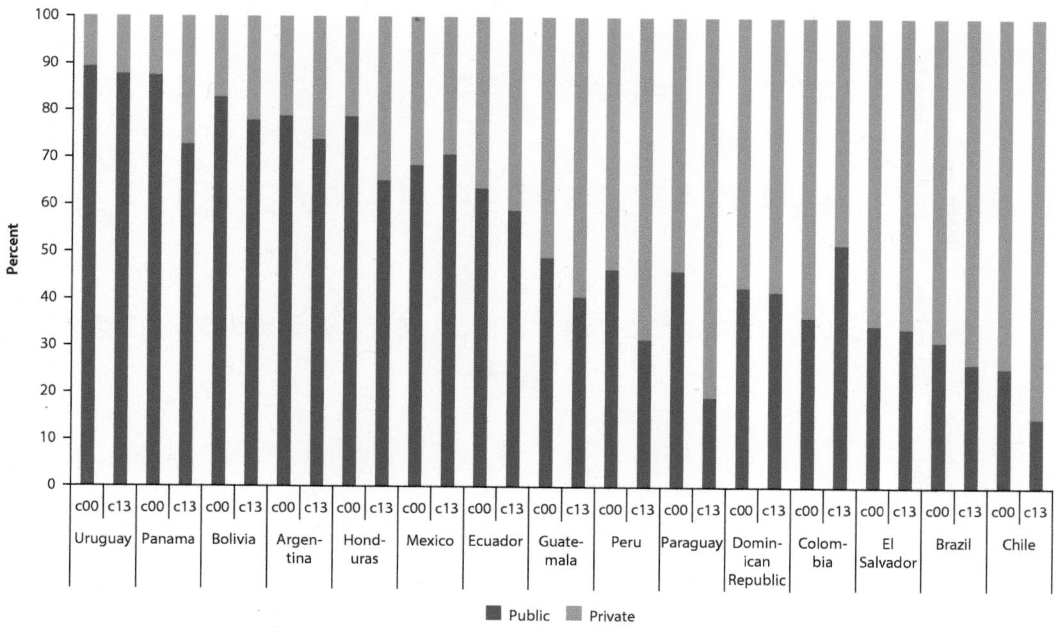

Source: Countries' administrative information and SEDLAC; see annex 5A for detailed information.
Note: Data pertain to the following years: Argentina (2000, 2013), Bolivia (2000, 2011), Brazil (2001, 2013), Chile (2005, 2015), Colombia (2000, 2013), Ecuador (2012, 2014), Mexico (2000, 2013), Peru (2005, 2013), and Uruguay (2000, 2014). Enrollment in graduate programs is not included. See country-specific notes of figure 5.5. We complement the administrative data with information from household surveys for Honduras, Guatemala, the Dominican Republic, and El Salvador. c00 = circa 2000; c13 = circa 2013.

Figure O.16 Enrollment Share of University and Nonuniversity HEIs, Latin America and the Caribbean, circa 2000 and 2013

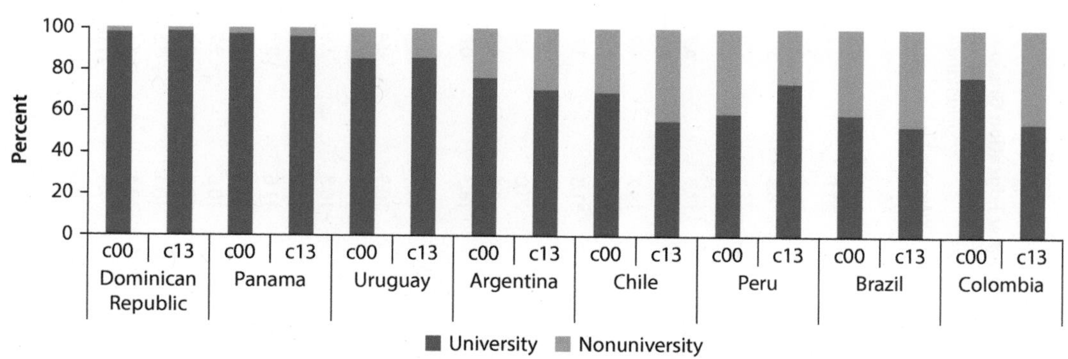

Source: Countries' administrative information; see annex 5A for detailed information.
Note: Data pertain to the following years: Argentina (2000, 2013), Brazil (2003, 2013), Chile (2005, 2015), Colombia (2000, 2013), the Dominican Republic (2006, 2011), Panama (2002, 2013), Peru (2005, 2013), and Uruguay (2000, 2014). Enrollment in graduate programs is not included. See annex 5B, table 5B.1, for details on the institutions included in the university and nonuniversity sector in each country. c00 = circa 2000; c13 = circa 2013.

Table O.1 Share of Higher Education Graduates by Field, circa 2013

	Education	*Humanities and arts*	*Social sciences, business, and law*	*Science*	*Engineering, manufacturing, and construction*	*Agriculture*	*Health and welfare*	*Services*	*Unspecified*
Argentina	16.4	9.9	35.7	8.1	6.0	2.5	17.9	3.4	0.0
Bolivia	24.0	2.2	33.2	4.9	10.8	5.6	17.4	0.5	1.7
Brazil	20.1	2.4	41.0	5.3	6.7	1.7	14.5	2.8	5.5
Chile	15.8	4.2	29.4	4.9	14.3	2.4	21.2	7.8	0.0
Colombia	8.3	3.5	54.1	4.0	18.7	1.7	7.3	2.3	0.0
Costa Rica	23.5	2.8	41.8	6.6	6.5	1.3	15.1	2.3	0.0
Cuba	23.6	1.0	29.2	2.7	1.4	2.1	32.5	6.3	1.2
Dominican Republic	17.7	4.7	46.8	4.6	9.8	0.7	14.0	0.6	1.1
Ecuador	21.2	4.1	43.0	6.1	8.8	2.4	10.9	3.6	0.0
El Salvador	18.7	4.7	35.9	1.0	21.2	1.4	17.0	0.1	0.0
Guatemala	24.7	1.0	37.4	2.6	14.1	7.3	12.8	0.0	0.0
Honduras	31.3	1.6	40.5	2.2	10.1	3.5	8.9	1.8	0.0
Mexico	12.5	4.4	44.7	5.5	21.3	1.7	9.0	0.7	0.1
Panama	25.0	5.8	34.7	5.8	10.1	0.5	9.9	8.2	0.0
Uruguay	3.9	4.0	40.9	7.8	7.8	5.1	27.6	2.9	0.0
Venezuela, RB	18.3	0.6	42.9	7.0	19.5	1.2	7.3	3.2	0.0
Average Latin America and the Caribbean	19.1	3.5	39.5	4.9	11.7	2.6	15.2	2.9	0.6
Indonesia	19.5	0.4	38.4	5.5	16.2	5.9	5.8		8.3
Malaysia	11.1	11.0	28.3	11.1	22.1	2.2	9.2	5.0	0.0
Philippines	16.8	1.9	34.1	13.9	11.6	2.4	8.6	5.8	4.8
Croatia	5.0	10.4	42.0	8.4	15.4	3.9	7.9	7.1	0.0
Czech Republic	11.6	8.4	35.9	10.4	12.9	3.8	10.3	5.4	1.3
Hungary	11.4	11.0	40.8	6.2	10.6	2.0	8.5	9.5	0.0
Lithuania	10.8	7.7	42.9	5.4	16.8	1.8	11.3	3.0	0.2
Poland	15.7	7.2	38.0	6.4	11.0	1.4	12.0	7.8	0.6
Turkey	10.1	8.5	46.7	8.6	12.3	3.2	5.7	4.9	0.0
Average comparators	12.4	7.4	38.6	8.4	14.3	2.9	8.8	6.1	1.7
United States	7.9	21.0	32.4	8.4	6.4	0.9	15.7	7.2	0.0
United Kingdom	9.9	16.1	29.9	16.2	9.0	0.9	15.7	1.5	0.8

Source: United Nations Educational, Scientific and Cultural Organization (UNESCO), http://data.uis.unesco.org/index.aspx?queryid=163.
Note: Average indicators are simple averages over the countries' indicators.

Returns Are High, But Declining and Heterogeneous

On average, the wage premium for higher education in Latin America and the Caribbean is high relative to that in the developed world. Higher education graduates can expect to earn, on average, 104 percent more than high school graduates, holding other worker characteristics constant. While many factors might contribute to these high premia (or Mincerian returns), a clear one is the still relatively low fraction of college-educated workers. Furthermore, even higher education dropouts enjoy a relatively large average earning premium of 35 percent relative to high school graduates (figure O.17). This high premium for incomplete higher education might in turn discourage students from completing higher education, an outcome to which long degrees and graduation requirements might contribute as well.[12]

Although they are high, average Mincerian returns to higher education relative to high school have actually declined since the 2000s, when they were equal to 115 percent. Most of this decline took place between 2000 and 2010. Messina and

Figure O.17 Mincerian Returns to Incomplete Higher Education versus Higher Education Degrees in Latin America and the Caribbean, Mid-2010s

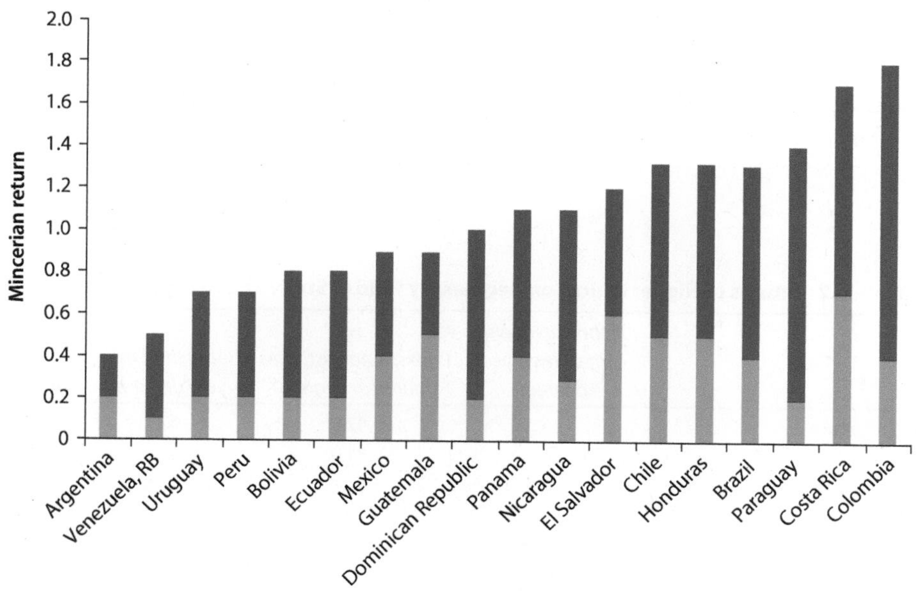

Source: World Bank calculations based on SEDLAC.
Note: The figure decomposes the return to a higher education degree (relative to complete high school) into two components: the return to some higher education (or incomplete higher education), and the additional return to completion. For example, in Uruguay, the return to complete higher education is equal to 70 percent; the return to incomplete higher education is equal to 20 percent; and the additional return to completing higher education (relative to not completing it) is 50 percentage points. The returns are computed as the exponential function of the coefficient estimated from the Mincer regression (minus 1). The estimation of the Mincer model corrects for self-selection into employment. The set of controls include gender, age and its square, urban area indicators, and regional indicators by country. When multiplied by 100, these returns are expressed in percent.

Silva (2017) study the related decline of higher education Mincerian returns relative to primary education, a phenomenon which could in principle be due to demand or supply factors. For instance, the greater supply of higher education graduates would, by itself, lead to lower Mincerian returns, as would the entry of lower ability students (receiving low-paying jobs afterward) into the system. While these supply-side factors have indeed played a role, there was also an increase in labor demand coupled with asymmetric responses of skilled and unskilled labor supplies. In particular, while the demand for both unskilled and skilled labor rose during the 2000s, the fact that the unskilled labor supply is less elastic than the skilled labor supply led to greater wage increases for unskilled than skilled workers. Institutional factors such as minimum wages contributed as well to the greater relative growth of wages for unskilled workers.

While Mincerian returns are informative of the higher education wage premium, they do not factor in the cost of higher education (including not only direct costs such as tuition but also the opportunity cost of salaries foregone by being in school). If, for instance, the net present value of higher education (that is, the expected salaries over a lifetime minus the higher education costs) exceeds the net present value of not pursuing higher education (and hence earning a high school graduate's salary) by 30 percent on average, then the average return to higher education is 30 percent.

When calculated in this fashion for the countries with available data, returns show a striking heterogeneity across fields and HEIs. In Chile, for instance, engineering and technology have the highest returns among universities' programs, followed by law, business, and science (table O.2). Education, in turn, has the lowest average returns, perhaps reflecting other job amenities (such as summers

Table O.2 Returns to Higher Education Degrees, by Field of Study and HEI Type, Chile

	Technical training centers (two-year degrees)	*Professional institutes (four-year degrees)*	*Universities (five-year degrees)*	*Overall*
Agriculture	35.3	42.5	62.7	52.5
Arts	66.1	31.0	49.0	41.2
Business management	57.1	54.6	126.8	78.2
Education	−2.4	9.5	12.7	9.6
Engineering and technology	109.6	99.8	163.5	125.8
Health	40.5	40.9	101.5	73.3
Humanities	−5.2	12.1	2.3	4.1
Law	61.3	38.6	128.5	115.1
Science	97.2	115.5	115.3	113.6
Social sciences	34.5	18.7	47.0	36.2
Total	**66.2**	**58.9**	**97.5**	**78.4**

Source: Espinoza and Urzúa 2016.
Note: Returns are expressed in percent; they are calculated as the net present value of higher education (net of tuition costs and foregone salaries while pursuing higher education). "Total" denotes the enrollment-weighted average over the fields. HEI = higher education institution.

off and stable employment), or simply reflecting low public spending in elementary and secondary levels along with low public value for teaching. Furthermore, about 10 percent of all students in Chile are enrolled in programs with negative expected returns, although this fraction also differs by field and HEI type (figure O.18).

Even within fields there is much return heterogeneity. Continuing with Chile, consider graduates from business programs. Although the average graduate from a bachelor's program has higher returns than the average short-cycle program graduate, being in the 25th percentile of the bachelor's program distribution of returns is quite similar to being in the 75th percentile of the short-cycle program distribution. In other words, the large heterogeneity in returns might render a bachelor's program no more valuable than a short-cycle program to some students.

Several Institutional Features Point to Potential Inefficiencies

These unsatisfactory outcomes, attained in spite of some reasonable inputs, calls into question the efficiency of the system, which is related to the incentives faced by the different agents. Some incentives might indeed foster inefficiencies. For instance, the region has a strong tradition of university autonomy

Figure O.18 Proportion of Students Facing Negative Expected Returns to Higher Education in Chile, by Field and HEI Type

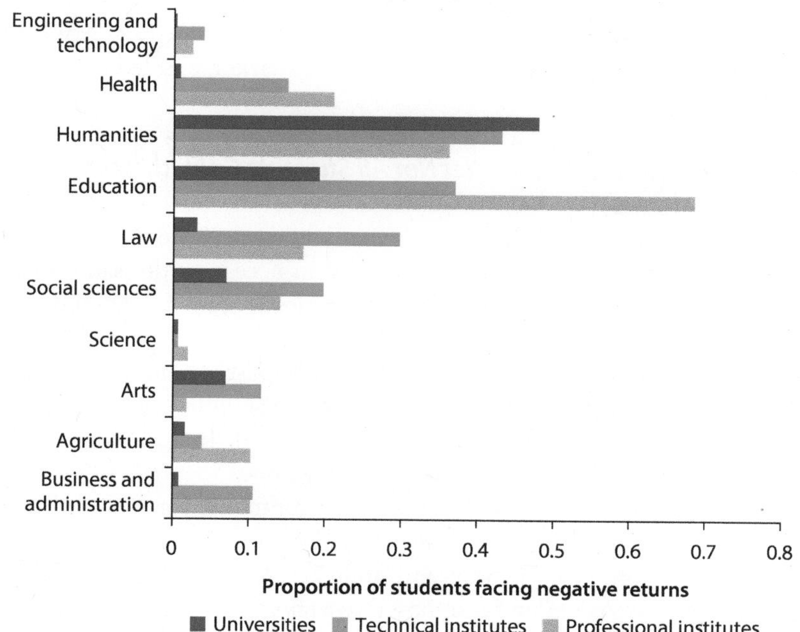

Source: Espinoza and Urzúa 2016.
Note: The figure shows, for each field and HEI type, the proportion of students facing negative expected returns. HEI = higher education institution.

from policy makers and government, a feature that makes it remarkably difficult to hold universities accountable for the public funding they receive. In addition, very little funding is competitively awarded to HEIs (whether public or private) for their research, a factor that might explain why universities in the region do not produce more graduates in science. Also, students in highly subsidized public HEIs are not held accountable for their outcomes; in some countries, students in public HEIs face no admission requirements, nor do they face a TTD limit. Furthermore, the fact that higher education programs are longer in many Latin American and Caribbean countries than in the developed world, and switching among them is harder, may constitute an obstacle to completion.[13]

Lessons Learned

In light of these stylized facts, it is important to take stock of lessons learned from our analytical research. Although this research focuses on only a few countries because of data availability, its lessons are likely applicable to other countries in the region.

Higher Education Access Grew as a Result of Supply and Demand

The access expansion was indeed an equilibrium outcome: fruit of the interaction of supply and demand. Demand for higher education rose with the increase in the number of high school graduates, the growth of personal income, and the removal of liquidity constraints through scholarships and loans. Supply of higher education grew as existing programs expanded and new programs and HEIs opened. Greater demand created the opportunity for new programs and HEIs to open, particularly to serve the "new" students; by creating new options, greater supply enticed new students to enter the market, and led others to alter their choices.

More Students Gained Access—Yet Not All Students Gained Access to the Same Options

Research on Colombia and Chile reveals that while many "new" students gained access to higher education, they did not all gain access to the same HEIs and programs. For bachelor's programs, both countries feature a high-end segment with selective admission and a low-end segment. High-ability students gained access to selective programs (most of which already existed before the expansion), while low-ability students gained access to less- (or non-) selective programs (many of which were created during the expansion). In addition, many low-ability students gained access to short-cycle programs.

Figures O.19 and O.20 illustrate these developments for Colombia, where public HEIs are heavily subsidized. Figure O.19 groups students into "student types" depending on their income and ability, and depicts the probability of choosing a bachelor's program (as opposed to a short-cycle program) conditional on attending college for each student type. As the figure shows, high-income, high-ability students are the most likely to choose a bachelor's program, and low-income, low-ability students are the least likely.

Figure O.19 Probability of Choosing a Bachelor's Program, Conditional on Going to College, Colombia, 2009

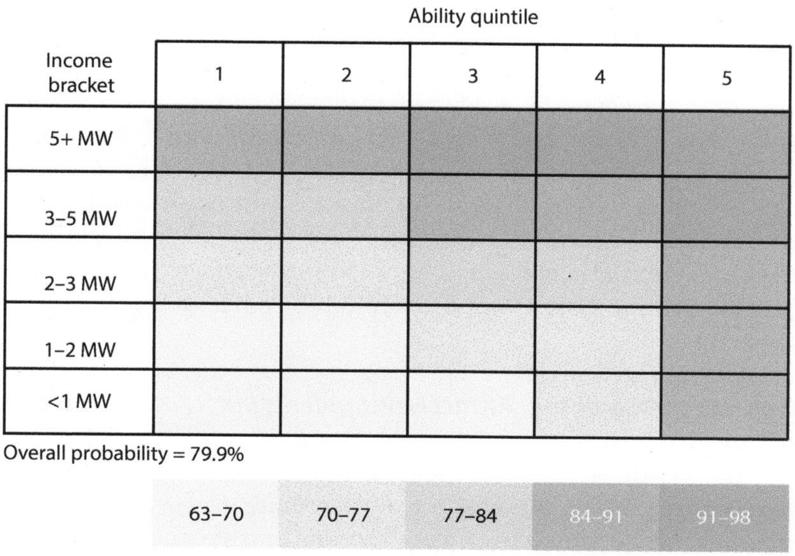

Ability quintile

Income bracket

1 2 3 4 5

5+ MW

3–5 MW

2–3 MW

1–2 MW

<1 MW

Overall probability = 79.9%

63–70 70–77 77–84 84–91 91–98

Source: Carranza and Ferreyra 2017.
Note: The figure shows the probability of choosing a bachelor's program among students who graduated from high school in 2009, and who enrolled within the five-year window following high school graduation. MW = minimum wage. Probabilities are expressed in percent.

Figure O.20 Probability of Attending Each HEI Type, Conditional on Choosing a Bachelor's Program, Colombia, 2009

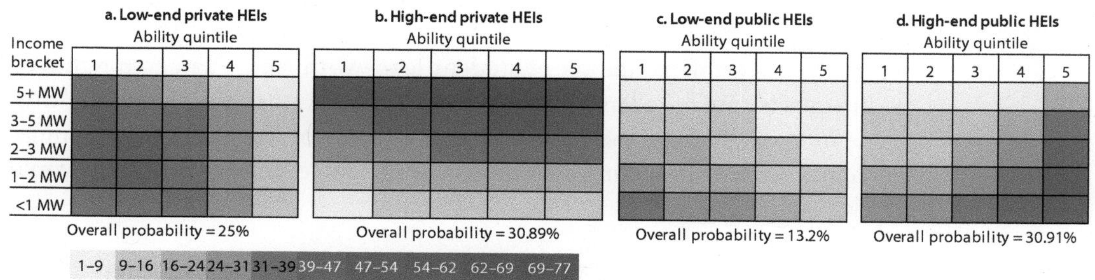

Source: Carranza and Ferreyra 2017.
Note: Probability pertains to first-year college students from the 2009 cohort (that is, high school graduates from 2009). Students are classified into "types"; a student type is a combination of income and ability. For each student type, probabilities, expressed in percent, add up to 100. MW = minimum wage.

Figure O.20, in turn, focuses on students enrolled in bachelor's programs. There is a clear sorting of students among HEI types depending on student income and ability. Broadly, high-end private HEIs attract high-income, high-ability students, whereas high-end public HEIs attract low-income, high-ability students. Low-end public and private HEIs attract low-income, low-ability students, although students in private low-end HEIs come from higher income families than students in public low-end HEIs.

Selective programs have remained selective throughout the expansion by continuing to serve high-ability students. Nonetheless, high-end HEIs in Colombia have also opened less-selective programs to serve lower ability students. In Chile, these students have been served by nonselective HEIs.

The fact that not all students gained access to the same options (largely because of differences in academic readiness and socioeconomic background) partly explains the heterogeneity in returns even for the same field. For instance, a law degree from a prestigious, selective HEI must have, on average, a higher return than a law degree from a low-end institution. Hence, attempts to raise social inclusion through higher education access can have only limited success in light of the heterogeneity in students, HEIs, and programs in the system, not to mention the heterogeneity of jobs in the labor market.

Not Only Did the Expansion Attract New Students But It Also Affected Their Choices

Besides affecting the *extensive margin* (that is, whether students enroll in higher education or not), the expansion affected the *intensive margin* (that is, the choices students make within the system, or their sorting across options), largely because of policy and supply-side changes.

For instance, throughout the expansion, overall, students in Colombia became more likely to choose short-cycle rather than bachelor's programs. Nonetheless, the highest ability students became *more* likely to choose bachelor's programs. Students with the highest income or ability became more likely than before to attend their usual choice of private HEIs, although high-ability, low-income students became less likely to attend their usual choice of selective public HEIs.

In Chile, the implementation of student loans with state guarantee removed liquidity constraints for a large number of low-income students. As a result, they became more likely to attend higher education; some of them also became more likely to pursue long programs, or programs with a lower return, than they would have chosen otherwise.

In Opening New Programs, HEIs Sought to Exploit New Opportunities

Detailed data from Colombia have enabled us to study the drivers of new program entry. HEIs are more likely to open a program in a particular field if they already have a presence in that field because they can exploit the same infrastructure. The new program might involve a repackaging of existing elements or a brand-new curriculum.

In Colombia, the behavior of low-end private HEIs has been a driving factor in other HEIs' program openings. Two things have happened in response to new programs opened by low-end private HEIs: (a) high-end private HEIs have opened similar programs yet at a higher tuition, thus attracting wealthier students; and (b) low-end public HEIs have opened similar programs yet at lower tuition, thus attracting lower income students. The preferred fields for new programs at HEI of all types are business, economics, and social science. In high-end public HEIs, the other most preferred fields for new programs are engineering and education.

Given their high fixed cost, opening new programs in science and technology was not profitable for private HEIs unless they were already offering them. From a strict cost-benefit analysis, these programs lead to economic losses because of their high cost and low enrollment. The same is true in the developed world, although competitive allocation of public funding to universities (both public and private) for research helps HEIs of all types offer more programs in science and technology.

Competitive Pressures Are Strongest in Midtier Programs

In countries with a relatively large private sector, the top-tier, highly selective HEIs are naturally isolated from competition of less-selective HEIs by virtue of admitting high-ability students. Highly selective HEIs compete among themselves, but not much with others outside their league. Similarly, the bottom tier, least-selective HEIs are somewhat isolated by virtue of attracting many students from outside the market. Again, these HEIs compete with each other but do not face much competition from higher tier HEIs.

In contrast, midtier HEIs are subject to the strongest competitive pressures. They face competition from more selective HEIs, which can lure their top students away. They also face competition from less selective HEIs, which can lure students away with the offer of nonacademic amenities (including, perhaps, a more convenient location). In addition, they compete among themselves. Perhaps for this reason, the number of programs has grown the most for students attending midtier HEIs, as illustrated in figure O.21 for Chile, mostly through the entry of new programs.

Such intense competition among midtier HEIs can lead both to positive and negative outcomes. On the one hand, as programs lose students to others' competition they lower admission standards to make up for enrollment losses: as a result, their peer ability suffers. On the other hand, programs might respond to competition by improving their offering: as a result, program quality might rise. Further research is needed to learn more about these outcomes.

Funding Mechanisms May Have Unintended Consequences

Two main tools are available to help remove students' liquidity constraints. The first is tuition subsidies or scholarships. When students receive a tuition subsidy, the HEI is reimbursed for the cost of its services. For instance, in a higher education system with subsidized tuition for public HEIs, the institutions receive public funding so that they can charge low (or zero) tuition. Alternatively, the subsidy might be given directly to the student, for her to use in the HEI of her choice. The second tool to remove liquidity constraints is student loans. While each tool admits many variations, it is useful to focus on the extreme cases of

Figure O.21 Change in Number of Degrees, by PSU Scores, Chile, 2007 and 2012

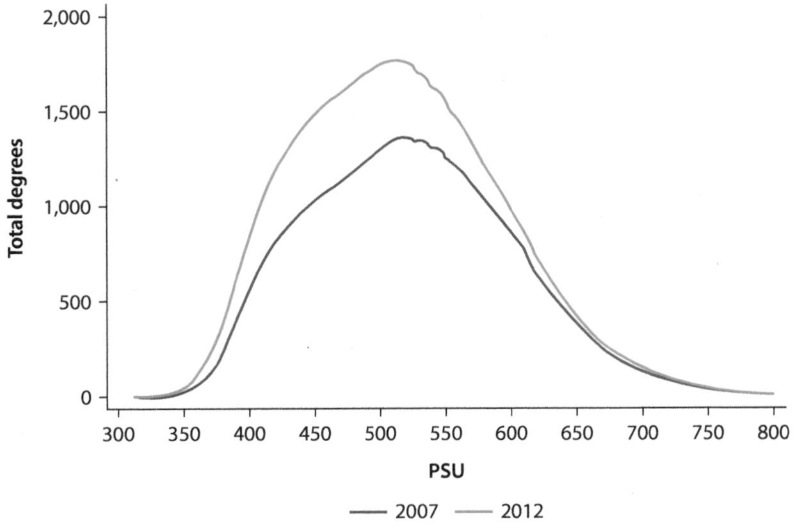

Source: Neilson et al. 2016.
Note: The PSU is the higher education entry exam; PSU scores are depicted in the horizontal axis. The figure shows the number of programs (degrees) available to students with a given PSU score in 2007 and 2012. PSU = Prueba de Selección Universitaria.

universal free tuition and nondefaultable student loans (or, more generally, loans with costly default). Many countries in the region provide at least one of these.

Simulations from a general equilibrium model indicate that both loans and universal free tuition have the potential to relax liquidity constraints, raise enrollment rates, and ultimately raise the percentage of skilled workers in the economy. However, according to our simulations, they are likely to do so to a different degree because they tend to create different incentives.

Nondefaultable loans create powerful incentives for student effort. They make the student internalize not only the cost of her education but also the risk of failing to graduate. A loan, then, induces financial responsibility on the part of the student. Yet precisely for this reason, only students who are likely to graduate take up loans, which explains why loans tend to expand enrollment to a lower extent than free tuition.

By itself, universal free tuition tends not to create such desirable incentives. With universal free tuition, the student no longer bears the cost of her education or the risk of failing to graduate. Hence, universal free tuition tends to attract many students who are likely to drop out. Furthermore, even some students who might succeed otherwise might take longer to graduate, or even fail.

While loans provided by a private institution have a relatively low fiscal cost,[14] universal free tuition is fiscally more costly because it requires fiscal resources to cover the cost of education—and the education, on average, takes longer, since TTD is higher under universal free tuition. Furthermore, universal free tuition requires fiscal resources to pay not only for the students that graduate but also for those that drop out.

Free tuition to students is not free to society, since society must pay taxes to finance free tuition. Since universal free tuition for all subsidizes some individuals who would be willing and able to pay for higher education, it may be an inefficient use of fiscal resources.

While policy makers might feel tempted to raise enrollment through free tuition without a concomitant increase in resources, the evidence for the United States shows that the resulting decline in per-student resources is associated with lower academic outcomes. This, in turn, could exacerbate the challenges generated by the entry of lower ability students. Remedial and developmental programs for less-prepared students, which might be viewed as a solution to the problem of low academic readiness, are fiscally costly as well.[15]

Given the role of students' responses to funding mechanisms, policy makers must try to design mechanisms that incentivize effort and graduation. Performance-based tuition subsidies for students who make satisfactory progress throughout college is one example. Indeed, the evidence suggests that such mechanisms deliver better academic outcomes than those without "strings attached."[16] The recent adoption of merit- and need-based financial aid programs, such as Ser Pilo Paga in Colombia and Beca 18 in Peru, is a step in this direction.

We Can Expect Only So Much from Higher Education

The region has great hopes for education as "the great equalizer," yet some sobering research findings tell a more complicated story. This section describes college-educated workers as "skilled," and we measure the "skill premium" as the ratio of the average wage of college graduates and high school graduates.

The working-age population (WAP) comprises individuals ages 25–65 years, or approximately 40 cohorts. Broadly speaking, each year one cohort retires and another enters, which means that about 1/40th of the WAP changes each year. Thus, raising the fraction of skilled population through higher education changes one cohort per year, or 1/40th of the whole WAP. Therefore, it takes either many years, or a radical increase in the fraction of skilled population among incoming cohorts, for higher education to effect substantive changes in the WAP. For the same reason, the reduction in the skill premium and wage inequality brought about by the greater share of skilled population is also slow.

Through simulations, we have investigated the long-term effect of increasing the number of college graduates by 50 percent in every cohort coming into the WAP from now on, and focused on individuals with at least a high school education, given our interest in the margin between high school and higher education. Given these countries' dropout rate, such increase in the number of college graduates would entail doubling higher education enrollment—a substantive feat that took about 10 years for these countries to accomplish.

In this scenario, over more than three decades, the fraction of skilled WAP (relative to all workers with at least a high school diploma) would rise from approximately 25 percent to 35 percent or 37 percent, and the skill premium would fall from 2.8 to 2.4. These effects are sizable, since they amount to a 50 percent increase in the fraction of the skilled population and a 14 percent decline in the skill premium. Even then, the fraction of the skilled population would remain well below that of the United States (47 percent), and the skill premium would remain well above the United States (1.7).

Although specific outcomes of these simulations are a consequence of model assumptions, the message remains that expanding the number of graduates (not merely enrollees) alone would have limited effects on skills and wage inequality and would take decades to materialize in full. This finding has two policy implications. First, in a region with an urgency to create and improve skilled human capital, the policy menu must include complementary reforms aimed at injecting speed and efficiency into the higher education process. Such reforms might include streamlining and shortening some programs, reviewing graduation requirements, and strengthening the connections between the university and the marketplace. A critical policy, of course, consists of raising academic readiness among high school graduates. While the region has made strides in the *quantity* of high school graduates—and this has been the main driver of higher education expansion—the region will not form skilled human capital at a fast rate unless it makes similar strides in the *quality* of high school graduates.

The second policy implication is that in its search for lower inequality, the policy maker cannot put all the eggs in the higher education basket. As Messina and Silva (2017) point out, although education explains 30 percent of the cross-sectional variation in wages in the region, and worker characteristics overall explain about 50 percent, the remaining 50 percent is explained by other factors, particularly firm heterogeneity. In other words, some individuals have "good" jobs in "good" firms, whereas others do not. The challenge for the policy maker, then, is to create an environment in which "good" firms can create "good" jobs and make "good," productive use of the skilled human capital formed through higher education.

Some Policy Considerations

The stylized facts depict the current crossroads of higher education in the region, and the analytical findings uncover some of the driving forces. Given the region's urgency to raise productivity in a low-growth, fiscally constrained environment, going past this crossroads requires the formation of skilled human capital rapidly and efficiently. Policy makers, however, must remain aware of both the challenges and limitations of higher education policy. They must also remain aware of the trade-offs between higher education access and completion, since one has the potential of undermining the other. In addressing these challenges and trade-offs, a role emerges for incentives, competition, monitoring, and information. While zooming in to the higher education sector is critical to sound higher education policy design, so is "zooming out" to (a) the secondary education system that prepares students for higher education, (b) the labor market in which higher education graduates will participate, and, of course, (c) the entire economy.

Inherent Challenges and Limitations of Higher Education Policy

Left to its own devices, the market will not achieve the social optimum of maximizing each person's potential and meeting the economy's skill needs because of the presence of externalities, liquidity constraints, information-related problems, and imperfect competition. Each of these distortions calls for a different set of policies. Broadly:

- Externalities call for government subsidies for higher education
- Liquidity constraints call either for government subsidies or for enabling student credit markets
- Information-related problems call for information provision and consumer protection
- Imperfect competition calls for enabling competition through student choice while also monitoring and regulating the sector

The presence of multiple distortions calls for multiple policy instruments. For instance, it is not enough for the policy maker to subsidize access to higher education; through her subsidies she must enable student choice among HEIs and programs, and these must be overseen at some level. The problem, of course, is that removing one distortion can aggravate another. For example, removing liquidity constraints through credit can indeed expand access, yet also invite the entry of low-quality HEIs and programs with considerable market power over a segment of uninformed consumers.

Sound policy, then, requires a delicate balance of multiple instruments. Not all instruments are created equal, though. The ultimate success of higher education policies depends on the behavior of higher education's key agents, namely students and HEIs. Thus, a useful criteria to choose among instruments is the extent to which they incentivize the desired behaviors and discourage others. The larger the scale of the policy, the more critical this consideration becomes to avoid negative, unintended effects.

Awareness of the unintended consequences of large-scale higher education policy is important. Equally important is awareness of the limitations of higher education as a social mobility tool. As the recent experience in the region demonstrates, broad access gives less-prepared students access to some lower quality higher education options, which, in turn, might lead to lower quality employment and perhaps some discontent. Furthermore, even if two students have the same subject matter competence despite having attended different HEIs, they might still face different job prospects because of other elements (for example, social and professional connections) or nonacademic skills (many of which were developed before higher education) that fall outside the scope of higher education.

Trade-Off between Higher Education Access and Completion

Providing access to higher education is a critical step toward forming skilled human capital. There are two main access paradigms: restricted access and open access. Restricted access rations access based on ability or financial means, whereas open access applies little or no rationing. Thus, restricted access systems may not grant access to students who are academically ready (for example, because of HEIs' capacity constraints or students' lack of financial means), whereas open access systems may grant access to students who are not academically ready.

When designing higher education systems, societies typically lean toward one of these paradigms (particularly through their public HEIs). Most higher education systems have some HEIs with restricted access, and others with open access. What is critical, though, is that each paradigm gives rise to consequential trade-offs. While restricted access regimes may be viewed by some as less fair than open access regimes, they may have higher completion rates by admitting academically ready students who are more likely to complete their studies—and by devoting more resources to each student. Furthermore, financial aid to low-income, academically ready students can substantially enhance the equity of these regimes.

Open access regimes, in turn, are viewed by many as providing a "second chance." For instance, students who received a low-quality secondary education, or who enrolled in higher education relatively late in life because of family responsibilities, benefit from open access regimes. Yet, precisely by enrolling a greater proportion of less-prepared students, open access regimes may have lower completion rates. Furthermore, because the HEIs attended by these students do not ration entry, enrollment may be too high relative to resources, thus leading to low per-student resources. The ensuing combination of students' low academic readiness and HEIs' inadequate per-student resources can lead to poor academic outcomes. Also, these HEIs might need additional resources not only to prevent a decline in per-student resources, but also to compensate for the students' lack of academic readiness (for example, through the provision of remedial education).

Thus, when choosing an access paradigm as part of its strategy to form human capital, societies must be aware of the trade-offs between access and completion. It is instructive to examine the experience of the United States, where the fraction of high school graduates enrolled in college rose from 48 percent for the class of 1972 to 70 percent for the class of 1992, yet the fraction of college students who completed their studies declined from 50.5 percent to 45.9 percent, respectively (Bound et al. 2010).

This outcome deterioration in the United States might have been due to students' declining academic readiness, or to factors related to collegiate characteristics (for example, HEIs' declining resources per student or the type of HEI first attended). The evidence indicates that most of the outcome deterioration can be attributed to a change in collegiate characteristics (Bound et al. 2010, 2012). In other words, expanding enrollment without a concomitant increase in resources—and mostly in open access HEIs (nonselective public HEIs and two-year HEIs)—has been the leading cause of the recent decline in completion rates in the United States.

Given Latin America and the Caribbean's need to form skilled human capital rapidly, there might be a role for the provision of additional support to students who are not academically ready, either through the provision of remedial education, or through other programs such as tutoring, mentoring, and advising. The important point is that—depending on the access paradigm embraced by a country—further access expansion may require additional resources (either from the public or the private sector) at least partly to compensate for the lower academic readiness of the "new" students. While societies may choose to devote such additional resources in higher education, they should remain aware of their opportunity cost, including the improvement of the primary and secondary education system that prepares the future higher education students.

Incentives, Competition and Choice, Monitoring, and Information

The evidence we have presented—and the incentives in some of these higher education systems—suggest that the systems might not be operating efficiently, and that there might be room for efficiency gains. In moving past the current crossroads, an important role arises for incentives, competition and choice, monitoring, and information.

Students who receive public funding must be given incentives to graduate—and to do it on time. Universal free tuition (especially when coupled with unrestricted admission) may not accomplish this goal, but performance-based tuition subsidies may. Loans with a default penalty may provide even stronger incentives. Given the current fiscal climate of limited public funds, carefully designed student loans may need to be part of the policy discussion. More broadly, the design of an efficient, responsible, and equitable funding system remains an important item in the higher education agenda for the region.

In addition, institutions must be given incentives to contribute to students' success: they must be given "skin in the game." Such incentives are not present, for instance, when public HEIs receive funding without accountability. They are not present either when private HEIs receive public funding (in the form of financial aid given to students) regardless of student outcomes.

Incentives are critical to addressing the worrisome fact that only one-half of enrolled students in the region have completed their degree by the age of 25–29 years, and that about one-half of all dropouts leave their programs in their first year. It is possible, for instance, that institutional or curricular features may contribute to this situation. For example, students in the region typically must choose a program in their first year in college as opposed to taking general education classes, as in the United States. If, after starting her program, a student realizes that the program is a poor match to her skills or preferences, she may have to start another program from scratch, or may be able to transfer only a few credits. While poor adaptation to higher education might lead some students to drop out of any system, curricular rigidities may lead even more students to drop out.[17]

In addition, academic advising and student support systems might not be as strong in Latin America and the Caribbean as in countries such as the United States, thus contributing to students' disorientation during their first year in college.

Furthermore, the fact that approximately 30 percent of all students who leave the system do so four years into it should call into question the length and appropriateness of the programs. While four years of coursework are not enough in many countries in the region for a student to receive an accountant's degree, perhaps they should suffice for a shorter program degree that prevents the student from leaving college with no degree at all.

Promoting variety and enabling competition among HEIs and programs can provide students with further choices and enable them to find their best-fitting option. Students, however, need the financial means to exercise choice. When public funding is restricted to public HEIs so that they can provide free or subsidized tuition, private HEIs are placed at a competitive disadvantage. Since some private HEIs and programs may be a better fit for some students than their public counterparts, this type of funding system restricts students' choices and limits competition. While public participation in higher education funding is motivated by the existence of externalities and liquidity constraints, it is not obvious that public funding should be mostly (or only) channeled towards public HEIs.

As in other areas of economic life characterized by pervasive information asymmetries, monitoring and regulation can improve outcomes. Both students and the policy maker can monitor institutions. Yet monitoring is more costly for some students than others. Thus, it is particularly necessary for the policy maker to monitor the HEIs attended by the "new" students, who might have less access to information or might have lower information-processing capacity (Ferreyra and Liang 2012). Thoughtful regulation and accreditation procedures, for instance, can accomplish this goal.

Monitoring and regulation are not sufficient, however, to improve outcomes. Only when a student has the ability to switch to another HEI are monitoring and regulation useful—an ability created by channeling at least some funding to students rather than institutions. Yet, monitoring can take place only in the presence of adequate information. Generating and disseminating information on programs' outcomes regarding completion, employment, and graduates' salaries are key in the new landscape, as is creating a culture in which students and families can expect to receive and act upon high-quality information. Chile, Colombia, and Peru have already taken steps in this direction.

Before and after Higher Education

As technological progress alters the structure of jobs and careers, individuals can expect to switch jobs more often throughout their lives—and even switch careers. Therefore, some higher education programs in the region may need to become shorter and more streamlined, and professional requirements may need to change to facilitate individuals' transitions among fields later in life.

While enhancing higher education is of great importance, the policy maker cannot overlook the pre- and postcollege stages. Higher education is more likely to produce good outcomes when it receives academically ready high school graduates. Moreover, higher education graduates can realize their productive potential only when enabled by their environment. For instance, one of the authors of this report has a friend who received a doctorate in molecular biology at a top research institution in the United States and worked as a postdoc at another top U.S. institution. She then went back to a top research institution in her home country in Latin America and the Caribbean. When she tried to run similar experiments to those she was conducting in the United States, she could not gain access to the necessary materials because of import restrictions in the economy. When she tried to download journal articles online, she found that the Internet connection was too slow, and that her institution did not have a subscription to several important journals. Getting to work in the morning was also a challenge because of recurrent transportation strikes. She found the lower expectations on the part of other researchers and assistants quite detrimental to the institution's morale. Thus, in only a few weeks since the return to her home country, she saw her productivity plummet, even though her human capital had not changed.

The message for the policy maker in the region, then, is that forming skilled human capital is not enough to raise productivity, growth, and equity unless an enabling environment is put in place as well. Once again, we can expect only so much from higher education.

Structure of the Report

Chapter 1 describes the recent higher education expansion. It documents the magnitude of the expansion, describes the "new" students, and examines patterns of higher education spending in the region relative to other regions. It examines a variety of private returns to higher education and provides evidence regarding public returns. Chapter 2 presents equity, quality, and variety indicators in higher education. It describes the recent equity gains, presents evidence regarding to quality, and documents the variety of programs and HEIs in the region. Chapter 3 focuses on wage-based returns to higher education, both complete and incomplete. It documents returns' recent average decline and their heterogeneity among fields and HEIs.

Chapter 4 examines the demand-side drivers of the recent expansion. It studies the admission and funding mechanisms in the region, and explores student sorting across programs and HEIs and HEIs' changes throughout the expansion. It also studies the unintended consequences of funding mechanisms. Chapter 5 examines the supply-side drivers of the expansion. It documents the supply-side growth in the region and studies the opening of new programs and the competitive strategies used by various HEI types. Chapter 6 provides a summary of institutional arrangements related to current higher education policy in the region. Chapter 7 concludes with policy implications from the analysis conducted in the report.

Notes

1. See the glossary for enrollment rate definitions.
2. Here, ability is proxied by academic readiness for college. In some countries, this is measured by high school graduation exams or college entrance exams.
3. Based on household survey data, in 2013 almost 80 percent of higher education students ages 18–24 years lived at home (namely, the student is either the child or grandchild of the household head). Student-level data for Colombia indicate that about three-quarters of students attend an HEI located in the same state where they attended high school.
4. For example, Hastings et al. (2016) describe that students tend to have noisy beliefs about programs' costs, although their average beliefs are correct. However, they overestimate the returns to their preferred programs.
5. See the glossary for the definition of *access rate*.
6. In some countries, class and exam schedules in public HEIs are often subject to disruptions caused by faculty or student strikes. Private HEIs thus offer a more tranquil, predictable environment. Parents who want to hold their children accountable find that the structured environment of a private university is helpful in this regard. Since private HEIs have an incentive to retain students for financial reasons, they are often more responsive to students' and parents' concerns.
7. See the glossary for the definition of *bachelor's* and *short-cycle* programs.
8. A student may drop out of a program and start a new one. If she also drops out from her second program and does not enroll in other programs afterward, then she drops out of the system. Hence, the fraction of students who drop out of the system is lower than the fraction that drops out of individual programs. We compute dropout rates from the system to facilitate comparisons with the United States.
9. Similarly, U.S. dropout rates are equal to 24 percent and 46 percent for students starting in four- and two-year HEIs, respectively.
10. This conjecture is supported by recent research from Maloney and Caicedo (2014) and Toivanen and Väänänen (2016).
11. Regarding engineers, Lederman et al. (2014) document that Latin American and Caribbean countries have fewer engineers than the median country and fewer than would be expected given their current level of development. Their measure (the number of engineering graduates per 1,000 inhabitants ages 15–24 years) is informative of the *stock* of engineers, whereas the share of higher education graduates from engineering, construction, and manufacturing is informative of the flow of engineers.
12. For instance, in some countries students must write a rather lengthy undergraduate thesis, with little assistance from the faculty, as a graduation requirement. Anecdotal evidence indicates that after completing their coursework, many students begin to work and never finish their thesis, which means that they never complete their degree.
13. For instance, the statutory length of business programs in many Latin American and Caribbean countries is five years (without including the undergraduate thesis that is sometimes required), relative to only four years in the United States. Students who wish to switch from one program to another (perhaps because their first program was not a good match to their preferences or ability) face more difficulties in many Latin American and Caribbean countries than elsewhere, given the lower overlap in the curriculum of alternative programs.

14. Loans made by private institutions may have a fiscal cost if they entail a publicly funded subsidy, or if they have a state guarantee.
15. See Bianchi (2016) and Bound et al. (2010, 2012) for evidence on the negative effect of lower resources on higher education outcomes. Bettinger et al. (2013) review the literature on remedial and developmental programs in higher education, which have yielded mixed results in the United States.
16. Dynarski and Scott-Clayton (2013) review the literature on higher education financial aid and conclude that performance-based financial aid is more effective in terms of college outcomes.
17. Bordon and Fu (2015) consider the potential effects in Chile of switching from the current system, in which students choose both an HEI and a program upon enrollment, to a system in which students choose an HEI first and a major later, after having spent time in college. They estimate that the new system would yield better program matches for students, particularly for female, low-income, or low-ability students (or a combination thereof).

References

Bettinger, E. A. Boatman, and B. Terry. 2013. "Student Supports: Developmental Education and Other Academic Programs." *The Future of Children* 23 (1): 93–115.

Bordon, P., and C. Fu. 2015. "College-Major Choice to College-then-Major Choice." *Review of Economic Studies* 82 (4): 1247–88.

Bound, J., M. Lovenheim, and S. Turner. 2010. "Why Have College Completion Rates Declined? An Analysis of Changing Student Preparation and Collegiate Resources." *American Economic Journal: Applied Economics* 2: 129–57.

———. 2012. "Increasing Time to Baccalaureate Degree in the United States." *Education Finance and Policy* 7 (4): 375–424.

Brunner, J. J. 1990. "Educación Superior en América Latina." Fondo de cultura Económica.

Carranza, J. E., and M. M. Ferreyra. 2017. "Increasing Higher Education Coverage: Supply Expansion and Student Sorting in Colombia." Background paper for this report.

Castleman, B. L. 2013. "Prompts, Personalization, and Pay-Offs: Strategies to Improve the Design and Delivery of College and Financial Aid Information." Working Paper, Center on Education Policy and Workforce Competitiveness. Charlottesville, VA.

Deming, D. J., and D. Figlio. 2016. "Accountability in U.S. Higher Education: Applying Lessons from K-12 Experience to Higher Education." *Journal of Economic Perspectives* 30 (3): 33–56.

Dynarski, S., and J. Scott-Clayton. 2013. "Financial Aid Policy: Lessons from Research." *The Future of Children* 23 (1): 67–91.

Espinoza, R., and S. Urzúa. 2015. "Las Consecuencias Económicas de un Sistema de Educación Superior Gratuito en Chile." Revista de Educación, N. 370. Madrid.

———. 2016. "Returns to Higher Education: Funding, Coverage and Quality." Background paper for this report.

Ferreira, F. H., J. Messina, J. Rigolini, L. F. López-Calva, M. A. Lugo, and R. Vakis. 2013. *Economic Mobility and The Rise of the Latin American Middle Class*. Washington, DC: World Bank.

Ferreyra, M. M., and P. Liang. 2012. "Information Asymmetry and Equilibrium Monitoring in Education." *Journal of Public Economics* 96 (1): 237–54.

Hastings, J. S., C. A. Nielson, A. Ramirez, and S. D. Zimmerman. 2016. "(Un) Informed College and Major Choice: Evidence from Linked Survey and Administrative Data." *Economics of Education Review* 51: 136–51.

Horn, L., X. Chen, and C. Chapman. 2003. *Getting Ready to Pay for College: What Students and Their Parents Know about the Cost of College Tuition and What They Are Doing to Find Out*. Statistical Report, National Center for Education Statistics. Washington, DC.

Hoxby, C. 2009. "The Changing Selectivity of American Colleges." *Journal of Economic Perspectives* 23 (4): 95–118.

Lederman, D., J. Messina, S. Pienknagura, and J. Rigolini. 2014. *Latin American Entrepreneurs*. Washington, DC: World Bank.

Maloney, W., and F. Caicedo. 2014. "Part II: Engineers, Innovative Capacity and Development in the Americas." Policy Research Working Paper 6814. World Bank, Washington, DC.

Melguizo, T., G. Zamarro, T. Velasco, and F. Sanchez. 2017. "The Methodological Challenges of Measuring Student Learning, Degree Attainment, and Early Labor Market Outcomes in Higher Education." *Journal of Research on Educational Effectiveness* 10 (2): 1–25.

Messina, J. and J. Silva. 2017. "Wage Inequality in Latin America: Understanding the Past to Prepare for the Future." World Bank, Washington DC. (forthcoming)

Neilson, C., J. Hasting, and S. Zimmerman. 2016. "Student Loan Policy and Higher Education Markets: Preliminary Evidence from Chile." Background paper for this report.

Shavelson, R. J., B. Dominguez, J. Marino, A. M. Mantilla, J. A. Morales, and E. Wiley. 2016. "On the Practices and Challenges of Measuring Higher Education Value Added: The Case of Colombia." *Assessment and Evaluation in Higher Education* 41(5): 695–720.

Skomsvold, P., A. Walton, and L. Berkner. 2011. "Web Tables: Six-Year Attainment, Persistence, Transfer, Retention, and Withdrawal Rates of Students Who Began Postsecondary Education in 2003–04." National Center for Education Statistics. Washington, DC.

Szekely, M. 2016. "Recent Trends in Higher Education in Latin America." Working Paper, Centro de Estudios Educativos y Sociales CEES.

Toivanen, O., and L. Väänänen. 2016. "Education and Innovation." *Review of Economics and Statistics* 98 (2): 382–96.

Tornatzky, L. G., R. H. Cutler, and J. Lee. 2002. "College Knowledge: What Latino Parents Need to Know and Why They Don't Know It." Tomás Rivera Policy Institute Report. Claremont, CA.

Introduction

In the pursuit of growth and equity, no country can afford to ignore higher education. Through higher education, a country forms skilled labor and builds the capacity to generate knowledge and innovation, which boosts productivity and economic growth. Since acquiring greater skills raises a person's productivity and her expected earnings, a good education system is also the basis for achieving greater equity and shared prosperity on a societal level. Particularly in societies mired with persistent and profound inequality, high-quality education can act as "the great equalizer": the ultimate channel of equal opportunities, and the ultimate hope for parents who long for a better future for their children.

In this study, we investigate three important aspects of higher education in Latin America and the Caribbean: *quality*, *variety*, and *equity*. A good higher education system offers quality, variety, and equity to maximize students' potential given their innate ability, interests, motivation, and academic readiness at the end of high school. Since people differ in these aspects, and the economy needs various types of skills, a *variety* of offerings allows students to find their best match. A good higher education system trains engineers as well as technicians—economists as well as administrative assistants. In addition, a good higher education system offers *quality* programs that maximize students' potential, given their best match. Since the mere availability of variety and quality does not guarantee students' access to or success in them, a higher education system displays *equity* when students have access to equal opportunities.

Societies vary in how they determine equity in higher education, since they differ in what they consider "fair." For instance, some societies consider it fair to give students of the same academic readiness access to the same opportunities, whereas others consider it fair to give all students access to the same opportunities, despite differences in their academic readiness or other characteristics. Regardless of their view of equity, higher education systems face the fact that quality, variety, and equity are interdependent. For instance, providing higher education access to disadvantaged students may improve equity, but possibly at the cost of quality if those students are limited to low-quality higher education options.

Hence, equity is best served by giving students access to high-quality programs at which they can succeed, an outcome that is more likely when a variety of programs are offered.

Higher education in the region has expanded dramatically in the last 15 years as the average gross enrollment rate (defined as the ratio between higher education enrollment and the population ages 18–24 years)[1] has grown from 21 percent to 43 percent between 2000 and 2013. Currently, the system includes approximately 20 million students, 10,000 institutions, and 60,000 programs. The higher education system has a rich history that dates back to the early 1500s, with the founding of the University of Santo Domingo, followed by the (then) Pontifical University of San Marcos (Lima) and the Royal and Pontifical University of Mexico (Brunner 1990).

Today, higher education is at a crossroads. The large expansion experienced since the early 2000s has given rise to a new, complex landscape. Concerned with access and social mobility, policy makers expanded the system at a time of economic growth, fiscal abundance, and a rising middle class. As a result, access grew for all students, but particularly those from the low- and middle-income segments. These "new" students, who were previously underrepresented in higher education, constitute a critical piece of the new landscape, as are the higher education institutions (HEIs) and programs serving them.

Concerns about quality loom over the large equity gains experienced by higher education systems in the region. The rapid expansion of the systems, the characteristics of the "new" students, and perhaps the lax regulation of some HEIs have led many to question the quality of their programs and, thus, the equity of a system in which not every student gains access to a high-quality option.

At this crossroads, Latin America and the Caribbean face an opportunity not to be missed. The policy decisions made 10 or 15 years ago have had profound consequences on today's environment. Today's decisions will have long-lasting, far-reaching consequences on the region's future as well.

Thus, in the remainder of this introduction we set the stage for the rest of the study by characterizing the role and capabilities of each agent in the higher education system (students, institutions, and the policy maker) as well as the distinctive characteristics of the higher education sector from an economic perspective. It is important to note that the study focuses on one role of the higher education system: the instruction of undergraduate students. While higher education systems have other roles (for example, the production and dissemination of research, the formation of graduate students and new researchers, and extension programs geared toward the community at large), not all HEIs take up these roles to the same extent, and there are scant data on these other roles. Furthermore, the instruction of undergraduate students is arguably the main role of HEIs in Latin America and the Caribbean. In addition, this study focuses mostly on the private returns to higher education. Although higher education yields returns to society as a whole, for data-related and technical reasons we restrict the scope to private returns.

Although higher education finance is an important aspect of higher education systems, a detailed study of this issue is beyond the scope of the current report.

Students, Institutions, and the Policy Maker

Because higher education is at a crossroads, it is important to recall what the agents in higher education (students and their families, HEIs, and the policy maker) can and cannot do, as well as their motives to engage.

The final outcome reached by a student in higher education (for example, employment, final GPA, or admission to graduate school) results from the contribution of multiple inputs. These include her effort, innate ability, and academic readiness. They also include inputs provided by the HEI, such as professors, peers, labs, and facilities. The important point is that individual academic readiness and effort are indeed inputs, and policies that merely give access to higher education without being mindful of students' academic readiness—or without providing incentives for student effort—will fall short of their potential benefits.

The possibility that students might not graduate brings us to another important point, namely that higher education is a risky investment. This risk affects some students more than others, since some students are less academically ready for higher education and more likely to drop out than others.

When making decisions, students and their families view higher education programs as "bundles" consisting of such elements as the program, peer students, student effort requirements, expected returns in the labor market, expected social and labor market connections, and distance to desirable locations. As this report documents, not all students care about these elements equally. For instance, high-ability students tend to care more about their peers' ability than their lower ability counterparts.[2] In addition, a distinctive regional feature is students' strong preference for attending an HEI close to home.[3] These two elements have important consequences on market structure.

While some students pursue higher education to improve their economic prospects, others seek the opportunity to learn a subject of their interest and are less concerned about economic payoffs. Still, others seek the "college experience," roughly defined as immersion in a new environment, with new peers, exposed to new ideas and perspectives. The multiplicity of goals is a challenge for the policy maker seeking to regulate the sector (Deming and Figlio 2016). Yet regardless of their goal, many students conduct a cost-benefit analysis when deciding whether to pursue higher education and what option to choose. If they attend college, they will incur the cost of tuition and other expenses, such as books and transportation, and will receive a college graduate's salary upon graduation. If they do not attend college, they will likely earn a high school graduate salary. The ability to design efficient, responsible, and equitable funding systems is perhaps the most obvious way for the policy maker to affect students' decisions, although it is not the only one.

Regardless of how the policy maker intervenes, the fact remains that her intervention is necessary because left to its own devices, the market will not achieve the social optimum of maximizing each person's potential and meeting the economy's skill needs. Several reasons contribute to this outcome. First, higher education provides a benefit not only to the person who receives it but also to society at large. Even when the market rewards a higher education graduate for her output, society also enjoys the contributions from her innovations, knowledge production, and research findings. Moreover, society benefits from the presence of higher education graduates in ways not fully rewarded by the market. For instance, these graduates might be more involved citizens and raise healthier children. In the presence of such externalities, students contemplating higher education will not internalize the full social benefits and will invest less in it than the social optimum.

Second, students with the greatest potential to benefit from a particular program may not be able to afford it. These liquidity constraints for talented individuals detract not only from equity but also from efficiency, since the economy fails to realize its full productive potential. A cautionary note: while liquidity constraints may be an obstacle to access, another may be the lack of academic readiness for higher education work. As documented in this report, students from lower income families tend to be less academically ready than those from higher income families, which may be evidence of an inequitable primary and secondary education system.

While the credit market could, in principle, mitigate short-term liquidity constraints, this market is imperfect. Higher education loans typically lack the collateral or guarantee required by financial institutions, since students borrow to finance an investment embodied in themselves. Moreover, a higher education loan is risky for a bank, since the bank only has noisy information on the loan's profitability. Similarly, the student may be uncertain over her graduation probability or the long-term returns of her higher education program. As a result, left to its own devices the credit market will play a smaller role, if any, in financing higher education than in the social optimum.

Third, higher education is a complex product characterized by strong information asymmetries, and it is difficult for students and parents to assess the quality and variety of offerings. Consider, for instance, a student interested in biology who is trying to choose a program suited for work in industry. She might not know what specific programs would train her better for industry than for research. She might see similar programs and not know how to differentiate among them, perhaps because the HEIs themselves choose not to reveal the relevant information. Or she might know that graduates from a particular program obtain high-paying jobs after graduation, yet not know whether this is due to the program's ability to select high-performing students, or to the rigor of its training and instruction. The ensuing lack of information leads some students to make suboptimal choices, such as enrolling in low-quality programs while also taking on heavy college loans.

To further complicate matters, some students and parents are better than others at information processing, namely at assessing the quality and variety of higher education programs, and at comparing long-term costs and benefits of alternative career paths and financing options. Such disparities, associated with parental background and education (Castleman 2013; Horn and others 2003; Tornatzky and others 2002), only exacerbate the inequities. Cognitive biases, too, prevent students from making sound decisions, by making them overestimate returns from some programs or be overconfident about their chances of success.[4] In Latin America and the Caribbean, where transferring across programs is rather difficult, the cost of making the wrong decision can be quite high. This raises the stakes on a decision in which there is no opportunity at learning by doing, given that most individuals make this decision only once (or just a few times) over their lifetime.

Information asymmetries, information-processing difficulties, cognitive biases, and decision-making costs can interfere with the higher education system's ability to form the skills required in the labor market. For example, an economy may suffer a shortage of computer programmers yet have a surplus of journalists. Even though market wages should act as indicators of relative scarcity to future graduates (that is, computer programmers should earn more, on average, than journalists), students may not use this information when making choices, or may not realize they lack the academic readiness necessary to pursue the higher paying program.

Fourth, higher education markets feature imperfect competition. Setting up and running an HEI is costly, a force that would naturally concentrate the system around relatively few providers and give them market power. The actual degree of concentration largely depends on legal and regulatory barriers to the entry of HEIs; if barriers are low, the system might experience considerable entry of new providers and relatively low concentration. Yet even if entry is plentiful, the fact that each HEI offers a differentiated product (for example, by geographic location, program type, student peer ability, curriculum focus, academic rigor, and expectations) allows HEIs to compete along multiple dimensions, and gives each HEI a certain degree of market power over the students that choose it.

For instance, most students in the region attend an HEI close to home. This gives HEIs a considerable market power in their geographic areas. Similarly, higher education markets in the United States were quite localized a few decades ago and, as they became geographically more integrated, they became more competitive (Hoxby 2009). Hence, although bringing higher education to additional locales can raise access for students in those places, special care is needed to prevent those HEIs from exploiting their natural market power by offering low-quality services.

Another instance of imperfect competition arises through tuition subsidies for students enrolled in public HEIs, a practice common to all countries in the region, some of which go as far as offering tuition-free public HEIs. When policy makers subsidize public HEIs but do not provide financial aid for private HEIs, they contribute to creating a captive demand for public HEIs, composed of students who have no other choice. While making education available to such students might be desirable, the ensuing market power for public HEIs deserves the policy maker's close attention.

Of much concern, too, is the market segment formed by students who are poorly informed about higher education programs and returns, are financially illiterate, and are academically unprepared for higher education. These students may be drawing from their families' meager savings or from student loans to finance their higher education. This segment naturally invites the entry of low-quality, high-price HEIs, and also deserves the policy maker's close attention.

Furthermore, in typical competitive markets, firm exit disciplines the market by forcing low-demand products (which, presumably, have the lowest quality) out of the market. Yet, a crucial difference between such markets and the higher education market is that the exit of an HEI can be quite costly for students, particularly those enrolled in the HEI. Societies, then, cannot afford frequent HEI exits.

Because students vary in income, ability, place of residence, gender, parental education, preferences, and goals pursued in higher education, there is room for the system to offer a wide range of higher education options. As a result, students *sort* across HEIs and programs. Sorting has three important consequences. The first is that not every student has access to the same options. Low-ability students, for instance, cannot gain access to selective programs, although this does not necessarily mean that their programs will be of low quality. Because high-ability students prefer attending higher education with other high-ability students, forcing some selective programs to admit lower ability students will only lead some high-ability students to switch to other programs.

The second consequence of sorting is that the market becomes segmented, and not every segment expands during an expansion. Since the selective segment expands mostly to admit high-ability students, it falls on the nonselective segment to admit lower ability students. Because there are many lower ability students, nonselective programs and HEIs will compete for them, sometimes fiercely.

The third consequence of sorting is that analytical or policy-related efforts on higher education must be mindful of the sector's vast heterogeneity and avoid one-size-fits-all approaches. Heterogeneity among students, institutions, and programs is a theme of our study.

Structure of the Report

Chapter 1 describes the recent higher education expansion. It documents the magnitude of the expansion, describes the "new" students, and examines patterns of higher education spending in the region relative to other regions. It examines multiple indicators of private returns to higher education and provides evidence regarding public returns. Chapter 2 presents equity, quality, and variety indicators in higher education. It describes the recent equity gains, presents evidence regarding to quality, and documents the variety of programs and HEIs in the region. Chapter 3 focuses on wage-based returns to higher education, both complete and incomplete. It documents returns' recent average decline and their heterogeneity among fields and HEIs.

Chapter 4 examines the demand-side drivers of the recent expansion. It studies the admission and funding mechanisms in the region, and explores student sorting across programs and HEIs. It also studies the unintended consequences of funding mechanisms. Chapter 5 examines the supply-side drivers of the expansion. It documents the supply-side growth in the region and studies the opening of new programs and the competitive strategies used by various HEI types. Chapter 6 provides a summary of institutional arrangements related to current higher education policy in the region. Chapter 7 concludes with policy implications from the analysis conducted in the report.

Notes

1. See the glossary for definitions of *gross enrollment rate* and *net enrollment rate.*
2. Here, ability is proxied by academic readiness for college. In some countries, this is measured by high school graduation exams or college entrance exams.
3. On the basis of household survey data, in 2013 almost 80 percent of higher education students ages 18–24 years lived at home (namely, the student is either the child or grandchild of the household head). Student-level data for Colombia indicate that about three-quarters of students attend an HEI located in the same state where they attend high school.
4. For example, Hastings and others (2016) describe that students tend to have noisy beliefs about programs' costs, although their average beliefs are correct. However, they overestimate the returns to their preferred programs.

References

Brunner, J. J. 1990. "Educación Superior en América Latina" ["Higher Education in Latin America"]. Fondo de Cultura Económica.

Castleman, B. L. 2013. "Prompts, Personalization, and Pay-Offs: Strategies to Improve the Design and Delivery of College and Financial Aid Information." Working paper, Center on Education Policy and Workforce Competitiveness, University of Virginia, Charlottesville.

Deming, D. J., and D. Figlio. 2016. "Accountability in U.S. Higher Education: Applying Lessons from K-12 Experience to Higher Education." *Journal of Economic Perspectives* 30 (3): 33–56.

Horn, L., X. Chen and C. Chapman. 2003. "Getting Ready to Pay for College, What Students and Their Parents Know About the Cost of College Tuition and What They Are Doing to Find Out." Statistical Report, National Center for Education Statistics, Institute of Education Sciences, Washington, DC.

Hastings, J. S., C. A. Nielson, A. Ramirez and S. D. Zimmerman. 2016. "(Un)informed College and Major Choice: Evidence from Linked Survey and Economic Data." *Economics of Education Review* 51: 136–151.

Hoxby, C. 2009. "The Changing Selectivity of American Colleges." *Journal of Economic Perspectives* 23 (4): 95–118.

Tornatzky, L. G., R. H. Cutler and J. Lee. 2002. "College Knowledge. What Latino Parents Need to Know and Why They Don't Know It." Report, Tomás Rivera Policy Institute, University of Southern California, Los Angeles.

CHAPTER 1

The Rapid Expansion of Higher Education in the New Century

Ciro Avitabile

Abstract

Starting from 2000, Latin America and the Caribbean have seen a large expansion in the share of skilled labor force that has been boosted by an unprecedented increase in the number of students enrolled in higher education. Simultaneously, the number of programs and institutions has significantly expanded. An increasing share of students comes from the bottom of the income distribution; these students display lower levels of academic readiness than higher-income students. Many countries are spending a significant share of resources in higher education relative to their possibilities, but the weight of public and private spending varies significantly across countries. Average private returns to the investment in higher education are still high but decreasing. There is little evidence that among individuals who belong to the same generation higher education generates positive externalities for those who did not make the investment, although evidence suggests that higher education can trigger intergenerational mobility. Therefore, the region can maximize the gains from its ongoing "demographic bonus" by forming skilled human capital; in so doing, speed in creating skilled labor force is critical, as is avoiding the creation of excess capacity.

Introduction

This chapter sets the stage for the analysis in the next chapters and summarizes the main trends in higher education in Latin America and the Caribbean. It discusses how the share of skilled labor force, enrollment in higher education, and completion rates have evolved over time. It then provides basic facts on higher education spending in the region. It discusses the evidence on some of the potential average private and social returns associated with higher education. It ends with a discussion on the role of higher education in maximizing the gains from the region's ongoing demographic bonus.

While the focus will be on the entire region, we will highlight the main differences across countries within the region, as well as differences in skilled labor force and enrollment associated to important sociodemographic characteristics such as gender and household income. Whenever possible, we will benchmark data with those of countries outside the region.

Trends in the Share of Skilled Labor Force, Higher Education Enrollment, and Completion Rates

The last two decades have seen a dramatic expansion in the share of skilled labor force in Latin America. In 1992, only 7.5 percent of the population ages 25–64 years had completed a higher education degree. The share went up to 9.7 percent in 2002 and to 13.5 percent in 2012. In 1992, only Peru had a share of the working-age population with a higher education degree above 15 percent. In 2012, four countries had a share of higher education graduates that exceeded 20 percent (see figure 1.1).

Similar to the pace of economic growth in the region, the pace of expansion in the share of skilled labor force was relatively slow between 1995 and 2002 and increased in the following decade (Messina and Silva, 2017).

In 2013 there were almost 20 million higher education students enrolled in about 60,000 programs in Latin America and the Caribbean.[1] In 1991 the enrollment rate in postsecondary education (ISCED 5 and 6) in the region was only 17 percent. Starting from 2000, the growth rate both in terms of students enrolled and programs is nothing less than staggering. As shown in figure 1.2, the gross enrollment rate increased from 21 percent to 40 percent between 2000 and 2010. For a comparison, Central Asia, which had the same baseline gross enrollment rate

Figure 1.1 Expansion in the Share of Skilled Working-Age Population, circa 1992, 2002, and 2012

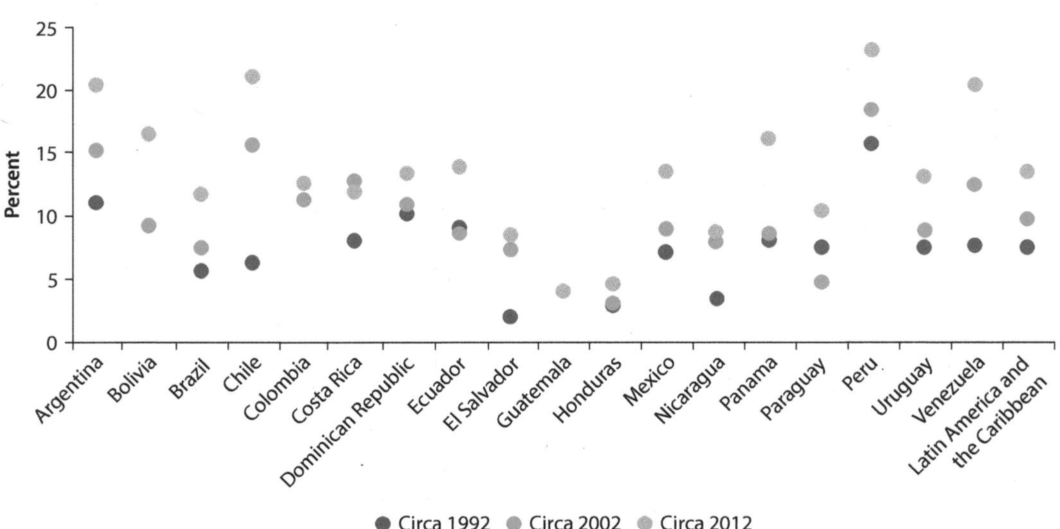

Source: World Bank calculations based on SEDLAC.
Note: The figure shows the share of the population ages 25–64 years that report completing higher education.

Figure 1.2 International Benchmarking of Gross Enrollment Rates, 2000, 2005, and 2010

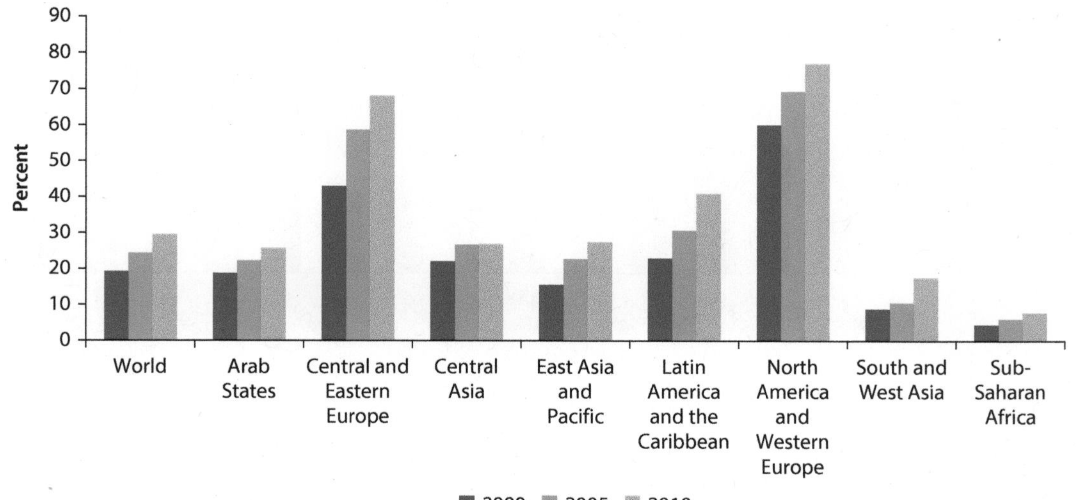

Source: United Nations Educational, Scientific and Cultural Organization, UNESCO. http://data.uis.unesco.org/?queryid=142.
Note: The figure shows the total enrollment in tertiary education (ISCED 5–8), regardless of age, expressed as a percentage of the total population of the five-year age group after leaving secondary school. For each region, the weighted average over the corresponding countries is given.

as Latin America and the Caribbean in 1992, reached 27 percent in 2010. Only South and West Asia have growth rates faster than that of Latin America and the Caribbean, and this might be partly explained by the former starting from a much lower baseline.

Evidence from household survey data shows that while Argentina, Uruguay, and Chile display gross enrollment rates in line with most Organisation of Economic Co-operation and Development (OECD) countries, Guatemala and Honduras display very low rates. Between 2000 and 2013 (figure 1.3), gross enrollment rates have grown most in Bolivia, Peru, and Chile. Remarkably, in Chile the expansion in higher education enrollment, when compared with the growth in gross domestic product (GDP) per capita, has been much faster than in countries such as France, Norway, and Sweden during their own major higher education expansions (see annex 1A, figure 1A.1). The picture does not change when looking at the net enrollment rate, a measure that reflects the participation of the official higher education age population (see annex 1B, figure 1B.1). Panama is the only country where enrollment rates declined between 2000 and 2013. There is no evidence that enrollment rates grew faster in countries with lowest baseline values in 2000.

The number of programs has more than doubled between 2000 and 2013, which can be partly explained by an increase in the number of higher education institutions (from 9,103 in 2000 to 13,844 in 2013) and partly by an increase in the offer of programs among existing institutions. The expansion of the supply in the region is discussed in chapter 5.[2]

The differences in enrollment rate over time and across countries can be largely explained by trends in upper secondary education completion rates,

Figure 1.3 Gross Enrollment Rate, circa 2000 and 2013

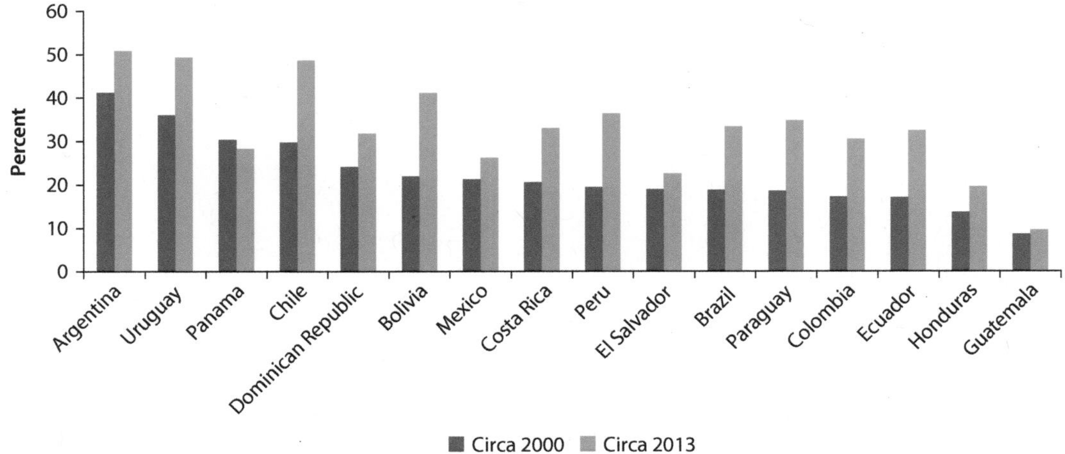

Source: World Bank calculations using SEDLAC databases.
Note: Gross enrollment rate refers to the total enrollment in higher education (ISCED 5–6) regardless of age, as a percentage of the population ages 18–24 years. Because of the change in survey coverage, we restricted the sample to 28 urban cities in Argentina, and the Asuncion and urban interior in Uruguay.

rather than by the increased entry rates of high school graduates into higher education.[3] Szekely (2016) finds that individuals born between 1990 and 1992 are 13 percentage points more likely to have ever enrolled in higher education than those born between 1970 and 1972. Out of this difference, 11 percentage points can be attributed to a higher probability of completing upper secondary education, and 2 percentage points to an increased probability of higher education enrollment conditional on high school completion.

On average, the graduation rate from upper secondary education in Latin America and the Caribbean increased from 32 percent in the early 1990s to 46 percent in late 2000 (Bassi, Busso, and Muñoz 2013). Furthermore, all countries have displayed significant improvements in upper secondary graduation rates, with Brazil, Colombia, and the República Bolivariana de Venezuela showing the steepest ones.

Higher education entry rates, in contrast, have not changed much on average, going from 49.5 percent in 2000 to 52.4 percent in 2013. In addition, entry rate changes have been very heterogeneous across countries. As shown in figure 1.4, entry rates went up in Chile, Colombia, Peru, and Ecuador; they declined in Argentina, Mexico, El Salvador, and Guatemala. While the fast growth in entry rates displayed by Colombia and Ecuador might be partly explained by their having the lowest rates at the baseline (both below 40 percent), that is not the case for Chile, which registered a 11 percentage point increase in spite of a relatively high entry rate (almost 48 percent) in 2000. The drop in entry rate in Guatemala is dramatic (from 52 percent in 2000 to 28.8 percent in 2013),

Figure 1.4 Entry Rate to Higher Education after High School Graduation, circa 2000 and 2013

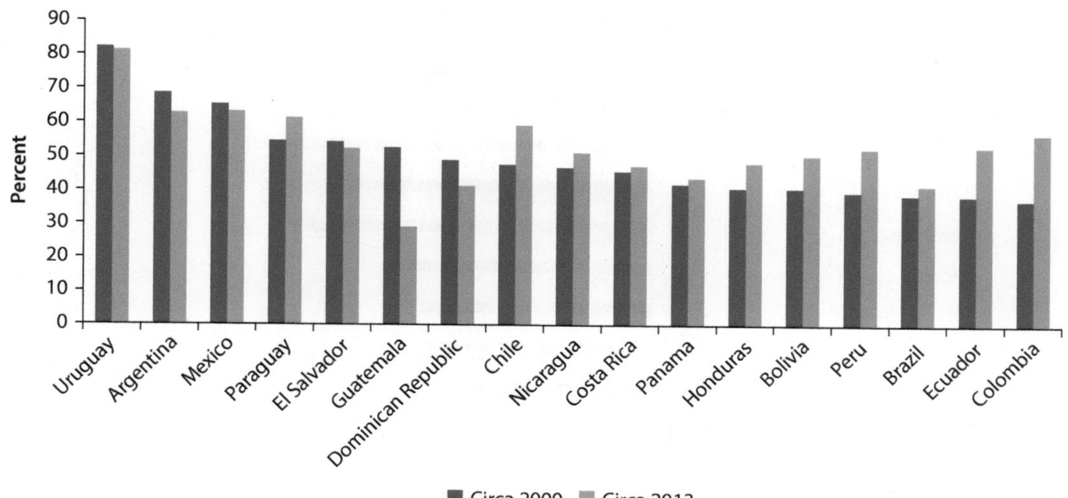

Source: World Bank calculations using SEDLAC databases.
Note: The entry rate is the percentage of population ages 18–24 years that have ever accessed higher education conditional on having graduated from high school. Because of the change in survey coverage, we restricted the sample of 28 urban cities in Argentina, and Asuncion and urban interior in Uruguay.

probably reflecting "selective" migration on the part of high school graduates. In particular, Adelman and Szekely (2016) find that in 2013, Guatemalan youth ages 18–25 years who migrated to the United States when they were at least 18 years old were more likely to have completed upper secondary school, or some higher education, than their counterparts at home.

There are large gaps in access associated to socioeconomic differences, but growth in access rates has been faster for students at the bottom of the income distribution and for women. The growth rate in access between 2000 and 2012 has been higher in the bottom quintile than in the top one (117 percent versus 24 percent), although there is large heterogeneity across countries. The gap between the top and bottom quintiles has shrunk in Chile, Bolivia, Mexico, and Argentina, but has widened in all the other countries (see figure 1.5).

In line with the evidence for developed countries (see Goldin, Katz, and Kuzmienko [2006] for the United States), in all the countries of the region, the share of female students enrolled in higher education is 50 percent or higher, with Ecuador displaying the lowest (50 percent) and Uruguay the highest (60 percent). As shown in figure 1.6, Guatemala, Chile, and Colombia have displayed remarkable increases in the share of female students enrolled in higher education between 2000 and 2013. Over this period, Paraguay, Argentina, and Ecuador have seen a reduction in the share of female students.

Cross-country differences in the share of female students cannot be accounted for by differences in the returns to higher education for women (discussed in chapter 3). When discussing the possible causes behind the increase in the share

Figure 1.5 Variation in Higher Education Access Rate, by Income Quintile, 2000–12

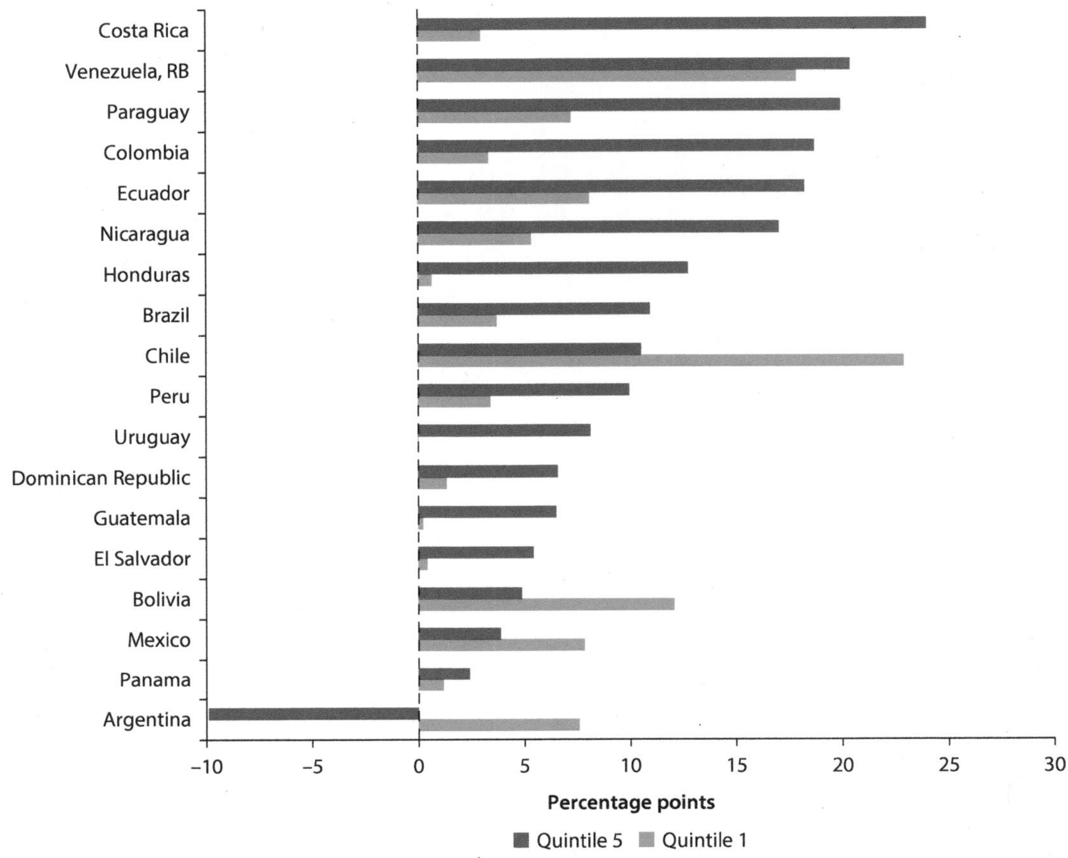

Source: World Bank calculations based on SEDLAC.
Note: Access rates are computed as the percentage of population ages 18–24 years that have ever had access to higher education. Because of the change in survey coverage, we restricted the sample of 28 urban cities in Argentina, and Asuncion and the urban interior in Uruguay.

of female college students in the United States, Goldin, Katz, and Kuziemko (2006) highlight the importance of changes in social norms and age at first marriage, as well as female students' improved performance in math and science in high school. These are the likely explanations behind both the trends in female education over time in Latin America and the Caribbean and the current variation in the female share across countries. However, a detailed analysis of the determinants of the gender differences goes beyond the scope of this chapter.

Low completion rates explain why the fraction of skilled population did not increase as much as the increase in enrollment. With higher education, it is difficult to distinguish the students who officially drop out from those who remain enrolled and could eventually finish their studies later. Using information in the household surveys on those who report incomplete higher education and are currently not studying, it is possible to build a proxy for completion rate.

Figure 1.6 Female Students in Higher Education, circa 2000 and 2013

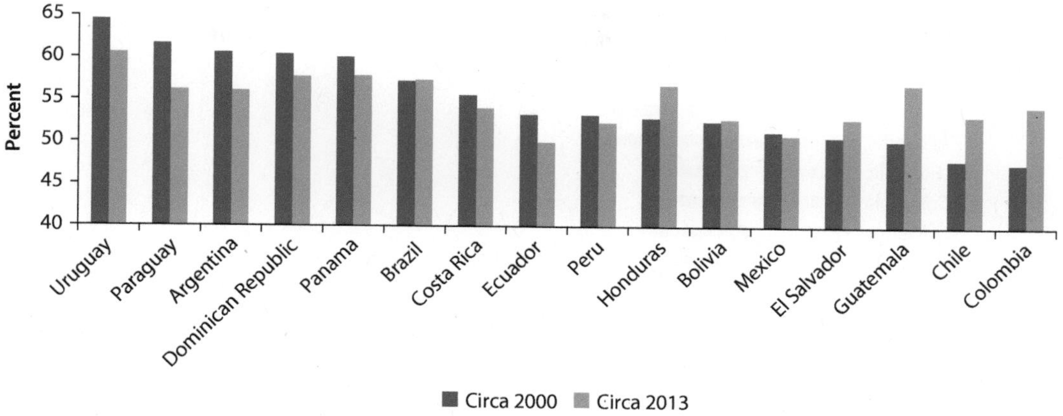

Source: World Bank calculations using SEDLAC databases.
Note: The figure depicts the percentage of higher education students aged 18–24 years who are female. Because of the change in survey coverage, we restricted the sample to 28 urban cities in Argentina, and Asuncion and the urban interior in Uruguay.

The average completion rate, defined as the percentage of individuals ages 25–29 years with complete higher education out of the total number of individuals with some college education, remains below 50 percent. In 2013, only Peru and Mexico had completion rates equal to 60 percent or higher and thus aligned with those of the United States (equal to 67 percent). In the full set of countries we find a very small (in absolute value) and negative correlation between enrollment and completion rates, lending little support to the hypothesis that countries that have higher enrollment rates (perhaps as a result of the recent expansion) have lower completion rates. We further discuss completion rates in Latin America and the Caribbean in chapter 2.

While we cannot benchmark completion rates in Latin America and the Caribbean against those in non-Latin American and Caribbean countries because of a lack of data, we are able to benchmark the gross graduation ratio. This indicator, developed by United Nations Educational, Scientific and Cultural Organization (UNESCO), is the ratio between the number of graduates from bachelor's and master's programs, and the number of individuals of theoretical graduation age (for instance, the number of individuals in the population ages 22–25 years). While a high graduation ratio might be due to a high higher education completion rate, it might also be due to a high upper secondary graduation rate, or a high higher education entry rate. Hence, the graduation ratio reflects the cumulative success of the educational system up to higher education.

Figure 1.7 shows the graduation ratio for Latin American and Caribbean countries, and for Europe and Central Asia and East Asia and Pacific comparators. The comparison is not encouraging for Latin America and the Caribbean, since most countries in that region lie below most of the comparators.

Figure 1.7 Gross Graduation Ratio, circa 2013

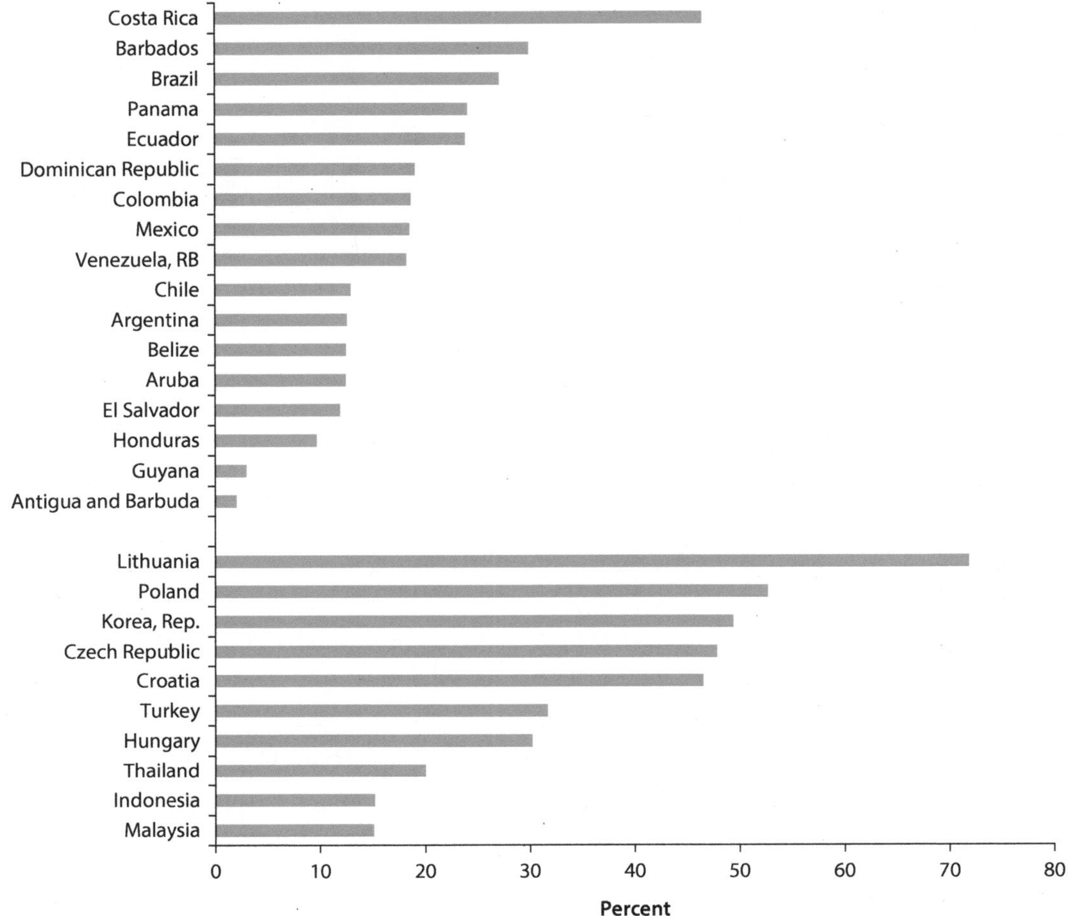

Source: United Nations Educational, Scientific and Cultural Organization, UNESCO. http://data.uis.unesco.org/index.aspx?queryid=161.
Note: Gross graduation ratio is calculated as the number of graduates from first degree programs (at ISCED 6 and 7) expressed as a percentage of the population of the theoretical graduation age of the most common first degree program.

"New" Students in the Higher Education System

As the share of individuals who enter higher education has increased, their average characteristics have changed. The most striking difference between students enrolled in early 2000 and in 2013 is the difference in the share of students belonging to the bottom of the income distribution. As shown in table 1.1, on average in the region the share of students in the bottom two quintiles increased from 10.5 percent in 2000 to 16.8 percent in 2013. Brazil has seen the largest increase in the share of students from the bottom two quintiles (from 3.4 percent in 2000 to 14.5 percent in 2013). Guatemala, Chile, and Bolivia have all at least doubled the share of students from the low end of the income distribution.

Table 1.1 Percentage of Higher Education Students, by Income Quintile, circa 2000 and 2013

	Before (circa 2000)				*After (circa 2013)*			
	1st	*2nd*	*4th*	*5th*	*1st*	*2nd*	*4th*	*5th*
Argentina	5.1	10.5	32.1	33.7	12.2	17.5	23.3	23.3
Bolivia	2.9	6.2	26.2	51.0	5.8	15.7	25.1	31.3
Brazil	1.2	2.2	21.4	68.2	5.3	9.2	28.6	40.3
Chile	5.6	8.2	27.9	40.0	14.9	19.0	21.2	25.1
Colombia	7.1	6.3	24.5	51.3	7.1	11.1	28.1	32.8
Costa Rica	2.9	5.6	27.4	53.9	6.1	8.9	28.3	40.2
Dominican Republic	4.1	9.1	23.8	51.8	6.0	10.4	22.0	45.2
Ecuador	5.5	9.0	24.9	46.3	7.0	12.6	25.1	36.6
El Salvador	1.7	4.3	21.1	61.8	2.5	7.4	27.4	46.3
Guatemala	2.4	0.8	11.7	81.7	3.5	3.6	10.0	78.0
Honduras	1.7	2.2	18.7	69.5	1.5	5.1	21.4	64.2
Mexico	6.0	8.0	26.9	45.2	10.6	11.9	26.9	32.7
Panama	3.0	5.0	29.9	43.8	4.1	8.8	26.4	39.3
Paraguay	1.5	4.7	25.6	58.7	4.9	12.5	25.8	39.9
Peru	3.2	10.3	27.6	40.9	6.8	14.0	26.7	32.5
Uruguay	1.4	6.4	27.1	50.1	1.5	7.4	28.7	46.7
Average Latin America and the Caribbean	**4.4**	**6.2**	**23.8**	**52.5**	**6.2**	**10.6**	**25**	**40.9**

Source: World Bank calculation based on SEDLAC databases.
Note: The table shows, for each year, the distribution of population of higher education students, ages 18–24 years, by family income quintile. The third quintile has been dropped in order to ease the exposition.

Students from the bottom of the income distribution might in principle differ from others along important sociodemographic characteristics and in terms of academic background. Although students ages 18–24 years enrolled in higher education in 2013 remain mostly urban, all the countries in the region, except Panama and Costa Rica, have witnessed (often modest) increases in the share of students from nonurban areas (figure 1.8).

The access of indigenous population to higher education has not changed since 2000. In Peru and Mexico, the countries with the largest shares, indigenous students accounted for 21.6 percent and 17.1 percent, respectively, in 2013. The fact that neither the share of urban nor indigenous students has changed in a significant way, in contrast with the substantial changes in the share of students coming from the bottom of the income distribution, suggests that the expansion in the enrollment has been mostly fueled by poor students living in urban areas.

Students belonging to low-income families are on average less academically ready than those from relatively well off families. Administrative data from standardized tests in Colombia and Brazil show that students belonging to the lowest segments of the income distribution tend to perform worse than others (figure 1.9).[4] In Colombia (figure 1.9a), among students whose family income is lower than the minimum wage, almost 54 percent are in the bottom two quintiles of the academic readiness distribution, and only 9 percent in the top quintile. In contrast, among those with an income five or more times higher

Figure 1.8 Higher Education Students Who Live in Urban Areas, circa 2000 and 2013

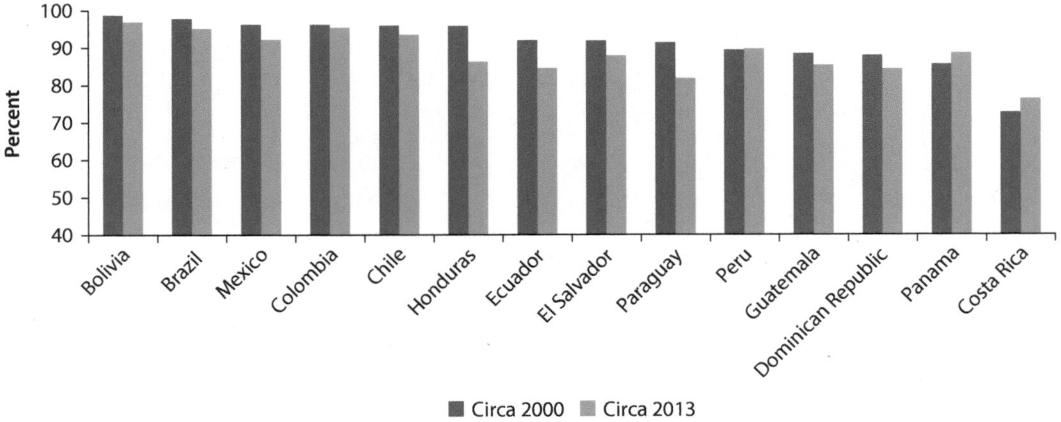

Source: World Bank calculations using SEDLAC databases.
Note: The figure depicts the percentage of higher education students, ages 18–24 years, that live in an urban area.

Figure 1.9 Ability Distribution Conditional on Income

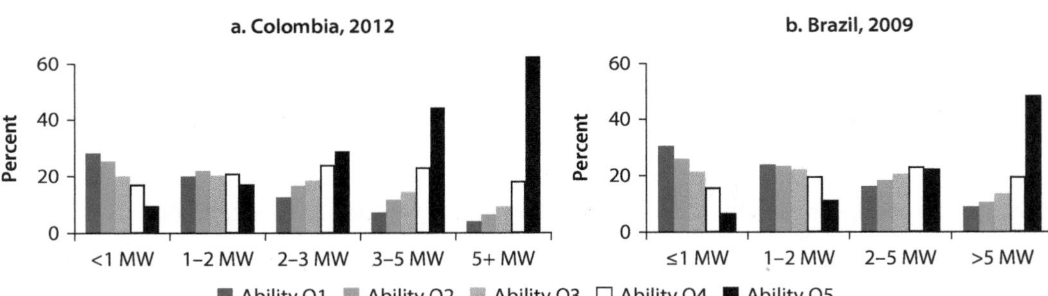

Source: Saber 11, National Assessment of Secondary Education, Brazil (ENEM).
Note: The panels show, for each family income bracket, the ability distribution in quintiles; thus, the height of the bars is the probability that a student in a particular income bracket is in the corresponding ability quintile. Ability quintiles are calculated using high school student's scores in Saber 11 test in 2012-second semester (Colombia) and ENEM test in 2009 (Brazil). MW = minimum wage.

than the minimum wage, only 11 percent are in the bottom two quintiles and 62 percent are in the top quintile of the ability distribution. The picture is very similar when we consider Brazil (figure 1.9b). This evidence suggests that since higher education enrollment in the bottom quintile of the income distribution has grown faster than in the top quintile during the first decade of 2000s, the share of students who are academically not ready has been increasing over time.

It is interesting to note that a comparison of 2000 and 2012 SABER 11 distribution by income brackets shows that among low-income students (with a family income of, at most, two times the minimum wage), the ability composition of high school graduates in 2012 is not different from the one of high school graduates in 2000 (figure 1.10).[5] However, among rich

Figure 1.10 Variation in the Income-Ability Relationship in Colombia, 2000 and 2012

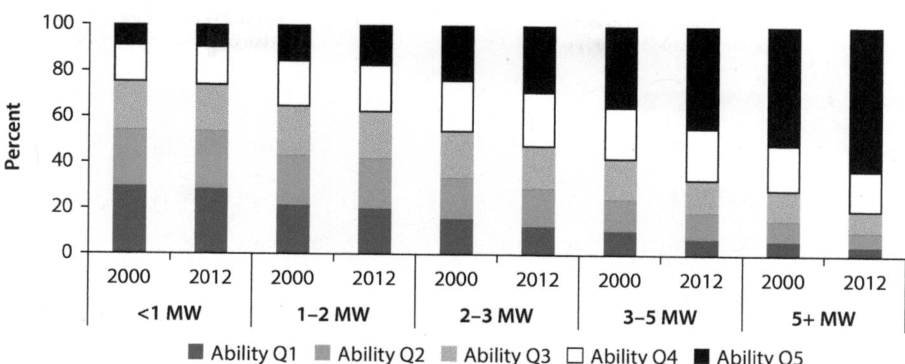

Source: Saber 11 data in 2000 and 2012.
Note: Ability distribution conditional on income. Ability quintiles are calculated using student's score in Saber 11 test in 2000-second semester and 2012-second semester. MW = minimum wage.

students (with an income at least three times higher than the minimum wage), the share of students scoring in the top quintile of the ability has increased from 51.4 percent in 2000 to 62.5 percent in 2012. Currently, a larger share of students is academically not ready, and the ability gap between rich and poor students has widened over time.

To summarize, during the recent higher education expansion in Latin America and the Caribbean, the share of a previously underrepresented type of student has risen—a student with relatively low income or ability. We use the term *new* to refer to this type of student throughout the report.

Spending in Higher Education

One potential explanation for the variation over time and across countries in higher education enrollment and completion is the amount of resources spent. Financial resources can also potentially contribute to explain the access gap between poor and rich students documented previously. While the financial resources invested can contribute only partly to improve educational attainments, it is virtually impossible to improve access and completion if limited public and private resources are invested.

For most countries in the region, per-student spending levels are relatively low when benchmarked to those of developed countries or comparator countries in East Asia and Pacific, although they are aligned with those of Eastern and Central Europe (see figure 1.11, panel a). For instance, the Latin American and Caribbean countries with the highest per-student spending, Mexico and Chile, spend less than US$8,000 per higher education student, approximately 20 percent less than that of South Korea or Indonesia, but well above that of Croatia and the Czech Republic.

Figure 1.11 Higher Education Spending, 2009

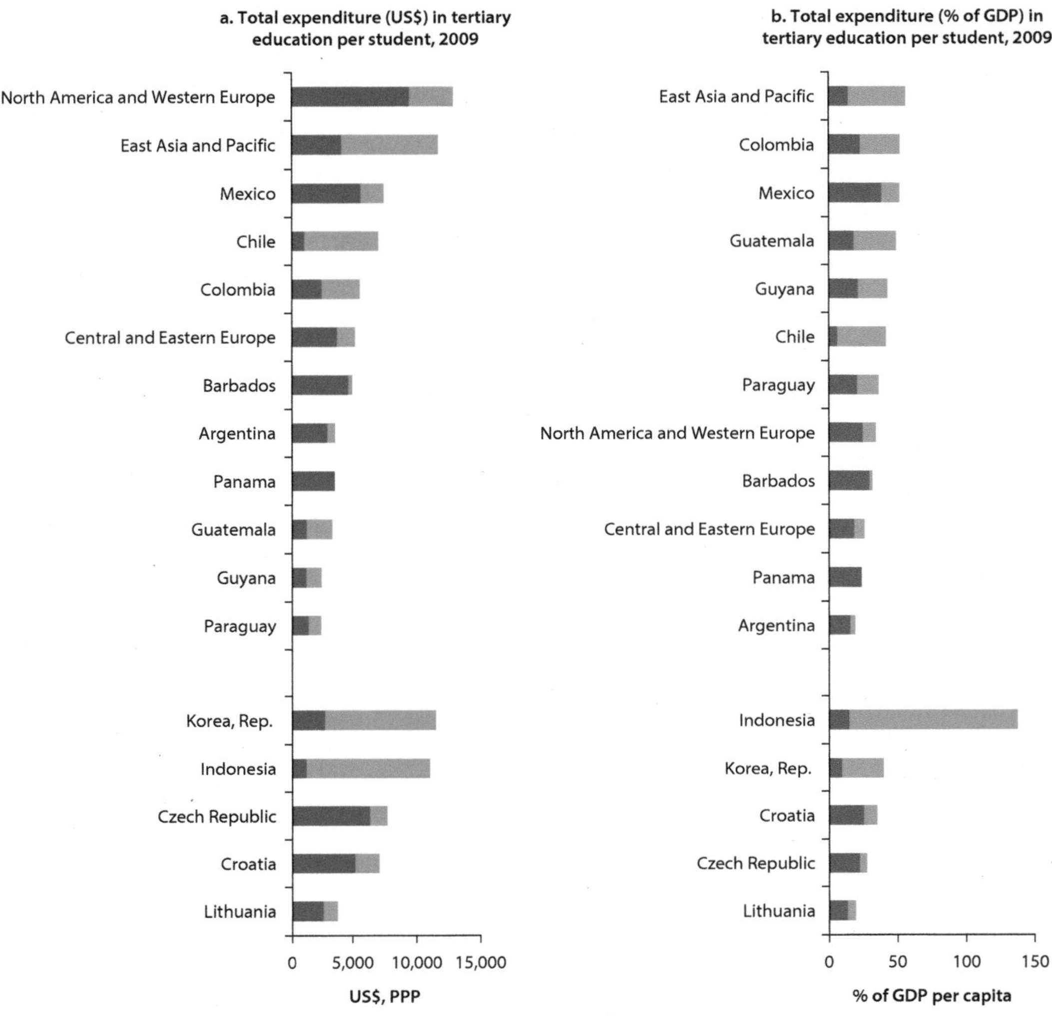

Source: World Bank calculations based on UNESCO Global Education Digest (GED) 2011 and World Development Indicators (WDI).
Note: Mexico is not included in the group of North American and Western Europe countries. East Asia and Pacific includes Australia, Indonesia, Japan, New Zealand and the Republic of Korea. PPP = purchasing power parity.

But, of course, differences in levels of spending might be misleading since most countries in the region have much lower GDP per capita than that of the United States and most Western European countries. When we examine the ratio of higher education spending to GDP per capita, the picture is different (figure 1.11, panel b). Many countries in the region display levels of higher education spending (relative to income) that fall below the East Asia and Pacific's average, but are well above those in the United States and Europe.

A lot of heterogeneity in the role of public funding exists across countries in the region. Whereas in Argentina, Panama, and Barbados, most higher education spending comes from public sources, this is not the case in other countries. Focusing on the countries with the highest per-student spending, we note that while in Mexico most spending comes from public sources, the opposite is true in Chile. Note, as well, that comparator countries in East Asia and Pacific rely mostly on private funding, whereas comparators in Eastern and Central Europe rely mostly on public funding. We return to the issue of higher education funding in chapter 4.

In 2013, with the only exception of Honduras, Argentina, Paraguay and St. Lucia, all the other countries for which data are available display a higher spending per student—in terms of GDP per capita—in higher education than in upper secondary. A similar trend is observed for most of the comparator countries (figure 1.12, panel a)

Between 2000 and 2010, the share of public spending per higher education student has been declining in most countries in the region, while the one for upper secondary education students has been increasing (17 percent in 2000 versus 23 percent in 2010). As discussed previously, since most of the increase in

Figure 1.12 Allocation of Public Spending, circa 2013

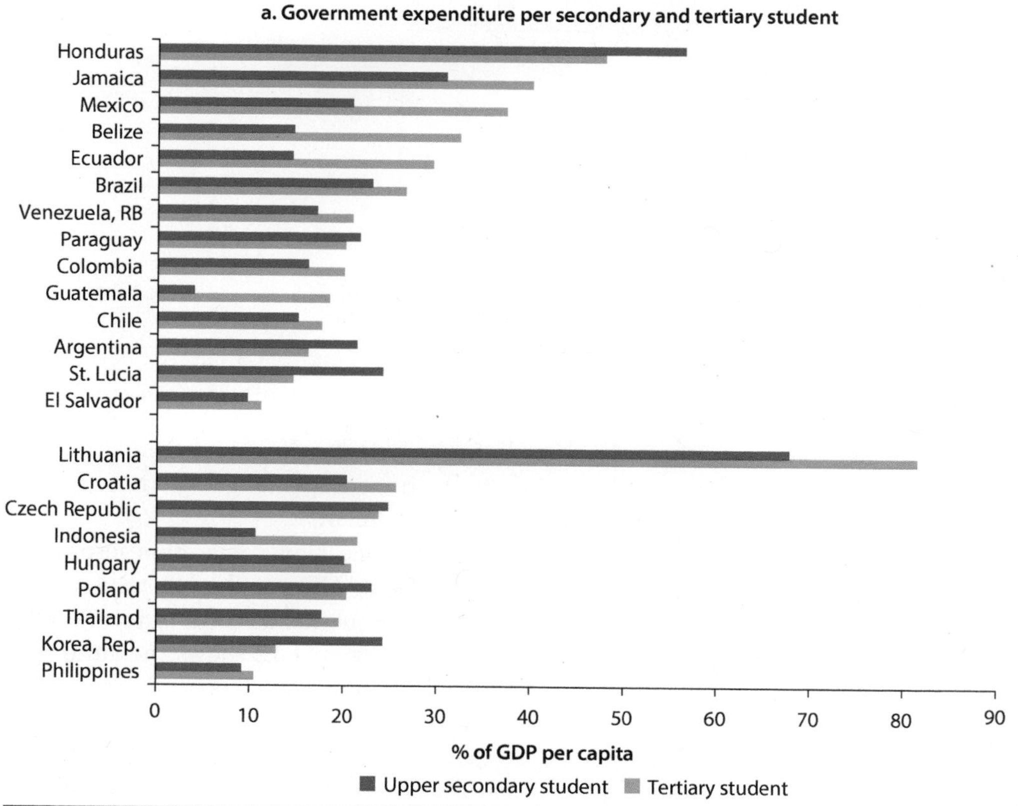

figure continues next page

Figure 1.12 Allocation of Public Spending, circa 2013 *(continued)*

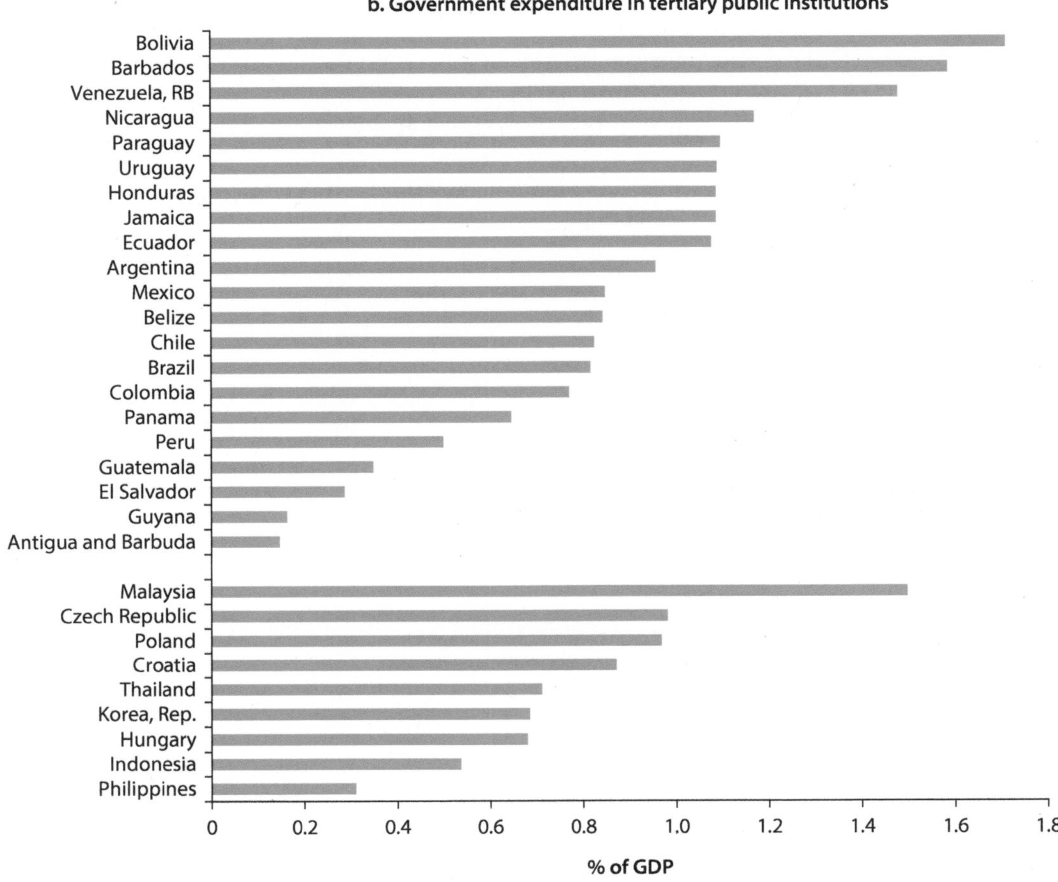

Source: United Nations Educational, Scientific and Cultural Organization, UNESCO. http://data.uis.unesco.org/index.aspx?queryid=189; http://data.uis.unesco.org/index.aspx?queryid=182.

higher education enrollment has been spurred by the increase in the upper secondary completion rate, this shift in government spending might not have had a detrimental effect on higher education enrollment.

Governments might subsidize access to public higher education institutions (HEIs) either through direct appropriations to the HEIs, or through tuition subsidies for the students. Governments might also subsidize access to private HEIs (usually through tuition subsidies). Panel b in figure 1.12 shows the amount of public spending (current and capital) in public institutions expressed as a percentage of GDP. Spending in public institutions (relative to income) is extremely high in Bolivia and Barbados, not only compared with other countries in the region but also to rich countries in East Asia and Pacific—(for example, Malaysia). Ecuador and Argentina, spend around 1 percent of the GDP, in line with the corresponding expenditure in the Czech Republic and Poland. Chile, Brazil, Mexico, and Colombia spend around 0.8 percent of the GDP in public institutions.

The share of higher education public spending devoted to wages varies across countries. In Argentina, Brazil, and Honduras, the wage bill absorbs more than 70 percent of the public spending in higher education, whereas in Colombia it represents only 46 percent of the spending. However higher wage bills are not necessarily associated with lower student-faculty ratios, which is indicative of higher education quality.[6] Brazil and Colombia have, on average, almost the same number of students per faculty (20 and 18, respectively), despite their large difference in the wage bill share. We return to the issue of student-faculty ratios in chapter 2.

Private Returns to Higher Education in Latin America and the Caribbean

The inflow of more educated workers into the labor force could potentially lower the labor market returns to higher education. In a simple demand and supply framework, an increase in the supply of skilled workers will lead to lower returns in the absence of a shift in the demand. In 2014, on average a higher education graduate in Latin America and the Caribbean earned 104 percent more than a high school graduate. The average premium varied from 49 percent in Argentina to 179 percent in Colombia.[7] The average wage premium for men and women was 104 and 99 percent, respectively.

Chapter 3 discusses in more detail the evolution of the wage premium between 2000 and 2012, and how the wage premium varies across fields of studies. The wage dispersion among higher education graduates, as measured by the standard deviations of the log hourly wage, is large and well above the wage dispersion among high school graduates in most countries (annex 1E, figure 1E.1). The high dispersion in the wage of higher education graduates is consistent with the large heterogeneity in returns documented in chapter 3.

The large higher education premium might also be explained by the fact that individuals who enroll in higher education have on average better cognitive and noncognitive skills than those who do not. Therefore, the large higher education premium might partly reflect skills acquired before entering higher education. There is a large body of evidence showing that both cognitive and noncognitive skills can shape individual educational choices and labor market outcomes, including wages (for example, Heckman and others 2006). The increase in the college wage premium over time in the United States has been linked to the increase in the returns to precollege cognitive skills (Murnane, Willett, and Levy 1995). Available data for Latin America and the Caribbean do not allow us to measure individual cognitive and noncognitive skills before entering higher education. To provide suggestive evidence on the role of these skills, we turn to data on cognitive and noncognitive skills collected by the World Bank as part of the STEP Skills Measurement program for 13 developing countries, including Colombia and Bolivia, in 2012. In both

Colombia and Bolivia, higher education graduates score much better that upper secondary graduates in terms of cognitive skills—as measured by the reading skills[8]—and marginally better in terms of noncognitive skills (see annex 1C, table 1C.1).[9] However, there is no evidence either for Bolivia or Colombia that differences in cognitive or noncognitive skills contribute to explain the higher education premium (see annex 1D, table 1D.1). However, this result requires a cautious interpretation. The lack of correlation might be explained, at least partly, by measurement error.

Individuals with higher education might enjoy benefits that go beyond the ones associated with higher wages. There is well established evidence for developed countries (for example, Cutler and Lleras-Muney 2010) that college educated individuals are in better health and display better health habits than noncollege graduates.[10] Evidence from the Demographic and Health Survey (DHS), which collects nationally representative data on health and population in developing countries, shows no association between education and health-related behavior. For instance, in line with other developing countries, the obesity rate in Latin America and the Caribbean for women with a higher education degree is not systematically lower than for women with lower levels of education (figure 1.13).

A traditional view of the marriage market suggests that higher wages should increase women's costs related to marriage and fertility. If that is the case, investing in higher education might generate a nonmonetary private cost

Figure 1.13 Education Levels and Health Behavior

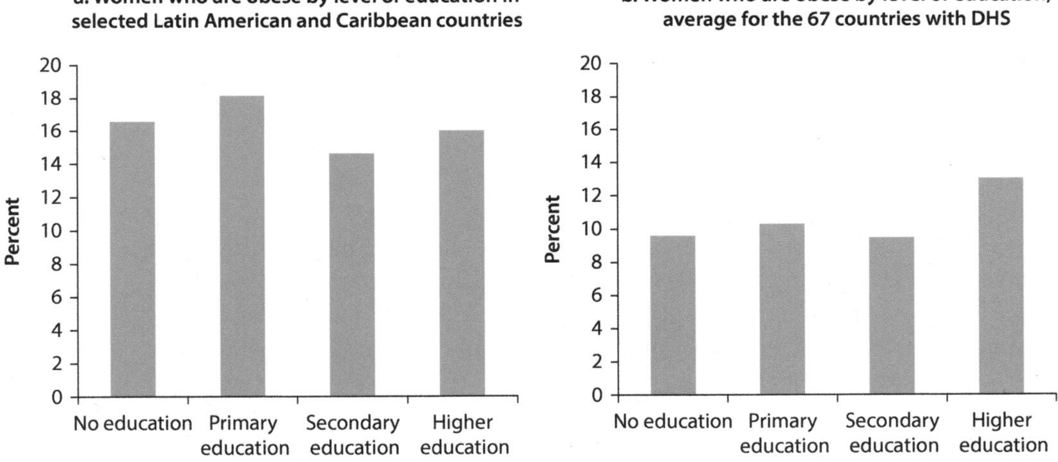

Source: Demographic and Health Surveys (DHS) Program database, ICF International for the U.S. Agency for International Development, http://dhsprogram.com/.
Note: The figure shows a simple average across countries. Data refer to the last year available. Women ages 15–49 years. The Latin American and Caribbean countries include Bolivia, Brazil, Colombia, the Dominican Republic, Guatemala, Guyana, Haiti, Honduras, Nicaragua, and Peru.

for women. Evidence from microdata for 18 countries shows that in 2012, 59 percent of the women ages 45–55 years with complete higher education were married, as opposed to 65 percent of the women with complete primary education (figure 1.14).[11] Among men in the same age group, 76 percent of those with complete primary and 77 of those with complete higher education were married. Ganguli, Hausmann, and Viarengo (2010) provide evidence that skilled women in Latin America and the Caribbean are more likely to "marry down"—marry men with a lower level of education—than skilled women in other countries.

The lower marriage rate among female higher education graduates in Latin America and the Caribbean is likely to be temporary. As technological progress allows married women with higher education degrees to buy market goods rather than producing them at home (Isen and Stevenson 2010), and social norms on female labor force participation change (Bertrand and others 2016), countries in Latin America and the Caribbean will likely follow the pattern of most developed countries, where women with higher education degree have higher marriage rates.[12]

Since male higher education graduates have a strong preference for female higher education graduates (about 60 percent are married to a higher education graduate), matching in the marriage market is likely to exacerbate income inequality between low-skilled and high-skilled workers.[13]

Figure 1.14 Higher Education and the Marriage Market, Latin America and the Caribbean

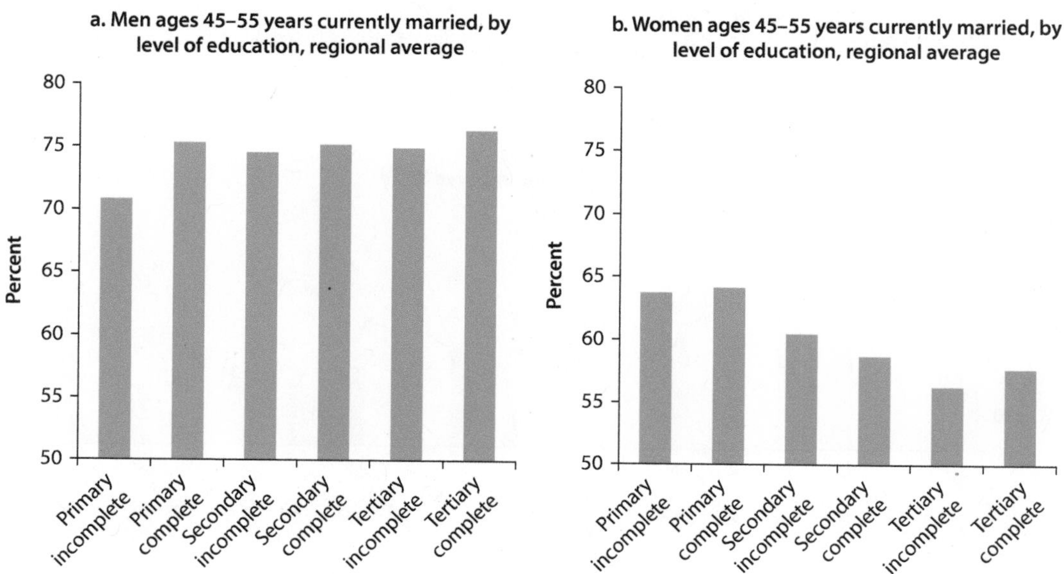

Source: World Bank calculations based on SEDLAC.
Note: The figure shows a simple average across countries. Data refer to year 2012 in all countries, except in Chile (2013), Guatemala (2011), Nicaragua (2009), and República Bolivariana de Venezuela (2011).

Social Returns and Costs of Higher Education

Theory predicts that increases in the overall level of education can benefit society in ways that are not fully reflected by individual benefits. Higher education rates might generate spillovers that may enhance productivity over and above the direct effect of education on individual productivity (Moretti 2004). Furthermore, increases in education also may reduce criminal participation (Lochner and Moretti 2004) and improve voters' political behavior (Milligan, Moretti, and Oreopoulos 2004). Understanding the extent of these externalities both across individuals belonging to the same generation and across generations is crucial to assess the efficiency of public investment in higher education. In this section we consider the externalities among individuals belonging to the same generation. The enforcement of tax compliance and social program eligibility is a major challenge in countries with large informal sectors. The persistently high level of informality poses a serious threat to the ability of Latin America and the Caribbean to boost growth (Loayza, Serven, and Sugawara 2009) and reduce inequality. From an individual perspective, informal workers are exposed to all types of risks (ill health, unemployment, disability, death, or poverty in old age). Based on household surveys, while average formality in the labor force in Latin America and the Caribbean is 52 percent, formality among those with complete higher education is 72 percent (Szekely 2016). Figure 1.15 shows the difference in formality rates between those with at least some higher education and those with lower other educational attainments. Higher education is associated with the highest share of formality in Honduras, the Dominican Republic, Guatemala, and Nicaragua, and with the lowest in Ecuador, Chile, Argentina, and Uruguay (Székely 2016).

The level of trust in other people[14] has been found to be positively correlated with (a) economic growth (Knack and Keefer 1997); (b) size of firms

Figure 1.15 Higher Education and the Formality Premium, circa 2013

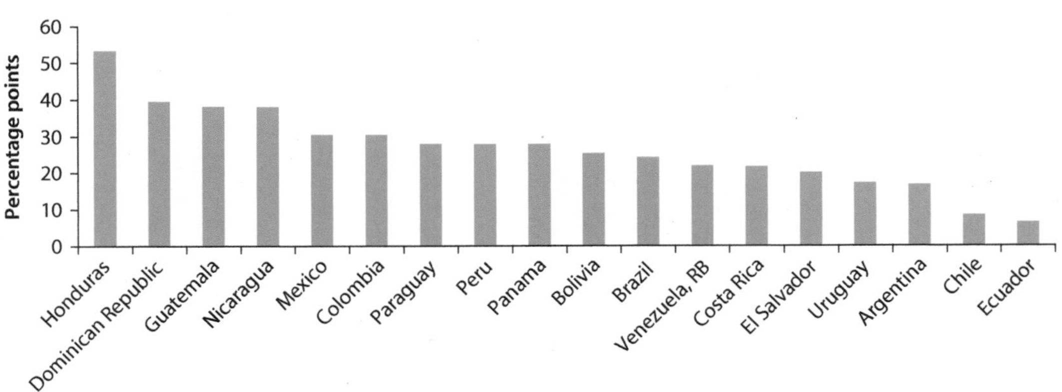

Source: Szekely 2016.
Note: The data show the difference in the formality rates between individuals with some higher education and those with lower attainment for the working-age population ages 25–65 years.

(La Porta and others 1997; Bloom, Sadun, and Van Reenen 2012); (c) financial development (Guiso and others 2004, 2008); and (d) international trade and investments (Cingano and Pinotti 2016).

Data from the World Values Survey (WVS) show that the level of trust among higher education graduates is about 50 percent higher than among individuals with lower levels of education (see annex 1F, figure 1F.1). There is instead no association between political participation, as proxied by the share of those who reported voting either in political or local elections in the WVS survey, and educational attainments (annex 1G, figure 1G.1). These results are consistent with the ones in Solis (2012), which for Chile finds no relationship between access to university and political participation, as measured by voter registration and affiliation with a political party.

In the absence of adequate economic opportunities, individuals who have completed higher education might be more likely to emigrate from their countries. This leads to a long-term loss of human capital for the country, the so-called "brain drain." Brain drain results in a loss of ideas and innovation, national investment in education, and tax revenues. Evidence in Mattoo, Neagu, and Özden (2008) and Marfouk (2007) suggests that, especially for small countries in Latin America and the Caribbean (for example, Jamaica, Haiti, and Guyana), as much as 80 percent of the university graduates leave their countries to move to the United States. On average, for Latin America and the Caribbean, 11 percent of the university graduates regularly live and work abroad. The overall share in the OECD is equal to 4 percent. Monetary returns to higher education do not seem sufficient to induce higher education graduates to stay in their own countries.

Brain drain has a huge cost for migrants as well. For example, among the Latin American migrants who arrived to the United States in the 1990s and have at least a college degree obtained at home, only 36 percent obtained a skilled job and another 26 percent has a semiskilled job (Ozden 2006).

Intergenerational Spillover of Higher Education

Higher education can have important implications on intergenerational mobility. Figure 1.16 shows the income quintiles for individuals born to parents with low educational attainments, depending on whether they earned a higher education degree or not, for a group of countries for which data are available. In a perfectly mobile society, a child would have an equal chance of ending up in any of the five quintiles as an adult. In Chile and Peru, among individuals born to parents with a low level of education, those without a higher education degree, have only a 10 percent probability of ending in the highest income quintile, but the probability is four times higher for those whose parents have a higher education degree (Brunori and others 2013).[15] In other words, an individual coming from a low socioeconomic status family without parents with a higher education degree will very likely remain in the lower part of the earnings distribution, whereas an individual with similar background but with parents with a higher education degree could just as easily land in the highest income quintile. While higher education completion is unlikely to be the only determinant of this difference, this evidence is suggestive of the importance of higher education in triggering intergenerational mobility.

Evidence from the DHS for a group of Latin American and Caribbean countries finds that infant mortality for parents with complete higher education is almost half that of those with complete primary (figure 1.17). This result is

Figure 1.16 Intergenerational Mobility for Individuals Born to Low-Educated Parents in Chile and Peru

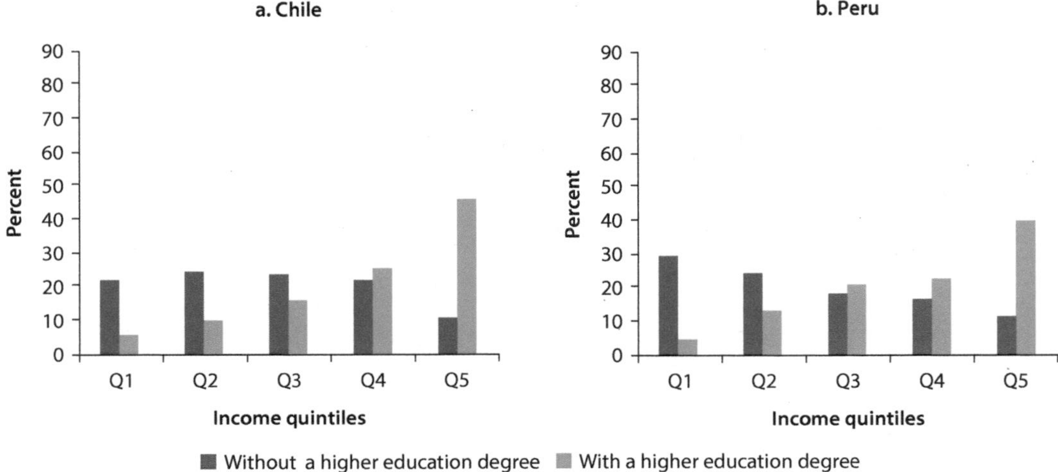

Source: World Bank calculations based on SEDLAC database.
Note: The figure depicts the probability of being in a particular income quintile by parental educational level. Adults born into lowest-education families are those household heads or spouses whose maximal parental education is less than complete primary. In Peru, the question about parental education is made either to the household head or the spouse.

Figure 1.17 Spillover on the Health of Future Generations in Latin America and the Caribbean

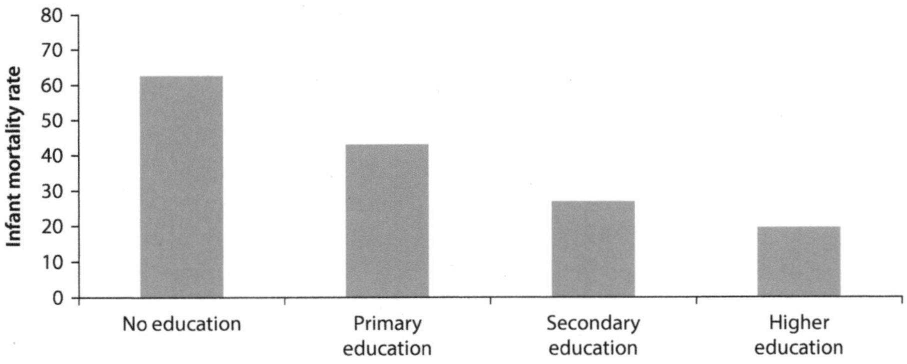

Source: Demographic and Health Surveys (DHS) Program database, ICF International for the U.S. Agency for International Development, http://dhsprogram.com/.
Note: The figure shows infant mortality rate by educational level. Data refer to the last year available. The Latin American and Caribbean countries include Bolivia, Brazil, Colombia, the Dominican Republic, Ecuador, El Salvador, Eritrea is in Africa, Guatemala, Guyana, Haiti, Honduras, Mexico, Nicaragua, Paraguay, and Peru. *Infant mortality rate* is defined as the number of deaths of infants under age one per 1,000 live births.

consistent with the existing evidence on the causal linkage between maternal investments and child health (Currie and Moretti 2002). Data from the WVS show that better educated parents tend to invest in their children's noncognitive skills importance more than less-educated parents since they believe more in these skills' importance. To the extent that healthier children go on to be more productive and more educated adults, higher education can have long lasting effect on intergenerational mobility.

Short Window of Opportunity

A country's dependency ratio is the ratio between the proportion of non-WAP and the WAP. Other characteristics equal, the higher the ratio, the higher the burden of nonworking dependents on those who work. Over the last decades, countries in Latin America and the Caribbean have experienced a constant decline in the dependency ratio (see figure 1.18). The dependency ratio is projected to further decline until 2020 or 2025, at which point it will begin to rise when smaller cohorts than before enter the WAP and larger cohorts exit.

The dependency ratio decline has given the region a "demographic bonus" by lowering the burden of dependents on those who work. Before the declining trend ends, the region could exploit this bonus by raising the skills and productivity of the WAP through higher education. Given the upcoming increase in the dependency ratio, raising the skills and productivity of the WAP would alleviate the burden of dependents on workers.

Expanding higher education over the next few years, rather than later on, would bring the additional benefit. In countries that rely mostly on public

Figure 1.18 Evolution of the Dependency Ratio, 1950–2050

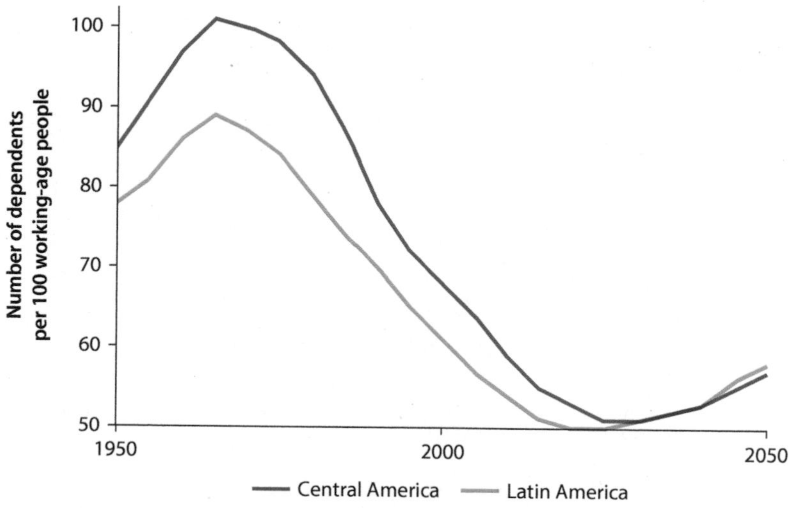

Source: De Hoyos and others 2016.
Note: The *dependency ratio* is defined as the ratio of the population ages 0–14 years and 65 years or more to the population ages 15–64 years.

funding for higher education, the per capita effort for taxpayers would be lower due to a larger tax base. Moreover, a better educated labor force is likely to attenuate the negative consequences of aging on labor productivity. For instance, individuals with higher education are more likely to continue working after retiring. According to 2014 household data, among individuals ages 65–74 years the average employment rate in the region is 39 percent among individuals with complete higher education, as opposed to 31 percent among individuals with complete secondary education.

Yet precisely because future cohorts are expected to be smaller, countries in the region may want to avoid expansions that leave them with higher education excess capacity in the future. For instance, chapter 4 presents simulation results for a large expansion in the number of college graduates. According to simulations for Brazil, even if the number of college graduates were to rise by 50 percent each year from now on (which, given current dropout rates, would require that enrollment approximately doubles each year), the share of skilled WAP among those with complete secondary education would rise from its current 25 percent up to 30 percent only by 2040, at which point the dependency rate is already projected to be rising.

While this 20 percent increase in the share of skilled population is substantial, the resulting share would still fall well below that of the developed world (in the United States, for example, this share is equal to 47 percent), and would be attained only after 20 years of continued effort. In other words, if the region is to exploit the demographic bonus before it ends, it must design its higher education expansion with care, choosing the tools that maximize skills and productivity in a fast and efficient manner, while avoiding the creation of excess capacity.

Annex 1A: Higher Education Enrollment Expansion and GDP Growth

Figure 1A.1 Higher Education Enrollment Expansion and GDP Growth

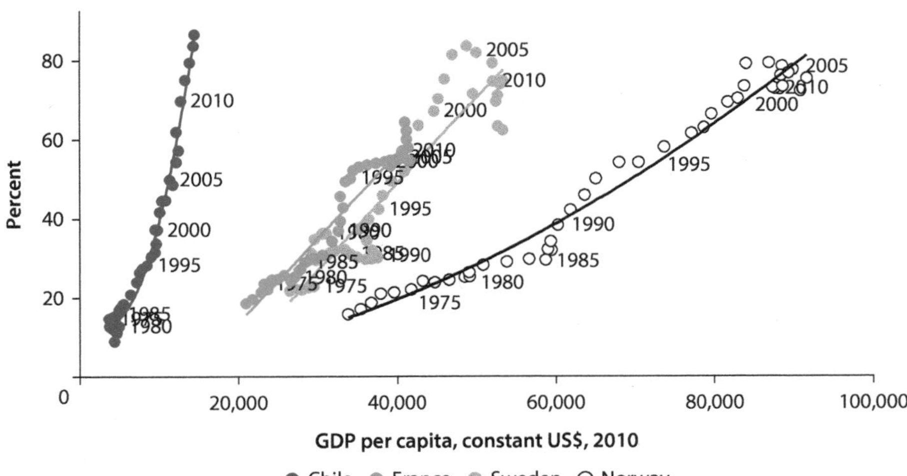

Source: Espinoza and Urzúa 2016.

Annex 1B: Net Enrollment Rate, circa 2000 and 2013

Figure 1B.1 Net Enrollment Rate, circa 2000 and 2013

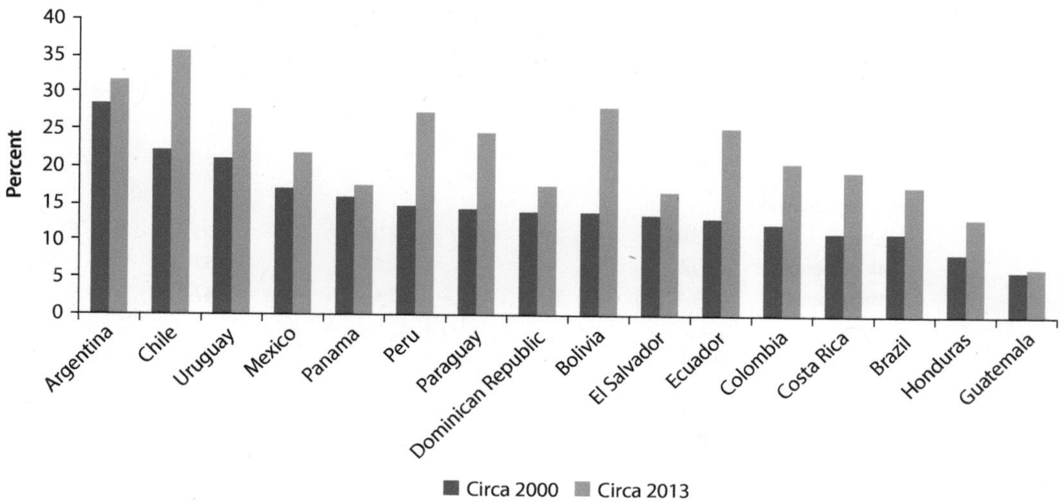

Source: World Bank calculations using SEDLAC databases.
Note: Because of the change in survey coverage, we restricted the sample to 28 urban cities in Argentina, and Asuncion and to the urban interior in Uruguay. Net enrollment rate is calculated as the percentage of individuals ages 18–24 years who are currently enrolled in higher education (ISCED 5–6).

Annex 1C: Cognitive and Noncognitive Skills, by Level of Education

Table 1C.1 Cognitive and Noncognitive Skills, by Level of Education

	Full sample	*Primary education or less*	*Lower secondary education*	*Upper secondary education*	*Higher education*
			Bolivia		
Reading skills					
Mean	1.32	0.52	0.34	0.94	1.81
10th percentile	0	0	0	0	0.8
90th percentile	2.7	2.56	1	2	2.9
Noncognitive skills					
Mean	2.96	2.77	2.8	2.89	3.06
10th percentile	2.47	2.27	2.27	2.47	2.67
90th percentile	3.4	3.27	3.27	3.33	3.47

table continues next page

Table 1C.1 Cognitive and Noncognitive Skills by Level of Education *(continued)*

	Full sample	*Primary education or less*	*Lower secondary education*	*Upper secondary education*	*Higher education*
			Colombia		
Reading skills					
Mean	1.68	0.86	1.26	1.88	2.49
10th percentile	0.3	0	0.1	1	1.8
90th percentile	2.8	1.9	2.2	2.8	3.22
Noncognitive skills					
Mean	3.02	2.91	2.97	3.05	3.12
10th percentile	2.6	2.53	2.53	2.67	2.73
90th percentile	3.47	3.33	3.4	3.47	3.47

Source: World Bank calculations based on STEP Skills Measurement program household surveys data.
Note: Both the reading skills and the noncognitive skills are defined over the range between 0 and 4. The reading skills indicators measure proficiency and related competencies. The noncognitive skills average four measures (each defined over the range 0–4): extraversion, conscientiousness, stability, and grit. The sample is restricted to men and women ages 25–55 years living in urban areas.

Annex 1D: Role of Cognitive and Noncognitive Skills in the Higher Education Premium

Table 1D.1 Role of Cognitive and Noncognitive Skills in the Higher Education Premium

Dependent variable: Log earnings per hour	*Bolivia*		*Colombia*	
Lower secondary education	0.209	0.170	0.170*	0.160*
	(0.149)	(0.151)	(0.093)	(0.094)
Upper secondary education	0.398***	0.366***	0.225***	0.201**
	(0.103)	(0.104)	(0.078)	(0.085)
Higher education	0.674***	0.636***	0.830***	0.792***
	(0.102)	(0.109)	(0.096)	(0.111)
Reading skills score		0.031		0.018
		(0.038)		(0.037)
Noncognitive skills score		−0.055		0.075
		(0.094)		(0.085)
N	1,139	1,129	1,216	1,216
R^2	0.133	0.131	0.131	0.132

Source: World Bank calculations based on STEP Skills Measurement program household surveys data.
*$p = .1$; **$p = .05$; ***$p = .001$.

Annex 1E: Wage Dispersion, by Education Level, circa 2014

Figure 1E.1 Wage Dispersion, by Education Level, circa 2014

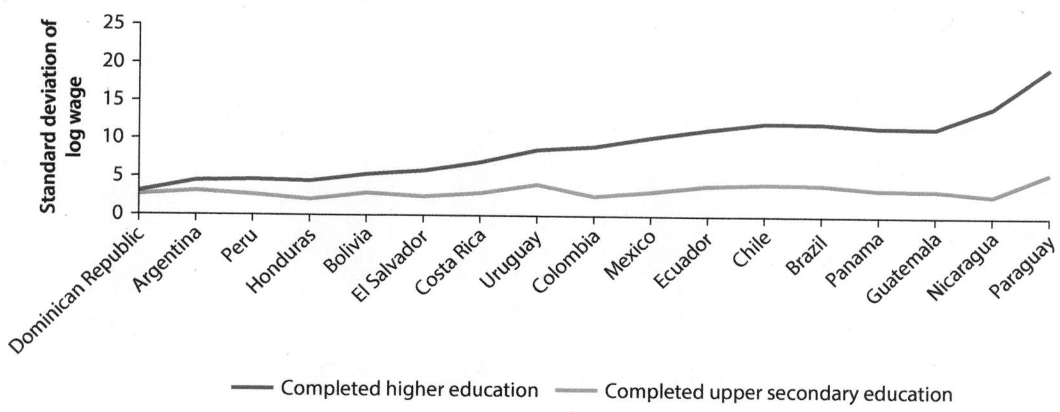

Source: World Bank calculations based on SEDLAC data.

Annex 1F: Trust, by Education Level

Figure 1F.1 Trust, by Education Level

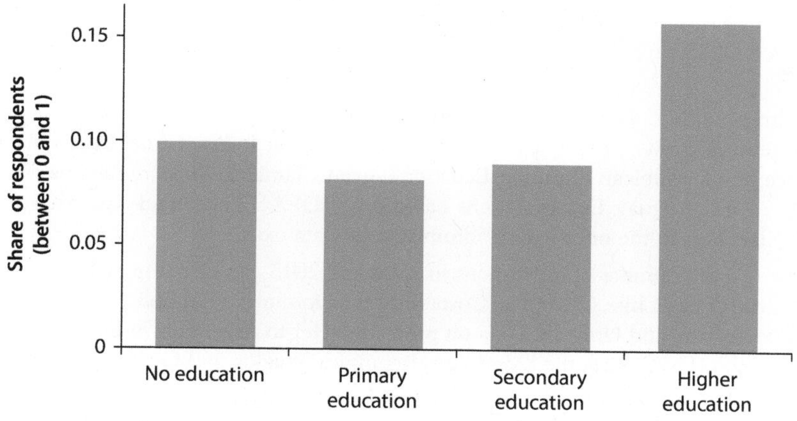

Source: World Values Survey 2010–14, World Values Survey Association, Stockholm, http://www.worldvaluessurvey.org.

Note: The figure shows a simple average across countries. Results are from the 6th wave of the World Values Survey. The nine Latin American and Caribbean countries covered are Argentina, Brazil, Chile, Colombia, Ecuador, Mexico, Peru, Trinidad and Tobago, and Uruguay. The variable Trust takes the value 1 for those who have reported that, generally speaking, they would say that most people can be trusted.

Annex 1G: Political Participation, by Education Level

Figure 1G.1 Political Participation, by Education Level

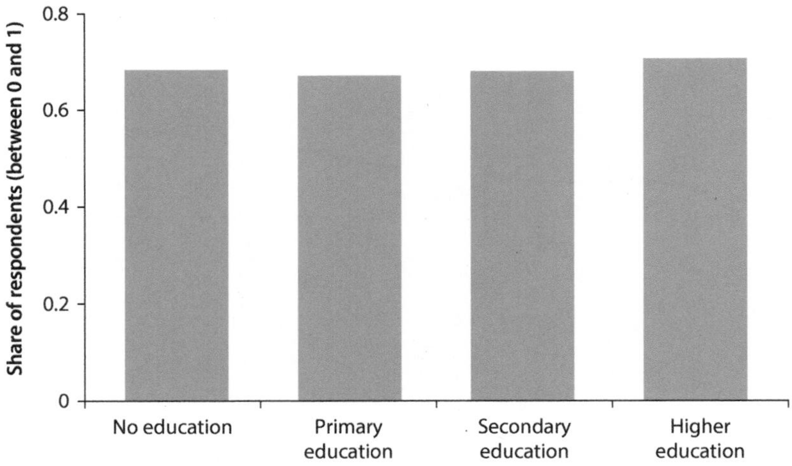

Source: World Values Survey 2010–14, World Values Survey Association, Stockholm, http://www.worldvaluessurvey.org.
Note: The figure shows a simple average across countries. Results are from the 6th wave of the World Values Survey. The nine Latin American and Caribbean countries covered are Argentina, Brazil, Chile, Colombia, Ecuador, Mexico, Peru, Trinidad and Tobago, and Uruguay. The variable Political Participation takes the value 1 for those who have reported having always voted, both in local and political elections.

Notes

1. Administrative data on enrollment were available for the following countries: Argentina, Bolivia, Brazil, the University of the West Indies, Chile, Colombia, Costa Rica, the Dominican Republic, Ecuador, Guyana, Jamaica, Mexico, Panama, Paraguay, Peru, and Uruguay. Extrapolations based on SEDLAC household data produce very similar rates to the ones where administrative data exist.
2. Data on the number of institutions in 2000 and 2013 can be compared for Argentina, Bolivia, Brazil, Chile, Colombia, Costa Rica, the Dominican Republic, Ecuador, Guyana, Mexico, Peru, and Uruguay. Data on programs refer to Argentina, Bolivia, Brazil, Chile, Colombia, Costa Rica, the Dominican Republic, Ecuador, and Guyana.
3. Throughout the book, we use the terms *upper secondary education* and *high school* interchangeably.
4. In Colombia, SABER 11 is mandatory and is taken by all high school graduates. In Brazil, ENEM is not mandatory, but is taken by students who wish to attend higher education since many HEIs use ENEM scores for admissions.
5. *MW* denotes minimum wage.
6. There is well established evidence that smaller class sizes in preprimary and primary education have a positive impact on student outcomes (for example, Krueger 1999) and the probability of attending college (Chetty, Friedman, and Rockoff 2014). Recent evidence (Bianchi 2015) finds for Italy that an increase in the student-faculty ratio has a moderate and statistically significant negative impact on university students' grades.

7. The average returns are computed from the estimated coefficients of a Mincer regression. The coefficient associated with the dummy variable "higher education degree" represents the average difference of (ln) monthly earnings between workers with that schooling level and the baseline category (workers with high school diploma), controlling for the rest of observable characteristics. The returns are computed as the exponential function of the coefficient minus one, and transformed in percentage points. The estimation of the Mincer model also considers the potential impact of self-selection into employment. The set of controls include gender, age, and its square, and a set of region dummies.
8. This a direct assessment of reading proficiency and related competencies scored on the same scale at the OECD's PIAAC (International Assessment of Adult Competencies).
9. The index averages five measures that capture extraversion, conscientiousness, openness, stability, and grit.
10. Clark and Royer (2013) show that a higher number of years of education lowers adult mortality.
11. These results are consistent with the evidence for Latin America and the Caribbean in Ganguli, Hausmann, and Viarengo (2010), which draws on a harmonized version of the Census data.
12. According to Pew Research Center, in the United States, 78 percent of college-educated women—as opposed to 40 percent of those with high school or less—who married for the first time between 2006 and 2010 could expect their marriages to last at least 20 years.
13. Kaufmann, Messner, and Solis (2013) find that attending a higher ranked university program has substantial returns in terms of partner quality for both sexes, but more pronounced for female students.
14. The question in the WWS reads as follows: "Generally speaking, would you say that most people can be trusted or that you cannot be too careful in dealing with people?"
15. Evidence in Brunori and others (2013) finds that in Peru and Brazil the intergenerational elasticity of earnings is more than three times higher than in Denmark and Finland.

References

Adelman, M., and M. Székely. 2016. "School Dropout in Central America. An Overview of Trends, Causes and Consequences, and Promising Interventions." Policy Research Working Paper 7561, World Bank, Washington, DC.

Bassi, M., M. Busso, and J. S. Muñoz. 2013. "Is the Glass Half Empty or Half Full? School Enrollment, Graduation, and Dropout Rates in Latin America." Research Department Publications IDB-WP-462, Inter-American Development Bank, Washington, DC.

Bertrand, M., P. Cortés, C. Olivetti, and J. Pan. 2016. "Social Norms, Labor Market Opportunities, and the Marriage Gap for Skilled Women." NBER Working Paper 22015, National Bureau of Economic Research, Cambridge, MA.

Bianchi, N. 2015. "The General Effects of Educational Expansion." Discussion Papers 15-008, Stanford Institute for Economic Policy Research, Stanford, CA.

Bloom, N., R. Sadun, and J. V. Reenen. 2012. "The Organization of Firms across Countries." *Quarterly Journal of Economics* 127 (4): 1663–705.

Brunori, P., F. Ferreira, and V. Peragine. 2013. "Inequality of Opportunity, Income Inequality and Economic Mobility: Some International Comparisons." Policy Research Working Paper Series 6304, World Bank, Washington, DC.

Chetty, R., J. N. Friedman, and J. E. Rockoff, 2014. "Measuring the Impacts of Teachers II: Teacher Value-Added and Student Outcomes in Adulthood." *American Economic Review* 104 (9): 2633–79.

Cingano, F., and P. Pinotti. 2016. "Trust, Firm Organization, and the Pattern of Comparative Advantage." *Journal of International Economics* 100: 1–13.

Clark, D., and H. Royer. 2013. "The Effect of Education on Adult Mortality and Health: Evidence from Britain." *American Economic Review* 103 (6): 2087–120.

Currie, J., and E. Moretti. 2002. "Mother's Education and the Intergenerational Transmission of Human Capital: Evidence from College Openings and Longitudinal Data." NBER Working Papers 9360, National Bureau of Economic Research, Cambridge, MA.

Cutler, D., and A. Lleras Muney. 2010. "Understanding Differences in Health Behaviors by Education." *Journal of Health Economics* 29 (1): 1–28.

de Hoyos, R., H. Rogers, and M. Székely. 2016. "Out of School and Out of Work: Risk and Opportunities for Latin America's Ninis." World Bank, Washington, DC. World Bank. https://openknowledge.worldbank.org/handle/10986/22349 License: CC BY 3.0 IGO.

Espinoza, R., and S. Urzúa. 2016. "Returns to Higher Education: Funding, Coverage and Quality." Background paper for this report.

Ganguli, I., R. Hausmann, and M. Viarengo. 2010. "Schooling Can't Buy Me Love: Marriage, Work, and the Gender Education Gap in Latin America." Working Paper Series rwp10-032, Harvard University, John F. Kennedy School of Government, Cambridge, MA.

Goldin, C., L. F. Katz, and I. Kuziemko. 2006. "The Homecoming of American College Women: The Reversal of the College Gender Gap." *Journal of Economic Perspectives* 20 (4): 133–56.

Guiso, L., P. Sapienza, and L. Zingales. 2004. "Does Local Financial Development Matter?" *The Quarterly Journal of Economics* 119 (3): 929–69.

———. 2008. "Trusting the Stock Market." *Journal of Finance* 63 (6): 2557–600.

Heckman, J. J., J. Stixrud, and S. Urzúa. 2006. "The Effects of Cognitive and Noncognitive Abilities on Labor Market Outcomes and Social Behavior." *Journal of Labor Economics* 24 (3): 411–82.

Isen, A., and B. Stevenson. 2010. "Women's Education and Family Behavior: Trends in Marriage, Divorce and Fertility." In *Demography and the Economy*, NBER Chapters, 107–40. National Bureau of Economic Research, Cambridge, MA.

Kaufmann, K., M. Messner, and A. Solis. 2013. "Returns to Elite Higher Education in the Marriage Market: Evidence from Chile." Working Papers 489, IGIER (Innocenzo Gasparini Institute for Economic Research), Bocconi University, Milan.

Knack, S., and P. Keefer. 1997. "Does Social Capital Have an Economic Payoff? A Cross-Country Investigation." *Quarterly Journal of Economics* 112 (4): 1251–88.

Krueger, A. 1999. "Experimental Estimates of Education Production Functions." *Quarterly Journal of Economics* 114 (2): 497–532.

La Porta, R., F. Lopez-De-Silanes, A. Shleifer, R. Vishny. 1997. "Trust in Large Organizations." *American Economic Review* 87 (2): 333–38.

Loayza, N. V., L. Serven, and N. Sugawara. 2009. "Informality in Latin America and the Caribbean." Policy Research Working Paper Series 4888, World Bank, Washington, DC.

Lochner, L., and E. Moretti, 2004. "The Effect of Education on Crime: Evidence from Prison Inmates, Arrests, and Self-Reports." *American Economic Review* 94 (1): 155–89.

Marfouk, A. 2007. "Brain Drain in Developing Countries." *World Bank Economic Review* 21 (2): 193–218.

Mattoo, A., I. C. Neagu, and C. Özden. 2008. "Brain Waste? Educated Immigrants in the US Labor Market." *Journal of Development Economics* 87 (2): 255–69.

Messina, J., and J. Silva. 2017. "Wage Inequality in Latin America: Understanding the Past to Prepare for the Future." World Bank, Washington DC.

Milligan, K., E. Moretti, and P. Oreopoulos. 2004. "Does Education Improve Citizenship? Evidence from the United States and the United Kingdom." *Journal of Public Economics* 88 (9–10): 1667–95.

Moretti, E. 2004. "Estimating the Social Return to Higher Education: Evidence from Longitudinal and Repeated Cross-Sectional Data." *Journal of Econometrics* 121 (1–2): 175–212.

Murnane, R. J., J. B. Willett, and F. Levy. 1995. "The Growing Importance of Cognitive Skills in Wage Determination." *Review of Economics and Statistics* 77 (2): 251–66.

Özden, Çaglar. 2006. "Brain Drain in Middle East and North Africa—The Patterns Under the Surface." United Nations Population, EGM/2006/10, New York, NY.

Psacharopoulos, G. 1994. "Returns to Investment in Education: A Global Update." *World Development* 22 (9): 1325–43.

Psacharopoulos, G., and H. A. Patrinos. 2004. "Returns to Investment in Education: A Further Update." *Education Economics* 12 (2): 111–34.

SEDLAC (Socioeconomic Database for Latin America and the Caribbean). Centro for Distributive, Labor and Social (CEDLAS), National University of La Plata, La Plata Argentina and World Bank, Washington, DC. (http://sedlac.econo.unlp.edu.ar/eng/).

Solis, A., 2012. "Does Higher Education Cause Political Participation? Evidence From a Regression Discontinuity Design." Working Paper Series 2013:13, Uppsala University, Department of Economics Uppsala.

Szekely, M. 2016. "Recent Trends in Higher Education in Latin America." Unpublished paper.

CHAPTER 2

Equity, Quality, and Variety of Higher Education

Francisco Haimovich Paz

Abstract

This chapter presents indicators of higher education quality, variety, and equity in the region and in individual countries. Access to higher education in Latin America and the Caribbean is, on average, four times more unequal than access to secondary education. Despite this tremendous inequality, there has been remarkable progress in the region in terms of expanding access to higher education to disadvantaged groups. In particular, we estimate that today, in comparison to 15 years ago, an additional 3 million young people belonging to the poorest 50 percent of the population have accessed higher education. The picture is less encouraging in terms of the quality of higher education. While measuring quality is extremely challenging, several indicators (including international academic rankings, per-student spending, and completion rates) suggest that the average quality in the region is moderate at best. On the other hand, the expansion in access to higher education was accompanied by an increase in variety. In 15 years, the higher education landscape in the region has become much more diversified. Many countries have seen the enrollment in short-cycle programs double and, in some cases, triple. In Brazil and Colombia more than 15 percent of the students are enrolled in distance learning programs. However, in many countries of the region, graduates are concentrated in relatively few fields of study, with little variety relative to developed nations.

Introduction

In this chapter we study access to higher education. Recall that we measure access as the proportion of individuals ages 18–24 years who have ever been enrolled in higher education (regardless of completion).[1] As it turns out, access to higher education in Latin American and the Caribbean is on average four times more unequal than access to secondary education. In particular, while the probability of accessing higher education is only 6 percent for young people in the poorest percentile, it grows to almost 70 percent in the richest percentile.

This association is particularly strong in Central American countries, where only 1 out of 100 young people in the poorest percentile has access to higher education.

Despite this tremendous inequality, there has been remarkable progress in the region in terms of expanding higher education access to disadvantaged groups. While the poorest 50 percent of the population (B50) represented only around 16 percent of higher education students circa 2000, this group comprised approximately 25 percent of higher education students circa 2012. By 2012, an additional 3 million B50 young people had gained access to higher education compared with 2000.

Contrary to the common belief that spending in higher education is highly regressive (since it is "mostly captured by the rich"), spending in higher education nowadays is at least slightly progressive. This means that if funded with a proportional income tax, the ex post income inequality slightly decreases. While it is true that richer young people are much more likely to be enrolled in higher education, their families also pay higher taxes. Our findings indicate that if higher education were funded by a proportional income tax, the poor would capture a larger share of the net benefits of higher education (that is, after discounting the proportional taxes).[2] Furthermore, a back of the envelope calculation indicates that the expenditures associated with expanding higher education coverage are four times more progressive than average expenditures in higher education, and almost as progressive as expenditures in secondary education.[3]

The picture is less encouraging in terms of the quality of higher education. Although measuring this is remarkably challenging, several indicators suggest that average higher education quality in Latin America and the Caribbean is moderate at best, compared with most other regions. According to Academic Ranking of World Universities (ARWU), less than 2 percent of the top 500 universities in the world are in Latin America and the Caribbean, the lowest regional representation after Africa. In most Latin American and Caribbean countries, per-student expenditure is between one-third and one-half of the expenditure in developed countries. Outcome indicators such as dropout rates and time-to-degree (TTD) are relatively high, suggesting than higher education spending is inefficient. All these challenges could be exacerbated as higher education coverage continues to grow at a rapid rate.

Even with rapid enrollment growth, most students enrolled in higher education were attending a four-year academic face-to-face program by early 2000. In the past 15 years, the higher education landscape in the region has become much more diversified. Many countries have seen the enrollment in two-year technical programs double and, in some cases, triple. More than 15 percent of higher education students are enrolled in distance learning programs in Brazil and Colombia. Graduates are concentrated in relatively few fields of study in many Latin American and Caribbean countries, with little variety compared to developed nations.

Equity

Who Has Access to Higher Education?

This section explores the socioeconomic profiles of students who have ever had access to higher education by analyzing the unconditional and conditional access gaps across groups. The analysis here focuses on individual and household characteristics, including family income, parental education, region of residence, ethnicity, and gender.

Unconditional gaps refer to the raw differences in access to higher education across groups, without controlling for any additional factor. For instance, these gaps capture the raw differences in access rates between young people from the fifth and first quintile, or between white and nonwhite groups. A more accurate picture can be drawn by looking at *conditional gaps*, that is, the access gaps across different groups holding constant other observable variables. For instance, it is likely that, to some extent, those with uneducated parents who belong to ethnic minorities and live in lagging regions have lower access to higher education for the same reason—namely, that they are poorer. To account for this, we use a regression analysis to compute the previous gaps but controlling for other correlated variables.[4]

The analysis begins by exploring simple unconditional gaps in access for different groups. The orange bars in figure 2.1 show these gaps for young people ages 18–24 years for the region as a whole. This simple exercise shows some important patterns:[5]

Family Income

Not surprisingly, income is strongly correlated with access to higher education. On average, young people from the fifth (richest) quintile are 45 percentage points more likely to attend higher education than those from the first (poorest) quintile. The differences are still large—around 39 percentage points—when comparing young people from the better-off households with those from middle-income households (fifth versus third quintile).

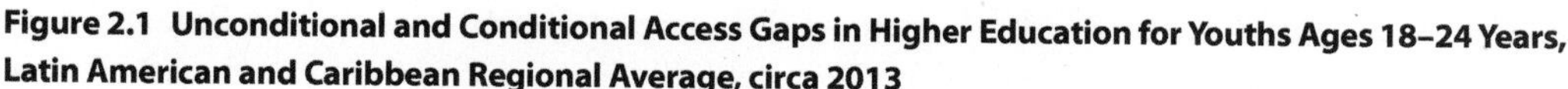

Figure 2.1 Unconditional and Conditional Access Gaps in Higher Education for Youths Ages 18–24 Years, Latin American and Caribbean Regional Average, circa 2013

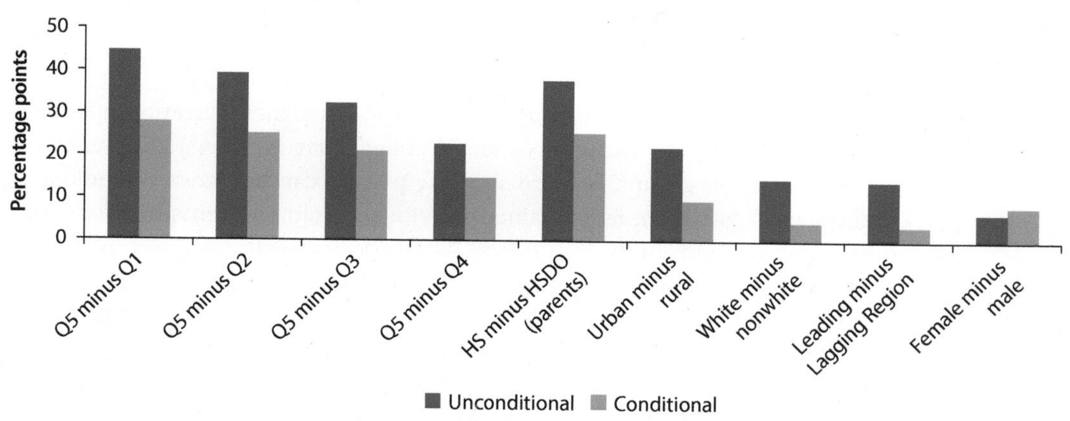

Source: World Bank calculations using SEDLAC.

Note: The figure shows a simple average across countries. HS = high school (completed); HSDO = high school drop out; Q = quintile (Q5 is the richest and Q1 is the poorest). Leading (or lagging) region stands for regions where higher education access is above (or below) the national access median. The conditional gaps were estimated using a linear probability model that regress access on a set of dummies capturing family income (quintiles of per capita income), parents' education, gender, ethnicity, region of residence, an urban dummy, and a full set of age dummies.

Parental Education

Parental education is also strongly associated with access to higher education. Young people whose parents have at least finished secondary education are, on average, 38 percentage points more likely to access higher education than those whose parents did not complete secondary education.[6]

Region of Residence

Access to higher education is also correlated with the region of residence, but this plays, on average, a secondary role. Young people living in the leading areas of the country in terms of access to higher education (that is, the regions where the access rate is above the national median access) are around 14 percentage points more likely to attend higher education. This average percentage, however, masks a lot of heterogeneity across countries. While in Argentina, Colombia, and Mexico these differences are around 5 percentage points, in countries like Honduras, Paraguay, and Peru the regional gaps grow to more than 20 percentage points.

Area of Residence

Young people living in urban areas are on average 22 percentage points more likely to attend higher education institutions (HEIs). The largest gaps are observed in Colombia and Bolivia, where urban youth are 35 percentage points more prone to attend HEIs.

Ethnicity

Nonwhite young people face a lower probability of accessing higher education. On average, for those countries with ethnicity information in our dataset, the probability of accessing higher education is around 15 percentage points smaller for disadvantaged ethnic groups.[7] The largest gap is observed in Brazil, where whites are 18 percentage points more likely to access higher education than nonwhite youths.

Gender

Women are 6 percentage points more likely to access higher education than men.

The above analysis focus on unconditional (that is, "raw") differences in access rates across groups. A more accurate picture can be drawn by looking at conditional gaps which, as explained previously, hold the remaining variables constant when computing those gaps. The results are summarized in the red bars in figure 2.1. This conditional analysis reinforces the previous conclusions. Family income and parental education are still the most important factors (although the gaps are one-third smaller). Regional, ethnic, and (to a lesser extent) urban gaps in access tend to vanish when holding other variables constant. This suggests that young people living in lagging regions and belonging to minority groups have less access to higher education because their parents tend to be poorer and less educated. The gender access gap is slightly larger when controlling for socioeconomic factors.

The Role of Secondary Completion Rates versus Entry Rates

Policy decisions are best informed by quantifying the extent to which access to higher education for disadvantaged young people is driven by their lower secondary completion rates in relationship to their lower entry rates into higher education. Secondary completion rates refers to the probability of graduating from upper secondary education (which is typically a prerequisite to be "eligible" to pursue a higher education degree). Entry rates, on the other hand, refer to the probability of accessing higher education conditional on completing upper secondary. The relative importance of each of these channels has critical policy implications. For instance, if the poor have particularly low secondary completion rates (SCRs), the potential equalizing impact of policies aimed at boosting the supply of higher education or relaxing tuition costs would be rather limited. On the contrary, if the poor chiefly differ in their entry rates to higher education (that is, the fraction of students who access higher education relative to those who finish upper secondary), the potential equalizing impact of such policies would be much larger.

This section uses a simple decomposition technique (Oaxaca-type decompositions, explained in annex 2A) to quantify the relative importance of both high school completion and higher education entry rates when explaining access gaps. We simulate how much access gaps would be reduced between two groups (for example, the poor and the rich) if both groups faced the same SCRs or the same entry rates to higher education. With these simulations, the access gaps can be exactly decomposed into two components: the share explained by differences in secondary completion rates (SCR effect), and the share explained by differences in the college entry rates (ER effect) (see annex 2A for details).[8]

The lower access to higher education of disadvantaged young people is explained to a large extent by their lower SCRs, as seen in figure 2.2. In particular, these differences explain, on average, around 56 percent of the gap between young people from the poorest and the richest quintiles. In addition, in countries such as Nicaragua and, surprisingly, Uruguay, the differences in SCRs explain around 81 percent of the gap.[9] When considering the first and fourth quintile, however, entry rates become more relevant. Still, the SCR effect explains at least 44 percent of these gaps.[10] On the other hand, the secondary completion rates also explain more than half of the access gap by region, areas of residence, gender, and ethnic group.

Role of Ability In Equity

The previous analysis indicates that a significant share of the access gaps observed in higher education are actually explained by "events" (that is, school dropout) that occur before reaching the higher education age. Indeed, the SCR effects estimated previously provide only a lower bound of the importance of the inequalities that arise before reaching the higher education age, since even the lower entry rates to higher education of the poor are partially driven by prior educational outcomes (such as their historical academic performance during secondary education).[11] In other words, in Latin America and the Caribbean at least

Figure 2.2 Decomposition of Access Gaps in Higher Education of Youths Ages 18–24 Years, Latin American and Caribbean Regional Average, circa 2013

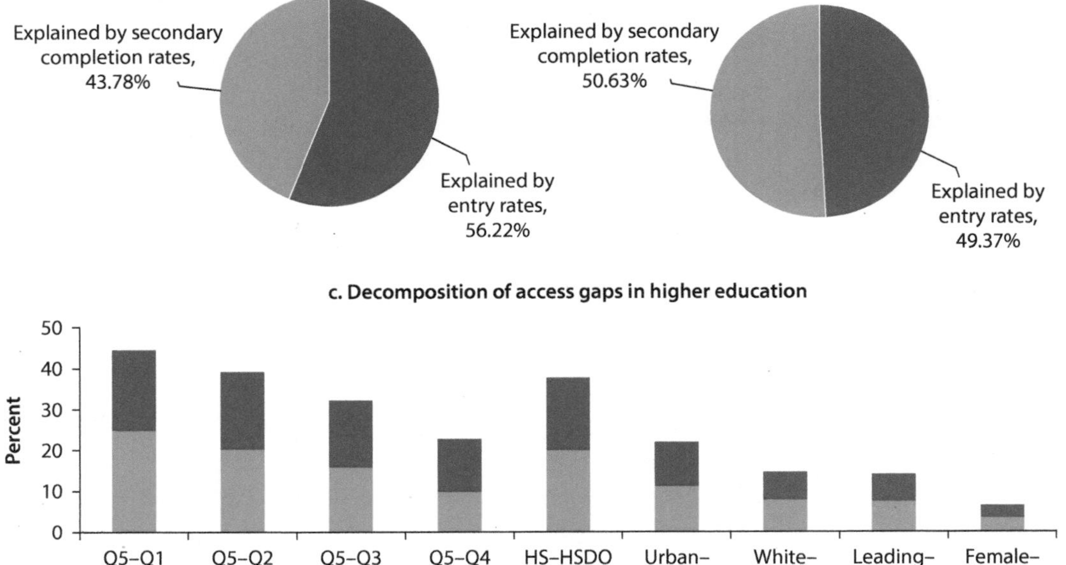

Source: World Bank calculations using SEDLAC.
Note: The figure shows a simple average across countries. HS = high school (completed); HSDO = high school drop out; Q = quintile (Q5 is the richest and Q1 is the poorest). Leading (or lagging) region refers to regions where higher education access is above (or below) the national access median.

56 percent of the higher education access gap between the poorest and the richest quintile is explained by "earlier educational inequalities."

To illustrate this, we use Colombia's rich student level data to estimate entry rates by income groups, but holding academic readiness constant.[12] In particular, we compare the entry rates of three groups of young people: high, middle. and low income.[13] The orange bars in figure 2.3 show the gap in entry rates without controlling for any other variable. Conditional on finishing secondary education, high-income young people are 44.9 percentage points more likely to enroll in higher education than low-income high school graduates. They are 13.9 percentage points more likely to enroll in higher education than middle-income young people. These gaps are strongly driven by differences in academic readiness and parental education. The gap between high- and low-income youths decreases by 41 percent when we hold academic readiness constant (from 44.9 percent to 26.5 percent).

When we further control for the education of mothers (which likely affects their children's preferences for enrolling in higher education) the gap decreases

Figure 2.3 Entry Rate Gaps and Academic Readiness in Colombia, 2009

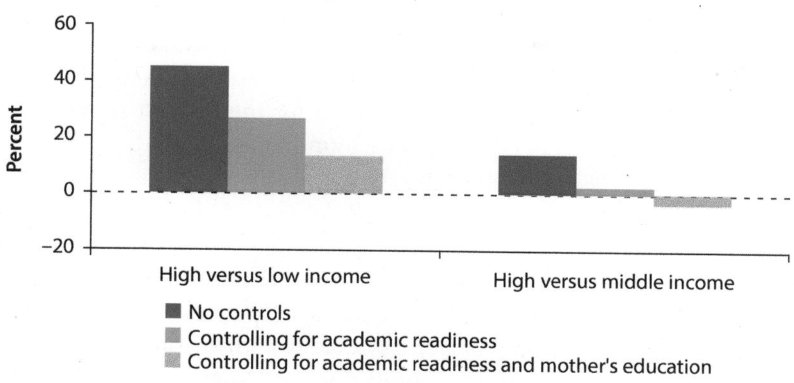

Source: World Bank calculations using Saber 11 and SPADIES.
Note: The sample consists of the cohort taking SABER 11 in 2009. High income: family income equal to 5 or more times the minimum wage. Middle income: family income 2 or 3 times the minimum wage. Low income: family income below minimum wage. Academic readiness is proxied by the standardized, by semester, SABER 11 score. We observe if the student enrolls in a higher education program at any time during the four years after graduation.

by an additional 29 percent (from 26.5 percent to 13.1 percent). In other words, around 70 percent of the gaps in the entry rates between high- and low-income young people could be accounted for by differences in academic readiness and parental education. On the other hand, the entry gap between high- and middle-income students decreases by 83 percent when we hold academic readiness constant (from 13.9 percent to 2.4 percent), and becomes negative when we further control for the education of mothers.

These results raise an important issue: whether unequal access necessarily means unfair access. Many societies would consider it fair if the available "seats" in HEIs were allocated according to academic readiness alone. Other societies might consider broader socioeconomic factors in determining higher education access. The results presented here, however, point out that policies targeting only the transition margin (that is, entry rates) are likely to have limited impact on the access to higher education of disadvantaged groups.

Measuring Inequality in Access: Huge Inequalities, but Rapid Progress

The income gaps discussed previously can be summarized with an index to facilitate comparisons across education levels and countries, and over time. Different methodologies can measure inequality in access (for example, Paes de Barros 2009). This section follows closely the methodology devised by Gasparini (2002), which measures inequality in access with a simple index and provides a straightforward graphical representation.

We measure inequality in the probability of accessing higher education across income percentiles. To do so, we first estimate (using locally weighted regressions) the probabilities of access across percentiles, and we then compute the Gini coefficient associated to the distribution of those probabilities. The larger this index (called G from now on), the larger the inequality. In particular, G equals zero when all groups have the same access probability, and equals 1 when only the richest percentile have access to higher education. We also illustrate this index graphically with the Lorenz curve associated with the index G (that is, the cumulative probability of accessing higher education for the poorest p percent of the population).[14] The technical details can be found in annex 2B.

Inequality in Access to Higher Education Relative to Other Educational Levels

Figure 2.4 shows the relation between income and access to different education levels (averaged across Latin America and the Caribbean). Access to higher education is strongly, and nonlinearly, associated with income. While less than 10 percent of young people in the poorest percentile have access to higher education, the access rate grows to 22 percent for the median percentile, and jumps to approximately 64 percent for the richest one. The income gradient is much stronger than in secondary education. In particular, access to secondary education grows "only" by 13 percentage points when comparing the median and richest percentile. On the other hand, since access to primary education is almost universal in Latin America and the Caribbean, the access rate is relatively flat with respect to income.

To measure the greater inequality in access to higher education, we compute the Gini coefficient associated with these probabilities. We find that, on average,

Figure 2.4 Access Rate across Percentiles of Household per Capita Income, Latin American and Caribbean Regional Average, circa 2012

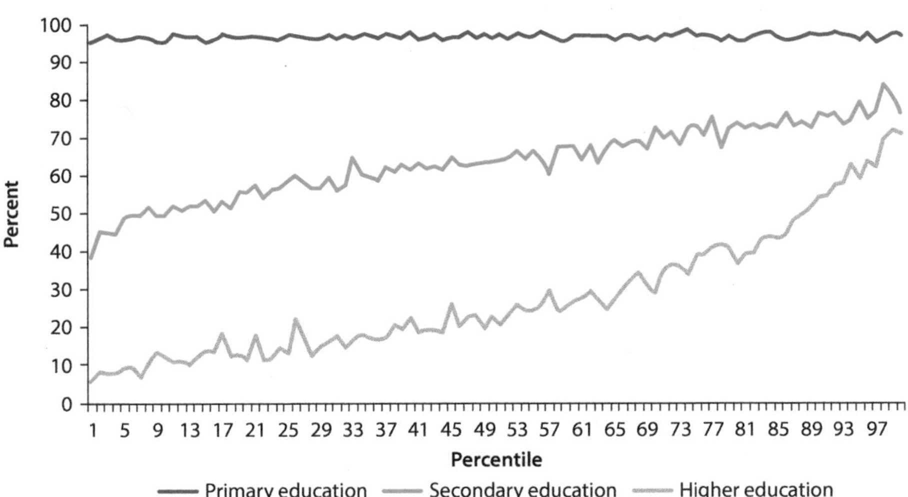

Source: World Bank calculations using SEDLAC.

Note: The access rate to higher education was computed as the share of individuals ages 18–24 years with incomplete or complete higher education. The access rate to secondary education was computed as the share of individuals ages 12–18 years with complete or incomplete secondary education. The access rate to primary education was computed as the share of individuals ages 6–12 years with complete or incomplete primary education.

access to higher education is four times more unequal than access to secondary education. Panel a and b of figure 2.5 report the Lorenz curves corresponding to each education level, averaged across Latin America and the Caribbean, and the corresponding Gini coefficients (see annex 2B for details). It is not surprising, given that access to primary is close to universal in Latin America and the Caribbean, that the Lorenz curve for primary education is close to the line of equality (Gini ≈ 0). The Lorenz curve for secondary education is slightly farther away from the line of equality, indicating that access to secondary education is moderately unequal (G=0.08). Higher education shows the highest level of inequality, with a Gini coefficient almost four times larger than that corresponding to secondary education (G=0.30).

Figure 2.5 Inequality in Access, by Education Level, in Latin American and Caribbean Countries

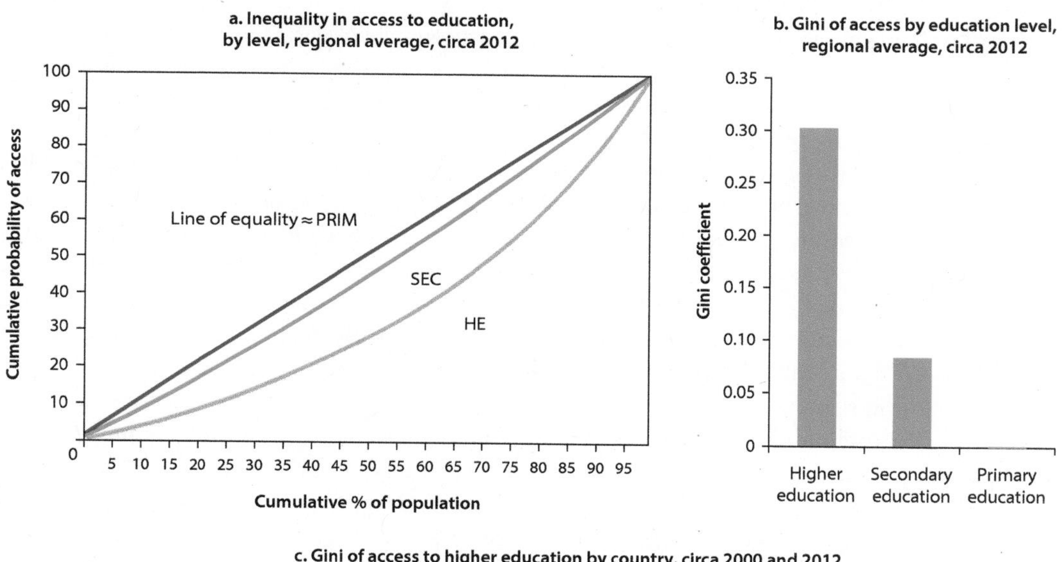

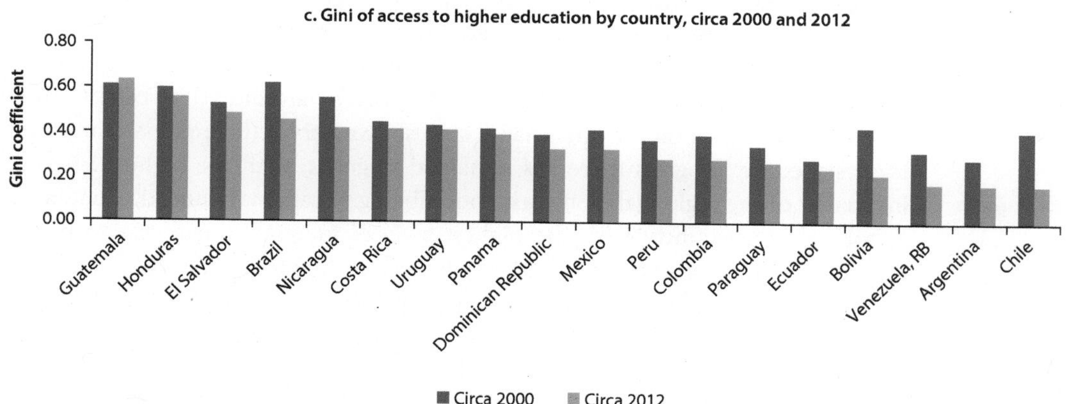

Source: World Bank calculations using SEDLAC.
Note: Panel a shows the Lorenz curve associated to the distribution of (smoothed) access rates to each education level across household per capita income (averaged across countries). Panel b shows the associated (average) Gini coefficients for each level. Panel c shows the Gini of the probability of accessing higher education for each country. HE = higher education; PRIM = primary education; SEC = secondary education.

As expected, there is substantial variation in inequality in access to higher education across countries, as shown in panel c. The largest levels of inequality are seen in Central American countries, which almost double the levels seen in South America. Access to higher education is particularly unequal in El Salvador (G=0.48), Honduras (G=0.55), and Guatemala (G=0.63). Among South American countries, the most unequal are Brazil and Uruguay (0.45 and 0.41, respectively). In contrast, the most equal higher education systems are found in Chile, Argentina, and República Bolivariana de Venezuela (G=0.17 in all three cases). As we will see in chapter 4, HE systems are organized quite differently in these countries. For example, two extreme cases, Honduras and Chile, have similar levels of income inequality, yet inequality in access to higher education is almost three times larger in Honduras than in Chile (G=0.55 versus G=0.17, respectively).[15]

Recent Progress in Equity

Although higher education is the educational level with the most unequal access in Latin America and the Caribbean, there has been substantial progress over the last 15 years, with increasing higher education participation among low- and particularly middle-income groups. Although access grew for all percentiles over this period (figure 2.6, panel a), it grew proportionally faster for low- and middle-income groups. One consequence is that while in 2000 only 16 percent of higher education students came from the poorest 50 percent of the population, they represented almost 25 percent of the students circa 2012. This progress has been remarkable in countries such as República Bolivariana de Venezuela, Argentina, and Chile, where the participation of the poorest 50 percent grew from about 23 percent to 25 percent in 2000 to around 40 percent in 2012. When looking at the region, we estimate that today, in comparison to 15 years ago, an additional 3 million of B50 young people gained access to higher education (panel c).

This remarkable progress is also captured by our index, which shows that inequality declined on average by almost by 23 percent over that time period. On average, the Gini coefficient went from 54 to 42 (figure 2.5, panel c). Progress has not been homogeneous across countries, however. Progress has been remarkable in countries such as Bolivia, República Bolivariana de Venezuela, Peru, and particularly Chile, where inequality in access declined by around 50 percent. Central American countries, on the other hand, have shown very little progress, if any, over the last decade. Progress there has remained stagnant, with the highest levels of inequality of the region (the only exception being Nicaragua). Indeed, Guatemala is not only the country with the highest level of inequality in access to higher education but it is also the one with the lowest decline in inequality.[16]

In box 2.1, we further analyze stories for a few countries. The key finding is that the bulk of the access increase came from different parts of the income distribution. In Chile most of the increase came from poor and middle-income groups. In Brazil, the increase is driven by the larger access of the upper middle class. In Honduras, the growth in access was larger for the richest percentiles. Furthermore, the poorest 20 percent of the population in Honduras showed a negligible improvement in access.

Figure 2.6 Expanding Access to the Poor, Youths Ages 18–24 Years, Latin American and Caribbean Countries, circa 2000 and 2012

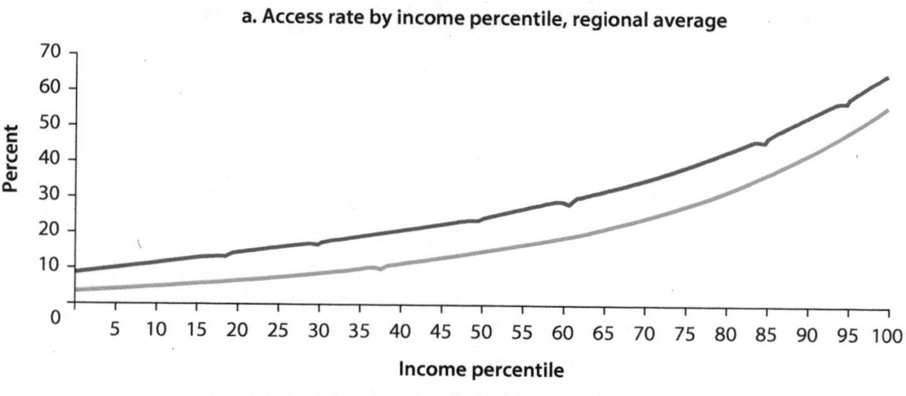

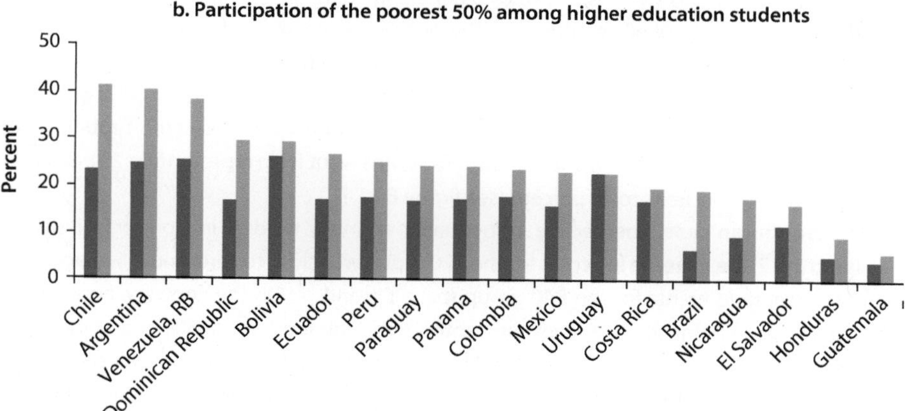

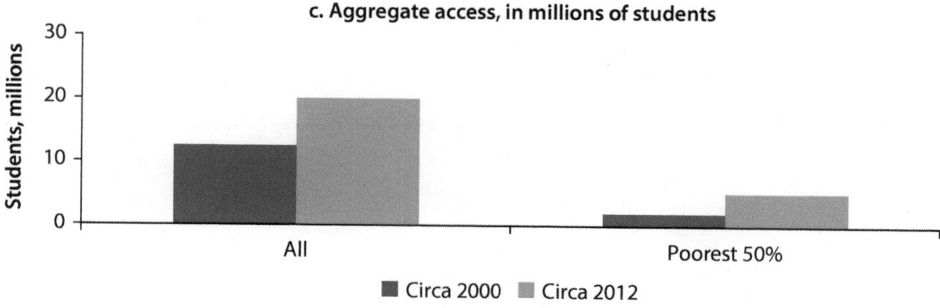

Source: Population estimates from Health Nutrition and Population Statistics, World Bank. World Bank calculations using SEDLAC.
Note: The sample in the figure is young people ages 18–24 years. Panel a shows the access rate by family income percentile (smoothed using locally weighted regressions). Panel b reports the share of higher education students that belong to the poorest 50 percent of the population. Panel c shows the approximated aggregate number of higher education students ages 18–24 years, and the aggregated number of higher education who belong to the poorest 50 percent of the population. This was estimated by multiplying the total population of the country by the share of the population ages 18–24 years who have access to higher education and who belong to a specific group—all young people or B50 young people.

Box 2.1 Improving Access to Higher Education in Brazil, Chile, and Honduras

The Brazilian case. The decline in inequality in access to higher education was also substantial in Brazil between 2001 and 2012 (panel a). The largest increment in access came from the middle and upper middle groups (the largest increase is observed around the 75th percentile of the income distribution, with an increment of approximately 13 percentage points; see panel b). One potential explanation is the expansion in the supply of private institutions over the last few years. The increase was also substantial for the B50 group, averaging more than 6 percentage points. This is huge considering that in 2001 the access rates for this group were close to zero (see figure B2.1.2).

The Chilean case. Chile is one of the most successful countries in terms of reducing inequality in access to higher education. This is largely explained by the introduction of government-backed student loans during 2006. Between 2000 and 2013 our index G declined by 24 points (from 41 to 17). This is driven by a general increase in the higher education access probability, which was chiefly captured by the poorest percentiles (see figure B2.1.1, panel a and b). The largest absolute increment in access is observed for the poorest 50 percent of the population, which faced an around 24 percentage increment in their likelihood of accessing higher education. The richest percentiles, on the other hand, only increased this probability by 13 percentage points. As a consequence, the B50 youths went from representing 23 percent of higher education students to 41 percent (see figure B2.1.1).

The Honduran case. The decline in inequality was very modest in Honduras. Between 2001 and 2012, the increase in access for the B20 group was close to zero, and it averaged less than 2 percentage points for the B40 group (panels a and b). On the contrary, access grew by 14 percentage points for the richest percentile. Although the poorest 50 percent increased their representation among higher education students during the last years by 4 percentage points, they represented only 10 percent of the students in 2012. Indeed, our index G declined by only 4 points over that period (from 59 to 55) (see figure B2.1.3).

Figure B2.1.1 Access to Higher Education and Change in Access Rate, by Income Percentile, Chile

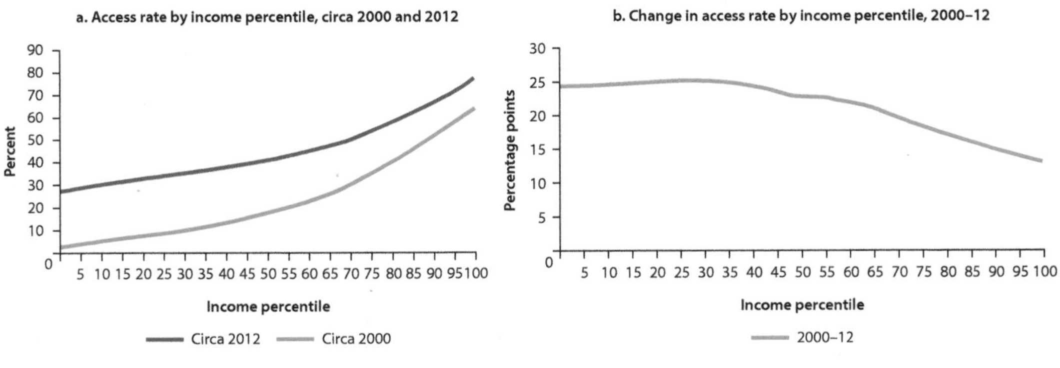

Source: World Bank calculations using SEDLAC.
Note: Percentile refers to the relative position in the per capita family income distribution.

box continues next page

Box 2.1 Improving Access to Higher Education in Chile, Brazil, and Honduras *(continued)*

Figure B2.1.2 Access to Higher Education and Change in Access Rate, by Income Percentile, Brazil

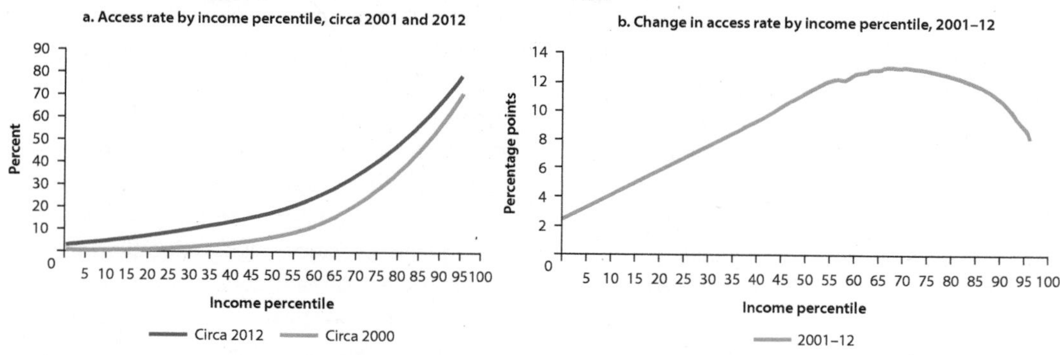

Source: World Bank calculations using SEDLAC.
Note: Percentile refers to the relative position in the per capita family income distribution.

Figure B2.1.3 Access to Higher Education and Change in Access Rate, by Income Percentile, Honduras

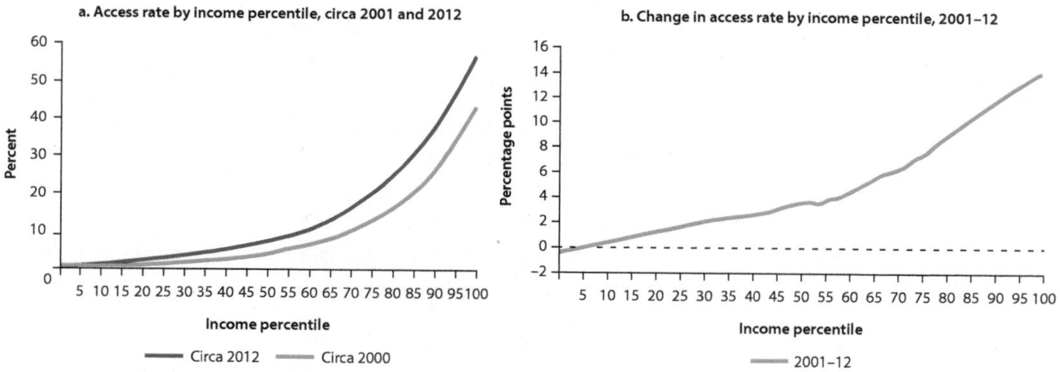

Source: World Bank calculations using SEDLAC.
Note: Percentile refers to the relative position in the per capita family income distribution.

Progressivity of Higher Education Spending

Contrary to the common belief that spending in higher education increases income inequality since it is "mostly captured by the richest youth," today, spending in higher education is (on average) slightly progressive. This means that if funded with a proportional income tax, ex post income inequality marginally decreases. Furthermore, a back of the envelope calculation indicates that the expenditures associated to expanding higher education coverage is four times more progressive than average expenditures, and almost as progressive as expenditures in secondary education (see box 2.2).

Box 2.2 Redistributive Effects of Public Spending in Higher Education

This analysis assumes that public expenditure in higher education involves an in-kind transference to those enrolled in higher education. Depending on how this transference is distributed across income quintiles (that is, depending on the access patterns in higher education by income) the ex post income (the ex ante income plus the transference) could be more equally or more unequally distributed. The advantage of this approach is that it can be implemented with basic information collected in most household surveys. This analysis distinguishes between the redistributive impact of the total spending in higher education (*average incidence*) and the spending associated to expanding the coverage of higher education (*marginal incidence*). This distinction is important since, while the richest are more likely to be enrolled in higher education (and hence they capture a large share of the *total* spending), middle-income students represent the larger share of the new students, and hence they capture a larger share of the *marginal* spending (see annex 2C for more details).

The average incidence analysis indicates that expenditures in higher education is slightly progressive. This means that if funded with a proportional income tax, ex post income inequality slightly decreases. To see this, panels a and c of figure B2.2.1 show both the average share of higher education spending captured by each quintile (under standard assumptions) and the tax burden that would be associated to the proportional tax. Under this funding scenario, while the poorest two quintiles would capture just 16 percent of the benefits of higher education, they would also pay only 10 percent of the tax. On the other hand, the richest quintile captures around 40 percent of the benefits (since they are more likely to enroll), but they would also pay around 60 percent of the tax.

Furthermore, a back of the envelope calculation indicates that the expenditure associated to expanding higher education coverage (that is, the marginal incidence) is much more progressive. As shown in panel b of figure B2.2.1, we estimate that the poorest two quintiles capture almost 30 percent of this expenditure, but they would still pay 10 percent of the costs

Figure B2.2.1 Distributive Incidence Analysis, Latin American and Caribbean Average, Youths Ages 18–24 Years, circa 2013

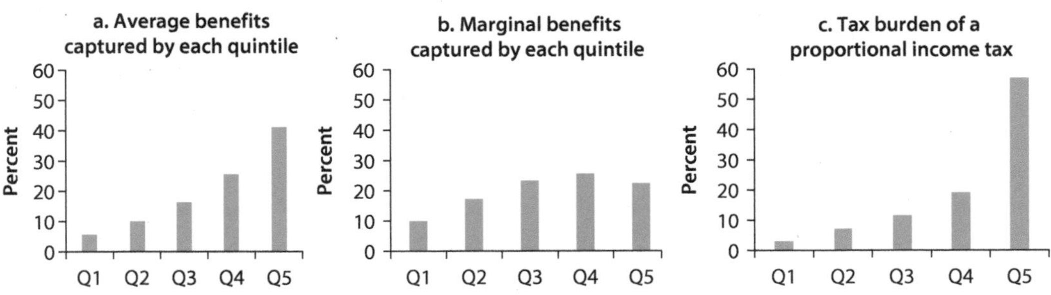

Source: World Bank calculations using SEDLAC.
Note: The details of the methodology are explained in annex 2B. The distribution of average benefits depends on the distribution across income quintiles of higher education students. The distribution of marginal benefits depends on the distribution of *new students*, which were roughly estimated using two cross-sectional datasets for each country with the methodology described in annex 2B.

box continues next page

Box 2.2 Redistributive Effects of Public Spending in Higher Education *(continued)*

Figure B2.2.2 Kakwani Index of Progressivity, Latin American and Caribbean Average, circa 2013

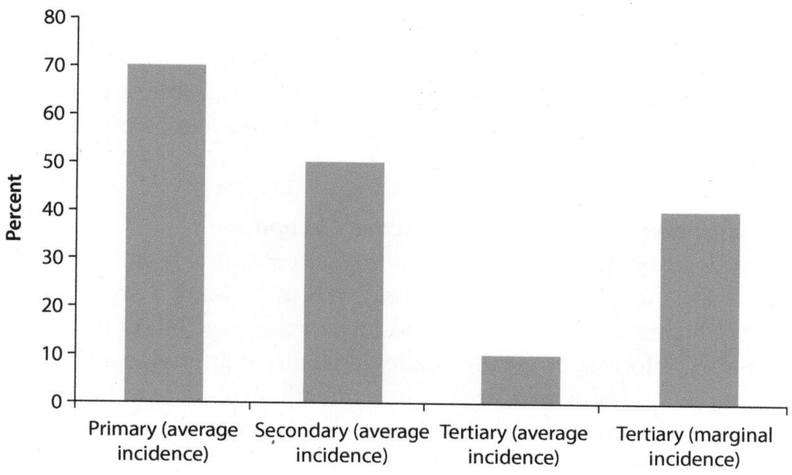

Source: World Bank calculations using SEDLAC.
Note: The details of the methodology are explained in annex 2C.

under the funding assumption. On the other hand, the share captured by the richest quintile is reduced to only 24 percent in this case, while they would pay 60 percent of the tax.

Figure B2.2.2, summarizes the results reporting the Kakwani index of progressivity. We also report the index for primary and secondary education as a benchmark. This index takes values in the range [−1,2]. A positive (negative) value means that the spending is progressive (regressive), and the larger the index, the larger the progressivity (that is, the impact on income inequality). While the Kakwani index is positive for both cases, it is around four times larger for the expenditures associated to expanding coverage in higher education (0.4 versus 0.1).

Quality

Greater access to higher education will lead to greater productivity only to the extent that HEIs provide a quality education. Ideally, one would like to measure quality of higher education programs as the value added of HEIs to outcomes such as end-of-college competence exams and graduates' wages. This exercise would require detailed data on both inputs and outputs to disentangle the contribution of all the inputs involved (among which HEI quality are only one part). For instance, if we measure higher education's output for a particular student as her score in an end-of-college competence exam, inputs consist of the student's ability, effort, academic readiness for higher education work, the ability and effort of her peers, and the HEI's value added through teaching, training, and provision of materials such as lab equipment.[17]

Unfortunately, this type of detailed data is not typically available in most countries. In this section we carry out a less ambitious exercise that documents differences in both inputs and outcomes across countries. Input measures includes students' academic readiness, per-student expenditures levels, faculty wages, and student-teacher ratios. The first two were discussed in chapter 1. Outcomes include wage returns to higher education (examined in chapter 3), completion rates, and TTD indicators. In addition, we report administrative indicators that document the existence and scope of accreditation systems, which are tools to ensure quality higher education (discussed in chapter 6). We finish by comparing the performance of LAC HEIs in world academic rankings.

Inputs

Higher Education Teaching Is an Attractive Occupation

Chapter 1 describes the main patterns in higher education spending. A common feature to all countries in the region is that a significant share of the public spending in higher education is directed toward the wage bill of university staff. Unfortunately, information on the quality of faculty is limited to a few countries. Hence, we rely on household surveys to indirectly explore whether faculty jobs are more attractive than the average jobs available for qualified workers (that is, those who graduated from higher education). In particular, we look at the relative wages of higher education professors as measured by the wage percentile of the median higher education professor in each country.[18] High relative wages could suggest that higher education professors are drawn from the pool of the most talented workers in the country. Of course, high salaries do not necessarily mean high quality. High salaries might reflect, for instance, that the faculty are unionized and have strong bargaining power.

In most Latin American and Caribbean countries, faculty jobs are among the top paying in the economy (above the 85 percentile), even when comparing them with the median graduate of higher education (see figure 2.7). In Brazil, for instance, wages of a median professor correspond to the 96th percentile, which means that only 4 percent of the workers have access to better paying jobs. In almost all of Latin America and the Caribbean, higher education professors earn more than other higher education graduates, with the exception of Nicaragua, Costa Rica, Argentina, and Uruguay. For comparison, in the United States, the income of the median professor corresponds to the 63th percentile, while the income of the median higher education graduate corresponds to the 73th percentile.

The higher income of higher education professors is not driven by longer hours of work. As shown in figure 2.8, higher education professors report shorter hours of work compared with workers with complete higher education and all workers. The average number of hours reported by higher education professors is 34.6 hours per week, as opposed to 41.4 for the workers with complete higher education.

Higher education professors are also less likely to work without the right to a pension in their main occupations (7.5 percent versus 43.5 percent among all workers), and less likely to work without the right to health insurance (8.5 percent versus 31.9 percent among all workers). This evidence suggests that the

Figure 2.7 Median Income Percentile of Higher Education Professors and Graduates, 2012

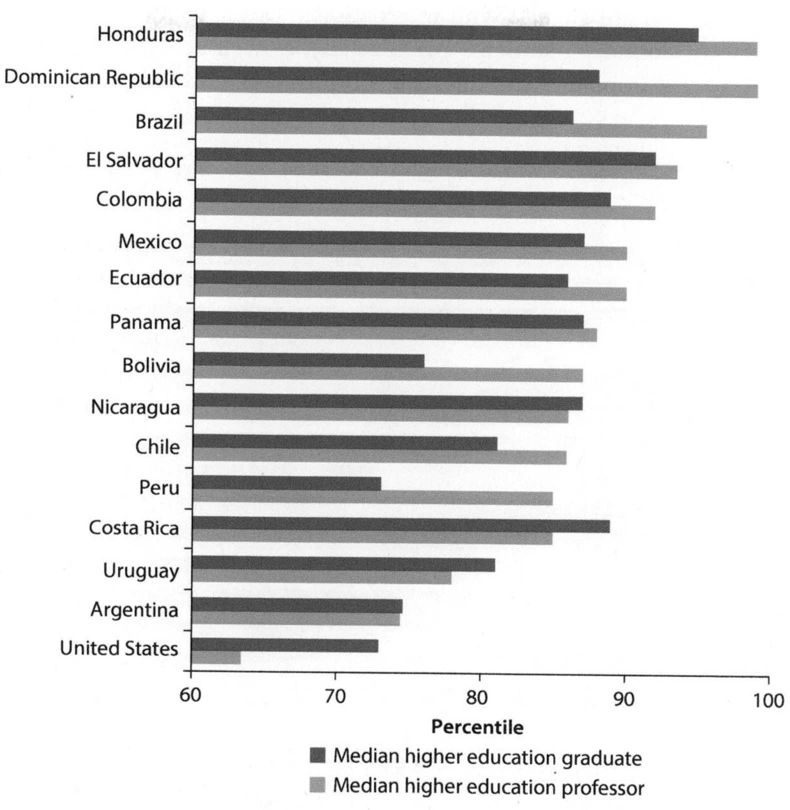

Source: World Bank calculations using SEDLAC (Latin America and the Caribbean) and IPUMS (United States).
Note: To identify professors in the household surveys, we combine information on main economic activity, sector of employment, and the level of education. Specifically, we consider an individual to be a professor if (a) she or he reports being employed as higher education professor; or (b) she or he reports being employed in higher education and has graduated from a higher education program.

benefits provided make faculty positions attractive for the region's most talented human resources.

For Bolivia, Brazil, and Colombia, we have information on the level of unionization of higher education professors. The average (30.4 percent) is much higher than for all other workers (9.9 percent). In Brazil and Bolivia, in 2012 more than 40 percent of the higher education professors reported being part of a union, as opposed to about 15 percent among all other workers. It is therefore difficult to rule out that the high monetary and nonmonetary premium described previously are, at least partly, the result of rent extraction of unionized workers.

Student-Faculty Ratios Are Aligned with International Standards

Holding teacher quality constant, lower student-faculty ratios are expected to raise student performance. Even in higher education, smaller classes allow teachers to promote active learning and interaction with their students, identify and support students that are lagging behind, and provide frequent and detailed feedback on students' work (Bianchi 2016). As shown in figure 2.9, most countries in the region are aligned with international standards in terms of student-teacher ratio (around 15 students per teacher), as well as those of comparator countries from Europe and Central Asia and East Asia and Pacific.

Figure 2.8 Average Weekly Work Hours for All Workers, Higher Education Professors, and Other Higher Education Graduates, 2012

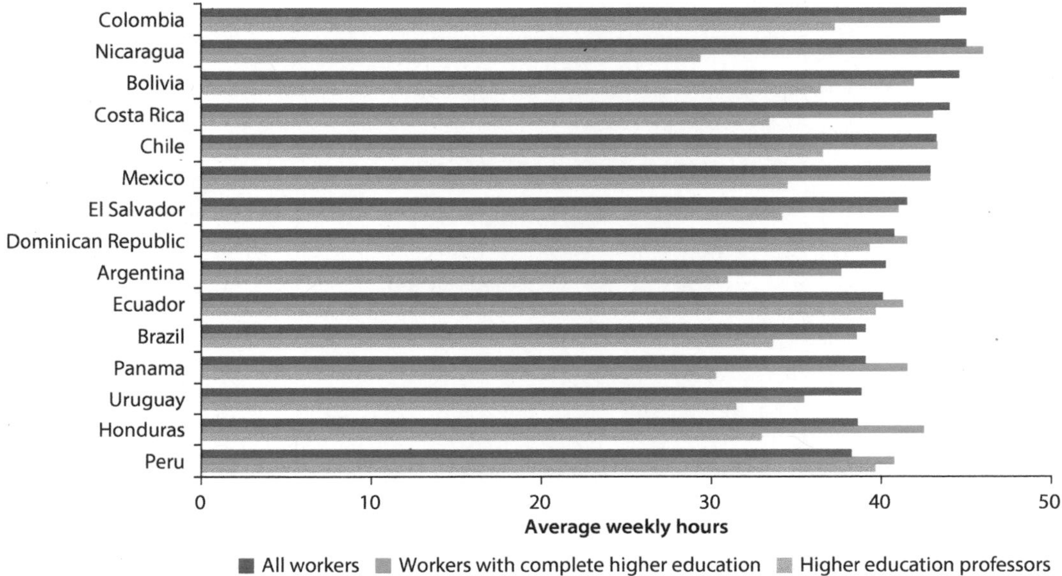

Source: World Bank calculations based on SEDLAC.

Figure 2.9 Student-Faculty Ratio, circa 2013

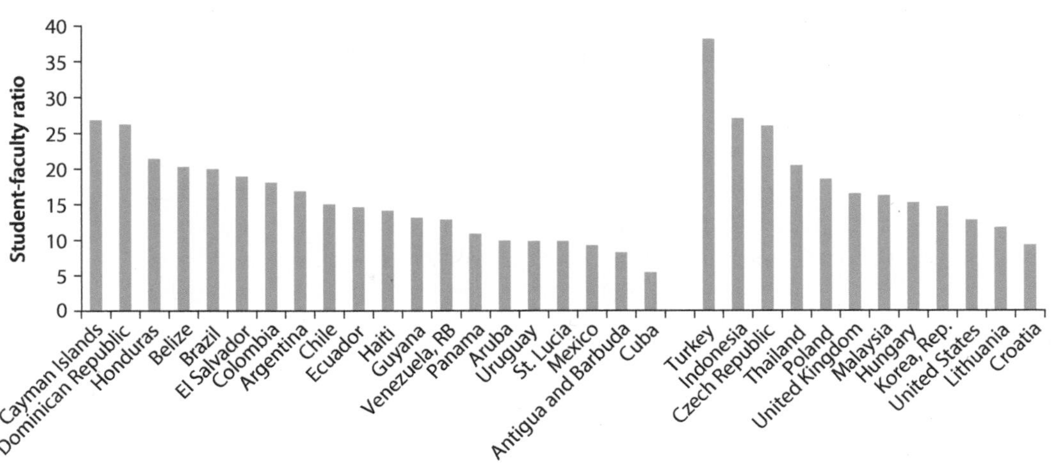

Source: United Nations Educational, Scientific and Cultural Organization, UNESCO. http://data.uis.unesco.org/index.aspx?queryid=180.

Outcomes

Completion Rates Are Low in Most Latin American and Caribbean Countries

A simple output indicator of the effectiveness of a higher education system is the completion rate of enrolled students. The completion rate forms an appealing statistic not only because it is simple and easy to understand but also because it measures a key goal of HEIs: what share of those who are seeking a degree succeeded? In addition, low completion rates indicate that a system is inefficient. Providing access to higher education is expensive, not only in terms of the direct costs but also in terms of both the opportunity costs of students and the potential negative externalities associated to congestions costs. Low completion rates mean that the society is bearing all these costs without achieving the expected outcomes. However, high completion rates might not mean higher quality. Indeed, completion rates can be boosted quite easily by relaxing graduation requirements (which could actually lead to lower higher education quality).

Completion rates are noticeably low in most Latin American and Caribbean countries. Figure 2.10 focuses on individuals ages 25–29 years who have ever enrolled in higher education. The figure shows, for each country, the fraction of individuals who have completed higher education, who have dropped out, and who are still enrolled but have not completed. On average, 46 percent of these individuals have completed higher education, 22 percent have dropped out, and 32 percent have not finished yet. Of these three indicators, completion is the most informative. The reason is that a student who is still studying might never graduate, but does not

Figure 2.10 Higher Education Completion Rates for Youths Ages 25–29 Years, in Latin America and the Caribbean, circa 2013

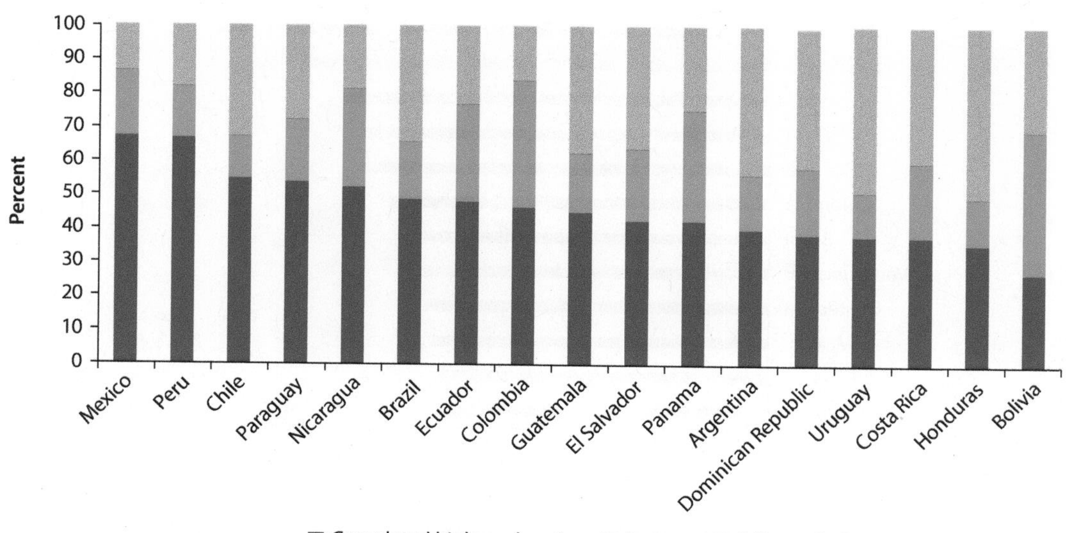

Source: World Bank calculations based on SEDLAC.
Note: Completion rates are estimated as the ratio between youths ages 25–29 years who completed a higher education program and the number of people ages 25–29 years who ever started a higher education program.

count as a dropout as long as he is still enrolled in higher education (which, in some countries, does not require making any kind of academic progress). When we look at the variation of completion rates across countries, we find that only Mexico and Peru display completion rates in line with the United States, equal to 67 percent.[19] Interestingly, the average completion rate of the region, on the contrary, is similar to that observed in open access, nonselective HEIs in the United States.[20]

Students Take Longer Than Necessary to Obtain Their Degrees

Another important indicator of the quality and efficiency of the system is TTD: the ratio between the effective duration of the programs (namely, the average time that students take to complete them) and the theoretical (statutory) duration. A large percentage of students taking longer than expected to complete their degrees leads to a significant waste of resources. In addition to the direct costs associated to extend enrollment, a longer TTD means that students have to wait longer to capture the returns to complete higher education education.

TTD estimates reveal inefficiencies in Latin American and Caribbean countries. The average TTD in the region (for countries with available data) is 1.36, which means that, on average, students spent around 36 percent more time than needed to complete their degrees (see figure 2.11). The outliers in the region are Honduras and Haiti, where students spent around twice the time needed to graduate. Interestingly, TTD is also large in some of the richest countries in the region, such as Argentina, Chile and Costa Rica, as well as in the United States.[21]

Figure 2.11 Time to Degree, Selected Countries, 2016

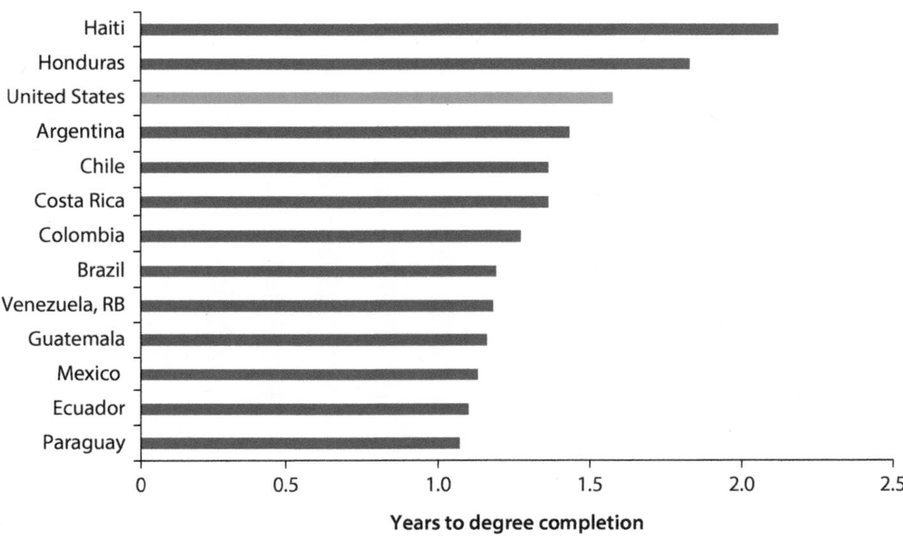

Source: World Bank survey to higher education authorities (see box 6.1), administrative data from Brazil and Colombia (see Ferreyra, Garriga, and Manuelli 2016), and Web Tables 2013-150, National Center for Education Statistics (NCES) for the United States.

Note: "Time to degree" is estimated as the ratio between the effective duration of the programs and the statutory duration. Data for the United States were collected in 2008, and data for Brazil were collected in 2012.

Quality Control and Assurance

The increase in the number and the variety of higher education programs and institutions has prompted education authorities to find mechanisms that can ensure quality. Certification and accreditation systems, either on a voluntary or compulsory basis, have become widespread. Chapter 6 discusses these systems.

In a paper written for this report, Avitabile and Cunha (2016) show that the share of accredited programs in Colombia has been increasing over time, as the proportion of accredited programs went from 6 percent in 2004 to 23 percent in 2013. Their findings suggest that programs are more likely to pursue an accreditation when they are in relatively more competitive markets and where there are fewer programs accredited. On average, programs that pursue accreditation do not have better students than those that do not do it. These results are potentially consistent with the hypothesis that in highly competitive markets, programs use the accreditation to differentiate themselves, but the informational value of accreditation is lower where there is a higher share of accredited programs.

In principle, there are different mechanisms through which the accreditation status might improve graduates' outcomes. First, it might help students and parents to identify better quality programs. In this case, the accreditation status would help higher quality programs to attract better students. Second, the requirements to become accredited might induce programs to improve the quality of the inputs in the learning production function, for example, teachers, managerial practices, and infrastructures. The accreditation status systems might work as a *signaling* device for employers, who might use information on accreditation status to make some inference on the quality of their applicants. In the last case, lower information asymmetries would allow employers to pay higher entry salaries, even in the absence of improved learning.

Avitabile and Cunha (2016) find for Colombia that the average entry scores for the cohorts that enter after a program's accreditation are not higher than those that entered before, once program time invariant characteristics are taken into account. They study the impact of accreditation on the level of knowledge (as measured by an exit exam) of recent higher education graduates and their labor market outcomes, as measured by the probability of employment and the hourly wage in the first year after graduation. They find that null effects after controlling for student initial level of ability and program time–invariant characteristics.

Overall, their results suggest that in the case of Colombia, parents and students are already aware of programs' quality, and that the quality of the inputs did not change as a result of the process. Nevertheless, the authors cannot rule out that the accreditation might improve the outcomes later in the working life. In contrast, the evidence for Chile for institutional accreditation, presented in chapter 3, suggests an extra year of accreditation is associated with an average increase of 5.6 percentage points on labor market monetary returns. In Chile, the positive returns to accreditation are driven by universities rather than other institutions.

Ranking Data

Rankings have become an increasingly popular tool to assess quality, both among students and policy makers. Ranking indicators suggest that the region might be lagging behind the rest of the developed world in higher education quality. For instance, data from the Top 500 ARWU, depicted in figure 2.12, panel a, show the small participation of the region among the top 500 universities in the world (less than 2 percent). In addition, regardless of the specific ranking, the region's top institutions do not belong among the world's top 100 (table 2.1). When averaging the positions in the four of the most well-known international rankings (*Times*, *US News*, ARWU, and QS World University Rankings), we find that the best-ranked institutions are the University of San Paulo, with an average ranking of 163; followed by the University of Buenos Aires, 293; and the National Autonomous University of Mexico, 305.

Figure 2.12 Universities in the ARWU Top 500, by Region, 2014

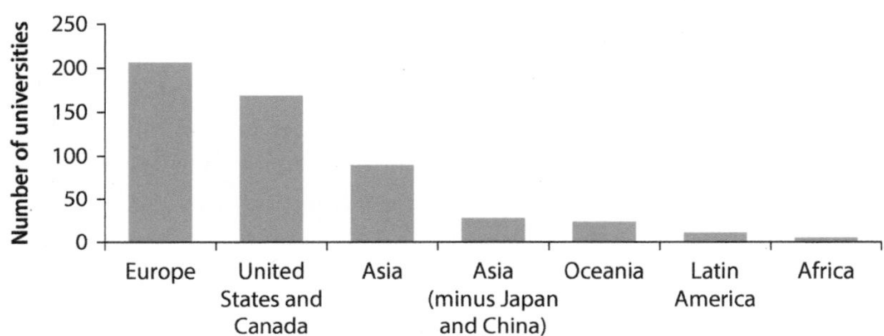

Source: Academic Ranking of World Universities (ARWU) 2014, Shanghai Ranking Consultancy, http://www.shanghairanking.com/.
Note: This figure shows the distribution by region of the top 500 universities according to the Academic Ranking of World Universities 2014.

Table 2.1 Average Ranking for Top Universities in Latin America and the Caribbean in Most Used Rankings, 2015

University	*Country*	*Average position*
University of Sao Paulo	Brazil	165
University of Buenos Aires	Argentina	293
National Autonomous University of Mexico	Mexico	305
University of Campinas	Brazil	307
Catholic University of Chile	Chile	375
Federal University of Rio de Janeiro	Brazil	375
University of Chile	Chile	396

Sources: Academic Ranking of World Universities (ARWU) 2015, Shanghai Ranking Consultancy, http://www.shanghairanking.com/; Quacquarelli Symonds (QS) World University Rankings 2015, https://www.topuniversities.com/qs-world-university-rankings; *Times* 2015; *US News and World Report* 2015.
Note: Only the universities that appear in at least three of these rankings were included. The average ranking position was calculated as the average of positions in each ranking (for those universities that did not appear in one of the rankings, it was assumed that their ranking was equal to lowest ranked university in the corresponding ranking).

We use the QS ranking of the top universities in Latin America and the Caribbean to analyze further the quality of universities within the region.[22] Figure 2.13 shows, for each country, the number of universities that rank among the top 50 universities in the region (divided by the total number of universities in the each country). While 13 percent of the universities in Chile belong to the top 50 universities of the region, between 8 percent and 9 percent of the universities in Argentina, Brazil, and República Bolivariana de Venezuela also rank among the top 50 universities. On the other hand, only 1 percent of the universities in Mexico and Peru appear among the top universities, and no university from Central America belong to this group.

Variety

In early 2000, the typical higher education student in Latin America and the Caribbean was attending a bachelor's face-to-face academic program, either in a public or private institution, depending on the country. The higher education sector has changed in the past 15 years, and now there are many different program and HEI profiles. Chapter 5 describes in detail how the higher education supply has changed, in terms of number of HEIs and programs, and how these changes have affected student sorting. This section aims at providing a snapshot of different dimensions in terms of student choice and program supply across the region.

Figure 2.13 Country-Level Percent of Universities That Belong to Latin America and the Caribbean's Top 50

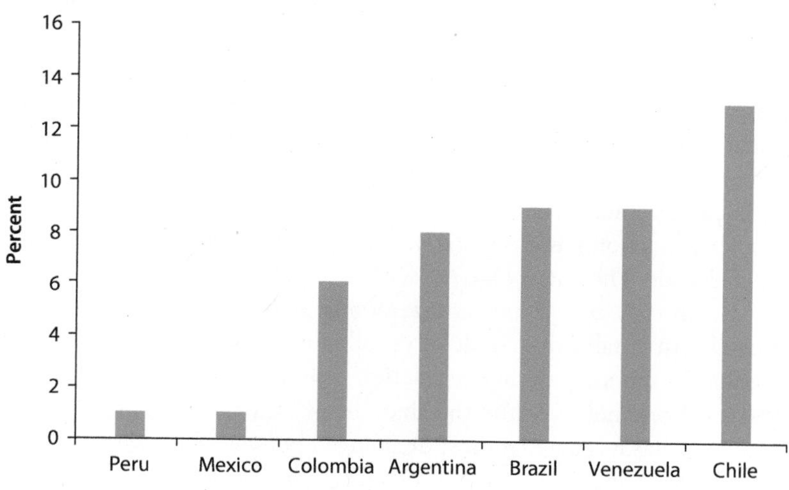

Source: World Bank calculations based on Quacquarelli Symonds (QS) Latin American University Rankings, 2015, https://www.topuniversities.com/qs-world-university-rankings, and World Bank survey to higher education authorities (see box 6.1).
Note: For each country, the figure shows the fraction of universities that belong to LAC's top 50. For instance, 6 percent of Colombia's universities are among the top 50 in LAC. The ranking is calculated as a weighted average of different elements: (a) academic reputation, (b) employer reputation, (c) faculty per student, (d) citations per paper, (e) papers per faculty, proportion of staff with PhDs, and web impact.

The share of students enrolled in private institutions increased from 46 percent in 2002 (circa) to 54 percent in 2013 (circa), with 10,657,388 students attending one of the 8,137 private institutions that were available, an increase from the 5,253 available in early 2000. Therefore, the expansion in private enrollment has been, at least partly, driven by a large expansion in supply. Private programs are on average much smaller than public ones (271 students enrolled versus 429), and they remain mostly focused on teaching. The expansion of the private sector can be partly explained by the fact that for-profit HEI are now allowed in at least seven countries in the region (Brunner and Ferrada 2011). Given the importance of the choice between public and private institutions, chapters 4 and 5 discuss the characteristics of students sorting into these institutions, and the evolution of supply over time.

Short-cycle higher education programs have played a key role in boosting the number of higher education graduates in the Organisation for Economic Co-operation and Development (OECD) countries. In 2012, roughly one-third of the population ages 25–34 years with a higher education degree in the OECD received a degree from a technical or vocational program. This is not the case in Latin American and the Caribbean. In the same year, according to the household surveys, only one-fifth of the students enrolled in higher education chose a short-cycle technical program, while the others preferred a bachelor's program. Administrative data on enrollment in short-cycle programs are available only for five countries, and they show that the number of students enrolled increased from 435,000 to 3 million between early 2000 and 2013.[23]

Using household data, Szekely (2016) documents that in 2013, on average 19.7 percent of the working-age population (WAP) has at least some higher education, disaggregated as follows: 9.4 percent of the WAP has completed a bachelor's program, 6.5 percent started but did not complete a bachelor's program, 2.7 percent has completed a short-cycle program, and 1.1 percent started but did not complete a short-cycle program (see figure 2.14). Thus, 81 percent and 19 percent of those enrolled in higher education chose a bachelor's and a short-cycle program, respectively. In 1995, 15 percent of the WAP had at least some higher education. Thus, over the past two decades, the stock of WAP with at least some higher education has grown by 4.7 percentage points, about 2.3 percentage points per decade. The share of WAP with at least some technical higher education has grown only by 0.2 percentage points. It is interesting to note that this growth is almost totally the result of enrollment in bachelor's programs, and is almost equal to the increase in the fraction of individuals with complete bachelor's degrees. Nonetheless, while the share of individuals with incomplete short-cycle programs has remained almost unchanged between the two years, the share of individuals with incomplete bachelor's programs has risen.

In 2013, Peru was the only country in the region where the share of the WAP enrolled in short-cycle programs was larger than the one enrolled in bachelor's programs (14.5 percent versus 13.2 percent). Together with Argentina (12 percent versus 19 percent) and Chile (8 percent versus 15.1 percent), these are the only three countries where short-cycle programs have higher enrollment

Figure 2.14 Bachelor's versus Short-Cycle Programs in Higher Education Expansion, Latin America and the Caribbean, circa 1995 and 2013

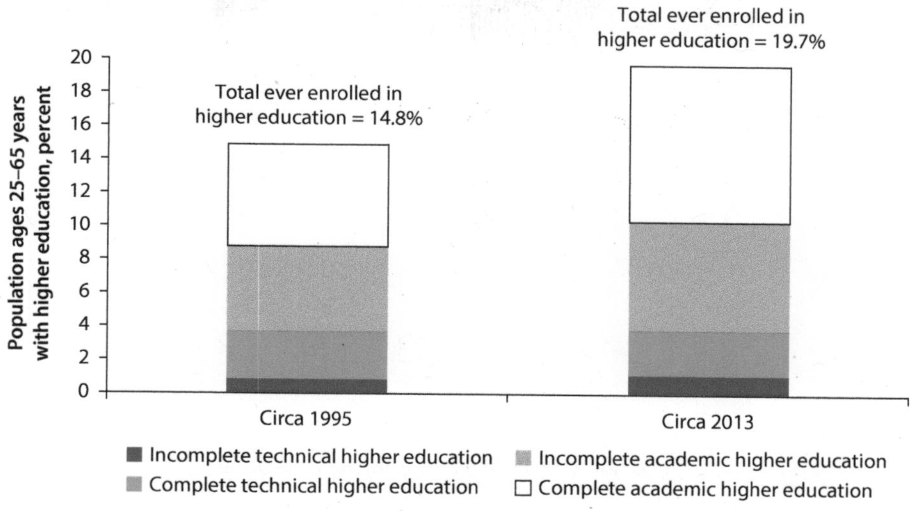

Source: Szekely 2016.
Note: Data show the simple average share of the working-age population that has ever enrolled in higher education across countries in the region. *Academic* refers to bachelor's programs; *technical* refers to short-cycle programs.

over enrollment in bachelor's programs. Szekely (2016) finds that, on average, 78 percent of the increase in the enrollment between 1995 and 2013 can be attributed to bachelor's programs.

Chapter 3 shows that both for Chile and Peru the labor market returns to technical (short-cycle) programs are large, and for some fields of study larger than for academic programs. The limited penetration of these programs is somewhat surprising, however. The preference for bachelor's programs is likely due to concerns about the quality of short-cycle programs, social norms, and lack of information about the potential labor market returns. Academic trajectories can also contribute to explain the imbalance: in 2012 the percentage of upper secondary students enrolled in technical programs was 15 percent in Latin America and the Caribbean, as opposed to 44 percent in the OECD (Avitabile, Bobba, and Pariguana 2015).

As chapter 3 will show, there is a large heterogeneity in labor market returns across different fields of study. Both in Chile and Peru, fields such as education and the humanities provide either close to zero or negative net returns, while engineering, law, and business provide returns that are much more than double than those of a high school degree.

Given this heterogeneity, it is important to examine the distribution of graduates across study fields in the region, presented in table 2.2. Almost 20 percent of the students graduate from an education-related field. This share is high not only compared with those in the United States (7.9 percent) and the United Kingdom (9.9 percent), but also to those in the comparator countries, where on

Table 2.2 Share of Higher Education Graduates by Field, circa 2013

	Education	*Humanities and arts*	*Social sciences business and law*	*Science*	*Engineering, manufacturing and construction*	*Agriculture*	*Health and welfare*	*Services*	*Unspecified*	*Shannon diversity index*
Argentina	16.4	9.9	35.7	8.1	6.0	2.5	17.9	3.4	0	1.782
Bolivia	24.0	2.2	33.2	4.9	10.8	5.6	17.4	0.5	1.7	1.669
Brazil	20.1	2.4	41.0	5.3	6.7	1.7	14.5	2.8	5.5	1.564
Chile	15.8	4.2	29.4	4.9	14.3	2.4	21.2	7.8	0	1.829
Colombia	8.3	3.5	54.1	4.0	18.7	1.7	7.3	2.3	0	1.447
Costa Rica	23.5	2.8	41.8	6.6	6.5	1.3	15.1	2.3	0	1.592
Cuba	23.6	1.0	29.2	2.7	1.4	2.1	32.5	6.3	1.2	1.526
Dominican Republic	17.7	4.7	46.8	4.6	9.8	0.7	14.0	0.6	1.1	1.516
Ecuador	21.2	4.1	43.0	6.1	8.8	2.4	10.9	3.6	0	1.656
El Salvador	18.7	4.7	35.9	1.0	21.2	1.4	17.0	0.1	0	1.567
Guatemala	24.7	1.0	37.4	2.6	14.1	7.3	12.8	0	0	1.586
Honduras	31.3	1.6	40.5	2.2	10.1	3.5	8.9	1.8	0	1.517
Mexico	12.5	4.4	44.7	5.5	21.3	1.7	9.0	0.7	0.1	1.568
Panama	25.0	5.8	34.7	5.8	10.1	0.5	9.9	8.2	0	1.738
Uruguay	3.9	4.0	40.9	7.8	7.8	5.1	27.6	2.9	0	1.629
Venezuela, RB	18.3	0.6	42.9	7.0	19.5	1.2	7.3	3.2	0	1.566
Average Latin America and the Caribbean	19.1	3.5	39.5	4.9	11.7	2.6	15.2	2.9	0.6	1.685
Indonesia	19.5	0.4	38.4	5.5	16.2	5.9	5.8		8.3	1.703
Malaysia	11.1	11.0	28.3	11.1	22.1	2.2	9.2	5.0	0	1.874
Philippines	16.8	1.9	34.1	13.9	11.6	2.4	8.6	5.8	4.8	1.878
Croatia	5.0	10.4	42.0	8.4	15.4	3.9	7.9	7.1	0	1.759
Czech Republic	11.6	8.4	35.9	10.4	12.9	3.8	10.3	5.4	1.3	1.898
Hungary	11.4	11.0	40.8	6.2	10.6	2.0	8.5	9.5	0	1.779
Lithuania	10.8	7.7	42.9	5.4	16.8	1.8	11.3	3.0	0.2	1.695
Poland	15.7	7.2	38.0	6.4	11.0	1.4	12.0	7.8	0.6	1.809
Turkey	10.1	8.5	46.7	8.6	12.3	3.2	5.7	4.9	0	1.687
Average comparators	12.4	7.4	38.6	8.4	14.3	2.9	8.8	6.1	1.7	1.863
United States	7.9	21.0	32.4	8.4	6.4	0.9	15.7	7.2	0	1.801
United Kingdom	9.9	16.1	29.9	16.2	9.0	0.9	15.7	1.5	0.8	1.832

Source: United Nations Educational, Scientific and Cultural Organization, UNESCO. http://data.uis.unesco.org/index.aspx?queryid=163.

average 12.4 percent of the students graduate from an education-related field. While education offers on average low labor market returns, many nonpecuniary benefits (including job stability, the relatively low number of working hours, and long vacations) might make teaching an attractive career (Mizala and Ñopo 2012). Moreover, as discussed in Bruns and Luque (2014), teaching might be the familiar choice to many first-generation higher education students. The share of graduates in education-related programs is disproportionally large in Central America (Honduras, Guatemala, Panama, and Costa Rica).

In line with the high returns in business and law, there is a large share of students opting for social sciences, business, and law (on average 39.4 percent). This is higher than shares in the United States (32.4 percent) and the United Kingdom (30 percent), although in line with those of comparator countries.

It is worrying that less than 5 percent of students graduate from science-related disciplines. This share is low not only compared with those in the United States and the United Kingdom but also to the average of the comparator countries, where 8.4 percent of graduates come from a science-related field. While the share of graduates from engineering, manufacturing, and construction (11.7 percent) is above that of the United States and the United Kingdom, it is below the average of the comparator countries (14.3 percent). As Lederman and others (2014) point out, students in the region have historically had greater tendency to focus on social science than students in places such as the United States or the United Kingdom. But, they also point out that the deficit of scientists and engineers in Latin America and the Caribbean may be related to the region's low innovation relative to that of upper-middle-income economies.[24] Given the low flow of graduates from these fields into the region's workforce, the deficit may persist for a while.[25]

It is a priori hard to assess whether there is an optimal distribution of graduates across fields, and what this distribution would look like. However, in principle it may be desirable to have a certain degree of diversity in the distribution of study fields to meet the needs of the labor market. To measure diversity of fields of study, we compute the Shannon diversity index for each country, with higher values associated to higher levels of diversity:

The index takes the following form (2.1):

$$H = -\sum_{i=1}^{N} p_i \, lnp_i \qquad (2.1)$$

where pi is the share of students choosing field i, and N is the number of possible fields. The Shannon index varies between 0, when the mass is concentrated in one option, and ln(N), when there is the same share of students for each field.

For the United States and the United Kingdom, the Shannon index takes the value 1.80 and 1.83, respectively, well above the Latin American and Caribbean average of 1.61. Most of the comparator countries display Shannon index values that are well above the Latin American and Caribbean average, with the

Czech Republic and the Philippines displaying very high scores (equal to 1.90 and 1.88, respectively). The only countries in the region that approach these high levels are Chile and Argentina, with Shannon index values equal to 1.83 and 1.78, respectively. In contrast, Colombia, Honduras, and the Dominican Republic are the countries with the lowest Shannon index values (equal to 1.45, 1.52, and 1.52, respectively).

Figure 2D.1, annex 2D, presents how the share of students per each field has evolved over time. The share of graduates in education has decreased almost in every country of the region, while the shares of those graduating from health or social sciences, business, and law have increased almost everywhere.

In summary, the findings suggest that, on average, the region shows a low level of diversity in terms of field choice, but students' choices seem largely consistent with the variation across fields in monetary returns.[26] Lack of diversity might be partly related to labor regulations that restrict the access to certain professions. For example, U.S. graduates who plan to enter teaching do not need a bachelor's degree in education. That is not the case in many Latin American and Caribbean countries, thus creating a strong ex ante incentive to choose education. However, ex post, graduates who are not able to find employment in their own field might struggle to find jobs in alternative fields. The relatively low level of diversity in the skills acquired by graduate students might be one of the reasons why Latin American and Caribbean firms are on average the ones that are most likely (34.2 percent) to report in the World Bank Enterprise Survey that inadequately educated workforce is one of the major constraints.

In 2001, the 5,359 students who were attending distance learning courses in Brazil accounted for only 0.18 percent of the students enrolled in higher education in the country. According to the 2013 administrative data, 1,153,572 students are enrolled in distance learning programs and represent almost 16 percent of the total enrollment. Brazil provides the best example for describing how distance learning has become a reality in the higher education landscape of the region. In all the countries for which sufficient data are available, distance learning represents a significant share of the students enrolled in higher education: Colombia (17 percent), Ecuador (12 percent), and Mexico (12 percent). Distance learning is not a prerogative of small and low-quality programs. Traditionally, well-regarded institutions have used distance learning to further diversify their offer. For instance, the Virtual University of the Instituto Tecnologico de Monterrey, started in 1997, has about 170,000 students in about 30 countries.

Annex 2A: Decomposing Access Gaps to Education

To quantify the relative importance of both completion and entry rates when explaining access gaps, we use Oaxaca-type decompositions. Intuitively, we simulate how much access gaps would be reduced between two groups (for example, the richest and poorest quintile) if both groups faced the same SCRs or the same entry rates to higher education. It turns out that, with these simulations, the access gaps can be exactly decomposed into two components: the share explained by differences in SCRs (SCR effect), and the share explained by differences in entry rates (ER effect).

The technique is simple. The first step is to notice that the access rate in higher education could be written as the product of SCRs and the entry rates. In other words, for a given age group, the enrollment rate in higher education could be written as the product of the share of students who completed secondary education, times the share of those students who accessed higher education (2A.1). Formally:

$$Access\ HE = SCR * ER, \tag{2A.1}$$

where SCR = secondary completion rates, and ER = entry rates. Then, the enrollment gap between two groups A and B (for example, the richest and poorest quintile) could be written as (2A.2):

$$GAP\ (A–B) = Access\ HE(A)–Access\ HE(B) = \mathrm{SCR}_A{\cdot}\mathrm{ER}_A - \mathrm{SCR}_B{\cdot}\mathrm{ER}_B \tag{2A.2}$$

Let's consider two cases: (2A.3) and (2A.4). If we add and subtract ($\mathrm{SCR}_B{\cdot}\mathrm{ER}_A$):

$$\begin{aligned} GAP\ (A–B) &= (\mathrm{SCR}_A{\cdot} - \mathrm{SCR}_B)\ \mathrm{ER}_A + (\mathrm{ER}_A - \mathrm{ER}_B)\ \mathrm{SCR}_B \\ &= SCR\ effect\ (i) + ER\ effect\ (i) \end{aligned} \tag{2A.3}$$

The first and second terms are the SCR and the CA effect, respectively. For instance, if both groups had the same SCR, then the gap would be reduced by ($\mathrm{SCR}_A{\cdot} - \mathrm{SCR}_B$) ER_A.

Alternatively, if we add and subtract ($\mathrm{SCR}_A{\cdot}\ \mathrm{ER}_B$):

$$\begin{aligned} GAP\ (A–B) &= (\mathrm{SCR}_A{\cdot} - \mathrm{SCR}_B)\ \mathrm{ER}_B + (\mathrm{ER}_A - \mathrm{ER}_B)\ \mathrm{SCR}_A \\ &= SCR\ effect\ (ii) + ER\ effect\ (ii) \end{aligned} \tag{2A.4}$$

The decomposition could change depending on the "path" chosen: (2A.3) or (2A.4). To avoid path dependence, we take the averages of (2A.3) and (2A.4), finding (2A.5):

$$\begin{aligned} GAP\ (A–B) &= (\mathrm{SCR}_A{\cdot} - \mathrm{SCR}_B)\ \overline{ER} + (\mathrm{ER}_A - \mathrm{ER}_B)\ \overline{SCR} \\ &= \overline{SCR\ effect} + \overline{ER\ effect} \end{aligned} \tag{2A.5}$$

This is an Oaxaca-type decomposition (see Blinder 1973; Oaxaca 1973). The first term in equation (2A.5) represents the share of the gap that could be explained by differences in SCRs between groups, and the second term represents the share that could be explained by differences in entry rates.

Annex 2B: Measuring Inequality in Access to Higher Education with the Gini Coefficient

The probability of having access to higher education is strongly correlated with household income. As shown in figure 2.6, while the probability of accessing higher education is only 8 percent for young people in the poorest percentile, it grows to 22 percent for the median percentile and to 64 percent for the richest percentile.

To compare the inequality in access to education across countries and over time, it is useful to summarize these inequalities with an index. A simple approach to measure how unequal higher education access is across income groups is to compute the Gini coefficient of the observed coverage rates by percentiles (which measures the probability of accessing higher education conditional on being in a given percentile). In short, the Gini coefficient measures how far we are from an "ideal" situation in which every youth faces the same probability of accessing higher education (a similar approach is proposed by Gasparini 2002).

Figure 2B.1 illustrates this exercise. The x-axis measures the *p* percentage of the population sorted by their probability of accessing school (that is, the level of education under analysis: primary, secondary, or higher education).[27] The y-axis measures the cumulative probability of accessing school. The red line is called the *Lorenz curve* of the observed distribution of probabilities, which simply measures the probability of accessing school accumulated by the *p* percent of the population. On the other hand, the blue line is a 45-degree

Figure 2B.1 Measuring Inequality in Access to Education

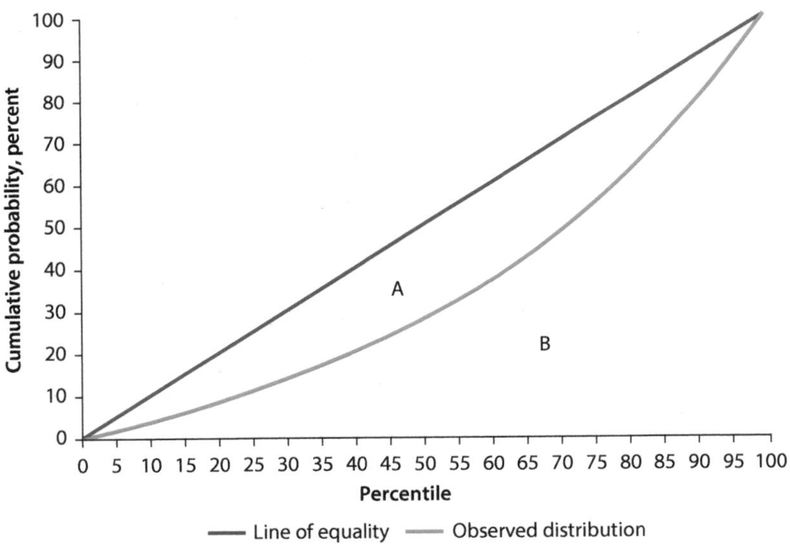

Source: World Bank calculations based on simulated data.
Note: Data show cumulative distribution of probability of the population being able to access school. The red line is the *Lorenz curve* of the observed distribution of probabilities, which measures the probability of accessing school accumulated by the *p* percent of the population. The blue line represents a hypothetical situation in which all income groups face the same probability of accessing school.

line that represents a hypothetical situation in which all income groups face the same probability of accessing school (that is, the *p* percent of the population accumulates *p* percent of the probability of accessing school, for every *p*). The further away the Lorenz curve is from the line of equality, the more unequal the access to school is. This is exactly what is measured by the Gini coefficient with the following formula (2B.1):

$$Gini\ coefficient = A\ /\ (A{+}B), \tag{2B.1}$$

where A is the area between the line of equality and the observed Lorenz curve, and B is the area below the Lorenz curve. The farther away we are from the line of equality, the larger A and the Gini are. In particular, the Gini coefficient is equal to one when B=0, and hence only the youths from the richest percentile attend school; and it is equal to zero when A=0, and hence the Lorenz curve is equal to the line of equality (that is, all percentiles face the same probability of attending school).

Annex 2C: Estimating the Redistributive Effect of Public Spending in Higher Education

Following Galiani and Gasparini (2012), we can approximate the direct redistributive effect of a program providing an in-kind transference (for example, access to school, a vaccine, etc.) by comparing the estimated income with the program (Y_i^c) with the counterfactual income in the absence of the program (Y_i^s). Let's assume that the income when the program exits could be written as follows (2C.1):

$$Y_i^c = Y_i^{mc} + t_i^e, \tag{2C.1}$$

where Y_i^c represents the total income of the individual (we are abstracting from household composition for simplicity), Y_i^{mc} stands for their market activities, and t_i^e stands for the monetary value of the in-kind transference from the government. On the other hand, the counterfactual income in the absence of the program is given by the following (2C.2):

$$Y_i^s = Y_i^{ms}, \tag{2C.2}$$

where Y_i^{ms} is the market value of their activities, and t_i^e is equal to zero in the absence of the program. The redistributive effect can be computed by comparing the income distribution under the program $\{Y_i^c\}$ with the simulated income distribution assuming that the program does not exist $\{Y_i^s\}$. The standard benefit incidence analysis assumes that the market income is the same with and without a program ($Y_i^{mc} = Y_i^{ms}$). Under this scenario, the redistributive impact of the in-kind transference can be measured as the following (2C.3):

$$I(\{Y_i^{mc} + t_i^e\}) - I(\{Y_i^{mc}\}), \tag{2C.3}$$

where I(.) is an index of inequality, such as the Gini coefficient in our case. The standard approach to estimate the monetary value of the in-kind transference t_i^e is to approximate by the average costs. Under these assumptions, the final incidence of the program is driven by the distribution of the in-kind transference across the income percentiles. In the case of higher education, the distributive impact is driven by the distribution of higher education students across income percentiles. While we could limit the analysis to those students enrolled only in public universities, we also include those enrolled in private universities: in many countries (for example, Chile) these students also receive significant subsidies from the government. Nevertheless, since it is clear that students enrolled in private universities are more concentrated on the richest percentiles than those enrolled in public universities, these estimations could be interpreted as a lower bound of the redistributive effect of higher education.

It can be shown that if higher education is financed with proportional (neutral) taxes, the ex post income inequality will decrease as long as the Kakwani index of progressivity is positive. This index takes values in the range [−1,2]. A positive (negative) value means that the spending is progressive (regressive), and the larger the index, the larger the progressivity. Formally (2C.4):

$$Kakwani\,index = \left\{Gini\left(Y_i^{mc}\right) - C\left(t_i^e\right)\right\}, \tag{2C.4}$$

where C(.) is the concentration index. The concentration index takes values between [−1; 1], with −1 corresponding to the case where the poorest percentile captures all the transfer t_i^e, and 1 to the case where the transfer is fully captured by the richest percentile. So, even if the spending is pro-rich (C(.)>0), it could have a positive redistributive effect if it is better distributed than income ($Gini\left(Y_i^{mc}\right) > C\left(t_i^e\right)$), which in turns means that *Kakwani index* > 0.

We also do a back of the envelope calculation to approximate the redistributive impact of the expenditures associated to expanding access to higher education. Following Van der Walle (2003), we can roughly estimate the marginal benefit captured by each income quintile as the following (2C.5):

$$M_q^e = \left(\frac{\Delta HE_q}{\Delta HE_{tot}}\right).100, \tag{2C.5}$$

where ΔHE_q is the estimated change in enrollment in higher education in quintile q between T=0 and T=1, and ΔHE_{tot} is the estimated change in the total enrollment in higher education. If we assume that a similar expansion will be funded with a neutral tax (with the current income distribution), then the redistributive impact of such expansion would be given by the following (2C.6):

$$Kakwani\ index = \left\{Gini\left(Y_q^{mc}\right) - C\left(M_q^e\right)\right\} \tag{2C.6}$$

Annex 2D: Change in Graduate Field Shares, Selected Latin American and Caribbean Countries, circa 2000–13

Figure 2D.1 Change in Graduate Field Shares, Selected Fields, circa 2000–13

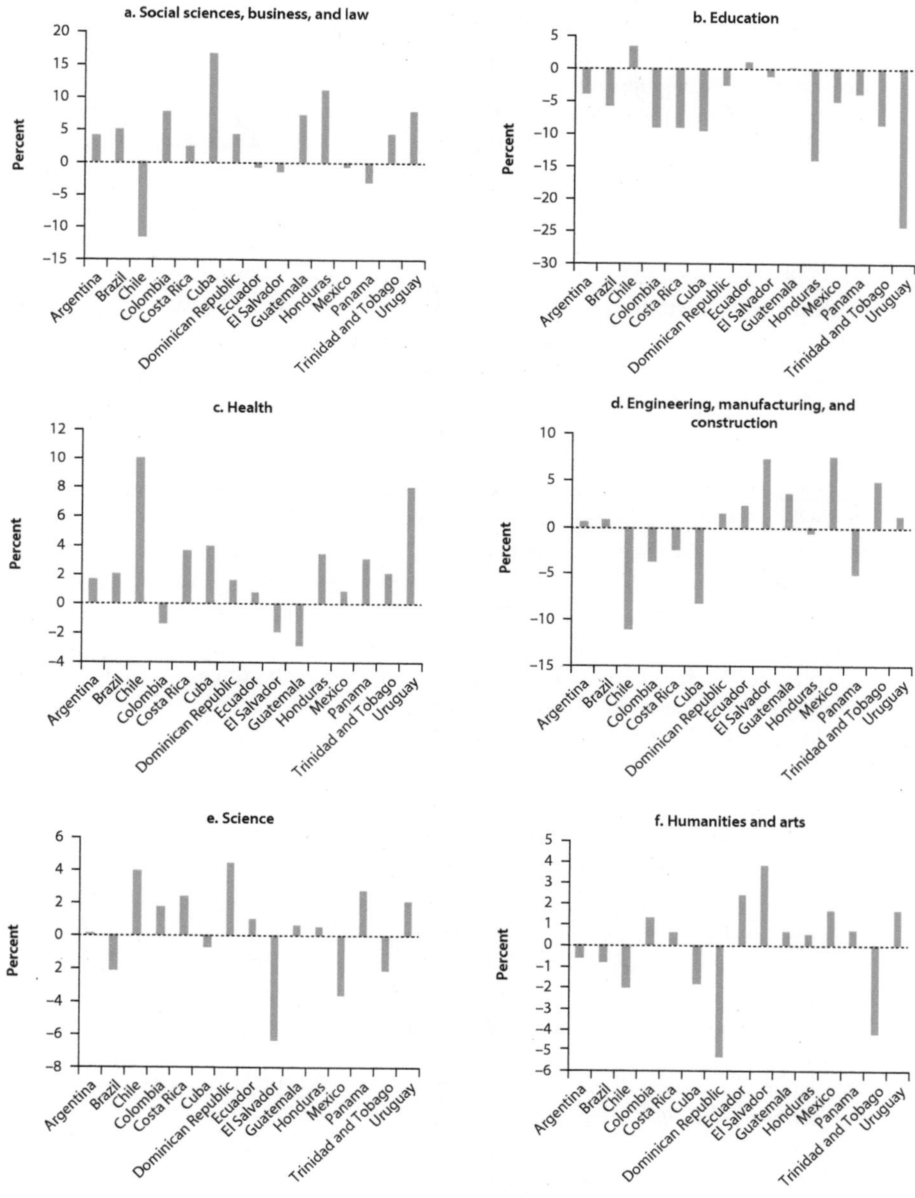

Source: World Bank calculations based on United Nations Educational, Scientific and Cultural Organization, UNESCO. http://data.uis.unesco.org/index.aspx?queryid=163.

Note: The figure presents the difference between circa 2000 and 2013 of the share of graduates in each field, in percentage points. Specific country years are as follows: Argentina (2006–13), Brazil (2001–12), Chile (2003–12), Colombia (2002–14), Costa Rica (2001–14), Cuba (2002–13), the Dominican Republic (2012–14), Ecuador (2007–13), El Salvador (2002–13), Guatemala (2002–07), Honduras (2003–14), Mexico (1999–2012), Panama (2002–13), Trinidad and Tobago (2000–04), Uruguay (2006–10).

Notes

1. See the glossary for the definition of *access rate*. In practice, this is the fraction of individuals ages 18–24 years with complete or incomplete higher education.
2. Hence, while the average implicit (or explicit) subsidy associated to public spending in higher education grows with family income because higher income individuals are more likely to enroll in higher education, when expressed as a share of the family income, the relative subsidy actually declines with family income. In other words, higher education is "pro-rich" but progressive. Other studies would refer to this subsidy as "not progressive" from the point of view of "absolute progressivity," but "progressive" from the point of view of "relative progressivity." See, for instance, Gasparini (2005).
3. In this case, using the terminology described earlier, higher education spending is both pro-poor and progressive.
4. In particular, the study estimates linear probability models, for each country, that regress access to higher education on a set of dummies capturing family income (quintiles of per capita income), parents' education, gender, ethnicity, region of residence, and a full set of age dummies.
5. An alternative way to explore the most relevant dimensions is to compare the (unconditional) predictive power of each variable. This is significant since it summarizes both the strength of the correlation and the variability of the dimension considered. We find that while family income or parents' education could (unconditionally) explain around 16 percent of the variation in access, regional differences, ethnicity, and gender could only account for 2 percent of the access differences.
6. We observe parental education only for those youths living with their parents (82 percent of this age group). This could raise some concerns regarding sample section bias, but we find that the results are similar when restricting the sample to those ages 18–20 years who are living with their parents (90 percent of this age group). In addition, the conditional analysis also allows to include the full sample of young people ages 18–24 years with a dummy for those with missing data. The conditional results are also robust to different samples and specifications.
7. This information is available only for Brazil, Guatemala, Nicaragua, and Peru.
8. See the glossary for the definitions of *entry rate* and *high school completion rate*.
9. While a plausible hypothesis is that the SCR effect plays a bigger role in poorer countries, the correlation between the poverty rate (using a US$4.0 per day purchasing power parity [PPP] poverty line) and the SCR effect is only 0.18. For instance, while there are countries such as Chile and Peru with relatively low poverty rates and low SCR effects (that is, SCR accounts for about 40 percent of the access gap), there are countries such as Argentina and Uruguay that also have relatively low poverty rates but considerably large SCR effects (that is, 72 percent and 81 percent of the gap, respectively). Furthermore, the SCR effects are poorly correlated with other key variables such as equity indicators or the size of the higher education system (as measured by net access rates) and access to free public higher education. Hence, the drivers of access gaps seem idiosyncratic as otherwise similar countries have different bottlenecks.
10. As expected, the share of the access gaps explained by secondary completion rates decreases monotonically with income. While the SCR effects explain around 56 percent of the access gap between the poorest and the richest quintile, it explains 52 percent, 49 percent, and 44 percent of the gaps between young people belonging to the richest quintile and those belonging to the second, third, and fourth quintile, respectively.

11. Furthermore, recent research documents that low academic readiness is in turn a function of early learning gaps that arise even before enrolling in primary education (for example, Cunha and others 2010).
12. We use SABER 11, which is the high school exit standardized test in Colombia. This test not only measures the academic readiness of students but it also gathers data on the socioeconomic background of parents.
13. Specifically, we define the groups as follows: (a) *high income:* family income equal to 5 or more times the minimum wage; (b) *middle income*: family income two to three times the minimum wage; (c) *low income*: family income below minimum wage.
14. The Lorenz curve provides a graphical representation of the index G. If access to higher education is not correlated with income, the poorest p percent of the population would accumulate p percent of the cumulative higher education access probability. In this scenario, the Lorenz curve would equal a 45-degree line (known as *the line of equality*). The further away the Lorenz curve is from line of equality, the more unequal the access to higher education is.
15. Income inequality refers to the Gini coefficient associated to the household per capita income (SEDLAC database 2013).
16. Besides being among the countries with the highest poverty rates in the region and the lowest secondary completion rates for the poor, Guatemala's limited supply of low-cost public universities is probably a key issue behind the high inequality in access to higher education. There exists only one public HEI (USAC) and 14 private universities. While students of private universities pay monthly fees between US$50 to US$700, the USAC charges around US$1 per month.
17. Two recent papers estimated value added models for HEIs in Colombia (Melguizo and others 2017; Shavelson and others 2016). Both papers conclude that these models are very sensitive to the choice of student outputs as well as the choice of the model.
18. To identify professors in the household surveys, we combine information on main economic activity, sector of employment, and the level of education. Specifically, we consider an individual to be a professor if (a) she or he reports being employed as higher education professor; or (b) she or he reports being employed in higher education and has graduated from a higher education program.
19. We calculate the U.S. completion rate based on the 2010 Current Population Survey (Flood and others 2015).
20. Among full-time, first-time students enrolled in public two-year colleges in the United States, only 35 percent graduate within five years (Scrivener and others 2015). Among full-time students enrolled in bachelor's programs in nonselective four-year HEIs, only 36 percent graduate within six years (Skomsvold and others 2015).
21. While we do not have an explanation for the fact that TTD is larger in the United States than in most countries in figure 2.11, given the lack of administrative or student level data for most Latin American and Caribbean countries, it is possible that the actual program duration might be longer in Latin America and the Caribbean. If the statutory duration of Latin American and Caribbean programs is longer, on average, than in the United States (for instance, five years rather than four), then the effective duration of programs in Latin America and the Caribbean is also longer than in the United States despite the smaller TTD for the former. With an average TTD of 1.36 for Latin America and the Caribbean and 1.58 for the United States, the average effective program duration is equal to 6.80 (= 5*1.36) and 6.32 (= 4*1.58) years, respectively.

22. The ranking is calculated as a weighted average of different elements: (a) academic reputation, (b) employer reputation, (c) faculty per student, (d) citations per paper, (e) papers per faculty, (f) proportion of staff with PhDs, and (g) web impact.
23. Argentina, Brazil, Chile, Colombia, and Mexico.
24. This conjecture is supported by recent research from Maloney and Caicedo (2014) and Toivanen and Vaananen (2016).
25. Regarding engineers, Lederman and others (2014) document that Latin American and Caribbean countries have fewer engineers than the median country and fewer than would be expected given their current level of development. Their measure, the number of engineering graduates per thousand people inhabitants ages 15–24 years, is informative of the stock of engineers, whereas the share of higher education graduates from engineering, construction, and manufacturing is informative of the flow of engineers.
26. Evidence in Avitabile and de Hoyos (2015) for Mexico and Hastings, Neilson, and Zimmerman (2015) for Chile finds that students on average have upwardly biased beliefs about the monetary returns to higher education.
27. Since the probability of accessing school typically increases monotonically with income, for simplicity, we will refer to the p percent of the population as the "poorest p percent of the population."

References

Avitabile, C., M. Bobba, and M. Pariguana. 2015. "High School Track Choice and Financial Constraints: Evidence from Urban Mexico." Policy Research Working Paper Series 7427, World Bank, Washington, DC.

Avitabile, C., and J. Cunha. 2016. "The Value of Accreditation in Higher Education: The Case of Colombia." Background paper for this report.

Avitabile, C., and R. de Hoyos Navarro. 2015. "The Heterogeneous Effect of Information on Student Performance: Evidence from a Randomized Control Trial in Mexico." Policy Research Working Paper Series 7422, World Bank, Washington, DC.

Bianchi, N. "The Indirect Effects of Educational Expansions: Evidence from a Large Enrollment Increase in STEM Majors." Working paper. Available at http://www.bianchinicola.com/research.html

Blinder, A. S. 1973. "Wage Discrimination: Reduced Form and Structural Estimates." *Journal of Human Resources* 8 (4): 436–55.

Brunner, J. J., and R. Ferrada (2011). *Educación superior en Iberoamerica: informe 2011*. CINDA, Santiago, Chile.

Bruns, B., and Javier Luque. 2014. "Great Teachers: How to Raise Student Learning in Latin America and the Caribbean (Advance Edition)." Washington, DC: World Bank.

Cunha, Flavio and Heckman, James J., 2010. "Investing in Our Young People," IZA Discussion Papers 5050, Institute for the Study of Labor (IZA).

Ferreyra, M. M., C. Garriga, and R. Manuelli. 2016. "General Equilibrium Effects of Higher Education Funding: The Case of Colombia and Brazil." Background paper for this report.

Galiani, M., and L. Gasparini. 2012. "El impacto Distributivo de las Políticas Sociales." CEDLAS Working Paper 130. CEDLAS, Universidad de La Plata, La Plata, Argentina.

Gasparini, L. C. 2002. "On the Measurement of Unfairness: An Application to High School Attendance in Argentina." *Social Choice and Welfare* 19 (4): 795–810.

Gasparini, L. 2005. "Pro-Poor and Progressive Growth in the Southern Cone: Evidence from Household Surveys." Working Paper, CEDLAS, Universidad Nacional de La Plata, La Plata, Argentina.

Hanushek, E. A., and Woessmann, L. 2010. "The Economics of International Differences in Educational Achievement." Working Paper 15949, National Bureau of Economic Research, Cambridge, MA.

Hastings, J., C. A. Neilson, and S. D. Zimmerman. 2015. "The Effects of Earnings Disclosure on College Enrollment Decisions." NBER Working Paper 21300, National Bureau of Economic Research, Cambridge, MA.

Lederman, D., J. Messina, S. Pienknagura, and J. Rigolini. 2014. "Latin American Entrepreneurs Many Firms but Little Innovation." World Bank, Washington, DC.

Maloney, W., and F. Caicedo. 2014. "Part II: Engineers, Innovative Capacity and Development in the Americas." Policy Research Working Paper 6814. World Bank, Washington, DC.

Mizala, A., and H. Ñopo. 2012. "Evolution of Teachers' Salaries in Latin America at the Turn of the 20th Century: How Much Are They (Under or Over) Paid?" IZA Discussion Paper 6806, Institute for the Study of Labor, Bonn.

Oaxaca, R. L. 1973. "Male-Female Wage Differentials in Urban Labor Markets." *International Economic Review* 14 (3): 693–709.

Paes de Barros, R. 2009. "Measuring Inequality of opportunities in Latin America and the Caribbean." World Bank, Washington, DC.

Sarah Flood, Miriam King, Steven Ruggles, and J. Robert Warren. Integrated Public Use Microdata Series, Current Population Survey: Version 4.0. [dataset]. Minneapolis: University of Minnesota, 2015. http://doi.org/10.18128/D030.V4.0.

Scrivener, S., Weiss, M. J., Ratledge, A., Rudd, T., Sommo, C., and Fresques, H. 2015. *Doubling Graduation Rates: Thee-Year Effects of CUNY's Accelerated Study in Associate Programs (ASAP) for Developmental Education Students*. New York: Manpower Demonstration Research Corporation (MDRC).

SEDLAC (Socioeconomic Database for Latin America and the Caribbean). CEDLAS, National University of La Plata, La Plata, Argentina, and World Bank, Washington, DC. (http://sedlac.econo.unlp.edu.ar/eng/).

Szekely, M. 2016. "Recent Trends in Higher Education in Latin America." Background paper for this report.

Skomsvold, P., A. Walton, and L. Berkner. 2011. "Web Tables: Six-Year Attainment, Persistence, Transfer, Retention, and Withdrawal Rates of Students Who Began Postsecondary Education in 2003–04." National Center for Education Statistics. Washington, DC

Toivanen, O., and L. Väänänen. 2016. "Education and Innovation." *Review of Economics and Statistics* 98 (2): 382–96.

Van der Walle, D. 2003. "Behavioral Incidence Analysis of Public Spending and Social Programs." In *Bourguignon and Pereira da Silva 2003 (editors). The Impact of Economic Policies on Poverty and Income Distribution*. New York: World Bank and Oxford University Press.

CHAPTER 3

The Economic Impact of Higher Education

Sergio Urzúa

Abstract

This chapter presents evidence on the economic impact of higher education in Latin America and the Caribbean. The text first examines the evolution of the Mincerian returns during the last decade. In the mid-2010s, the estimated premium to a higher education degree is 104 percent (relative to a high school diploma), which implies a reduction of 11 percentage points since early 2000s. The estimated premium to incomplete higher education, on the other hand, is 35 percent in the mid-2010s, also declining over the last decade (6 percentage points). The chapter then presents returns on lifetime earnings net of tuition and opportunity costs. By combining administrative records from two countries from the region (Chile and Peru), it reports large heterogeneity in the returns to higher education degrees. The evidence even suggests negative net benefits for some degrees and institutions. The results vary across students' socioeconomic characteristics and proxies of quality in the system. We conclude with a discussion of the implications of our findings.

Introduction

As documented in previous chapters, Latin America and the Caribbean have expanded the coverage of higher education during the last two decades. In 1991, the gross enrollment rate in postsecondary education (ISCED 5 and 6) in the region was only 17 percent, but it had reached 43 percent by 2012. Chile and Colombia emerge as two good examples of this trend. In the same period, their enrollment rates in higher education more than tripled. By 2012 both countries had reached enrollment rates comparable to the levels observed in many developed nations. More recently, Peru joined Chile and Colombia in their efforts to increase coverage. All the evidence suggests that this pattern will continue and extend throughout the region.

These achievements have been received with optimism in the region, particularly among policy makers. Most of the expansion has come from rising high school graduation rates and, at least to some extent, from public policies designed to facilitate access to the system and promote human capital accumulation in economies with large deficits of productive labor. Greater financial support for students and the geographical expansion of higher education institutions (HEIs) during the first decade of the new millennium are examples of these efforts in the region.[1]

And, of course, a greater access to higher education was expected to bring significant economic and equity gains. In particular, public policies were designed and implemented under the assumption that first generations of college graduates, particularly those coming from vulnerable households, would be shielded against the effects of poverty and inequality. However, this optimistic view is now being weakened. There is a growing concern that the expansion in coverage has been accompanied by a deterioration in the quality of the system. This phenomenon explains, at least partially, the massive student protests observed in Chile and Colombia during the last five years.

Concerns about the decline in the quality of higher education are common in the public and academic debate in the region. As explained in Messina and Silva (2017), this phenomenon could be the result of multiple factors, including (a) new marginal students accessing higher education less well prepared, (b) stress on the system, which lowers the average quality of all new graduates, (c) slow adjustments in curricula to changing demands for skills, and (d) new institutions offering lower value added diplomas.

The overall reduction in the Mincerian returns to higher education in Latin America and the Caribbean has been indicated as one of the potential manifestations of the degradation of the higher education system (Aedo and Walker 2012; Lustig, López-Calva, and Ortiz-Juarez 2013; Rodriguez and others 2016). For instance, Camacho, Messina, and Uribe (2016) document that the expansion and democratization of the system explains the declining returns to higher education in the 2000s in Colombia. This implies that the marginal student accessing higher education is less well prepared (after accounting for self-selection into different programs).

The objective of this chapter is twofold. First, we analyze the economic returns to higher education in Latin America and the Caribbean using conventional empirical strategies, and document the decline in returns. Second, we follow the literature and provide a theoretical framework to evaluate the return to higher education. By using publicly available data on tuition costs and estimations for future earnings, we estimate the economic impact of higher education programs in Chile and Peru. These calculations complement the more conventional estimates of the returns to higher education,[2] and illustrate their variation by field, HEI, and program type.

The simple but comprehensive economic approach and the use of publicly available data make our methodology easy to understand. Our framework allows for calculations that can be easily replicated by families, students, researchers, and policy makers. In this context, our analysis is consistent with the idea that more and better information about the future labor market outcomes associated with different career paths should be at the core of the efforts to expand access to higher education in the region.

Economic Impact of Higher Education

There is a long-standing theoretical and empirical literature that concerns the economic value of education. The conventional empirical strategy comes from the seminal contributions of Gary Becker and Jacob Mincer (Becker and Chiswick 1966; Mincer 1974). The idea is simple. The comparison of average (ln) adult earnings between individuals with different schooling levels (for example, years of education), but identical characteristics otherwise, should inform about the economic benefits of education. In this section, we present estimates of the returns to higher education for different Latin American countries. Box 3.1 describes the Mincer model in detail.

To avoid the natural difficulties associated with the heterogeneity of definitions of *higher education* throughout Latin America, our empirical analysis is carried out using the set of homogenized household survey of the World Bank and CEDLAS (Centro de Estudios Distributivo, Laborales y Sociales). Figure 3.1 presents the results.

The findings document the large Mincerian economic returns associated with a higher education degree in the region. It ranges from 49 percent (Argentina) to 179 percent (Colombia), with an average of 104 percent. This implies that, on average, monthly earnings of workers with a degree from an HEI more than double those obtained by workers with a high school graduates.

Box 3.1 The Mincer Regression

If Y denotes (ln) adult earnings, S represents years of education, and X is a set of variables, including labor market experience and its square, the coefficient β from the regression model (B3.1.1):

$$Y = \alpha + \beta S + \gamma X + \varepsilon \tag{B3.1.1}$$

represents the average difference in (ln) earnings between workers with S and S-1 years of education, controlling for the rest of observable characteristics. The returns can be computed as the exponential function of the coefficient (minus 1). For small returns, β can be directly interpreted the return to one year of education.

To capture the return to a higher education degree, we relax the assumption of a linear effect of education on earnings, and estimate a Mincer model of the form (B3.1.2):

$$Y = \alpha + \sum_{s=1}^{S} \beta_s D_s + \gamma X + \varepsilon \tag{B3.1.2}$$

where D_s is a binary variable that takes a value of 1 if the individual reports the schooling level s as her final educational attainment, and 0 otherwise. The set of schooling levels (S) considered include (a) primary education, (b) secondary education (high school diploma), (c) higher education without a degree, and (d) higher education with a degree.

Figure 3.1 Mincerian Returns to a Higher Education Degree in Latin America and the Caribbean, Mid-2010s

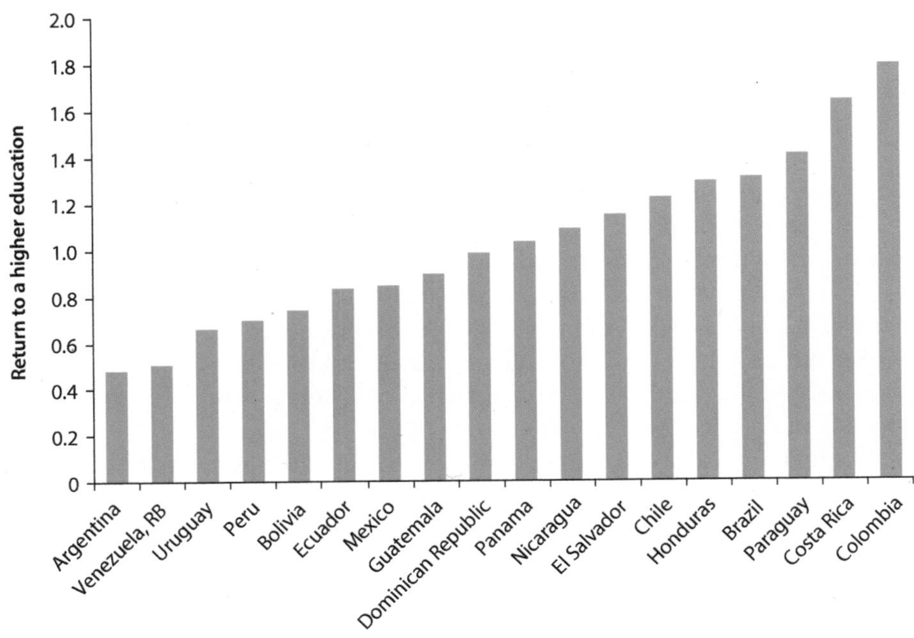

Source: World Bank calculations based on SEDLAC.
Note: The figure reports the return to a higher education degree relative to the alternative of a high school diploma. The returns are estimated using Mincer regression models. The coefficient associated with the dummy variable "higher education degree" represents the average difference of (ln) monthly earnings between workers with that schooling level and the baseline category (workers with high school diploma), controlling for the rest of observable characteristics. The returns are computed as the exponential function of the coefficient minus 1. The estimation of the Mincer model also considers the potential impact of self-selection into employment. The set of controls include gender, age and its square, urban area indicators, and regional indicators by country.

Expectations of better labor market outcomes, as suggested by the high private average returns depicted in figure 3.1, may have been the drivers supporting the expansion of higher education in the region. Nevertheless, behind the averages hides significant heterogeneity in returns across different groups. Table 3.1 documents the gender differences in Mincerian returns computed from equation (3.2) estimated by gender.

In 11 out of 18 countries, the Mincerian return to a higher education degree is higher for males than females, and the average regional gender gap is 15 percent. The largest differences in favor of males emerge in Argentina, Chile, Mexico, and Guatemala, while the Dominican Republic, República Bolivariana de Venezuela, Ecuador, and Panama have the largest differences favoring females.

And heterogeneity emerges across schooling attainment as well. For example, as reported in chapter 2, a large fraction of students leave the system before completing their degrees. Thus, would mere enrollment also secure positive returns? In other words, how important is graduating from an HEI relative to just enrolling in the system? Figure 3.2 compares the results associated with the two options.

Table 3.1 Gender Gaps in the Mincerian Returns to a Higher Degree in Latin America and the Caribbean, Mid-2010s
Percent

Country	*Difference Males versus Females*	*Country*	*Difference Males versus Females*
Dominican Republic	−54	Uruguay	17
Venezuela, RB	−24	Paraguay	20
Ecuador	−18	Peru	20
Panama	−13	El Salvador	21
Nicaragua	−5	Costa Rica	30
Colombia	−4	Argentina	34
Brazil	−2	Chile	41
Bolivia	3	Mexico	92
Honduras	5	Guatemala	108

Source: World Bank calculations based on SEDLAC.
Note: The table compares the returns to a higher education degree estimated for males and females. Specifically, if r_M and r_F denote the returns for males and females, respectively, the table presents $(r_M/r_f-1) \times 100$. The returns are computed as the exponential function of the coefficient estimated from the Mincer regression (minus 1). The estimation of the Mincer model also considers the potential impact of self-selection into employment. The set of controls include gender, age and its square, and a set of region dummies.

Figure 3.2 Minceriann Returns to Incomplete Higher Education versus Higher Education Degrees in Latin America and the Caribbean, Mid-2010s

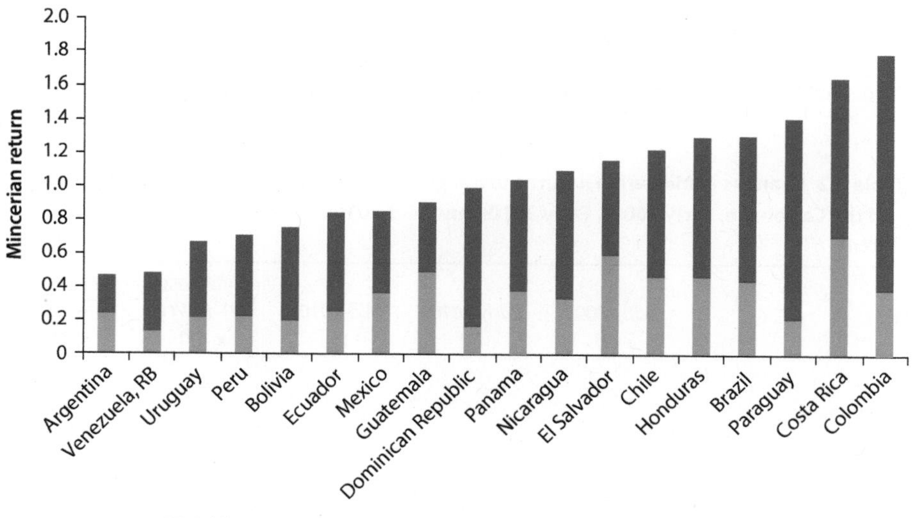

Source: World Bank calculations based on SEDLAC.
Note: The figure decomposes the return to a higher education degree (relative to complete high school) into two components: the return to some higher education (or incomplete higher education), and the additional return to completion. For instance, in Uruguay, the return to complete higher education is equal to 70 percent; the return to incomplete higher education is equal to 20 percent; and the additional return to completing higher education (relative to not completing it) is 50 percentage points. The returns are computed as the exponential function of the coefficient estimated from the Mincer regression (minus 1). The estimation of the Mincer model corrects for self-selection into employment. The set of controls include gender, age and its square, urban area indicators, and regional indicators by country. When multiplied by 100, these returns are expressed in percent.

For the region, the estimated average return to incomplete higher education (individuals who enroll but drop out before obtaining the degree) is 35 percent (relative to secondary education), with positive returns for each country included in the analysis. This suggests that enrolling in HEIs in Latin America and not obtaining a degree would lead to significant differences in labor income. The average premium from completion, on the other hand, is 69 percent, with the largest returns found in Colombia (140 percent) and Paraguay (120 percent), and the smallest in Argentina (25 percent) and República Bolivariana de Venezuela (37 percent). However, as discussed later in the chapter, this conclusion needs further qualifications.

Mincerian Returns to Higher Education Over Time

During the last decade, the evolution of Mincerian returns to a higher education degree relative to a high school diploma has been characterized by a stable decline. While in the early 2000s the average return in the region was approximately 115 percent (relative to secondary education), in recent years it has decreased to 104 percent, a reduction of 11 percentage points, with 11 countries experiencing negative variations. Table 3.2 presents these results.

It is worth noting that although South American countries experienced, in general, reductions in Mincerian returns, for many Central America nations the evolution of the returns displayed the opposite results.

On the basis of our estimates (table 3.2), the Plurinational State of Bolivia reports the largest reductions in Mincerian returns. Although in early 2000s the estimated premium to a higher education degree was 217 percent in the country, by mid-2010s it was only 76 percent, implying a 65 percent reduction (or 142 percentage points). Argentina (50 percent), Chile (30 percent),

Table 3.2 Changes in Mincerian Returns to a Higher Education Degree in Latin America and the Caribbean, Early 2000s, Early 2010s, and Mid-2010s
Percent

	Early 2000s (1)	*Early 2010s (2)*	*Mid-2010s (3)*	*Difference ((2)–(1))/(1) x 100*	*Difference ((3)–(1))/(1) x 100*
Bolivia	217	93	75	−57	−65
Argentina	99	59	49	−40	−50
Chile	174	147	122	−16	−30
Uruguay	89	87	66	−2	−25
Mexico	112	78	85	−31	−24
Dominican Republic	129	115	99	−10	−23
Panama	127	104	103	−18	−18
Brazil	152	141	131	−7	−14
Peru	85	61	71	−28	−17
Ecuador	95	96	84	2	−11
Venezuela, RB	53	43	51	−7	−3

table continues next page

Table 3.2 Changes in Mincerian Returns to a Higher Education Degree in Latin America and the Caribbean, Early 2000s, Early 2010s and Mid-2010s *(continued)*

	Early 2000s (1)	*Early 2010s (2)*	*Mid-2010s (3)*	*Difference ((2)–(1))/(1) x 100*	*Difference ((3)–(1))/(1) x 100*
El Salvador	111	124	115	12	4
Guatemala	85	103	90	22	6
Colombia	156	207	180	33	15
Nicaragua	89	104	110	16	23
Honduras	102	129	130	26	27
Paraguay	110	103	141	−6	29
Costa Rica	93	126	165	36	78

Source: World Bank calculation based on SEDLAC.
Note: The table presents the returns to a higher education degree for three different time periods. For Argentina, the Plurinational State of Bolivia, Chile, Costa Rica, the Dominican Republic, Ecuador, Guatemala, Mexico, Panama, Peru, El Salvador, Uruguay and República Bolivariana de Venezuela, early 2000s refers to information collected during 2000. For Brazil, Colombia, Honduras, Nicaragua, Paraguay is 2001. For Argentina, Colombia, Costa Rica, the Dominican Republic, Ecuador, Honduras, Mexico, Panama, Peru, Paraguay, El Salvador, Uruguay and República Bolivariana de Venezuela, early 2010s refers to 2010, for Nicaragua it refers to 2009; while for the Plurinational State of Bolivia, Brazil and Chile it refers to 2011. For Argentina and Chile, mid-2010s refers to 2013, while for the Plurinational State of Bolivia, Brazil, Colombia, Costa Rica, the Dominican Republic, Ecuador, Guatemala, Honduras, Mexico, Nicaragua, Panama, Peru, Paraguay, and Uruguay refers to 2014. Because of data limitations, in the case of República Bolivariana de Venezuela, mid-2010s refers to 2011. The returns are computed as the exponential function of the respective coefficient estimated from the *Mincer* regression (minus 1). The estimation of the Mincer model also considers the potential impact of self-selection into employment. The set of controls include gender, age and its square, urban area indicators, and regional indicators per country.

and Uruguay (25 percent) follow the Plurinational State of Bolivia in the ranking. Interestingly, the comparison of the early 2000s (column 1), early 2010s (column 2), and mid-2010s (column 3) estimates suggests that most of the reductions emerged before 2010.

On the other hand, only seven nations show positive trends in the Mincerian returns to higher education (table 3.2). Among them, Costa Rica emerges as the country with the largest increase (from 93 percent to 165 percent). Paraguay, Honduras, and Nicaragua, on the other hand, report increases above 20 percent of the early 2000 returns. As before, the analysis of the results from the three periods confirms that most of the changes occurred during the first decade of the new millennium.

Multiple factors could explain the overall negative trend in returns. Economic theory suggests that the recent expansion of higher education systems, which has translated into an increasing supply of highly skilled individuals, should have contributed to the phenomenon (Lustig, López-Calva, and Ortiz-Juarez 2013). Their democratization – the expansion towards middle and low socioeconomic groups – could have also played an important role (Camacho, Messina, and Uribe 2016). In addition, recent evidence has identified the natural resources boom as a potential force behind the trends, since it boosted the demand for unskilled labor in the region. And regardless of the driving factor, the reduction in Mincerian returns has also been, at least partially, linked to the decline in income inequality observed in Latin America during the last decade (Messina and Silva, 2017).

Does the negative trend also characterize the evolution of the Mincerian returns to attend higher education? As figure 3.2 shows, during the mid-2010s and throughout the region, the "alternative" of attending higher education but not obtaining a degree has been associated with positive returns. However, given the general decline in returns to higher education degrees, the documented expansion of the system and the large dropout rates characterizing the region, it is important to examine its dynamics. Figure 3.3 compares the changes between early 2000s and mid-2010s in the returns to some higher education and higher education degrees.

On average, while the Mincerian return to a degree reduced 11 percentage points in the last 10 years, the return to "some higher education" declined in 6 percentage points (equivalent to a 15 percent reduction). Moreover, 14 out of the 18 analyzed countries show decreasing returns to incomplete higher education.

Figure 3.3 Changes in Mincerian Returns to Higher Education, Mid-2010s versus Early 2000s

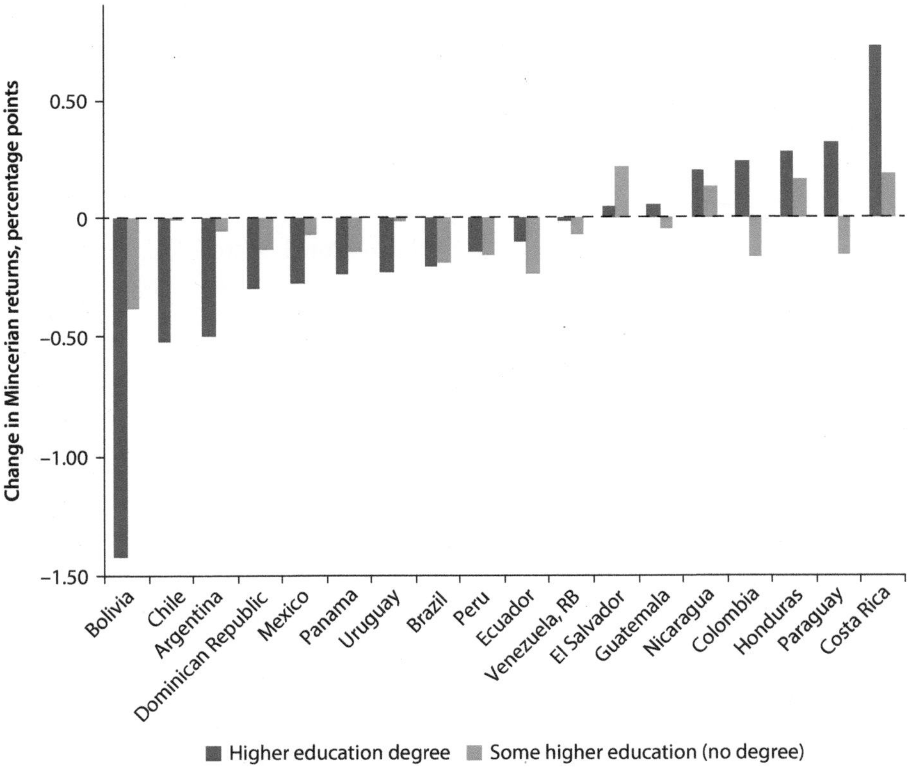

Source: World Bank calculation based on SEDLAC.

Note: The figure compares the changes in the returns to a higher education degree and to some higher education (no degree) for two different time periods: early 2000s and early 2010s. The returns are computed as the exponential function of the respective coefficient estimated from the Mincer regression (minus 1). The estimation of the Mincer model also considers the potential impact of self-selection into employment. The set of controls include gender, age and its square, urban area indicators, and a set of regional indicators by country. "Some higher education (or incomplete)" refers to the situation in which an individual enrolls in a program but does not complete it. This category is typically reported in household surveys, and it is reported for any type of higher education institution (HEI) (technical, vocational, or university degree).

In Guatemala, Colombia, and Paraguay, while the return to a higher education degree increased over time, for those dropping out the trend reversed.

Overall, these results should alert policy makers since the penalization of not obtaining a degree after enrolling in an HEI is increasing throughout Latin America.

Although informative, in general, the average returns to education calculated from the Mincer model do not fully capture critical elements associated with the economic benefits of a higher education degree. For example, they do not directly take into account the direct and indirect costs of higher education.[3] Moreover, given the characteristics of the data (cross-sections) and dependent variables used in the estimation (monthly earnings), the Mincerian returns inform about the economic impact of education in a specific unit of time (for example, month), not assessing the long-term impact of the human capital accumulation process. Furthermore, given the high levels of income inequality in the region, focusing on average returns might not provide a complete picture of the returns to higher education. Therefore, in what follows, we complement the previous evidence with new estimates of net and heterogeneous returns to a higher education degree on lifetime earnings.

Tuition and Opportunity Costs and the Impact of Higher Education on Lifetime Earnings

What are the implications of incorporating tuition and opportunity costs when estimating the economic impact of a higher education degree? How important is a life-cycle perspective for the economic analysis of the student's decision to pursue a specific degree? Given the large dispersion of labor income in the region, how heterogeneous are the returns to higher education? To answer these questions, we extend the conventional Mincerian approach, and we focus on the identification of heterogeneous financial net returns to higher education on lifetime earnings (Camacho, Messina, and Uribe 2016; Espinoza and Urzúa 2016; Gonzalez-Velosa and others 2014; Urzúa 2012).[4]

We rely on publicly available data and attempt to replicate what students and their families could do to evaluate the returns to a degree in a specific degree offered by a particular type of HEI. Provided the information is available, the calculations carried out here can be carried out by anybody, including students and their families, since they do not rely on complex methodologies. This section, and the next, draw heavily on Espinoza and Urzúa (2016), written for this report.

Defining the Net Economic Impact of Higher Education on Lifetime Earnings

The estimation of the (ex post) net economic returns to higher education on lifetime earnings might not only provide evidence on the overall long-term effects of the positive trends in enrollment rates but also help to understand and assess the way individuals are making enrollment decisions.

Consider the schooling decision problem of an individual who, after completing secondary education, is deciding whether to pursue a higher education degree. For the sake of clarity, assume that she is weighing the alternatives of enrolling in program *i* in higher institution *j* versus the alternative of searching for a job right after obtaining a high school diploma. In making the decision, the agent anticipates that, depending on the duration and costs of the program, the higher education alternative will involve delaying labor income until graduating and paying her investment while in school. Under the alternative, on the other hand, she could potentially start receiving income immediately. However, she anticipates that a higher education degree most likely will increase her earnings over her life cycle compared to the option of not enrolling and starting to work. Thus, the difference in lifetime earnings in favor of "higher education" could compensate its costs, leaning her toward that option. In this section, we try to recreate this analysis. In particular, if we denote by *NPV(i,j)* the discounted net value of future earnings obtained after graduating from program *i* in institution *j* (net of tuition costs), and *NPV* the present value of earnings associated with the alternative of "not pursuing higher education studies after high school graduation," we subsequently compute $(NPV(i,j)/NPV-1) \times 100$. See box 3.2 for further details.

Quantifying the Impact of Higher Education

As extensively discussed in the literature, the self-selection of individuals into different education levels generally prevents the interpretation of mean differences in earnings across education groups as the causal effect of schooling (Card 2001; Heckman and Vytlacil 2007). To take this into account, we first define the parameter of interest. Given the main objective of this chapter, we focus on the difference between the lifetime earnings associated with a higher education degree and the lifetime earnings of the "high school" alternative,

---

Box 3.2 Net Returns to Higher Education on Lifetime Earnings

From an economic perspective, the decision to enroll in higher education should involve, to some extent, the comparison of the financial benefits and costs associated with the alternative versus the option of working after obtaining a high school diploma. For the sake of clarity, let's assume the individual is weighing the alternatives of enrolling in program *i* in higher institution *j* versus start working. For simplicity, we assume that all programs are offered across all types of HEIs. Then, the overall supply of HEI degrees is the set of all possible tuples *(i,j)*. In this context, if we let *NPV(i,j)* represent the discounted value of future annual earnings obtained after graduating from program *i* in institution *j* (net of tuition costs), and *NPV* be the present value of earnings associated with the alternative of "not pursuing higher education studies after high school graduation," the individual should base,

box continues next page

Box 3.2 Net Returns to Higher Education on Lifetime Earnings *(continued)*

at least partially, her decision upon whether *NPV(i,j)* is larger or smaller than *NPV*. This logic motives the following definition of the return to program *i* obtained in institution *j* as:

$$r(i,j)=\frac{NPV(i,j)-NPV}{NPV}, \tag{B3.2.1}$$

with

$$NPV(i,j)=\sum_{t=d_{ij}+1}^{R}\frac{Y_{i,j}(t)}{(1+r)^t}-\sum_{t=1}^{d_{ij}}\frac{C_{i,j}}{(1+r)^t}, \tag{B3.2.2}$$

$$NPV=\sum_{t=1}^{R}\frac{Y_{hs}(t)}{(1+r)^t}, \tag{B3.2.3}$$

where $Y_{i,j}(t)$ represents the annual labor income *t* years after graduation from program i at institution *j*; $C_{i,j}$ denotes annual tuition costs, which are assumed constant over time; *r* is the discount rate; d_{ij} is the program's formal duration; and *R* is the number of years between the moment the student enters the program and her retirement. Likewise, $Y_{hs}(t)$ represents the income level *t* years after high school graduation. The main empirical challenge is the estimation of $Y_{i,j}(t)$, $t = 1,...,R$. We use multiple realizations of $Y_{i,j}(\overline{t})$, that is, average earnings $\overline{t}$ after graduation, to extrapolate and estimate series of labor earnings until retirement (age of 65). Annex 3A describes this procedure. Espinoza and Urzúa (2016) include differences in employment rates across education levels in the computation of the net present values. Other risk-adjusted returns, for example the sharpe ratio, could be also computed in the context of this framework.

---

but for those individuals that end up attending and, eventually, graduating from HEIs. Formally, this parameter is defined as the Treatment Effect on the Treated (Heckman and Vytlacil 2007).

The empirical identification of this treatment parameter involves the estimation of the lifetime earnings of individuals with a higher education degree but as high school graduates. Different empirical strategies impose different assumptions leading to the estimation of this counterfactual outcome. For example, one alternative would be the substitution of this term by the average net present discounted value estimated from the sample of high school graduates without college experience. This, however, would produce biased and inconsistent results because of self-selection (Willis and Rosen 1979). Instead, we use lifetime earnings estimated at different percentiles of the income distribution of workers with high school degrees (without any higher education experience). Box 3.3 presents a formal discussion on the net returns to higher education on lifetime earnings.

Effectively, this strategy allows us to assess the potential role of selection, since we could compare the observed average labor market outcomes of higher

Box 3.3 Net Returns to Higher Education on Lifetime Earnings

The treatment effect of interest is (B3.3.1):

$$\Delta(i,j) = E[NPV(i,j,k) - NPV(k)|D(i,j,k) = 1]$$
$$= E[NPV(i,j,k)|D(i,j,k) = 1] - E[NPV(k)|D(i,j,k) = 1], \tag{B3.3.1}$$

where $D(i,j,k)$ is an indicator function, such that $D(i,j,k) = 1$ if individual k graduates from program i in institution j, and $D(i,j,k) = 0$ otherwise. Notice that the second expectation is unobserved. It represents the expected net present discounted value associated with the alternative high school degree but calculated for those individuals with a higher education degree (from program i in institution j). One alternative would be the substitution of this term by the average net present discounted value estimated from the sample of high school graduates (high school graduates) without college experience. This, however, would produce biased and inconsistent results because of the self-selection of individuals into higher education degrees and institutions (Willis and Rosen 1979). Thus, we use a different strategy. Following the logic in Neal (2004), we proxy $E[NPV(k)|D(i,j,k) = 1]$ with different percentiles of the distribution of earnings. Thus, we define NPV_p as the discounted value associated with the alternative of not pursuing higher education studies after completing secondary education, where the subscript p refers to the p-*th* percentile of the income distribution of workers with high school degrees (without any higher education experience). Formally (B3.3.2),

$$NPV_p = \sum_{t=1}^{R} \frac{Y_{p,hs}(t)}{(1+r)^t}, \tag{B3.3.2}$$

where $Y_{p,hs}(t)$ represents the income level of the p-*th* percentile after t years of high school graduation. In this way, by modifying p we can empirically assess the potential role of selection as we could compare the observed average labor market outcomes of higher education graduates with those from different percentiles of the income distribution of high school graduates. Conceptually, this approach assumes that the relevant comparison group for those obtaining a college degree is not the average high school graduate, but high school graduates obtaining earnings in the p-*th* percentile of the distribution.

education graduates to those from different percentiles of the income distribution of high school graduates. Our empirical results use the 75th percentile. Therefore, we assume that the average individual obtaining a higher education degree would have received earnings closed to the 75th percentile of the earnings distribution of high school graduates had she not accessed higher education. We discuss how our results are robust to the use of different percentiles.[5]

Our estimated returns must be interpreted with caution, however. They are intended to identify the average economic gain of those individuals obtaining a specific higher education degree versus their alternative of becoming a worker with a high school degree. In this context, our estimates represent none of the following: (a) the average effect of the marginal individual who is indifferent between higher education and high school (Carneiro, Heckman, and Vytlacil 2011); (b) the internal rate of return (Heckman, Lochner and Todd 2006); and (c) the treatment effects in a multinomial choice setup (Rodriguez, Urzúa, and Reyes 2016). Nevertheless, they do inform about the economic impact of obtaining a higher education degree for those individuals pursuing it. Given the significant expansion of higher education in the region, this is a parameter relevant to policy makers.

Sources of Information

The computation of the net returns described previously requires degree-specific information on tuition costs, the duration of programs, and labor market outcomes for higher education graduates. Traditional sources of information, such as household surveys, do not contain all these dimensions. We focus on Chile and Peru, where high-quality administrative data on higher education enrollment and job market outcomes are available, allowing the estimation of heterogeneous net returns.

Chile

We employ four different sources of information. The primary dataset comes from the Higher Education Information Service (*Servicio de Información de Educación Superior* or SIES). This source contains student-level administrative records from all public or private HEIs in the country, including institutions offering two-year degrees (*centros de formación tecnica* [CFTs], technical training centers); four-year college degrees (*institutos profesionales* [IPs], professional institutes); and five-year college degrees (universities).[6] The list of variables includes type of HEI program, its duration and tuition costs, gender, age, region of residence, high school characteristics, socioeconomic status (SES), and high school GPA. We analyze the information from all students who first enrolled in HEIs in 2012.

Our second source is the Comisión Nacional de Acreditación (CNA, National Accreditation Commission), the institution granting accreditation status to HEIs (and academic programs) in Chile. Accreditation status is granted based on the multiple external evaluations assessing the mission and objectives of the HEI, its quality assurance policies and protocols, and its capacity to adjust and function based on its statutes and ordinances. At the end of the evaluation process, accreditation status is granted using the following taxonomy: 0 years of accreditation (unaccredited), 2–3 years (sufficient), 4–5 years (satisfactory), or 6–7 years (outstanding). Therefore, from CNA we obtain years of accreditation for each HEI or academic program.

The third source is the website mifuturo.cl, which provides official information on labor income four years after graduation for 1,069 higher education programs.[7] The fourth source is employment rates for different types of HEI graduates and average earnings for high school graduates, obtained from the 2013 Chilean household survey CASEN.

We distinguish 10 different fields of study. The taxonomy follows the International Standard Classification of Education: Fields of Education and

Table 3.3 Descriptive Statistics, Higher Education Institutions in Chile

	Type of HEI		
	Technical training centers (two-year degrees)	*Professional institutes (four-year degrees)*	*Universities (five-year degrees)*
Supply side			
Number of HEIs	56	40	58
Number of fields	191	141	434
Average tuition (US$)	2,602	2,694	5,423
Average duration	2.42	3.18	4.60
Number of campuses	167	178	219
Average years of accreditation	1.24	1.68	3.33
Demand side			
Number of students	62,282	111,240	152,832
Total enrollment (%)	19.1	34.1	46.8
Female (%)	52	51	52
Average PSU score	406.55	412.06	519.95
Student composition (%)			
Public schools	45	41	28
Voucher schools	53	56	56
Private schools	2	3	16
Total	100	100	100

Source: Espinoza and Urzúa 2016.
Note: HEI = higher education institution; PSU = Prueba de Selección Universitaria (College Admission Exam).

Training (ISCED-F), with adjustments made by the Ministry of Education of Chile. Table 3.3 presents descriptive statistics.

Universities have the highest average tuition costs and longest programs (averages are computed over programs based on the information from SIES), and attract students with higher scores in the national college admission test (Prueba de Selección Universitaria, PSU, Chile's college admission exam) than technical training centers and professional institutes.[8] And while 16 percent of the students attending universities graduated from private high schools, this group represents only 2 and 3 percent of the student body attending technical training centers and professional institutes, respectively. This illustrates the important sorting across types of HEIs in Chile.

Peru

The government's website portal, www.ponteencarrera.pe, is the primary source of information. It gathers detailed data on 3,957 higher education programs, including program-specific tuition costs, duration, and total enrollment; and campus location.[9] The information is reported for three different types of HEIs: universities; *instituciones de educación superior tecnológica* ([IESTs], technological institutes); and *institutos de educación superior* ([IESs], higher education institutes). The latter two offer technical and vocational programs, which are typically shorter and less expensive than those offered by universities, so they are merged into the "vocational/technical" category. The website also reports a selectivity index (the ratio of the number of admitted students to the number of applicants), which seeks to provide information on the demand for each specific degree, a proxy for quality.[10] The data also contains information on graduates' average monthly earnings over the first four years after graduation. However, this information is available only for 424 programs. For expositional clarity we present evidence for six fields of study.

A second data source is the 2014 Peruvian national household survey ENAHO (National Household survey). As in the case of Chile, from this survey we construct labor income for individuals without higher education degrees. We also generate employment rates at different levels of education. Table 3.4 shows descriptive statistics of the program level data.

It is worth mentioning that unlike in Chile, individual-level administrative information is not available in Peru. Hence we estimate only economic returns at the program levels.

Average Returns to Higher Education in Chile

As described above, to compute net returns we contrast the average net present values of a specific field and HEI type and the alternative of not pursuing higher education studies. For the latter alternative we use earnings for the 75th percentile of the distribution (p=0.75 in equation B.3.3.2).[11] Given that we are analyzing the counterfactual outcomes of individuals who ended up obtaining a higher education degree, we consider this percentile (instead of the average or the median of the distribution) as a sensible proxy for their labor market outcomes in the event of not pursuing higher education.

Table 3.5 displays the returns by field (agriculture, arts, business management, education, engineering and technology, health, humanities, law, science, and social sciences) and type of HEI (CFT, or technical training center; IP, or

Table 3.4 Descriptive Statistics, Higher Education Institutions in Peru

	University	*Vocational/technical*	*Total*
Institutions			
Number of HEIs	121	748	869
Public (%)	32.2	47.3	45.2
Market share (%)	55.5	44.5	
Programs			
Number of programs	1,519	2,438	3,957
Duration years (average)	5.13	3.05	3.85
Annual tuition (US$)	1,243.4	433.5	744.9
Enrollment (average)	120.2	62.2	85
Selectivity (%)	62.6	82.6	74.7
Annual salary (US$)	4,999	3,449	4,045

Source: Espinoza and Urzúa 2016

Note: The Vocational/technical category includes *institutos de educación superior tecnológico* (IESTs) and *institutos superiores de educación* (ISEs). HEI = higher education institution.

Table 3.5 Returns to Higher Education Degrees in Chile, by Field of Study and HEI Type
Percent

	Type of HEI			
	Technical training centers (two-year degrees)	*Professional institutes (four-year degrees)*	*Universities (five-year degrees)*	*Overall*
Agriculture	35.3	42.5	62.7	52.5
Arts	66.1	31.0	49.0	41.2
Business management	57.1	54.6	126.8	78.2
Education	−2.4	9.5	12.7	9.6
Engineering and technology	109.6	99.8	163.5	125.8
Health	40.5	40.9	101.5	73.3
Humanities	−5.2	12.1	2.3	4.1
Law	61.3	38.6	128.5	115.1
Science	97.2	115.5	115.3	113.6
Social Sciences	34.5	18.7	47.0	36.2
Total	66.2	58.9	97.5	78.4

Source: Espinoza and Urzúa 2016.
Note: HEI = higher education institution.

professional institute; or university). The results suggest that the highest returns are associated with five-year degrees in the fields of business management, law, science, and engineering and technology. This last field also concentrates the highest results across types of HEIs. Interestingly, results in chapter 2 show that a significant fraction of the graduates in the region obtain degrees in the fields of business and law. Hence, our evidence suggests that students, at least to some extent, are choosing fields rationally.

Two other interesting results emerge from the table. First, there is substantial heterogeneity both across fields of study and HEI type. For example, while the average student following a university degree in engineering and technology expects a return of more than 160 percent, the average student enrolled in the same type of institution but pursuing a degree in humanities expects a return of 2.3 percent.

Second, returns in some fields and HEI (especially CFT) are negative. Pursuing an education degree in a CFT has associated an average net return of −2 percent. This means that, on average, these higher education graduates would have been better off (in financial terms) if they had not pursued that degree and instead entered the labor force after graduating from high school.[12]

Figures 3.4 and 3.5 examine these two points. Figure 3.4 (panels a, b, and c) depicts the distributions of the estimated returns by field and HEI type. In particular, the panels show the estimated average return along with the return of the students in the 25th and 75th percentile of the distribution (of returns). Each panel documents large heterogeneity.

Moreover, it is important to point out that low-return university degrees (figure 3.4, panel c) might not necessarily be preferable to average- and high-return two- and four-year degrees (figure 3.4, panels a and b, respectively). For instance, the 25th percentile return from a university law degree is quite similar to the

Figure 3.4 Heterogeneity in the Returns to Higher Education in Chile, by Field of Study and Type of HEI

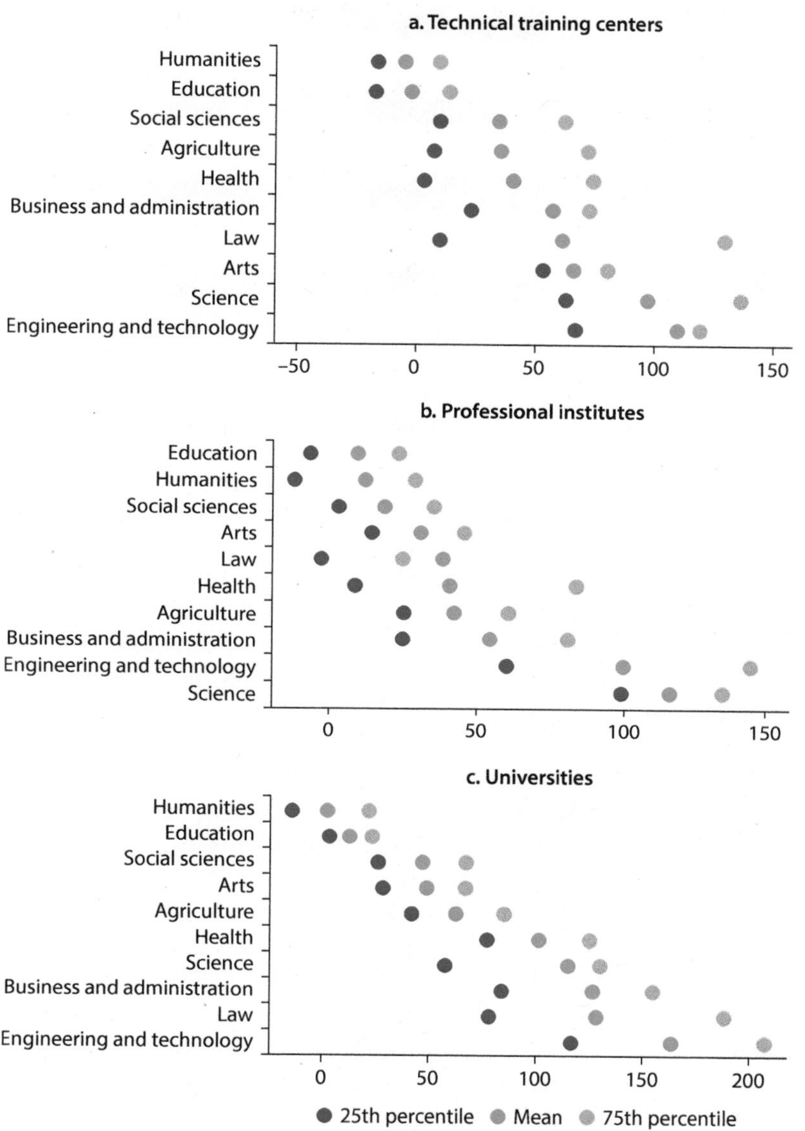

Source: Espinoza and Urzúa 2016.

average return from a CFT degree in the same field. Likewise, the 25th percentile return from a university business degree is similar to the 75th percentile return from an IP degree in the same field. These results might explain the stable increase of enrollment in IPs relative to universities in Chile observed until recently.[13]

Figure 3.5 explores the incidence of low-returns to higher education using the information from the 2012 freshman class (overall system). It displays the fraction of students that could face negative net returns.

Figure 3.5 Negative Returns to Higher Education in Chile

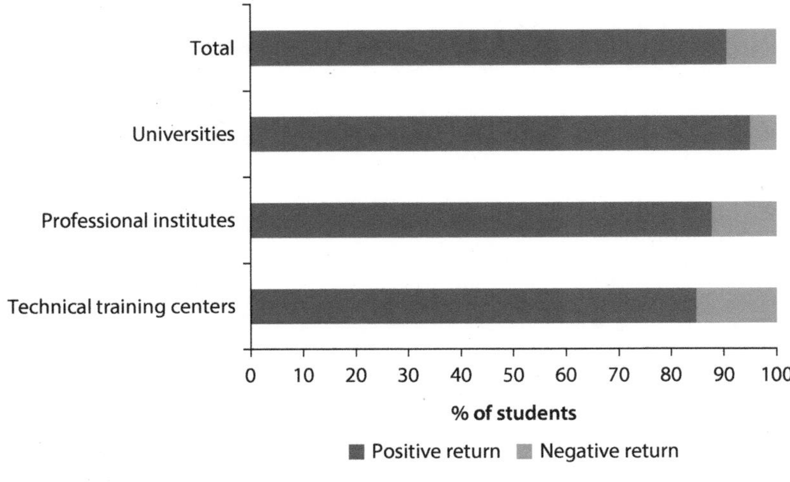

Source: Espinoza and Urzúa 2016.

The fraction is significantly higher in CFTs and IPs relative to universities.[14] Overall, this implies that approximately 7 percent of the students who started higher education in 2012 attended programs identified as having negative average returns (3.7 percent attended programs with returns below −10 percent). It is important to note that almost 75 percent of these students obtained high school degrees from low-SES high schools (that is, schools where at least half of student body is of low SES).

Figure 3.6 presents similar results by field of study. Note that from the new students belonging to the 2012 cohort, more than 30 percent of those pursuing degrees in humanities are enrolled in institutions reporting negative returns.

To further illustrate the large heterogeneity across degrees and the mechanisms delivering negative returns, figure 3.7 depicts the estimated average streams of earnings for graduates in the fields of education (panel a) and technology and engineering (panel b). The figure also includes the streams of earnings associated with a high school diploma (high school graduates) at different levels (percentiles) of the income distribution of this group.

For future higher education graduates, earnings are negative during the first few years since they must pay tuition costs. Later we discuss the implications of alternative funding regimes that could imply that students do not have to pay tuition costs out of pocket. After graduation, earnings become positive, displaying a concave profile as predicted by the Mincer model. Among high school graduates, there are no negative earnings during the first few years, since we assume they start working immediately after obtaining the high school diploma. Furthermore, for them the figure presents the estimated profiles associated with three different percentiles of the income distribution. They are not as concave as the one observed among higher education graduates.

Figure 3.6 Percentage of Students Who Could Face Negative Returns to Higher Education in Chile, by Field of Study and HEI Type

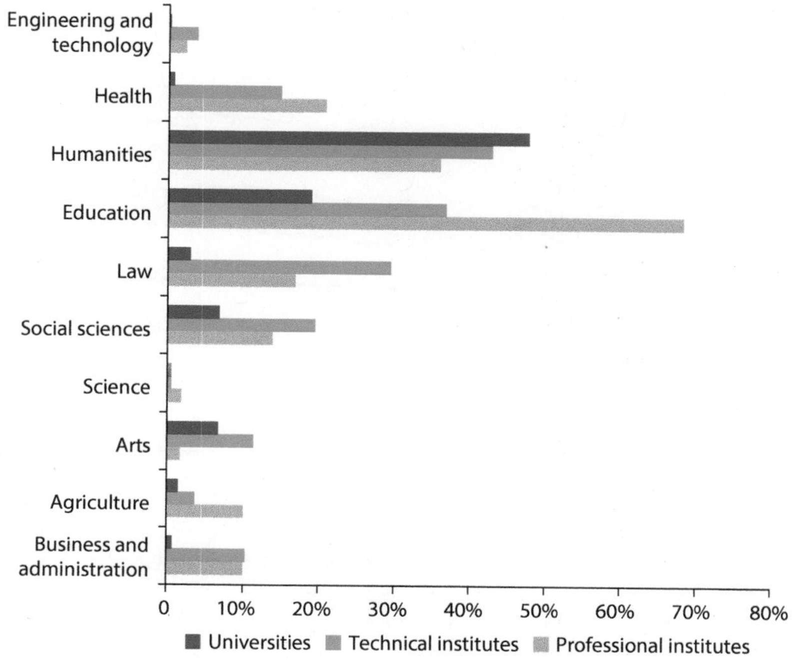

Source: Espinoza and Urzúa 2016.
Note: HEI = higher education institution.

While degrees in education have relatively low earnings, which imply low or even negative returns, technology and engineering programs have high salaries compared with those of high school graduates.

Average Returns to Higher Education in Peru

As reported in table 3.6, the estimated returns in Peru are substantially lower than those reported for Chile. The overall return to a higher education degree is 36.8 percent (78.4 percent for Chile). This is consistent with the evidence on Mincerian returns, and it might suggest that returns to education are structurally lower in Peru. Moreover, even though estimates still show some degree of heterogeneity across fields of study, they tend to be more homogeneous than in Chile. This might be due to the fact that the information in Peru is available only at the program level and, consequently, the estimates reported are obtained using more aggregate data than in the case of Chile.

The field that exhibits the highest returns is sciences, engineering, and manufacturing (58.5 percent), while education programs show negative returns (table 3.6). Interestingly, the estimated returns to degrees in the fields of health; business and management; and sciences, engineering, and manufacturing

Figure 3.7 Age-Earnings Profiles for Selected Degrees in Chile
Millions of pesos

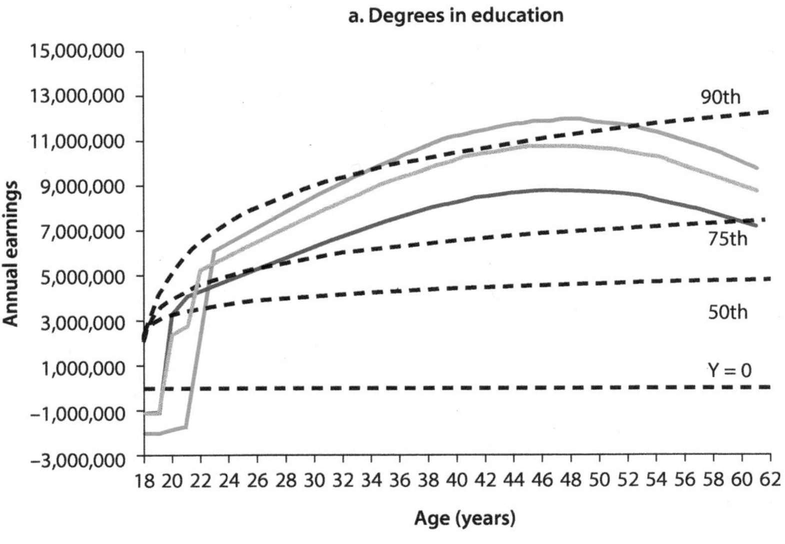

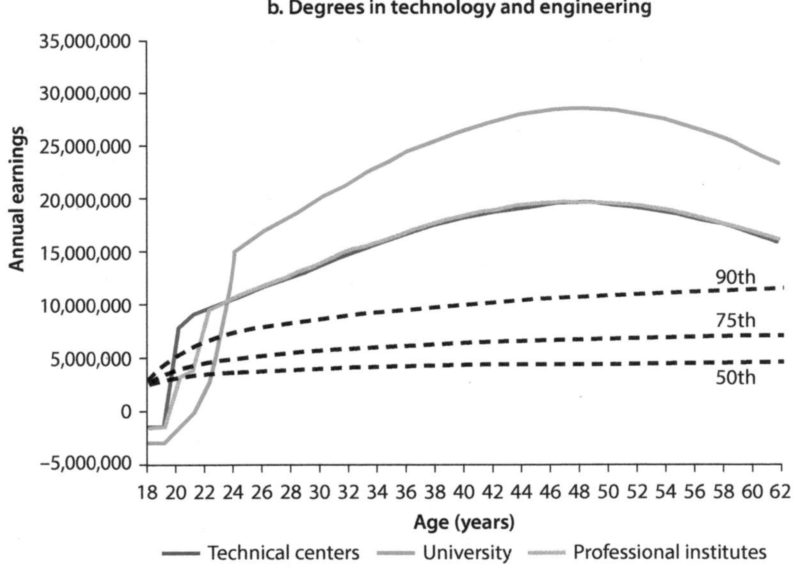

Source: Espinoza and Urzúa 2016.
Note: Dashed lines show the earning trends for high school graduates (HSG) and their income distribution (50th, 75th, and 90th percentiles). CLP = Chilean pesos; HSG = high school graduate.

are higher among vocational or technical institutions than among universities, suggesting that low-tuition and short programs might not necessarily be penalized by the market.

Figure 3.8 also illustrates the large heterogeneity in returns, but distinguishing between public and private HEIs. In general, higher education degrees

Table 3.6 Returns to Higher Education Degrees, by Field of Study and HEI Type, Peru
Percent

	HEI type (%)		
	Vocational or technical	*University*	*Overall*
Arts and architecture	16.3	47.9	34.6
Business and management	31.9	24.3	28.6
Education	−18.5	−18.5	−18.5
Health	31.3	7.1	18.8
Sciences, engineering, and manufacturing	70.7	49.4	58.5
Social sciences and communications	11.6	27.8	27.6
Other	50.5	33.0	43.2
Total	44.7	30.5	36.8

Source: Espinoza and Urzúa 2016.
Note: HEI = higher education institution.

Figure 3.8 Returns to Higher Education Degrees in Peru, by Field of Study and Type of HEI

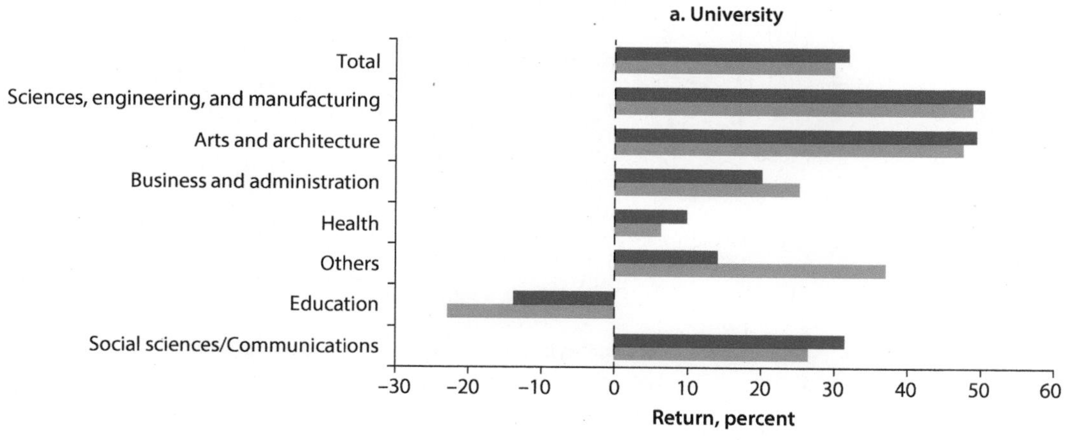

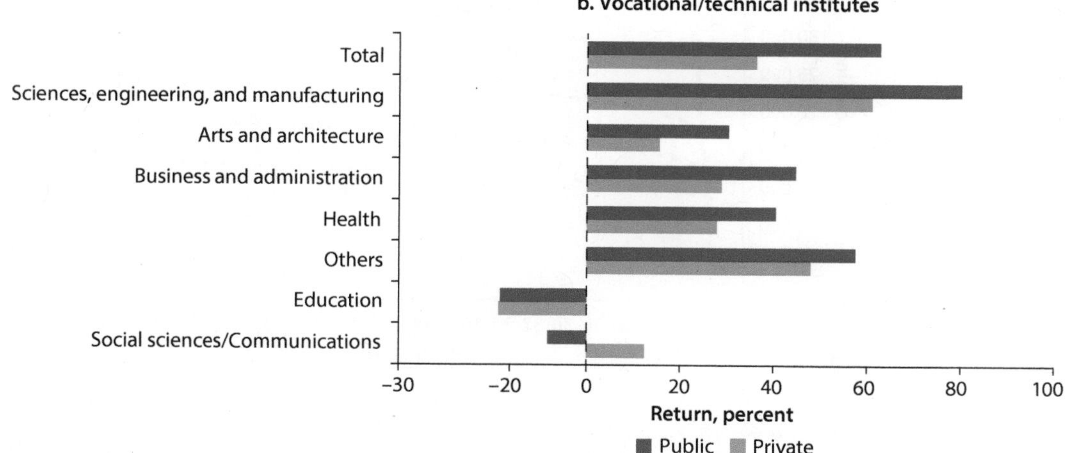

Source: Espinoza and Urzúa 2016.

granted by public institutions show higher returns than degrees granted by private institutions. However, private universities show better performances in business and management; health; and sciences, engineering, and manufacturing programs. The same is true for degrees in social sciences and communications granted by private vocational or technical institutes.

Figure 3.9 depicts the estimated streams of earnings for two different degrees: education (panel a) and science, engineering, and manufacturing (panel b).

Figure 3.9 Age-Earnings Profiles for Selected Degrees in Peru
Centimos

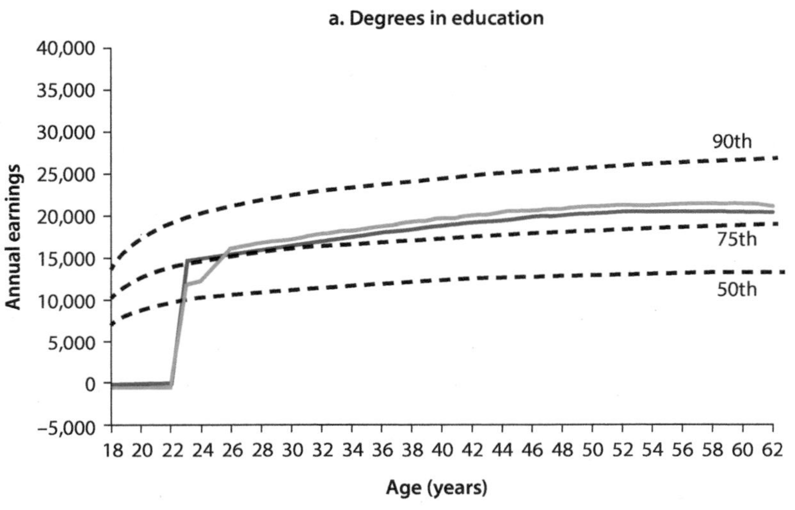

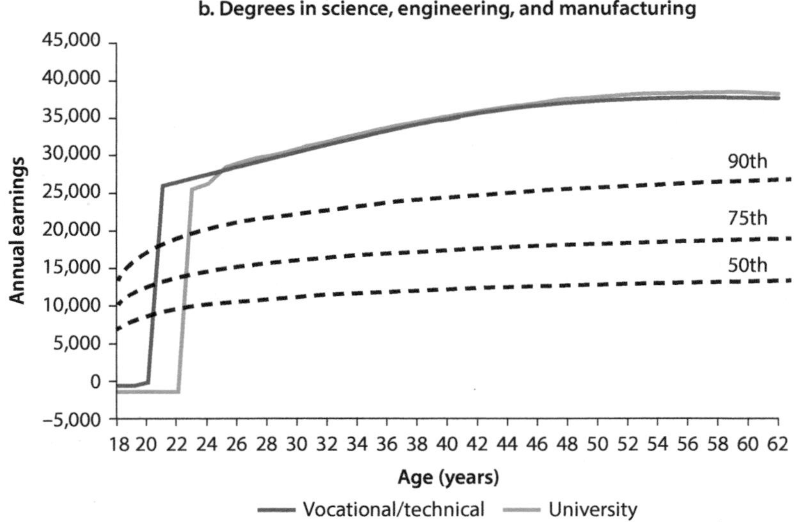

Source: Espinoza and Urzúa 2016.
Note: Dashed lines show the earning trends for high school graduates (HSG) and their income distribution (50th, 75th, and 90th percentiles).

The dashed lines show the estimated streams of earning of high school graduates at three percentiles of the group's income distribution (90, 75, and the median).

Panel a of figure 3.9 illustrates how poorly graduates of education programs from HEIs perform in the labor market compared with high school graduates. Individuals with these higher education degrees earn higher salaries than those in the 75th percentile, but never earn more than those in the 90th. This explains the negative returns reported in table 3.6. Graduates from science, engineering, and manufacturing programs, in contrast, earn substantially more than high school graduates.

Quality Measures and Returns

National accreditation systems gather and report information that can be used to construct variables measuring the quality and relevance of HEIs (and academic programs). In what follows we examine the data available for Peru and Chile, and analyze whether proxies for quality correlates with the returns to higher education. Box 3.4 describes the empirical model.

In the case of Chile, we use the estimated individual-level returns to specific degrees examined earlier and CNA institution-level data on years of accreditations to empirically assess this relationship. Column (1) of table 3.7 presents the estimated effect of years of accreditation on returns (β). We estimate that an extra year of accreditation is associated with an increase of 5.6 percentage points on returns. Columns (2) and (3) present similar estimates by type of institution. The largest estimated coefficient is found among universities. The impact of accreditation on returns among training centers and professional institutes is small in magnitude and even negative. This suggests that, when it comes to degrees granted by these institutions the labor market in Chile might not recognize accreditation as a good proxy for quality. The opposite seems to be true among degrees granted by universities.

Box 3.4 Empirical Association between Net Returns and Accreditation Status

To investigate the empirical association between the net return to a degree in field *i* obtained from institution *k* and the proxy for quality, *Q(j)*, we estimate the following regression model (B3.4.1):

$$r_p(i,j) = \alpha + \beta Q(j) + \pi(i) + \mu(j) + \varepsilon(i,j), \qquad \text{(B3.4.1)}$$

where $r_p(i,j)$ is the net return (obtained using the methodology described in Box 3.2), $\pi(i)$ and $\mu(j)$ are field and HEI type fixed-effects, respectively, and $\varepsilon(i,j)$ is the error term. β is the parameter of interest.

Unfortunately, the information from Peru does not include proper program or HEI quality measures. However, the selectivity index can be interpreted as a proxy variable for quality. We define a program that admits less than one-third of its applicants as "highly selective" (presumably those of the highest quality), those admitting between one- and two-thirds of their pool of applicants as "moderately selective," and those admitting more than two-thirds as "nonselective" (presumably admitting those students of the lowest quality). Table 3.8 presents the returns to higher education degrees by program selectivity levels and type of HEI.

Table 3.7 Effect of Quality on Labor Market Returns, Chile

	(1)	*(2)*	*(3)*
Accreditation	0.056***	–	–
	(0.001)	–	–
Accreditation × CFT	–	0.005***	−0.004***
(baseline)	–	(0.001)	(0.001)
Accreditation × IP	–	−0.023***	−0.005***
	–	(0.001)	(0.001)
Accreditation × university	–	0.121***	0.134***
	–	(0.13)	(0.14)
Field FE	Yes	Yes	Yes
Field × HEI FE	No	No	Yes
Constant	0.202***	0.394***	0.373***
	(0.004)	(0.005)	(0.006)
R^2	0.51	0.54	0.56
N	307,242	307,242	307,242

Source: Espinoza and Urzúa 2016.
Note: CFT = *centros de formación técnica* (technical training centers); HEI = higher education institution; IP = *institutos profesionales* (professional institutes).
* = significant at the .1 level. ** = significant at the .05 level. *** = significant at .01 level.

Table 3.8 Average Returns in Peru, by Program Selectivity and HEI Type
Percent

	Vocational or technical			*University*		
	Highly selective	*Moderately selective*	*Nonselective*	*Highly selective*	*Moderately selective*	*Nonselective*
Arts and architecture	5.0	29.1	16.5	65.9	39.4	42.2
Business and management	49.9	44.6	30.1	23.4	62.8	18.4
Education	–	−25.0	−17.3	−18.0	−21.3	−16.7
Health	32.5	40.1	30.3	11.4	6.7	6.3
Sciences, engineering, and manufacturing	80.5	75.9	69.6	60.4	63.0	41.6
Social sciences and communications	–	56.6	8.9	38.6	67.7	15.3
Others	–	56.5	55.1	–	18.8	35.6
Total	66.1	54.6	43.0	42.5	45.6	23.6

Source: Espinoza and Urzúa 2016.
Note: HEI = higher education institution. – = not available.

As shown in table 3.8, we do not find a clear pattern linking the degree of selectivity and net returns. For universities, the overall results suggest a premium for highly and moderately selective over nonselective institutions, Similar findings are observed for vocational or technical institutions.

Overall, the results from Chile and Peru suggest no robust association between proxies for quality and returns to degrees. In the case of Chile, years of accreditation are positively correlated only for university degrees. For Peru, the results suggest only a vague connection between selectivity and returns for both types of institutions.[15]

Implications for Financing Higher Education in Latin America

Higher education in Latin America faces enormous financial challenges. The bulk of the higher education funds comes from the state budget (Brunner and Hurtado 2011), and increasing government expenditures have sustained the recent expansions of the higher education systems across the region. Figure 3.10 presents the public expenditure per higher education student as a percentage of gross domestic product (GDP) per capita in a set of countries from the region.

The level of public expenditure as percentage of GDP (per capita) is 24.8 percent in Great Britain, 21 percent in Australia, and 8.8 percent in the Republic of Korea (UNESCO). The comparison of these percentages with those reported in figure 3.10 demonstrates the high levels of public expenditure

Figure 3.10 Public Expenditure per Higher Education Student as a Share of GDP per Capita in Selected Latin American and Caribbean Countries

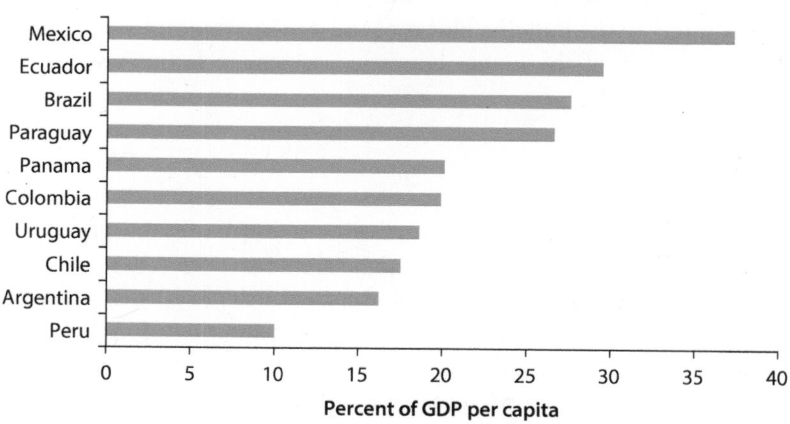

Source: United Nations Educational, Scientifical and Cultural Organization, UNESCO. http://data.uis.unesco.org/index.aspx?queryid=189.

Note: Average total (current, capital, and transfers) general government expenditure per higher education student, expressed as a percentage of GDP per capita, calculated as follows: divide total government expenditure for a higher education by its total enrollment, divide again by GDP per capita, and multiply by 100. For Mexico, Argentina, Chile, and Colombia, the information corresponds to 2013; for Panama, Paraguay, and Ecuador, 2012; Brazil, Mexico, and Peru, 2010; and Uruguay, 2006. For more information, consult the UNESCO Institute of Statistics website: http://www.uis.unesco.org/Education/. Chapter 1 presents a similar figure (including data for comparator countries), but for a different year.

(per student) observed throughout the region. In addition, as discussed in chapter 1, different countries (for example, Colombia, Chile, and Peru) have complemented the public efforts with major private contributions from students and their families.

Despite the increasing fiscal (and private) liabilities and the expansion of higher education, structural reforms aimed at implementing efficient and equitable funding systems have been rare in Latin America and the Caribbean. We expect the needs for structural reforms will accelerate as economic growth throughout the region slows down. In particular, to sustain and extend the current efforts, countries will be forced to find new sources of resources. Furthermore, in light of the evidence on net returns reported above, as higher education systems continue expanding, reforms will also emerge as policy responses to potential private risks associated with the decision to enroll in higher education.

On the other hand, although funding systems for higher education in Latin America and the Caribbean are idiosyncratic, in general, they rely on both institutional (or traditional) and student-based funds, with most of the resources to institutions allocated based on negotiated funding, that is, on the basis of the amounts institutions had received in the past and their lobbying efforts (Albrecht and Ziderman 1992). This, together with the current and future expansion of the system, an increasing private participation in financing higher education, limited public resources, and the political obstacles of changing the existing mechanisms, will put the design of efficient funding systems at the forefront of the public debate. Chapter 4 analyzes this.

Better funding mechanisms containing risk-sharing mechanisms and information policies communicating the financial implications of investing in higher education should be the building blocks of the structural reforms that will sustain a healthy expansion of the higher education system in Latin America and the Caribbean.[16]

Conclusions

Latin American and Caribbean countries have implemented policies aimed at promoting access to higher education, and many more will continue doing so in the years to come. However, despite its political returns, the empirical evidence on economic returns to education suggests caution in continuing this strategy, particularly if effective quality assurance mechanisms are not in place. The intuition is simple. To a large extent, the new generations of (marginal) higher education students had access to a low-quality primary and secondary education. Therefore, for this group, not any higher education system would guarantee a more promising future. Only a system designed to effectively alleviate their lack of skills and provide them with the capacities to success in the labor market would protect them against adverse economic circumstances.

Our empirical results have important implications for public policies. They confirm the importance of further efforts to construct and disseminate information on the performance of higher education graduates in the labor market. The evidence also calls into question the long-term benefits of blind policies seeking to expand coverage of higher education without assuring its quality and relevance.

Annex 3A: Methodology

The estimation labor income over the life-cycle. A main empirical challenge is the estimation of earnings *t* years after graduation, $Y_{i,j}(t)$, t = 1 ... *R*. We use the information on $Y_{i,j}(\overline{t})$, that is average earnings $\overline{t}$ years after graduation to extrapolate and estimate series of labor earnings until retirement (age 65 years). To do this, we consider the following steps:

1. From household surveys we estimate the following Mincer equation (3A.1):

$$ln\ Y_i = \alpha + \beta_1 \times Age_i + \beta_2 \times Age_i^2 + \varepsilon_i \qquad (3A.1)$$

   from the sample of individuals ages 24–65 years, with a postsecondary degree but who are not attending HEIs.
2. Because our administrative records contain earnings information only for $t = \overline{t}$, we define $Y_{i,j}(\overline{t})$ as the initial earnings and use the estimates from equation (B3.1.1) to predict $Y_{i,j}(t), \forall\ t \neq \overline{t}$ as follows (3A.2):

$$\widehat{Y_{i,j}(t)} = \widehat{Y}_{i,j}(t-1) \times exp\left(\widehat{\beta_1} + 2\widehat{\beta_2} \times (t-1)\right), \qquad (3A.2)$$

3. This procedure is replicated for workers with different types of degrees. Specifically, we estimate separate equations using the samples of workers with university degrees, four-year degrees, and two-year degrees. This allows us to estimate different earning patterns along the working life.
4. The earnings of workers who do not attend higher education, $Y_p(t)$, is estimated using a flexible functional form and data from the household surveys in Chile and Peru.
5. All earnings estimates are weighted by the probability of being employed in certain period, $e_{i,j}(t)$. Because of data availability, we assume $e_{i,j}(t) = e(t)$ for all workers graduating from the same type of HEI. When employment rates are not reported in the data (like in Peru), we nonparametrically estimate it from the household survey. If the data reports employment rates at a given point in time[17] (at $t = \overline{t}$), we estimate $e_{i,j}(t) \forall t \neq \overline{t}$ using a similar procedure as with the earnings. From the household surveys we first estimate the probability of being employed at age *t* as follows (3A.3):

$$P_i = \alpha + \gamma_1 \times Age_i + \gamma_2 \times Age_i^2 + \varepsilon_i, \qquad (3A.3)$$

We use $e_{i,j}(\bar{t})$ to estimate $e_{i,j}(t), \forall t \neq \bar{t}$ as follows (3A.4):

$$\widehat{e_{i,j}}(t) = \widehat{\alpha} + \widehat{\gamma_1} \times (Age_{HS} + d_{ij} + t) + \widehat{\gamma_2} \times (Age_{HS} + d_{ij} + t)^2, \qquad (3A.4)$$

where Age_{HS} is the age at which the student graduated from high school (assumed to be 18 if unknown), and d_{ij} is the duration of program i at institution j.

Missing data. Datasets do not often report all income and tuition information, which are key variables to estimate the returns to education. Instead of restricting the sample size to those programs with complete information, we predict the missing values of tuition (C) and graduates income (Y). We first estimate two linear models as follows (3A.5, 3A.6):

$$Y_{i,j}(\bar{t}) = \delta_0 + X_{i,j}\delta_1 + \varepsilon_{i,j}, \qquad (3A.5)$$

$$C_{i,j} = \theta_0 + X_{i,j}\theta_1 + \varepsilon_{i,j}, \qquad (3A.6)$$

where $\varepsilon_{i,j}$ is an idiosyncratic error term and the vector $X_{i,j}$ contains program and institution characteristics such as program's duration, HEI type, field of study fixed effects, and institution fixed effects. We the use the estimated parameters to predict the missing values of $Y_{i,j}(\bar{t})$ and $C_{i,j}$ as follows (3A.7, 3A.8):

$$\widehat{Y_{i,j}}(\bar{t}) = \widehat{\delta_0} + X_{i,j}\widehat{\delta_1}, \qquad (3A.7)$$

$$\widehat{C_{i,j}} = \widehat{\theta_0} + X_{i,j}\widehat{\theta_1} \qquad (3A.8)$$

Despite the limitations imposed by the underlying assumptions, the resulting estimates from equation (B3.2.1) allows us to compare the financial net returns of pursuing a degree in field *i* in institution *j* versus the alternative of not pursuing that specific degree and entering the labor force as a high school graduate. The estimates take into account both the monetary and opportunity costs of higher education.

Annex 3B: Mincer and Employment Regressions in Chile

Table 3B.1 Mincer Regressions, Chile

	Technical centers	*Professional institutes*	*Universities*
Age	0.062***	0.065***	0.094***
	−0.007	−0.006	−0.004
Age^2	−0.001***	−0.001***	−0.001***
	(0.000)	(0.000)	(0.000)
Constant	11.590***	11.566***	11.371***
	−0.152	−0.124	−0.093
R^2	0.04	0.04	0.06
N	2691	4643	11028

Source: Espinoza and Urzúa 2016.
Note: Estimation results of equation (3A.1) in annex 3A.
* = significant at the .1 level. ** = significant at the .05 level. *** = significant at the .01 level.

Table 3B.2 Employment Regressions, Chile

	Technical centers	*Professional institutes*	*Universities*
Age	0.037***	0.036***	0.049***
	(0.003)	(0.002)	(0.001)
Age^2	−0.000***	−0.000***	−0.001***
	(0.000)	(0.000)	(0.000)
Constant	0.065	0.094**	−0.163***
	(0.061)	(0.048)	(0.030)
R^2	0.06	0.06	0.15
N	3,544	6,141	14,188

Source: Espinoza and Urzúa 2016.
Note: Estimation results of equation (3A.5) in annex 3A. CFTs = *centros de formación técnica* (technical training centers); IPs = *institutos profesionales* (professional institutes).
* = significant at the .1 level. ** = significant at the .05 level. *** = significant at the .01 level.

Annex 3C: Missing Data Estimation

Table 3C.1 Missing Data Regressions, Chile

	Dependent variable		
	Earnings	*Tuition*	*Duration*
Agriculture	−220,057.388***	288,975.387***	1.215***
	(61,387.798)	(75,215.190)	(0.200)
Arts	−277,323.987***	321,282.902***	0.698***
	(53,856.764)	(70,041.717)	(0.179)
Science	−136,876.021*	−142,201.771	0.694***
	(78,434.517)	(100,393.461)	(0.261)
Social sciences	−289,436.501***	11,775.528	0.082
	(45,584.232)	(59,009.102)	(0.155)
Law	101,351.249*	197,037.620***	1.607***
	(53,480.905)	(64,116.622)	(0.176)
Education	−409,802.793***	−270,520.128***	−0.372**
	(45,984.358)	(56,234.308)	(0.147)
Humanities	−574,775.800***	−258,903.917**	−0.521*
	(95,813.777)	(112,521.793)	(0.292)
Health	−24,069.067	390,443.194***	−0.027
	(48,984.589)	(58,697.246)	(0.152)
Engineering and technology	215,296.860***	100,443.905*	0.514***
	(44,523.689)	(55,659.206)	(0.145)
Constant	−220,057.388***	288,975.387***	1.215***
	(61,387.798)	(75,215.190)	(0.200)
Region fixed-effects	Yes	Yes	Yes
HEI fixed-effects	Yes	Yes	Yes
R^2	0.78	0.92	0.85
N	387	540	505

Source: Espinoza and Urzúa 2016.
Note: Estimation results of equations (3A.5) (earnings) and (3A.6) (tuition) in annex 3A. HEI = higher education institution.
* = significant at the .1 level. ** = significant at the .05 level. *** = significant at the .01 level.

Notes

1. For example, between 2009 and 2013, the amount of public resources allocated to student financial aid in Chile increased from US$495 million to US$1.458 million, respectively. And for Colombia, the amounts (loans and subsidies) went from US$44 million to US$382 million between 2003 and 2010, respectively.
2. The literature analyzing the returns to education is vast. Recent papers analyzing this topic include Arcidiacono (2004); Binelli (2008); Bouillon, Legovini, and Lustig (2005); Bound and Turner (2011); Grogger and Eide (1995); Heckman and Li (2004); Kane and Rouse (1995); Kaufmann (2014); Kirkebøen, Leuven, and Mogstad (2016); Lindley and Machin (2011); Manacorda, Sanchez-Parama, and Schady (2010); Rodriguez, Urzúa, and Reyes (2016); and Rodney, Li and Lovenheim (2016).
3. The interpretation of Mincerian coefficients as the return to education is possible only under strong assumptions. More precisely, only after imposing the absence of direct costs of college, no loss of work life with schooling, and a multiplicative separable structure between schooling and experience components in earnings, the conventional Mincer coefficient can be interpreted as the internal rate of return (Card 2001; Heckman, Lochner, and Todd 2008).
4. See Espinoza and Urzúa (2016), Gonzalez-Velosa and others (2014), and Urzúa (2012) for a further discussion of the empirical strategy used in this section. Using rich administrative data from Colombia, Camacho, Messina, and Uribe (2016) document heterogeneous effects of higher education on labor market outcomes by type of program. Kirkebøen, Leuven and Mogstad (2016) analyze the effects of students' choices of type of postsecondary education (field of study) on labor market outcomes. The study documents significant heterogeneity on the returns to different fields in Norway, even after controlling for institutional differences and quality of peer groups. Even though the identification strategies used in these studies differ from the empirical strategy used in this chapter, the results are consistent.
5. Rodriguez, Urzúa, and Reyes (2016) present a semi-structural model of endogenous higher education choices and labor market outcomes for Chile. They document significant endogenous sorting based on observed and unobserved variables across higher education institutions, confirming that the comparison of the average higher education graduates and the average high school graduates would be inappropriate.
6. The SIES is a public entity within the Ministry of Education that manages official higher education statistics.
7. Using the ISCED classification, earnings are reported by institution and field of study. To match this information with the individual-level enrollment data, we aggregate the estimates by type of institution and field of study. Thus, although we are not fully exploiting the variation across the 557 degrees available, we are able to capture heterogeneity given the differences in duration of degrees and tuition costs across fields and HEI types.
8. The PSU is the national college admission test. It consists of four sections (mathematics, language, science, and history), and its scores are standardized (average of 500 points and a standard deviation of 110).
9. The website ponteencarrera.pe is a joint initiative of the Departments of Education and Labor of Peru and a private corporation (IPAE Acción Empresarial). It was first launched in 2015.
10. The work attempting to quantitatively measure quality in higher education combines input factors and outcome measures (for example, reputation, entrance examination

scores and admissions selectivity, financial resources, graduation rates, graduates' employment and earnings, and other attributes that can easily be measured but that say little about student learning), adjusted for in preexisting characteristics (Matsudaira 2016). In this context, the ratio of the number of admitted students to the number of applicants should be interpreted as an imperfect and indirect measure of HEI quality. Collecting and generating meaningful quality indicators in higher education is one of crucial challenges for Peru and the region.

11. This allows us to estimate returns for all students entering the higher education system in 2012. Tables 3B.1 and 3B.2 in Annex 3B present the estimates of the Mincer regression (equation 3A.1 in Annex 3A) and the employment rate equation (equation 3A.3) allowing the estimation of the earnings sequences. Table 3C.1 in Annex 3C presents the estimates of equations (3A.5) and (3A.6) (see Annex 3A), which allow the prediction of tuition and earnings when data values are missing.
12. Espinoza and Urzúa (2016) present similar results but after incorporating differences in employment in the calculation of the Net Present Values. The results are qualitatively similar.
13. In 2012, 174,371 freshman students enrolled in IPs and CFTs, whereas 158,907 enrolled in universities. In 2006, the same difference was 40,000 but in favor of universities.
14. Heterogeneous net returns by field and type of HEI have been also documented for Colombia. Using administrative information from Observatorio Laboral para Educación (http://www.graduadoscolombia.edu.co), Gonzalez-Velosa and others (2015) show significant heterogeneity across fields of study and institutions. Some degrees yield quite high rates of return (for example, law). There is, however, a significant dispersion. For example, technical degrees can yield positive or negative returns depending on the HEI. As a result, a non-negligible fraction of graduates from the higher education system run the risk of obtaining negative net economic returns. Camacho, Messina, and Uribe (2016) also document heterogeneous results by type of program. For a comprehensive analysis of the field choice in college and its implications see Altonji, Arcidiacono, and Maurel (2015) and references therein. For a discussion on funding mechanisms for higher education in the context of heterogeneous returns see Espinoza and Urzúa (2015a,b).
15. MacLeod and others (2016) show that college reputation is correlated with graduates' earnings growth. This suggests the existence of other channels through which the labor market learns about institution's value added and the ability of its graduates.
16. Several studies have documented that families and students do not have enough information about tuition costs and the application process, and that this awareness is positively related with students' grade level and parents' education level and income (Castleman 2013; Horn, Chen, and Chapman 2003; Hoxby and Turner 2015; Tornatzky, Cutler, and Lee 2002). The literature has also shown that the high degree of complexity that families face when applying to the financial aid systems may discourage students from applying to higher education institutions (Avery and Kane 2004; Castleman 2013; Dynarski and Scott-Clayton 2006; Dynarski and Wiederspan 2012). For Latin America, Hastings and others (2016) explore the way students form beliefs about earnings and cost outcomes at different institutions and majors and how these beliefs relate to degree choice and persistence. They find that students appear to systematically overestimate earnings outcomes.
17. The Chilean data report the employment rate one year after graduating from the program.

References

Acemoglu, D., and J. Angrist. 2000. "How Large Are Human-Capital Externalities? Evidence from Compulsory Schooling Laws." *NBER Macroeconomics Annual* 15: 9–59.

Aedo, C., and I. Walker. 2012. *Skills for the 21st Century in Latin America and the Caribbean*. Directions in Development. Washington, DC: World Bank.

Albrecht, D., and A. Ziderman. 1992. "Funding Mechanisms for Higher Education." World Bank Discussion Papers, No 153, World Bank, Washington, DC.

Altonji, J., P. Arcidiacono, and A. Maurel. 2016. "The Analysis of Field Choice in College and Graduate School: Determinants and Wage Effect." In *Handbook of the Economics of Education*, edited by E. A. Hanushek, S. Machin, and L. Woessmann, 305–96. Vol. 5. Oxford, U.K.: Elsevier.

Andrews, R. J., J. Li, and M. F. Lovenheim. 2014. "Heterogeneous Paths Through College: Detailed Patterns and Relationships with Graduation and Earnings." *Economics of Education Review* 42: 93–108.

Archibald, R. B., and D. H. Feldman. 2010. *Why Does College Cost So Much?* Oxford University Press, Oxford, U.K.

Arcidiacono, P. 2004. "Ability Sorting and the Returns to College Major." *Journal of Econometrics* 121 (1–2): 343–75.

Avery, C., and T. J. Kane. 2004. "Student Perceptions of College Opportunities. The Boston COACH Program." In *College Choices: The Economics of Where to Go, When to Go, and How to Pay For It*, edited by C. Hoxby, 355–394. Chicago, IL: University of Chicago Press.

Becker, G. S., and Chiswick, B. R. 1966. "Education and the Distribution of Earnings." *American Economic Review* 56: 358–69.

Binelli, C. 2008. "Returns to Education and Increasing Wage Inequality in Latin America." Working Paper 3008, Rimini Centre for Economic Analysis, Rimini, Italy.

Bouillon, C., A. Legovini, and N. Lustig. 2005. "Can Education Explain Changes in Income Inequality in Mexico?" In *The Microeconomics of Income Distribution Dynamics in East Asia and Latin America*, edited by F. Bourguignon, F. Ferreira, and N. Lustig, Washington, DC: World Bank.

Bound, J., and S. E. Turner. 2011. "Dropouts and Diplomas: The Divergence in Collegiate Outcomes." In *Handbook of the Economics of Education*, edited by E. A. Hanushek, S. Machin, and L. Woessmann, 573–613. Vol. 4. Oxford, U.K.: Elsevier.

Brunner, J. J., & R. Ferrada. 2011. *Educación superior en Iberoamerica: informe 2011*. CINDA, Santiago, Chile.

Camacho, A., J. Messina, and J. Uribe. 2016. "The Expansion of Higher Education in Colombia: Bad Students or Bad Programs?" Manuscript, Inter-American Development Bank, Washington, DC.

Card, D. 2001. "Estimating the Return to Schooling: Progress on Some Persistent Econometric Problems." *Econometrica* 69 (5): 1127–60.

Carneiro, P., J. J. Heckman, and E. J. Vytlacil. 2011. "Estimating Marginal Returns to Education." *American Economic Review* 101 (6): 2754–81.

Castleman, B. L. (2013). "Prompts, personalization, and pay-offs: Strategies to improve the design and delivery of college and financial aid information." Working Paper No. 14,

Center for Education Policy and Workforce Competitiveness, University of Virginia, Charlottesville.

Dynarski, S., and J. E. Scott-Clayton. "The Cost of Complexity in Federal Student Aid: Lessons from Optimal Tax Theory and Behavioral Economics." *National Tax Journal* 59 (2): 319–56.

Dynarski, S., and M. Wiederspan. 2012. "Student Aid Simplification: Looking Back and Looking Ahead." *National Tax Journal* 65 (1): 211–34.

Espinoza, R., and S. Urzúa. 2015a. "The Economic Consequences of Implementing Tuition-Free Tertiary Education in Chile." *Revista de Educación* 370: 10–37.

———. 2015b. "On the Inappropriateness of Levying a Graduate Tax to Finance a Tuition-Free Higher Education." *Economía y Política* 2 (2): 77–106.

———. 2016. "Returns to Higher Education: Funding, Coverage and Quality." Background paper for this report.

Gallego, F. 2011. "Skill Premium in Chile: Studying Skill Upgrading in the South." *World Development* 40 (3): 594–609.

Gonzalez-Veloso, C., G. Rucci, M. Sarzosa, and S. Urzúa. 2015. "Returns to Higher Education in Chile and Colombia." Working Paper 587, Inter-American Development Bank, Washington, DC.

Grogger, J., and E. Eide. 1995. "Changes in College Skills and the Rise in the College Wage Premium." *Journal of Human Resources* 30 (2): 280–310.

Hastings, J., C. A. Neilson, A. Ramirez, and S. D. Zimmerman. 2016. "(Un) Informed College and Major Choice: Evidence from Linked Survey and Administrative Data." *Economics of Education Review* 53: 159–63.

Heckman, J. J. and E. J. Vytlacil. 2007. "Causal Models, Structural Models and Econometric Policy Evaluation." In *Handbook of Econometrics*, edited by J. J. Heckman and E. E. Leamer, Vol. 6. Elsevier, Amsterdam.

Heckman, J., L. Lochner, and P. Todd. 2008. "Earning Functions and Rates of Return," *Journal of Human Capital* 2 (1): 1–31.

Heckman, James J., and Xuesong Li. 2004. "Selection Bias, Comparative Advantage and Heterogeneous Returns to Education: Evidence from China in 2000." *Pacific Economic Review* 9 (3): 155–71.

Horn, Laura, Xianglei Chen, and Chris Chapman. 2003. *Getting Ready to Pay for College: What Students and Their Parents Know About the Cost of College Tuition and What They Are Doing to Find Out*. Washington, D.C.: National Center for Education Statistics, Institute of Education Sciences, U.S. Department of Education.

Hoxby, Caroline M., and Sarah Turner. 2015. "What High-Achieving Low-Income Students Know about College." *American Economic Review* 105 (5): 514–17.

Kane, T. J., and C. E. Rouse. 1995. "Labor-Market Returns to Two- and Four-Year College." *American Economic Review* 85 (3): 600–14.

Kaufmann, K. M. 2014. "Understanding the Income Gradient in College Attendance in Mexico: The Role of Heterogeneity in Expected Returns." *Quantitative Economics* 5 (3): 583–630.

Kirkebøen, L., E. Leuven, and M. Mogstad. 2016. "Field of Study, Earnings, and Self-Selection." *Quarterly Journal of Economics* 131 (3): 1057–1111.

Lindley, J., and S. Machin. 2011. "Rising Wage Inequality and Postgraduate Education." Discussion Paper 5981, IZA, Bonn, Germany.

Lustig, N., L. F. López-Calva, and E. Ortiz-Juarez. 2013. "Deconstructing the Decline in Inequality in Latin America." Tulane Economics Working Paper Series 1314, Tulane University, New Orleans.

MacLeod, W. B., E. Riehl, J. E. Saavedra, and M. Urquiola. Forthcoming. "The Big Sort: College Reputation and Labor Market Outcomes." *American Economic Journal: Applied Economics*.

Manacorda, M., C. Sanchez-Parama, and N. Schady. 2010. "Change in the Returns to Education in Latin America: The Role of Demand and Supply of Skills." *Industrial and Labor Relations* 63 (2): 307–26.

Matsudaira, J. 2016. "Defining and Measuring Institutional Quality in Higher Education." Paper presented at the Quality in Undergraduate Education Conference, National Academies of Sciences, Engineering and Medicine, Washington, DC., December.

Messina, J., and J. Silva. 2017. "Wage Inequality in Latin America: Understanding the Past to Prepare for the Future." World Bank, Washington, DC.

Moretti, E. 2004. "Estimating the Social Return to Higher Education: Evidence From Longitudinal and Repeated Cross-Sectional Data." *Journal of Econometrics* 121 (1–2).

Mincer, Jacob. 1974. "Schooling, Experience, and Earnings." National Bureau of Economic Research, Cambridge, MA.

Neal, D. 2004. "The Measured Black-White Wage Gap among Women Is Too Small." *Journal of Political Economy* 112 (1): 2.

Rodney, A., J. Li, and M. Lovenheim. 2014. "Heterogeneous Paths through College: Detailed Patterns and Relationships with Graduation and Earnings." *Economics of Education Review* 42: 93–108.

Rodriguez, J., S. Urzúa, and L. Reyes. 2016. "Heterogeneous Economic Returns to Postsecondary Degrees: Evidence from Chile." *Journal of Human Resources* 51 (2).

Rojas, E., T. Rau, and S. Urzúa. 2013. "Loans for Higher Education: Does the Dream Come True?" NBER Working Paper 19138, National Bureau of Economic Research, Cambridge, MA.

Tornatzky, Louis, Richard Cutler, and Jongho Lee. 2002. *College Knowledge: What Latino Parents Need to Know and Why They Don't Know It*. Los Angeles, CA: Tomas Rivera Policy Institute.

Urzúa, S. 2012. "La Rentabilidad de la Educación Superior en Chile. Revisión de la base de 30 años de Políticas Públicas." *Estudios Públicos* 125.

Vedder, R. 2004. *Going Broke by Degree: Why College Costs Too Much*. Washington, DC: AEI Publications.

Willis, R. J., and S. Rosen. 1979. "Education and Self-Selection." *Journal of Political Economy* 87 (5): S7–S36.

CHAPTER 4

The Demand Side of the Higher Education Expansion

María Marta Ferreyra

Abstract

Both demand and supply have contributed to the expansion of higher education access in the region. In most countries, access rates grew mainly because of rising high school graduation rates, although in some countries, such as Colombia, their main driver were the rising college entry rates on the part of high school graduates. A case study of Colombia shows that low-income, high-ability students accounted for much of the enrollment growth, and thus the expansion contributed to equity and efficiency. In Colombia, students sort based on income and ability across bachelor's and short-cycle programs, across high- and low-end public and private higher education institutions (HEIs), and across new and existing programs. Most of the Colombian expansion was due to factors related to supply and policy resulting in a greater entry rate on the part of high school graduates. Simulations that are based on a structural general equilibrium model show that large-scale attempts to expand higher education access through free tuition or student loans have quite different effects, some of them unintended. Whereas loans create incentives for student effort, free tuition does not. Furthermore, free tuition attracts students who are not likely to graduate, thus raising dropout rates along with enrollment rates, and is fiscally more costly. In the long term, even large higher education expansions may not have large effects on the skill composition or skill premium. Furthermore, the region might miss its current demographic bonus unless its young population becomes more skilled.

Introduction

The recent expansion of access to higher education in Latin America and the Caribbean is both a demand and a supply phenomenon. On the demand side, the increase in the number of high school graduates—and the increased capacity to pay for higher education (through greater parental income, tuition subsidies, credit, or scholarships)—has led more students to enroll in higher education. On the supply side, the increased capacity in the system (through the entry of new HEIs and programs and existing program expansions) gave HEIs the ability to serve the increased demand. It is important to note that if the system had not been able to absorb additional students, access would not have risen.

In this chapter we focus on demand-side aspects of the recent expansion. To gain access to higher education, a student must be admitted by an HEI and have the means to pay for it. We begin by describing the admission and funding mechanisms used in the region. A specific demand-side driver is the rise in high school graduation rates. Thus, in "Role of Recent Access-Expanding Policies," we decompose the observed expansion in access rates into two portions: (a) as a result of the increase in high school graduation rates, and (b) as a result of the increase in higher education entry rates on the part of high school graduates.

In "Increased Access for Whom, and To What?" we investigate whether "new" students attracted by the expansion are similar to those who were already in the system, and what HEIs and programs are chosen by the "new" students. We answer these questions for Colombia, focusing on whether greater access to higher education has also provided students with access to quality and variety.

Although the recent expansion in Colombia has been sizable, it might have been driven merely by the increase in the number of high school graduates. Hence, we decompose the recent expansion into a portion as a result of changes in the size and characteristics of the population of prospective students and another as a result of changes in the supply structure and policies. Furthermore, we examine students' sorting patterns across the various higher education options.

Funding increases for higher education are usually aimed at expanding access. Nonetheless, funding mechanisms create incentives for HEIs and students, the response to which can undermine the mechanisms' original intent. Thus, in "Unintended Effects of Demand-Related Policy Interventions," we explore the unintended effects of two alternative mechanisms: free tuition and credit. Besides affecting enrollment rates, these policies can affect the characteristics of students who enroll in higher education and their effort during college, as well as dropout rates. Furthermore, these policies can affect the share of skilled workers (that is, workers who have completed higher education) in the population and the college premium, thus affecting income inequality as well.

Because the effects of alternative funding regimes are mediated by student responses to the very incentives created by those regimes, funding reforms can have muted effects on the number of higher education graduates. Even if incentives are designed to maximize these effects, they raise an important question: How large of a funding increase is needed to expand the skilled workforce and lower wage inequality substantially? We examine this issue, followed by a conclusion.

Variety of Admission and Funding Mechanisms in the Region

There is a wide variation in admission mechanisms in the region, both within and across countries. Table 4A.1 in annex 4A summarizes admission mechanisms by country and HEI type (public or private). In general, private HEIs establish their own admission criteria, sometimes similar to that of public HEIs. As for public

HEIs, most countries rely on a test-based system. Some countries rely on a standardized test used by all public HEIs (as in Chile and Ecuador) or by many of them (as in Brazil, Colombia, and Mexico). Even when such a standardized test exists, public HEIs in some countries supplement the standardized test with other elements, or give their own exam.

The only countries with unrestricted, open admission to public HEIs are Argentina, Bolivia, Uruguay, and República Bolivariana de Venezuela. Although some HEIs in these countries apply specific criteria for certain programs, such as medicine or music in Uruguay, or require the approval of pre-university courses, as in Universidad de Buenos Aires, Argentina, admission is unrestricted for the vast majority of programs and HEIs.

Student funding mechanisms also vary in the region, both within and across countries. Table 4B.1 in annex 4B summarizes funding mechanisms by country and HEI type. As the table shows, every country subsidizes higher education in some way. Subsidy mechanisms include free or subsidized tuition at public HEIs, subsidized loans, merit- or need-based scholarships, and subsidies for nontuition expenses such as housing, food, or transportation. Box 4.1 discusses the broad issue of financing mechanisms for the ongoing and future higher education expansion.

Broadly speaking, the region currently displays two models of public funding for higher education. The first model consists of providing free (or almost free) tuition at public HEIs, but no funding for students in private HEIs.

Box 4.1 Funding Mechanisms Supporting the Ongoing and Future Expansions

Properly designed higher education funding mechanisms are building blocks of more efficient and equitable higher education systems.

Although funding systems for higher education in the region are idiosyncratic (Brunner and Hurtado 2011; de Fanelli 2008), the vast majority of these systems combines private and public sources of funding. Public funds are channeled either to the HEIs or to the students. The allocation of funding to public HEIs is often based on historical precedent as well as the HEIs' lobbying efforts (Albrecht and Ziderman 1992). This allocation mechanism (and the political barriers to modify it), the limited public resources for higher education, and the increasing role of private funding in higher education finance are likely to put the design of efficient funding systems at the forefront of the public debate, given the funding needed to support the ongoing higher education expansion.

Ideally, higher education funding systems would not only support a menu of relevant and high-quality programs but also promote competition among HEIs and align the incentives of families, students, and other stakeholders. In particular, given the evidence on heterogeneous returns reported in chapter 3, there might be an important role for risk-sharing mechanisms, and for the dissemination of information on the financial implications of investing in higher education.[a]

box continues next page

Box 4.1 Funding Mechanisms Supporting the Ongoing and Future Expansion *(continued)*

Nonetheless, the exact structure of higher education funding systems depends on country-specific needs and objectives. In determining these and adopting the reforms necessary to support the ongoing higher education expansion, policy makers will confront critical questions such as these:

- Should public HEIs charge tuition?
- Who should pay for higher education?
- What are the private and social returns to higher education?
- What is the opportunity cost of the resources allocated to higher education?
- How should public funding be distributed among students and institutions?
- What should be the relative importance of private sources of funding versus public ones?
- Is the menu of higher education programs consistent with the needs of the productive system?
- Is the system equitable and financially sustainable?

In the resulting higher education funding system, a key piece will be the set of funding mechanisms used to support the increasing demand for higher education. In general, this set could include one or several of the following options. (Note that this list includes funding mechanisms, as opposed to expenditure programs. For instance, general taxes can be used to pay for financial aid programs, such as scholarships, or to pay for direct appropriations to the HEIs.)

Regular student loans. These resemble conventional commercial loans, and are usually provided by commercial banks. They do not include flexible payback schemes. They can incorporate government subsidies that lead, for instance, to lower interest rates.

Student loans with income-contingent payback schemes. These provide students with funding for tuition or other expenses. Their defining characteristic is that repayment depends on the borrowers' capacity to pay. In general, state guarantees are needed in these schemes. Private entities (for example, commercial banks) as well as governments might provide these loans.

Private funding. This includes options such as using family assets or personal savings, and taking on consumption loans from commercial banks.

Graduate income taxes. These are taxes on individuals who graduate from higher education. In principle, this tax would allow education to be free of payment at the point of delivery. The amount paid by an individual does not depend on the cost of her education. Thus, a graduate tax is different from a loan.

Other taxes. Resources from income or corporate taxes would fund higher education.

Each funding mechanism involves trade-offs. For instance, Espinoza and Urzúa (2015) discuss the trade-offs between graduate taxes versus student loans. Similarly, each expenditure program involves trade-offs. The final choice of funding sources and mechanisms—and of expenditures programs—will affect the efficiency, equity, and sustainability of the overall higher education system.

a. The literature has documented students lack information on tuition costs and the application process (Castleman 2013; Horn, Chen, and Chapman 2003; Hoxby and Turner 2015; Tornatzky, Cutler, and Lee 2002). The literature has also evidenced the high degree of complexity faced by families when applying to financial aid systems and how this may discourage students from applying to higher education institutions (Avery and Kane 2004; Castleman 2013; Dynarski and Scott-Clayton 2006; Dynarski and Wiederspan 2012). For Latin America, Hastings and others (2016) explore the way students form beliefs about earnings and cost outcomes at different institutions and majors and how these beliefs relate to degree choice and persistence. They find that students appear to systematically overestimate earnings outcomes for past graduates.

Public HEIs capture the majority of higher education students in these countries (Argentina, Bolivia, Ecuador, Mexico, Panama, and Uruguay).[1] The second model consists of charging tuition at public HEIs yet providing funding for students at private HEIs through scholarships and loans. In these countries, private HEIs capture the majority of higher education students. Brazil is a hybrid case, where public HEIs are free but highly selective and capture only 28 percent of the market, and where public funding is available for students attending private HEIs through grants and loans.

Countries where public HEIs charge tuition provide tuition subsidies at public HEIs or subsidies for nontuition expenses. In Colombia, for instance, public HEIs not only charge a relatively low tuition (equal, on average, to less than one-fifth of the average tuition in private HEIs) but also provide tuition discounts based on financial need and performance after the student's first year. As a result of these various subsidies, affordability of public HEIs is generally not viewed as an issue in the region.

Credit for higher education is available in a number of countries, such as Brazil, Chile, Colombia, Costa Rica, Ecuador, and Peru. In Chile, loans have been given by commercial banks since 2006 and have had a state guarantee. In the remaining countries that provide credit, loans are given directly by some public institution (such as Instituto Colombiano de Crédito Educativo y Estudios Técnicos en el Exterior [ICETEX] in Colombia or Banco del Pacifico in Ecuador). These loans require students to have a private guarantor, a factor which might deter many students from pursuing the loan.

Role of Recent Access-Expanding Policies

Although the Latin American and Caribbean average access rate rose from 18 percent to 28 percent between 2000 and 2013, there is considerable variation in the rate of increase across countries.[2] The access rate grew by about 20 percentage points in Bolivia, Chile, Colombia, and Peru, yet by less than 5 percentage points in El Salvador and Argentina, and even fell slightly in Guatemala.

As discussed in chapter 1, higher education access could in principle rise because of a greater number of high school graduates or because of a greater propensity of high school graduates to enroll in higher education (that is, a greater entry rate).[3] By definition, policies aimed at expanding access to higher education raise the entry rate. Hence, the relative importance of the entry rate in the recent expansion illustrates the role of access-expanding policies.

A decomposition of the observed access rate growth shows that, on average, 78 percent of the growth in the region was due to greater high school graduation.[4] In other words, the rise in the entry rate had only a minor role in the recent expansion.

Nonetheless, figure 4.1 shows that the entry rate had a more prominent role in some countries than in others. The increase in the entry rate accounts for more than half of the access rate growth in Colombia and Ecuador, and has had a large role in Peru and Chile as well. In contrast, the decline in entry rate would have

Figure 4.1 Decomposition of Changes in the Higher Education Access Rate, Latin American and Caribbean Countries, 2000–13

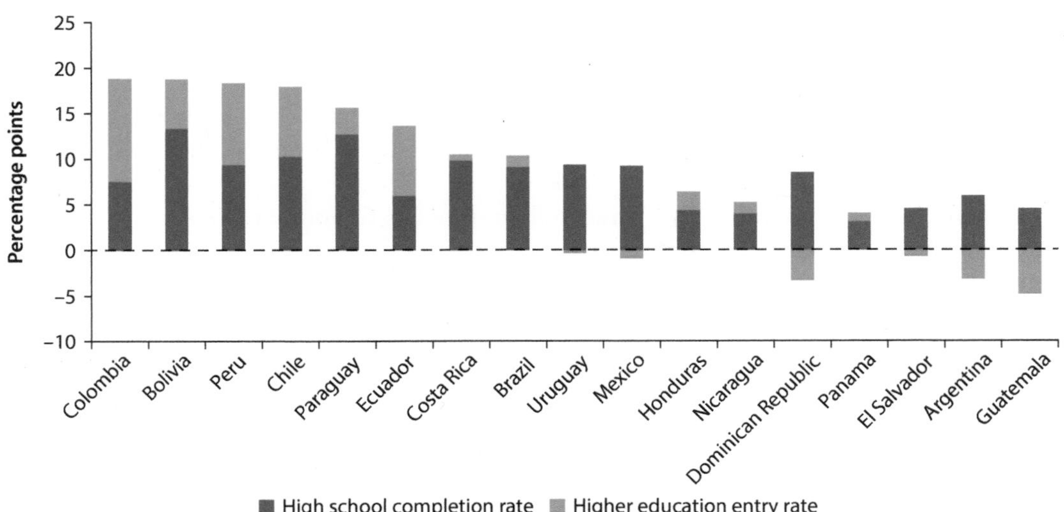

Source: World Bank calculations based on SEDLAC.
Note: The vertical bars show the change in access rate, in percentage points. Change is computed as the difference between circa 2013 and circa 2000. In each bar, the orange portion corresponds to the change explained by higher education entry rate and the blue portion corresponds to the change explained by the secondary school completion rate.

led to a lower access rate in countries like Argentina and Guatemala if the high school graduation rate had not risen.

Overall, countries with the largest expansion are those where the entry rate has played the greatest role. Not surprisingly, these countries implemented deliberate policies to expand higher education access. For instance, Chile implemented state guaranteed loans in 2006; Ecuador expanded public HEIs after 2009; and Colombia implemented multiple policies described in detail later in this chapter. Interestingly, the market share of private HEIs is relatively large in the countries with the greatest expansion. Furthermore, by adopting policies to facilitate access to privates HEIs, these countries relied on the private sector to help boost higher education access.[5]

Increased Access for Whom, and to What?

As described in chapter 1, increased access has attracted "new" students into the system. An important question is what kind of options students are gaining access to, and whether they are gaining access to quality and variety. Thus, in this section we draw heavily on Carranza and Ferreyra (2016), who examine these issues for the recent higher education expansion in Colombia in a paper written for this report.

Colombia constitutes an interesting case study for several reasons. Relative to other countries, the Colombian higher education market is quite evenly split between public and private institutions. Both sectors include selective and nonselective institutions (precise definitions are given below). It is important to note that admission to many HEIs is largely determined by the score in a standardized, mandatory test taken by high school graduates: SABER 11. Thus, whether a student gains access to a particular HEI or program largely depends on her ability, broadly understood as her academic readiness for higher education as measured by the high school exit exam. Moreover, public HEIs in Colombia are heavily subsidized.

Colombia has implemented a multi-pronged approach at expanding higher education access. It modified funding for public HEIs to link it more closely with performance on goals such as enrollment and regional impact. It expanded the menu of programs offered by Servicio Nacional de Aprendizaje (SENA, National Learning Service), a public institution for vocational and technical training. Although SENA is not an HEI, it started to offer short-cycle higher education programs throughout the whole country. In addition, Colombia created *centros regionales para educacion superior* (CERES), which means "regional centers for higher education." These are partnerships between HEIs, local authorities, and firms aimed at expanding higher education in regions with few or no higher education options. Colombia expanded its student loan system by increasing funding for ICETEX, the public institution providing student loans. Moreover, loan terms became more favorable through lower interest rates (which have been equal to zero since 2011 for low-income students), and easier guarantor requirements.

Recent Expansion in Colombia

As mentioned before, higher education access expanded rapidly in Colombia between 2000 and 2013. Since much of our analysis does not include SENA because of data limitations, here we examine two sets of enrollment trends: one including only HEIs, and another including HEIs as well as SENA's higher education programs.

Figure 4.2 shows that enrollment in HEIs almost doubled over that time period, and total higher education enrollment more than doubled when including SENA. Until approximately 2005, SENA had very little enrollment and public HEIs grew faster than private HEIs. Since then, SENA has been growing quickly while enrollment in public HEIs has not grown much. Growth in private HEIs, in turn, has accelerated since 2010.

Enrollment grew in both short-cycle (*tecnicos y tecnologicos*) and bachelor's (*universitarios*) programs, as shown in figure 4.3. Nonetheless, the latter grew more in absolute terms. The current market share of bachelor's programs is 83 percent of total enrollment in HEIs, and 68 percent of total enrollment (including SENA). In the analysis that follows we do not include SENA because we rely on student-level data, which are not available for SENA programs. Thus, our analysis provides a lower bound of the expansion of the higher education system in general and of short-cycle programs in particular.

We examine *access to variety* by looking at three dimensions. The first is program type (short-cycle and bachelor's programs). The second corresponds to new and existing programs among bachelor's programs. The third pertains to the geographic

Figure 4.2 Total Enrollment in Public and Private HEIs, Colombia, 2000–13

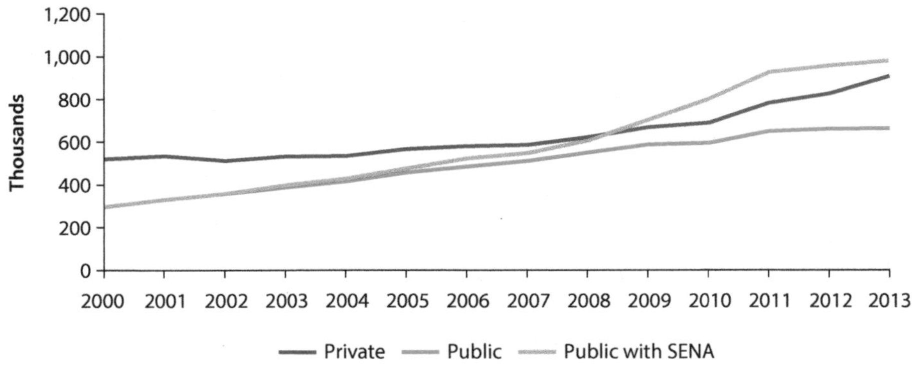

Source: Carranza and Ferreyra 2017.
Note: Private is enrollment in private HEIs. *Public* is enrollment in public HEIs (hence excluding SENA). *Public with SENA* is enrollment in public HEIs and in SENA's higher education programs. HEI = higher education institution. SENA = Servicio Nacional de Aprendizaje (National Learning Service).

Figure 4.3 Total Enrollment in Short-Cycle and Bachelor's Programs, by Program Type, Colombia, 2000–13

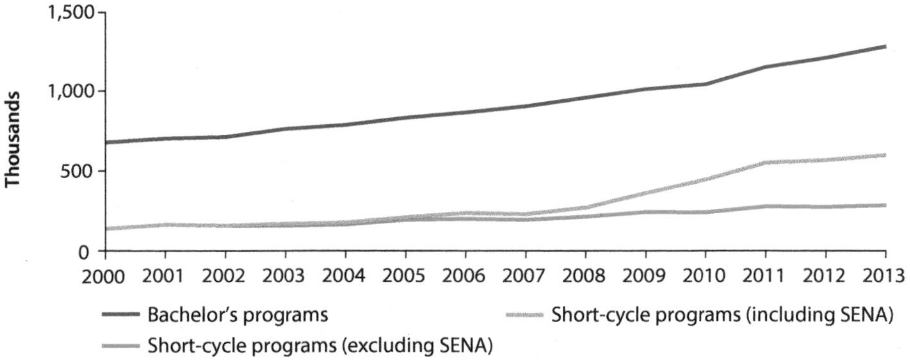

Source: Carranza and Ferreyra 2017.
Note: HEI = higher education institution; SENA = Servicio Nacional de Aprendizaje (National Learning Service).

location of programs and, hence, students. We consider a program "new" when it has zero enrollment of first-year students every semester between 2000 and 2005 but has positive enrollment of first-year students after 2005. A program might be considered new for the institution but not necessarily for the system. For instance, when an HEI opens its first business administration program, the program is new for the institution but not for the system. In contrast, when a HEI opens the first human–computer interaction program in the country, the program is new both for the HEI and the system. Most new programs belong to the first type.

Two differences stand out between new and existing programs.[6] First, 5 percent of existing programs are taught online relative to 10 percent of new programs. Second, the distribution of programs across fields is different between new and existing programs. While 30 percent of new programs cover economics and business, only 21 percent of existing programs do. Similarly, new programs are more likely than existing to cover social sciences (20 percent versus 17 percent) and arts (7 percent versus 4 percent). In contrast, new programs are less likely to cover these fields than existing programs: engineering (22 percent versus 28 percent), education (11 percent versus 16 percent), and health (4 percent versus 9 percent).

As in the rest of Latin America and the Caribbean, students tend to attend higher education close to home. For instance, 73 percent of students from the 2009 cohort in Colombia attend an HEI located in their same department (or state) of residence at the time of finishing high school. Because students tend to live at home while enrolled in higher education, the expansion of offerings in noncentral locations can help improve access. Thus, the share of students attending HEIs outside metropolitan areas grew from 17 percent in 2000 to 23 percent in 2013, mostly because of the growth of public HEIs outside metropolitan areas.

To examine access to quality, we classify HEIs into "low end" and "high end."[7] We consider four HEI types: high-end public, low-end public, high-end private, and low-end private. As figure 4.4 shows for bachelor's programs, all four HEI types gained enrollment between 2000 and 2013, although high-end public HEIs and low-end private HEIs gained the most.

Who Are the "New" Students in the System?

Our analysis compares two student cohorts that enter higher education toward the beginning and end, respectively, of the study period. We examine students taking SABER 11 in 2000 (and entering higher education any time in the window 2001–05), and students taking SABER 11 in 2009 (and entering higher education any time in the window 2010–14).[8] We label these groups the "2000 cohort" and "2009 cohort," respectively.[9]

High school graduates and first-year college students from the 2000 cohort are quite different from those in the 2009 cohort, both in number and characteristics.

Figure 4.4 Total Enrollment in Bachelor's Programs, by HEI Type, Colombia, 2000–13

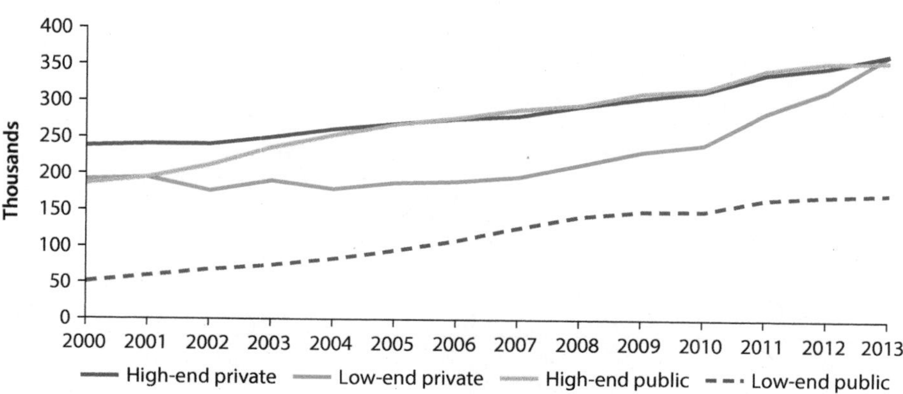

Source: Carranza and Ferreyra 2017.

Table 4.1 shows average demographic and socioeconomic characteristics for high school graduates and for students going to college from the 2000 and 2009 cohorts. As the table shows, the 2009 cohort of high school graduates is 30 percent larger than that of the 2000 cohort. Compared with the 2000 cohort, on average, high school graduates in the 2009 cohort have lower family income, are more likely to be female, and have more educated mothers. A comparison between first-year college students from the 2000 and 2009 cohorts shows that the 2009 cohort is about 85 percent larger. As is the case with high school graduates, on average, college students from the 2009 cohort have lower family income, are more likely to be female, and have more educated mothers than college students from the 2000 cohort. Furthermore, their average ability is lower.

To facilitate our analysis, we focus on two main student characteristics, namely family income and student ability. We define a "student type" as a combination of income and ability, and the "student type space" as the set of all such combinations.

Table 4.2 depicts the joint distribution of income and ability among high school graduates and college students in the 2000 cohort (panels a and b, respectively) and in the 2009 cohort (panels c and d, respectively).[10] Note that among high school graduates in both 2000 and 2009, the higher the income, the higher the probability of being in the top ability quintiles.[11] In other words, higher

Table 4.1 Characteristics of High School Graduates and First-Year College Students from the 2000 and 2009 Cohorts, Colombia

	High school graduates			*First-year college students*		
	2000 cohort	*2009 cohort*	*Difference*	*2000 cohort*	*2009 cohort*	*Difference*
	(1)	*(2)*	*(2)–(1)*	*(3)*	*(4)*	*(4)–(3)*
Average SABER 11 score standardized	0.001	0.001	0.001	0.493	0.404	−0.088***
Family income						
5+ MW	0.083	0.058	−0.025***	0.168	0.096	−0.072***
3–5 MW	0.100	0.078	−0.022***	0.175	0.128	−0.047***
2–3 MW	0.185	0.159	−0.026***	0.235	0.215	−0.020***
1–2 MW	0.401	0.427	0.026***	0.325	0.400	0.075***
<1 MW	0.231	0.277	0.046***	0.097	0.161	0.064***
Age	17.329	17.442	0.113***	16.812	17.065	0.253***
Female	0.522	0.535	0.013***	0.513	0.526	0.013***
Mother's education						
Primary education	0.499	0.358	−0.141***	0.295	0.207	−0.088***
Secondary education	0.296	0.433	0.137***	0.328	0.455	0.127***
Short-cycle program	0.109	0.088	−0.022***	0.187	0.134	−0.053
At least bachelor's program	0.095	0.121	0.026***	0.190	0.204	0.014***
Works in high school	0.087	0.087	−0.000	0.049	0.057	0.008***
Observations	419,113	541,162		118,141	219,731	

Source: Carranza and Ferreyra 2017.
Note: Income is self-reported by the student. Students' Saber 11 score is standardized by semester-year, with zero mean and unit standard deviation. MW = minimum wage.
****p* = .01.

Table 4.2 Distribution of High School Graduates and First-Year College Students, by Income and Ability, Colombia, 2000 and 2009

		Year: 2000											
		a. High school graduates						*b. First-year college students*					
Income bracket		*Ability quintile*						*Ability quintile*					
		1	*2*	*3*	*4*	*5*	*Total*	*1*	*2*	*3*	*4*	*5*	*Total*
5+ MW	Relative (%)	0.54	0.73	1.03	1.63	4.27	8.2	0.78	1.21	2.04	3.6	9.98	17.61
3–5 MW	Relative (%)	1.1	1.4	1.76	2.26	3.34	9.86	1.18	1.88	2.75	4.19	7.63	17.63
2–3 MW	Relative (%)	2.98	3.37	3.7	4.14	4.13	18.32	2.08	3.14	4.12	5.71	8.1	23.14
1–2 MW	Relative (%)	8.77	8.84	8.61	8	5.92	40.14	3.6	4.87	6.23	7.89	9.39	31.97
<1 MW	Relative (%)	6.98	5.84	4.93	3.76	1.98	23.48	1.49	1.74	1.97	2.24	2.19	9.64
Total	Absolute	82,871	82,113	81,497	80,527	79,909	406,917	9,669	13,606	18,130	25,029	39,511	105,945
	Relative (%)	20	20.18	20.03	19.79	19.64	100	9	12.84	17.11	23.62	37.29	100

		Year: 2009											
		c. High school graduates						*d. First-year college students*					
Income bracket		*Ability quintile*						*Ability quintile*					
		1	*2*	*3*	*4*	*5*	*Total*	*1*	*2*	*3*	*4*	*5*	*Total*
5+ MW	Relative (%)	0.25	0.39	0.61	1.12	3.44	5.81	0.32	0.59	0.99	1.91	6.1	9.92
3-5 MW	Relative (%)	0.69	0.94	1.26	1.8	3.02	7.71	0.73	1.26	1.91	3.1	5.77	12.76
2-3 MW	Relative (%)	2.28	2.68	3.1	3.68	4.05	15.79	1.83	2.78	3.83	5.53	7.34	21.31
1-2 MW	Relative (%)	9.24	9.23	9.1	8.58	6.62	42.77	4.62	6.5	8.18	10.05	10.48	39.83
<1 MW	Relative (%)	7.78	6.93	5.97	4.68	2.56	27.92	2.41	3.09	3.57	3.88	3.24	16.18
Total	Absolute	105,932	105,545	104,869	103,955	103,090	523,391	20,235	29,045	37,734	50,001	67,256	204,271
	Relative (%)	20	20.17	20.04	19.86	19.7	100	10	14.22	18.47	24.48	32.92	100

Source: Carranza and Ferreyra 2017.
Note: Ability quintiles are based on standardized (by semester-year) Saber 11 scores. MW = minimum wage.

income students are more academically ready for higher education than their lower income counterparts.

Table 4.2 provides a clear example of the student body changes that have happened throughout the region. Students from the lowest two income brackets represent a greater share of high school graduates in 2009 than in 2000. Similarly, students from the lowest two income brackets, and from the lowest four ability quintiles, represent a greater share of college students in 2009 than in 2000.

Panel a of table 4.3 shows the observed increase in higher education enrollment by student type, and panel b shows the contribution of each student type to the total enrollment growth. As panel a shows, almost all student types increased their enrollment between 2000 and 2009. Nonetheless, two student groups account for most of the enrollment growth. The first group is that of low-income, high-ability students (from the bottom two income brackets and the top two ability quintiles), who account for 34 percent of the enrollment growth. The second group is that of low-income, low-ability students (from the bottom two income brackets and the bottom two ability quintiles), who account for 22 percent of the enrollment growth.

These two student groups have made different choices within the HEI system and have been served by different HEIs, as we will see shortly. Nonetheless, the fact that low-income and *high-ability* students account for a large share of the enrollment growth means that the expansion has enhanced both equity and efficiency. As we argue below, this development has been closely related with the expansion of high-end public HEIs.

To What Are Students Gaining Access?

As the higher education system expands, an important issue is the type of options to which students gain access, and whether these have changed over time. Thus, we now focus on students' choice patterns. These are captured by students' probabilities of choosing different options: namely, by their sorting across those options.

Changes in sorting patterns are related to higher education supply and policy. As an example, consider the case of low-income, low-ability students. This student type may have become more likely to attend short-cycle programs instead of not enrolling in college at all. What can explain this choice probability change? If we assume that students' preferences over the various options remain constant over time, then changes in choice probabilities could be due to changes in supply structure. In our example, HEIs may have created new short-cycle programs, or they may have increased the attractiveness of short-cycle programs (for example, by developing career placement services for graduates from short-cycle degrees). A particular instance of increased attractiveness (although not solely because of changes in supply structure) is that of rising returns. Yet, changes in choice probability could also be due to policy changes, as would be the case in our example if new tuition subsidies were implemented for short-cycle programs. Thus, we broadly interpret sorting changes as the outcome of supply and policy changes.

Table 4.3 Change in Higher Education Enrollment between the 2000 and 2009 Cohorts, Colombia

	a. Enrollment change between 2000 and 2009						*b. Share of total change (%)*					
Income	*Ability quintile*						*Ability quintile*					
bracket	*1*	*2*	*3*	*4*	*5*	*Total*	*1*	*2*	*3*	*4*	*5*	*Total*
5+ MW	−171	−72	−139	101	1,888	1,607	−0.17	−0.07	−0.14	0.10	1.92	1.63
3–5 MW	254	573	979	1,894	3,692	7,392	0.26	0.58	1.00	1.93	3.75	7.52
2–3 MW	1,523	2,363	3,447	5,258	6,417	19,008	1.55	2.40	3.51	5.35	6.53	19.33
1–2 MW	5,619	8,111	10,119	12,166	11,462	47,477	5.71	8.25	10.29	12.37	11.66	48.29
<1 MW	3,341	4,464	5,198	5,553	4,286	22,842	3.40	4.54	5.29	5.65	4.36	23.23
Total	10,566	15,439	19,604	24,972	27,745	98,326	10.75	15.70	19.94	25.40	28.22	100

	c. Enrollment change attributable to demand changes						*d. Percent of enrollment change attributable to demand changes*					
Income	*Ability quintile*						*Ability quintile*					
bracket	*1*	*2*	*3*	*4*	*5*	*Total*	*1*	*2*	*3*	*4*	*5*	*Total*
5+ MW	−358	−444	−554	−664	−1,209	−3,229	209.26	616.34	398.84	−657.76	−64.03	−200.95
3–5 MW	−188	−168	−99	247	1,200	992	−74.01	−29.40	−10.10	13.06	32.51	13.42
2–3 MW	149	386	685	1,332	2,530	5,081	9.79	16.34	19.87	25.33	39.42	26.73
1–2 MW	1,716	2,255	2,993	3,849	4,870	15,682	30.53	27.80	29.58	31.64	42.49	33.03
<1 MW	816	1,158	1,324	1,577	1,631	6,506	24.41	25.93	25.47	28.41	38.05	28.48
Total	2,135	3,187	4,349	6,341	9,022	25,032	20.20	20.64	22.18	25.39	32.52	25.46

Source: Carranza and Ferreyra 2017.

Note: Panel a shows the enrollment change for each student type. Panel b shows the percent of the overall enrollment change accounted for by each student type. Panel c shows the enrollment change for each student type, attributable to demand-related factors. Panel d shows the percent of enrollment change, for each student type, attributable to demand-related factors. MW = minimum wage.

We will return shortly to this interpretation to decompose enrollment growth into demand- and supply- (or policy)-related drivers.

Sorting into College

Figure 4.5 uses color patterns to depict each student type's probability of attending college in 2009 (panel a), and the percentage point change in this probability between 2000 and 2009 (panel b). Overall, the share of high school graduates going on to college has risen from 26 percent to 39 percent, and, as panel b shows, the probability of going to college has risen for all student types.[12]

Unlike the average country in the region, Colombia experienced a large increase in the higher education entry rate. While this by itself would have led to an expansion in higher education enrollment, the number of high school graduates also grew substantially. The decomposition presented later in this chapter will separate the role of these two elements in the overall enrollment expansion, enrollment growth in specific programs and HEI types, and enrollment growth by student type.

Student types differ vastly in their college enrollment probability. As panel a of figure 4.5 shows, income raises the college enrollment probability for a given ability, and ability raises the college enrollment probability for a given income. As expected, students in the upper triangle of the type space are more likely to go to college than those in the lower triangle. The college enrollment probability is highest (at approximately 70 percent) for students with the highest income and ability, and lowest (at approximately 12 percent) for students with the lowest income and ability.

Although the probability of college enrollment rose for all student types, it rose more for some types than for others. Panel b of figure 4.5 shows that the

Figure 4.5 Probability of Enrolling in Higher Education, Colombia, 2000 and 2009

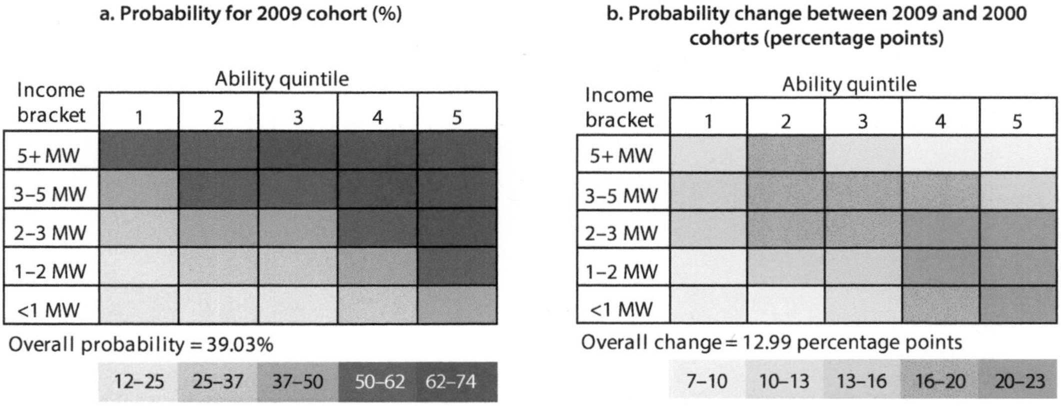

a. Probability for 2009 cohort (%)

b. Probability change between 2009 and 2000 cohorts (percentage points)

Source: Carranza and Ferreyra 2017.

Note: In panel a, probability pertains to first-year students from the 2009 cohort. In panel b, the difference is calculated as the 2009 cohort's probability minus the 2000 cohort's probability. MW = minimum wage.

smallest changes in college enrollment probability are for the students who in 2009 are either most or least likely to enroll in college. In contrast, students with the highest ability and lowest income have experienced the greatest gains in college enrollment probability.

These developments have enhanced both equity and efficiency. Still, there is room for further gains, since not all students with the highest ability are equally likely to enroll in college.

Sorting into Short-Cycle versus Bachelor's Programs

Figure 4.6 explores sorting into short-cycle or bachelor's programs conditional on going to college. Patterns of sorting into college, and into bachelor's and short-cycle programs, are similar, as reflected by the similarity between figure 4.5, panel a, and figure 4.6, panel a. Students with the highest ability and income have the highest probability of enrolling in a bachelor's program (about 95 percent), whereas students with the lowest ability and income have the lowest (about 65 percent).

On average, students have become less likely to attend bachelor's programs conditional on going to college (and hence more likely to attend short-cycle programs), since the conditional probability of enrolling in a bachelor's program has fallen by 2.34 percentage points between 2000 and 2009. Nonetheless, the probability has risen for high-ability students (who were already the most likely to attend bachelor's programs) and fallen for low-ability students. Thus, sorting changes have strengthened the preexisting sorting patterns between short-cycle and bachelor's programs.

Figure 4.6 Probability of Choosing a Bachelor's Program, Conditional on Going to College, Colombia, 2000 and 2009

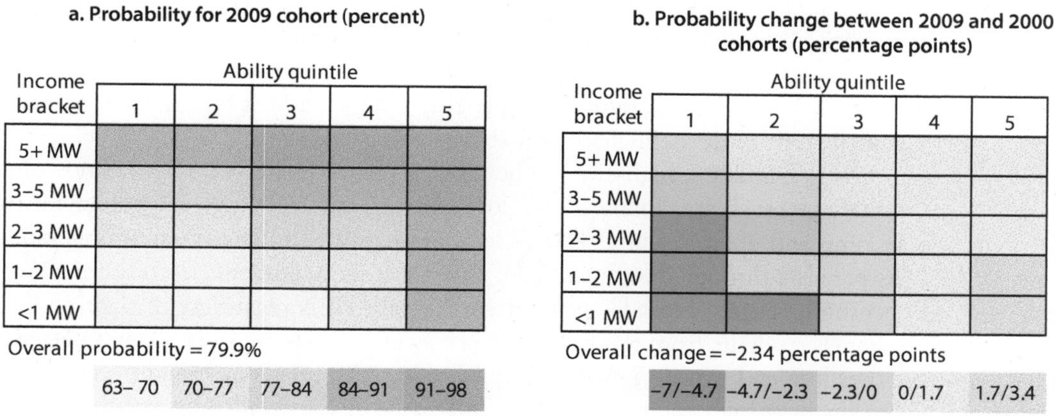

a. Probability for 2009 cohort (percent)

Income bracket
Ability quintile
1 2 3 4 5
5+ MW
3–5 MW
2–3 MW
1–2 MW
<1 MW
Overall probability = 79.9%
63–70 70–77 77–84 84–91 91–98

b. Probability change between 2009 and 2000 cohorts (percentage points)

Income bracket
Ability quintile
1 2 3 4 5
5+ MW
3–5 MW
2–3 MW
1–2 MW
<1 MW
Overall change = −2.34 percentage points
−7/−4.7 −4.7/−2.3 −2.3/0 0/1.7 1.7/3.4

Source: Carranza and Ferreyra 2017.
Note: Panel a shows the probability of choosing a bachelor's program among students who graduated from high school in 2009 and who enrolled within the five-year window after high school graduation. In panel b, the difference is calculated as the 2009 cohort's probability minus the 2000 cohort's probability. MW = minimum wage.

Figure 4.7 Probability of Enrolling in a New Program for the 2009 Cohort, Conditional on Enrolling in a Bachelor's Program in Colombia
Percent

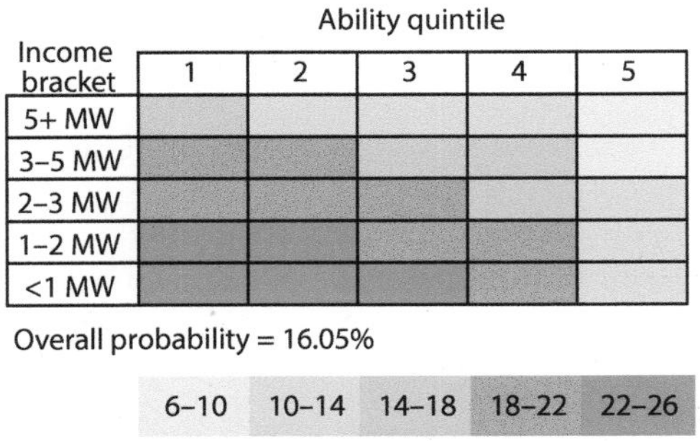

Income bracket	Ability quintile 1	2	3	4	5
5+ MW					
3–5 MW					
2–3 MW					
1–2 MW					
<1 MW					

Overall probability = 16.05%

6–10	10–14	14–18	18–22	22–26

Source: Carranza and Ferreyra 2017.
Note: Probability pertains to first-year students from the 2009 cohort. MW = minimum wage.

Sorting into New versus Existing Programs

Low-income, low-ability students are most likely to enroll in a new program. The probability of enrolling in a new (rather than an existing) program, conditional on choosing a bachelor's program, is shown in figure 4.7. Low-income, low-ability students (who are the least likely to enroll in college or in a bachelor's program conditional on college enrollment) are the most likely to enroll in a new program.

Sorting by HEI Type

Since different HEIs specialize in students of different incomes and abilities, students sort across HEI types. Figure 4.8 depicts sorting patterns by showing each student type's probability of choosing a given HEI type in 2009 (panels a through d), and the percentage point change in these probabilities (panels e through h). For a particular student type, the addition of choice probabilities is equal to 1. In addition, figure 4.8 (panel i) shows the HEI type chosen by each student type with the highest probability.

Overall, in 2009, high-end public and high-end private HEIs have almost the same market share, followed by low-end private and low-end public HEIs. Income and ability each affect student sorting, but so does their combination. As panels a through d and panel i of figure 4.8 show, students from the top two income levels are most likely to attend private HEIs regardless of their ability, whereas students from the bottom three income levels are most likely to attend either low-end private HEIs (if they have low ability) or high-end public HEIs (if they have high ability). Only students with the lowest income and the lowest ability are most likely to attend low-end public HEIs. Although high-end HEIs are the top choice for high-ability students, they are also the top choice for some low-ability students, particularly in the case of high-end private HEIs.

Figure 4.8 Probability of Attending Each HEI Type, Conditional on Choosing a Bachelor's Program in Colombia, 2000 and 2009

a. Low-end private, 2009 cohort (Percent)

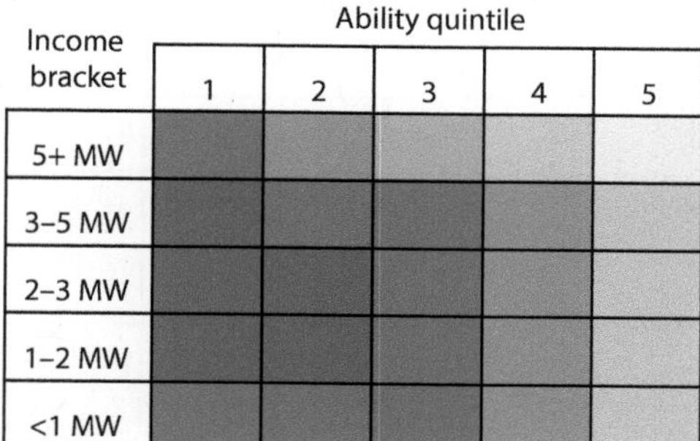

Overall probability = 25%

b. High-end private, 2009 cohort (Percent)

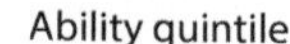

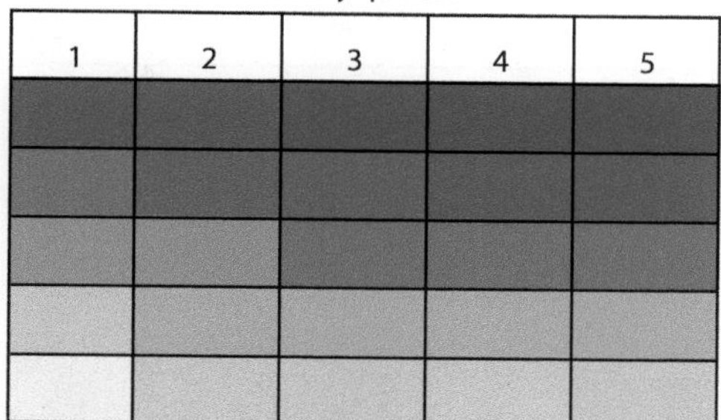

Overall probability = 30.89%

1–9 | 9-16 | 16-24 | 24-31 | 31-39 | 39-47 | 47-54 | 54-62 | 62-69 | 69-77

c. Low-end public, 2009 cohort (Percent)

Ability quintile

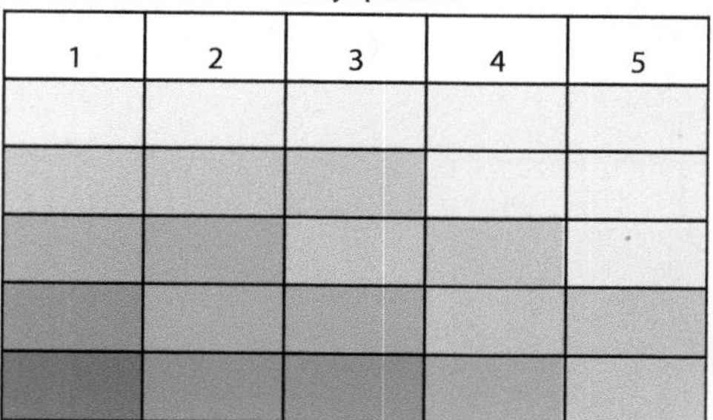

Overall probability = 13.2%

d. High-end public, 2009 cohort (Percent)

Ability quintile

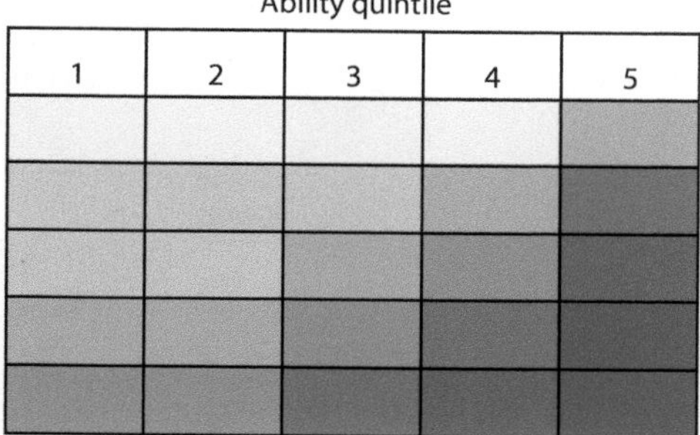

Overall probability = 30.91%

e. Change between 2000 and 2009 low-end private (percentage points)

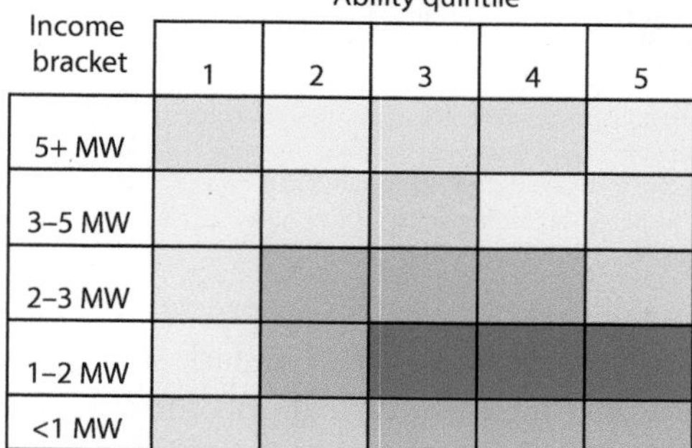

Overall change = 3.31 percentage points

f. Change between 2000 and 2009 high-end private (percentage points)

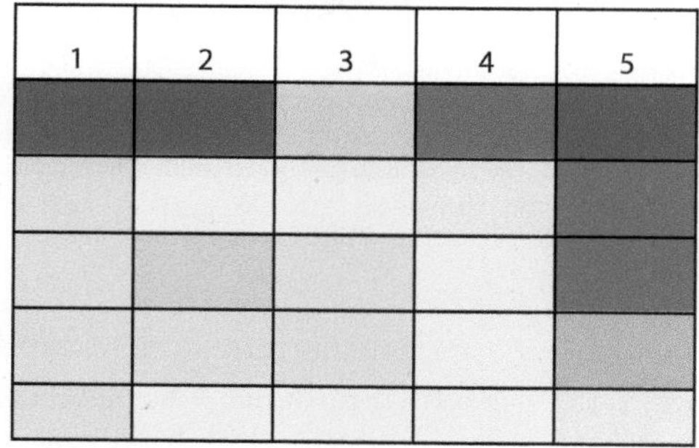

Overall change = –5.39 percentage points

–10 to –8 | -8 to –6 | –6 to –4 | –4 to –2 | –2 to 0 | 0–1 | 1–3 | 3–4 | 4–5 | 5–6

figure continues next page

Figure 4.8 Probability of Attending Each HEI Type, Conditional on Choosing a Bachelor's Program in Colombia, 2000 and 2009 *(continued)*

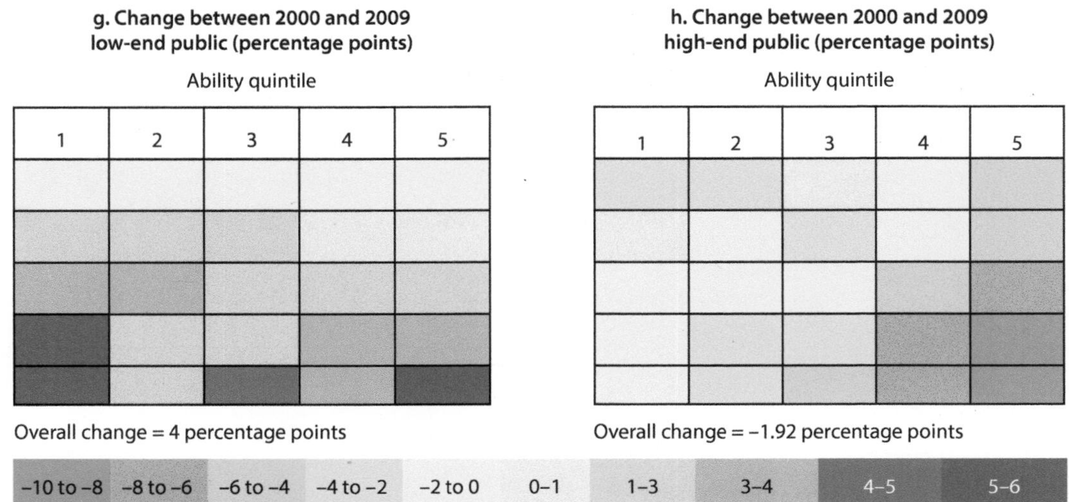

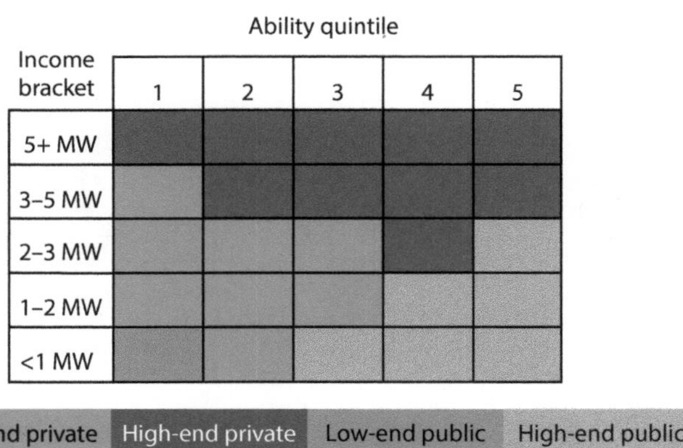

Source: Carranza and Ferreyra 2017.
Note: HEIs are classified into four types: low-end private, high-end private, low-end public, high-end public. In panels a through d, probability pertains to first-year students from the 2009 cohort (that is, high school graduates from 2009). Students are classified into "types"; a student type is a combination of income and ability. For each student type, probabilities add up to 100. In panels e through h, the difference is calculated as the 2009 cohort's probability minus the 2000 cohort's probability. Panel i shows the HEI type most frequently chosen by each student type (that is, the modal choice). HEI = higher education institution; MW = minimum wage.

Splitting the student type space into four regions reveals a stark sorting, as shown in figure 4.8, panel c. We observe that high-ability, high-income students mostly attend high-end private HEIs. High-ability, low-income students mostly attend high-end public HEIs. Low-ability, low-income students mostly attend low-end private (and, to a lesser extent, low-end public) HEIs. Low-ability, high-income students, who represent a very small fraction of the student population, attend high- and low-end private HEIs.

These sorting patterns have important implications for low-ability students, whose share in the higher education student body has risen, though these implications differ by student income. Low-income, low-ability students (who are mostly enrolled in low-end HEIs, particularly private) are the least likely to enroll in college, the most likely to choose a short-cycle rather than a bachelor's program, and the most likely to choose a new program when enrolling in a bachelor's program. Thus, low-end HEIs seem to provide these students with an opportunity to enroll in a bachelor's program should they choose to do so, particularly through new programs. On the opposite end of the income spectrum, the fact that many high-income, low-ability students attend high-end private HEIs suggests that these HEIs serve two distinct market segments: high-ability students through existing programs, and low-ability students through new programs. We will return to this topic in chapter 5.

Overall, students have become less likely to attend high-end HEIs, yet probability change patterns between 2000 and 2009 are nuanced. As panel b shows, high-ability, low-income students have become less likely to attend their typical choice of high-end public HEIs. In contrast, students with the highest income or the highest ability have become even more likely to attend high-end private HEIs.

Decomposing Enrollment Growth

The greater propensity of students to enroll in college would by itself lead to enrollment growth. But would it alone explain the observed enrollment growth? Similarly, the increase in the number of high school graduates would also lead to greater college enrollment (assuming the system is capable of absorbing the additional students). But would it alone explain the observed enrollment growth?

To answer these questions, we decompose the enrollment growth into two portions. The first portion is due to the increase in the number of high school graduates and the change in their characteristics (namely, because of changes in observed demand shifters). The second portion is due to the increase in students' propensity to enroll in college or to choose specific higher education options. Given our rich data on student characteristics, we can plausibly assume that we observe all demand shifters. Hence, we can interpret our decomposition as disentangling the role of demand-side factors, associated with changes in the number and characteristics of high school graduates, and supply-and-policy-factors, associated with changes in the conditional enrollment rate and sorting patterns. Broadly, the latter also includes changes in programs' attractiveness, including changes in returns.

We apply our decomposition to enrollment changes in the system as a whole, in short-cycle and bachelor's programs, in new and existing programs, and in the various HEI types. Beginning with enrollment changes in the whole system, panel c in table 4.3 shows the enrollment change attributable to demand, and panel d shows the fraction of the total enrollment change attributable to demand based on our decomposition.

Overall, demand has a relatively small role explaining enrollment growth, since only 25 percent of the total enrollment growth between 2000 and 2009 is attributable to demand. In other words, if the higher education system had merely expanded to absorb the additional students while keeping the entry enrollment rate constant, we would have seen only 25 percent of the actual enrollment growth. The role of demand is strongest among low-income students and high-ability students, who account for the largest share of the enrollment expansion. Furthermore, we will see shortly that the role of demand varies among programs and HEI types as well.

Thus, supply and policy changes have played a critical role in the recent higher education expansion. While the supply structure and offerings have indeed changed in Colombia (as described in chapter 5), multiple policies to expand access have been implemented as well.

Although both short-cycle and bachelor's programs gained enrollment, they did so by attracting different student types. For each student type, figure 4.9 depicts the enrollment change in short-cycle programs, existing bachelor's programs, and new bachelor's programs. Of these program types, existing bachelor's programs grew the most. While students from the second-lowest income bracket account for most of the enrollment growth, short-cycle programs have grown by drawing on lower ability students than bachelor's programs. In turn, existing bachelor's programs have grown by drawing on higher ability students than new bachelor's programs.

Demand explains less than half of the growth of each program type, as it accounts for 42 percent, 22 percent, and 18 percent of the enrollment growth in existing bachelor's, new bachelor's, and short-cycle programs, respectively. Thus, supply and policy have had their greatest role in the expansion of new bachelor's and short-cycle programs, through which the system has acquired greater variety and has raised the enrollment rate of low-income, low-ability students. As a consequence, greater variety has contributed to greater equity.

Figure 4.10 shows the enrollment expansion in short-cycle programs (already shown in figure 4.9), and in bachelor's programs at each HEI type. More than half of the enrollment gains for each of these five options comes from the bottom three income brackets. Although low-end public and private HEIs have similar

Figure 4.9 Enrollment Expansion in Short-Cycle Programs, Existing Bachelor's Programs, and New Bachelor's Programs in Colombia

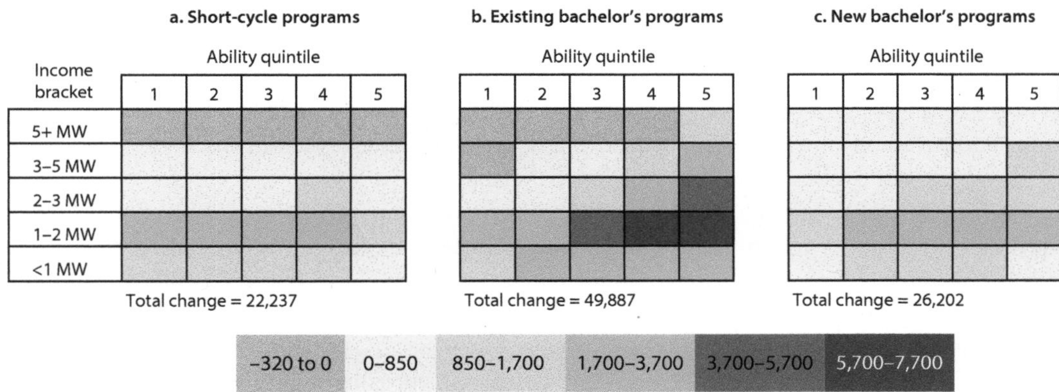

Source: Carranza and Ferreyra 2017.
Note: Expansion expressed in number of students. Change computed between the 2000 and 2009 cohorts. MW = minimum wage.

Figure 4.10 Expansion in Enrollment, by HEI Type, in Colombia

a. Short-cycle programs

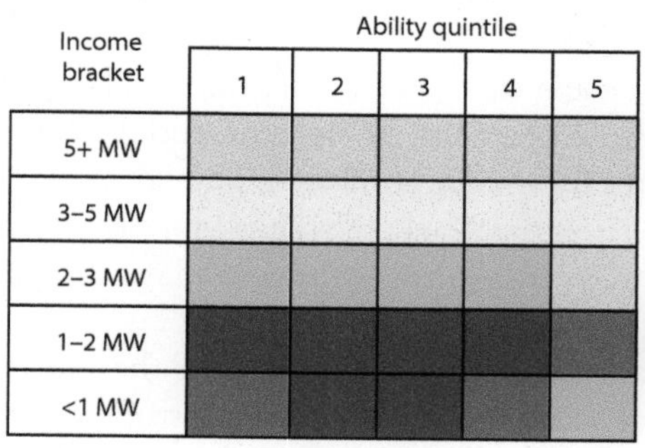

Total change = 22,237

b. Bachelor's low-end private

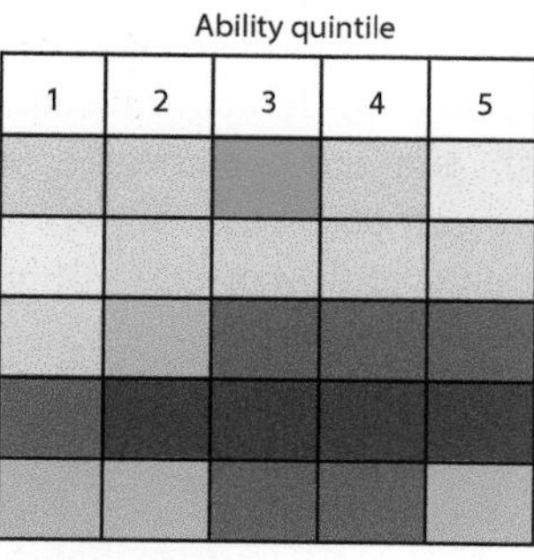

Total change = 21,906

c. Bachelor's high-end private

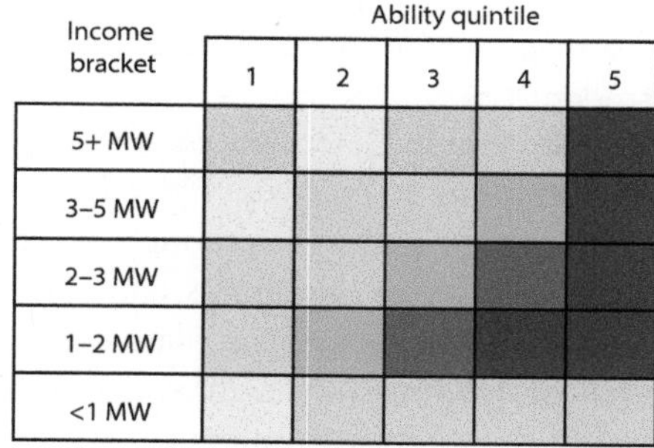

Total change = 18,808

d. Bachelor's low-end public

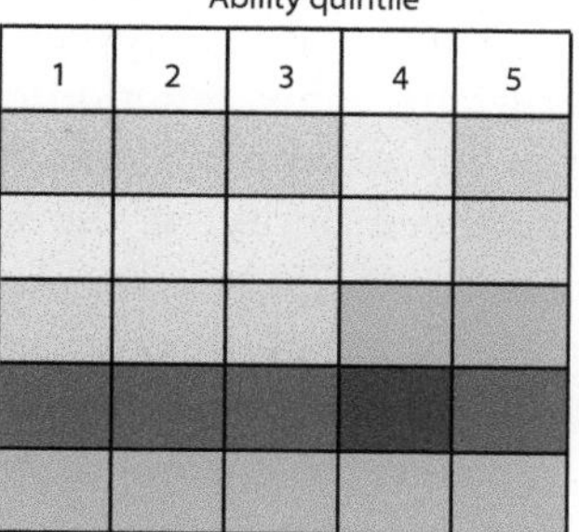

Total change = 13,524

e. Bachelor's high-end public

Income bracket

Ability quintile

1 2 3 4 5

5+ MW

3–5 MW

2–3 MW

1–2 MW

<1 MW

Total change = 21,851

−163 to −80 | −80 to 0 | 0–170 | 170–500 | 500–1,000 | 1,000–1,600 | 1,600–4,700

Source: Carranza and Ferreyra 2017.

Note: Expansion expressed in number of students. Change computed between the 2000 and 2009 cohorts. MW = minimum wage

growth patterns, low-end private HEIs grow by drawing in slightly higher income and higher ability students than low-end public HEIs. High-end public and private HEIs grow by drawing in students of similar ability, yet high-end private HEIs attract students of higher income.

Once again, demand accounts for less than half of the observed expansion. Overall, demand explains 24 percent, 26 percent, 31 percent, and 30 percent of the expansion of bachelor's programs in low-end private, high-end private, low-end public, and high-end public HEIs, respectively. Although supply and policy explain most of the expansion in these institutions, demand plays the greatest role in public HEIs.

To summarize, two groups of students account for most of the enrollment expansion in Colombia: low income students, and high ability students. Hence, the expansion has enhanced both equity and efficiency. Conditional on enrolling in college, students have become more likely to enroll in short-cycle programs. In turn, students attending bachelor's programs have become less likely to attend existing programs in favor of new ones, and less likely to choose high-end HEIs. Overall, student sorting reveals a market segmentation whereby different HEIs and programs compete for different student types.

From our decomposition analyses we learn that in Colombia, supply and policy explain the majority of the observed enrollment changes. Overall, demand explains about 25 percent of the enrollment expansion, although it explains about 40 percent of the expansion of existing bachelor's programs, and 30 percent of the expansion of public HEIs. Among student types, demand plays the greatest role explaining the enrollment growth of low-income, high-ability students: namely, those who account for the greatest share of the enrollment growth.

Unintended Effects of Demand-Related Policy Interventions

Besides affecting enrollment rates, funding mechanisms can have other effects as well. For example, broadening access to higher education through greater funding can lead to the entry of students who lack the academic preparation to succeed. Thus, along with an increase in enrollment rates, a funding expansion can also lead to an increase in the number of dropouts. In addition, a funding expansion can be fiscally costly if financed with public resources.

In this section we explore the general equilibrium effects of funding mechanisms. These effects include the impact on dropout rates, student work while in college, the skill composition of the population and college premium, income inequality, and fiscal costs and revenues. Although often unintended, these effects can undermine the effectiveness of the funding mechanism and must then be taken into account by the policy maker.

An important theme of this section is that expanding access to higher education does not necessarily mean expanding the size of the skilled population (namely, those with complete higher education), because students may not complete their course of study. Indeed, as we saw in chapter 2, for every two students ages 25–29 years that gain access to higher education, only one (approximately)

Box 4.2 Structural Models in Policy Analysis

Structural models reflect the structure of a problem by capturing the decision making of the relevant agents as a function of their preferences, endowment, prices, and opportunities. Since policies often change prices and opportunities, these models can be used to predict individuals' responses to such changes.

To ensure that structural models indeed capture key aspects of the problem of interest, quantitative methods are applied to make the models' predictions about an actual setting resemble the setting as much as possible. Because of the models' complexity, such methods are often computationally involved.

Even the most sophisticated structural models are limited in the aspects of a problem they can capture before losing tractability. Hence, structural models are best viewed as indicating the direction of effects of a particular policy or economic shock, their approximate magnitude, and their driving forces.

completes her course of study and joins the ranks of the skilled population. Furthermore, the fraction of individuals completing higher education has fallen over time despite the fact that access has risen. Although, on average, the access rate for individuals ages 25–29 years is higher than for those ages 60–65 years (28 vs. 12 percent), their completion rate is lower (50 vs. 73 percent).

This section draws heavily on Ferreyra, Garriga, and Manuelli (2016), written for this report. The authors develop a structural model of college enrollment and completion, work while in college, and labor market outcomes. They use the model to quantify the general equilibrium effects of alternative funding mechanisms in Colombia and Brazil. Structural models are powerful because they enable us to conduct simulations for policies that may not have been implemented yet and learn about their potential outcomes. In the absence of these models, the policy maker would only be able to learn about already implemented policies, which are just a subset of all possible (and perhaps desirable) policies. Furthermore, structural models illuminate the channels through which policies operate, thereby providing valuable guidance for policy design.

Current Setting in Colombia and Brazil

In this section, using data for circa 2012, we focus on bachelor's programs in Colombia and Brazil, which account for more than 80 percent of the enrollment in each country.[13] Table 4C.1 in Annex 4C presents relevant information for these countries and for the United States for comparison purposes.

As this table shows, Colombia has a net enrollment rate of 20 percent, and 48 percent of students are enrolled in a public HEI. There is almost no private credit for higher education in Colombia. The main loan program for higher education is the government-sponsored ICETEX. Eligibility to ICETEX is determined by family income and student academic performance. As of 2012, only 11 percent of first-year students were using these loans.[14] Thus, while access to public HEIs is facilitated by heavy public subsidies, access to private HEIs largely depends on students' own financial resources. It is of interest, then, to examine the effects of providing additional funding options.

Expanding funding options for higher education might be even more necessary in Brazil. The net enrollment rate in Brazil is equal to 16 percent. Only 27 percent of students are enrolled in public HEIs, which are free and highly selective. There is a government-run loan program, Fundo de Financiamento Estudantil (FIES, Student Finance Fund), for the remaining 73 percent of students, who are enrolled in the private sector. This program was expanded in 2009 and has been subject to recent modifications as well. Given the income eligibility rules for the program, most high school graduates qualified for FIES in 2012. The program features subsidized interest rates and generous repayment terms. In 2012, 22 percent of incoming private HEI students (and 11.5 percent of all private HEI students) were using FIES. In addition, Brazil has a tuition discount program, Programa Universidade para Todos (ProUni), targeted to low-income students. In 2012, ProUni covered about 10 percent of all private HEI students. In total, FIES and ProUni covered approximately 21 percent of all private HEI students in 2012.

While public sector higher education is free in Brazil, its small size renders funding for private HEIs all the more important. Thus, analyzing alternative funding mechanisms is of great interest.

Returns to higher education in Brazil and Colombia are very high by international standards. The skill premium (defined here as the ratio of the average wage for college graduates and the average wage for high school graduates) is 2.77 in Brazil and 2.7 in Colombia, but only 1.67 in the United States. An important reason behind the high skill premium in Brazil and Colombia is the low percentage of skilled (that is, college-educated) working-age population in those countries, equal to 11 percent and 13 percent, respectively, in contrast with 42 percent in the United States. In the model presented next we focus on the working-age population with at least a high school diploma. Relative to this population, Brazil and Colombia still have a low fraction of skilled workers (equal to 26 percent and 27 percent, respectively) in comparison with the United States, which has 47 percent of skilled workers.

A Model to Analyze General Equilibrium Effects

The model used to analyze general equilibrium effects captures the main components of students' decisions, particularly those affected by the incentives created by alternative policies. The model considers the decisions made by high school graduates who are heterogeneous in their ability (including not just innate talent but, more broadly, academic readiness for higher education) and family income. A high school graduate decides whether to enroll in college and join the workforce at the end of college as a "skilled worker," or join the workforce right away as an "unskilled worker." In the model, the higher education sector is competitive and can expand as needed to absorb additional students. Once they join the workforce, students work until retirement (assumed to take place at age 60 years).

Firms use labor and capital, and their production level depends on the amount of capital and labor (skilled and unskilled) that they use. Skilled labor is more productive than unskilled labor and hence commands a wage premium. The ratio of skilled workers' wages to unskilled workers' wages is the "skill premium," which is a function of the supply and demand of each type of workers. For instance, policies that raise the supply of skilled workers are expected to lower the skill premium.

In the model, the workforce is divided into "young" and "old" workers (or "inexperienced" and "experienced," corresponding to age brackets 25–35 years and 36–60 years, respectively) to denote different experience levels. Every year, some individuals retire from the workforce and others enter.

Since experience raises productivity, skilled older workers command a wage premium relative to skilled young workers, and similarly for unskilled workers. The model also includes a government that runs a balanced budget and collects lump-sum taxes when needed to pay for higher education expenses.

Students choose how to spend their time during college and how to fund college. During college, a student must complete a number of required credits to graduate and must do so within a stipulated time. At any time during her college career a student is free to drop out and join the workforce as an unskilled worker. During college, she can use her time to study, work, or enjoy leisure. We can think of studying as exerting effort toward the completion of the required credits. Funding for college may come from parental income, working while in college, government grants, and college loans. We assume that college loans are nondefaultable and must be repaid in full after college regardless of whether the student graduates or not.

A student's progress toward completion is a function of her ability and effort, which vary across students. We assume that higher ability students are more productive in their efforts. Early on in college, students find out their "college ability": namely, whether they are suited to pursue higher education given their initial experience in college. If a student's college ability is too low, she may decide to drop out.

A student can choose to work while in college. She would do so to alleviate liquidity constraints or to reduce the burden of future repayments in case she has a college loan. However, working while in college reduces the amount of time available to study and hence extends the time-to-degree (TTD) (that is, delays graduation) or even prevents college completion altogether.

Some students may not complete college. The model captures the fact that some students face the risk of not graduating either because of a low "college ability" or because of an insufficient time to study as a result of working while in college. If we assume that college ability is positively associated with academic readiness, then students with low academic readiness, on average, face a greater risk of dropping out, as do students who work.

For some students, the best decision might be not to enroll in college. When deciding whether to go to college, a high school graduate considers the costs of benefits of going to college, the trade-offs involved in working while in college,

Table 4.4 Baseline and Counterfactuals for Colombia, circa 2012

		Model		
	Data	*Baseline*	*Loan*	*Free tuition*
Education				
Enrollment rate (%)	41.5	38.6	39.5	53.0
Dropout rate (%)	39.0	23.1	20.7	43.5
Time-to-degree	1.28	1.1	1.0	1.15
Labor market				
Skilled workers (%)	27.2	27.6	31.4	33.5
Skill premium	2.72	2.6	2.45	2.38

Source: Ferreyra, Garriga, and Manuelli 2016.
Note: *Data* reflect actual data; *baseline* is the predicted equilibrium without policy simulations; *loan* reflects the outcome of implementing private loans for higher education; *free tuition* reflects the outcome of publicly funded free tuition for all students. Time-to-degree is the average ratio between the actual time taken by students to obtain their degree, and the statutory duration of the program. The skill premium is the ratio of skilled and unskilled workers' wages.

the risk of finding out that her "college ability" is low, and her parental income and academic readiness. As a result, low-ability students may not find it optimal to enroll in college because of their relatively high risk of dropping out, and low-income students may not be able to overcome their liquidity constraints.

In equilibrium, students, workers, and firms make their best possible decisions, and the government runs a balanced budget. The equilibrium is *stationary*: all aggregates and prices are stable over time, as is the amount of workers of each skill and age group.

The model is parameterized to replicate key features of the data, and then used to simulate alternative funding regimes. Table 4.4 presents such key features (column 1) along with the model's predicted values (column 2). The model fits most aspects of the data (including others not shown in the table) reasonably well. However, it underpredicts the dropout rate, most likely as a result of institutional features not included in the model.[15] Despite this quantitative underprediction, *qualitative* predictions for dropout rates remain valid.

Simulating Alternative Funding Mechanisms

Two alternative programs are considered for Colombia: the implementation of a college loan and free tuition. In these simulations, loans are provided by private financial institutions, without government intervention. Thus, they do not utilize fiscal resources. In contrast, providing free tuition to students requires fiscal resources. In what follows, *baseline* refers to the version of the model that replicates the data (without conducting any simulation). For simplicity we eliminate the distinction between public and private HEIs, and assume only one type of HEI that charges the average tuition.

Table 4.4 presents results for the loan program (column 3). Results for the loan should be compared with those from the baseline. While Colombia currently has ICETEX loans, this simulation considers the implementation of a loan available to all students. The simulated loan does not contain subsidies, offers the same terms to all borrowers, and, for simplicity, charges the market interest rate.

The goal of the simulation is to illustrate the incentives created by nondefaultable loans. The fact that private credit markets minimally provide student loans in the region and require some form of state intervention (in the form of state-guarantee or publicly provided loans) might suggest that this simulation is not interesting. However, we wish to highlight the first-order incentives created by nondefaultable loans regardless of whether they are provided by public or private institutions, and to contrast them with those created by free tuition.

Loans raise enrollment rates, and lower dropout rates and TTD. As table 4.4 shows, the availability of loans raises the enrollment rate modestly, from 38.6 percent to 39.5 percent. It is interesting to note that loans reduce the dropout rate and TTD.[16] Two forces contribute to this outcome. First, loans reduce the need to work while in college for some students and hence lower the dropout rate and TTD. Second, students who take up loans know they will have to repay them regardless of whether they graduate or not, and that payback will be easier with a college degree than with only a high school diploma. They also know that the longer they take to graduate, the more debt they accumulate. As a result, they exert effort to graduate in a timely manner.

Since the effect on the enrollment rate is modest, loans have a relatively modest effect on the fraction of skilled population, which rises from 27.6 percent to 31.4 percent. The increased supply of skilled population leads to a decline (also modest) in the skill premium, from 2.6 to 2.45.

Free tuition raises enrollment rates; even then, not everybody chooses to attend college. Column 4 of table 4.4 presents results for free tuition funded with lump-sum taxes paid by all workers. Free tuition leads to a larger increase in enrollment rates than the loan program, as we would expect from a program that drives the direct cost of college to zero. Note, however, that the enrollment rate is still well below 100 percent. In other words, even if the direct cost of college is zero, some students may choose not to enroll either because the cost of effort and the risk of dropping out are too high for them given their ability, or because their opportunity cost is too high given their family income.

Unlike the loan program, which lowers the dropout rate and TTD, free tuition raises both. Two forces contribute to this outcome. First, by alleviating the liquidity constraint, free tuition enables many low-income students to enroll in college, yet these students tend to be less academically ready than those already enrolled in college. As a result, they either take longer to complete their degree, or are more likely to drop out. Second, the loan program creates an incentive for students to graduate, yet free tuition does not.

Free tuition also raises the percentage of skilled workers, but has a higher fiscal cost than loans. Free tuition's net effect of increasing both enrollment and dropout rates is an increase in the percentage of skilled workers, which rises from 27.6 percent to 33.5 percent. This increase is larger than that triggered by loans, yet the fiscal cost of free tuition is also higher than the fiscal cost of loans (which is zero). Free tuition requires fiscal resources to pay not only for the students that graduate but also those for those who drop out. Even graduating students consume more fiscal resources than with loans, because on average they take longer to graduate.

Free tuition has important fiscal implications. Free tuition to students is not free to society, since society must pay taxes to finance free tuition. Since free tuition for all subsidizes some individuals who would be willing and able to pay for higher education, it is an inefficient use of fiscal resources.

To summarize, both loans and free tuition relax liquidity constraints, raise enrollment rates, and raise the percentage of skilled workers. However, they do so to a different extent because they create different incentives. Nondefaultable loans create powerful incentives for student effort. They make the student internalize not only the cost of her education but also the risk of failing to graduate. A loan, then, induces financial responsibility on the part of the student. Yet, precisely for this reason, only students who are likely to graduate take up loans, which explains why loans expand enrollment to a lower extent than free tuition.

Free tuition, in contrast, does not create these incentives. With free tuition, the student no longer bears the cost of her education or the risk of failing to graduate. Hence, free tuition attracts many students who are likely to drop out. Furthermore, even some students who might succeed otherwise might take longer to graduate or even fail given the incentives created by free tuition.

Although the loans considered in these simulations have no fiscal cost, free tuition is fiscally costly.[17] While governments might feel tempted to raise enrollment through free tuition without a concomitant increase in resources, the evidence shows that the resulting decline in per-student resources is associated with lower academic outcomes.[18] This, in turn, could exacerbate the challenges generated by the entry of lower ability students into the system.

To be sure, the exact effect of loans depends on loan design. More generally, the design of funding mechanisms is critical to the incentives they create. Loans create financial responsibility to the extent that borrowers cannot default on them, or that default is costly (for example, through credit score degradation).[19] The take-up rate of loans can be boosted by adding a subsidy component to the loan or by providing more favorable repayment terms. Furthermore, take-up rates might not be high when public education is already heavily subsidized and widely available, as in Colombia.

Given the role of students' responses to funding mechanisms, it is important to design mechanisms that incentivize effort and graduation, and thus attract students who are likely to succeed. An example is tuition subsidies for students with high levels of academic readiness or satisfactory progress throughout college. Indeed, empirical evidence shows that financial aid tied to academic achievement raises the latter more than unconditional aid.[20] Furthermore, the policy maker might decide to spend the same amount of fiscal resources as she would under free tuition for all, but with higher per-student spending because of the lower number of subsidy recipients. The fiscal cost of this policy could be further lowered, if needed, by adopting a means-tested tuition subsidy that provides greater subsidy to lower income students, to avoid subsidizing high-income students who would be able to pay for tuition on their own.

Empirical Evidence on Dropout and Completion Rates

Since higher education expansion may have the unintended effect of raising dropout rates, we now examine related evidence. Two caveats are in order. First, an important assumption in the model is that the academic standards required for graduation remain constant throughout the higher education expansion. In reality, such standards might have fallen during the expansion, particularly in countries with lax oversight of private HEIs or poor incentives for public HEIs. This is because, with other things being equal, private HEIs have incentives to keep students enrolled (and graduate them) to collect tuition. Moreover, public HEIs whose funding is tied to enrollment face a similar incentive.

Second, the fact that the expansion is recent does not allow us to examine its effect on dropout rates. Nonetheless, we can look at a recent cohort and examine the variation in dropout rates and academic progress among students of different income and ability. Here, we focus on the 2006 cohort in Colombia. To provide context, we compare with students from the 2003–04 cohort in the United States based on Skomsvold, Walton, and Berkner (2011).[21]

For bachelor's programs, we first look at dropout rates from the higher education system within a certain time window since initial enrollment.[22] A student drops out from the system when she drops out from the last program she has ever enrolled in, without ever having graduated from any program. For instance, a student may drop out from her first program and enroll in a second one. When she drops out from the first, she is counted as a dropout from a program, but only when she drops out from the second is she considered a dropout from the system. Since students might drop out from a program but graduate from subsequent ones, dropout rates from the system are lower than those from a program. The dropout rate from the system for students pursuing bachelor's programs is equal to 37 percent in Colombia and 24 percent in the United States. The dropout rate from a program in Colombia is equal to 51 percent which, as expected, is higher than the dropout rate from the system. For comparability with the United States, we focus on dropout rates from the system for students who started in bachelor's programs, unless otherwise indicated.

Low income students, and low ability students account now for a greater share of higher education enrollment in Colombia. Panels a and b from figure 4.11 show that such students are indeed at greater risk of dropping out than their more advantaged counterparts.[23] Panel c shows that for a given ability level, lower income students are generally more likely to drop out; for a given income level, lower ability students are more likely to drop out. Furthermore, students with the lowest income and ability are about twice as likely to drop out as students with the highest income and ability.

Dropout rates vary not only among students, but also among programs. Figure 4.12 shows the variation in dropout rates from the program across program areas. For instance, while 41 percent of students enrolled in health

Figure 4.11 Dropout Rates from the System in Colombia, by Student Ability and Family Income, 2006

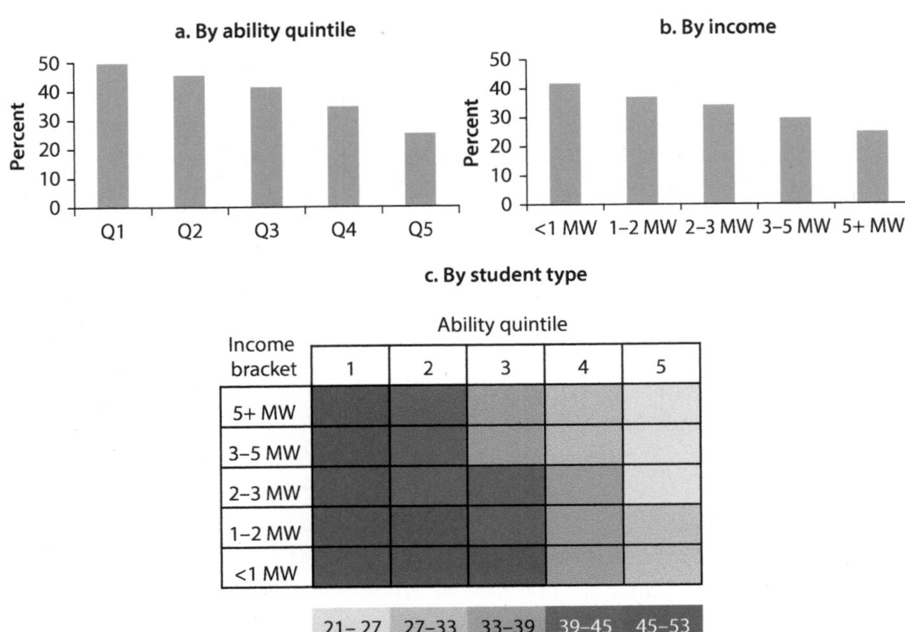

Source: World Bank calculations based on SPADIES and Saber 11. Cohort starting a bachelor's program in the first semester of 2006.

Note: A student is considered a dropout from the system if he or she is not enrolled in any program on the 14th or 15th semester since the beginning of the first program he or she started and has not graduated from any previous program. MW = minimum wage; Q = quintile.

Figure 4.12 Dropout Rates from the Program, by Area of Study in Colombia, 2006

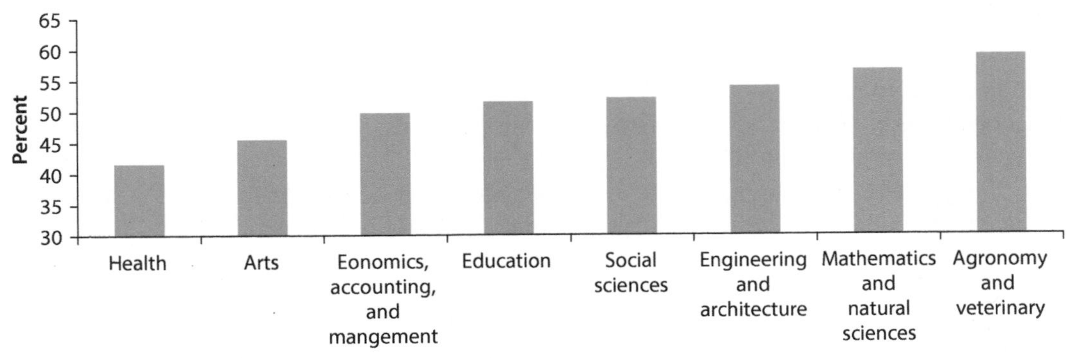

Source: World Bank calculation based on SPADIES.

Note: The figure shows the percentage of students that drop out by area of study, for students starting a bachelor's program in the first semester of 2006.

programs drop out, the fraction climbs up to almost 60 percent among agronomy and veterinary students.

An interesting difference between Colombia and the United States pertains to dropout timing. As figure 4.13 shows, almost 36 percent of the students who drop out from the system do so during their first year. In contrast, in the United States, students who drop out from the system are almost equally likely to do so at any time during their first 5 years in college.

The difference in dropout timing between Colombia and the US suggests the existence of an institutional or curricular feature that may cause higher early dropout rates in Colombia. One possibility is the fact that in Latin America and the Caribbean, students must choose a program in their first year in college as opposed to taking general education classes as in the United States. If, after starting the program, a student realizes that the program is a poor match to her skills or preferences, she may have to start another program from scratch, or might not be able to transfer credits easily. While poor adaptation to higher education might lead some students to drop out in any higher education system, these curricular rigidities may lead even more students to drop out. Since 35 percent of the students who drop out from their first bachelor's program start a different program afterward, a substantial fraction of students might indeed be affected by such rigidities.[24] In addition, academic advising and student support systems might not be as strong in Latin America and the Caribbean as in the United States, thus contributing to students' disorientation during their first year in college.

Despite the concentration of dropouts at the beginning of their college career, the fact remains that about 30 percent of those who drop out do so after their fourth year. In other words, about 10 percent (approximately equal to 0.30 * 0.37) of all students drop out after spending at least four years in college. Furthermore, the vast majority of these students have completed about 85 percent of their required coursework by the time they drop out. While we do not know the reasons for these students' withdrawal from the system, possible graduation impediments

Figure 4.13 Percent of Students Who Drop Out of the Higher Education System in Each Year, Relative to All Dropouts in Colombia, 2006

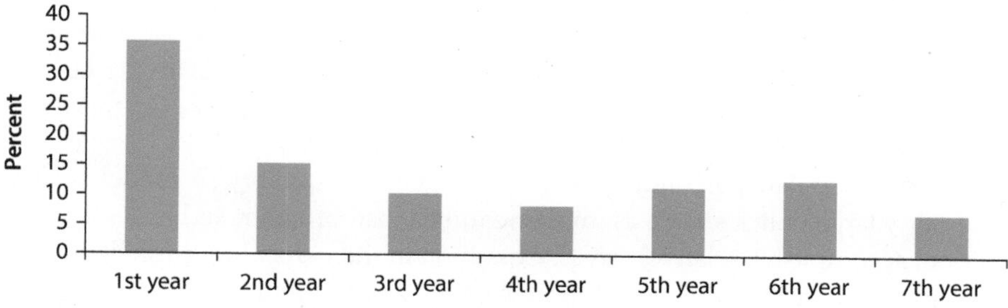

Source: World Bank calculations based on SPADIES.
Note: The figure shows the percentage of students who drop out in each year of college, relative to all students who drop out. For example, 35.5 percent of all students who drop out do so during their first year. Sample: students who start their first bachelor's program in the first semester of 2006.

Figure 4.14 Completion Rate Gap between the Top Income Quintile and the Bottom Two Quintiles in Latin America and the Caribbean, circa 2013

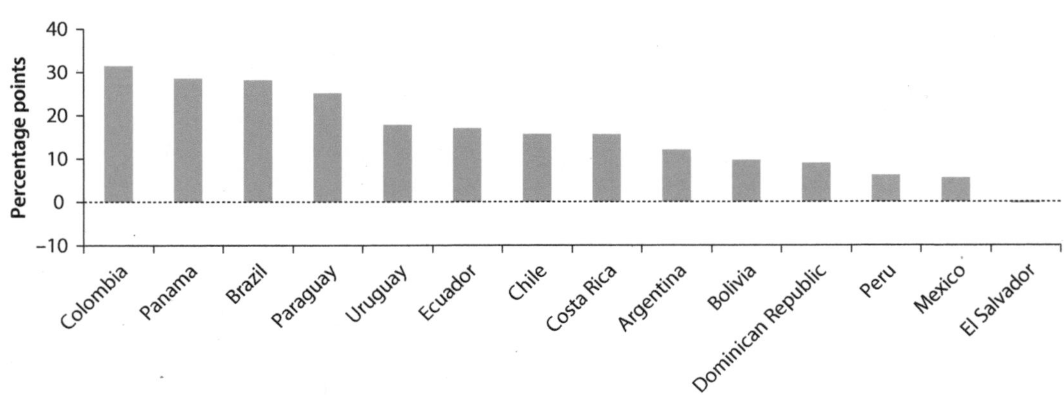

Source: World Bank calculations based on SEDLAC.

might include additional graduation requirements (such as a foreign language exam, or an undergraduate thesis), or the fact that the student has begun full-time work (perhaps as a result of an internship) and no longer has time to study.

Since much of the recent expansion in Colombia has consisted of students enrolling in short-cycle programs, it is interesting to note that dropout rates from short-cycle programs are higher than those from bachelor's programs (64 percent versus 51 percent). This is similar to the United States, where dropout rates from short-cycle and bachelor's programs are equal to 46 percent and 24 percent, respectively.

The completion gaps in Colombia among students from different backgrounds are present in other countries as well. As figure 4.14 shows, there is a substantial completion gap between the top and the bottom income quintiles in the whole region. Hence, while the region has made equity gains by raising access among the bottom income quintiles, completion is not equal.[25]

To summarize, we have presented evidence that the additional students that a free (or highly subsidized) tuition system would attract are quite likely to drop out. Furthermore, a large fraction of students drop out of the system during their first year because of possible institutional rigidities that render it costly for students to switch programs to seek a better match, and that further raise fiscal costs.

Long-Run Labor Market Effects: Skills, Returns, and Inequality

The policy simulations conducted with our general equilibrium model suggest that fairly large policies, such as implementing a loan program and providing free tuition, accomplish a relatively small expansion in the percentage of skilled workers and a relatively small reduction in the college premium. While these effects lead to a reduction in wage inequality, this reduction is also relatively small.

Therefore, we pursue two objectives in this subsection. The first is to study the long-run consequences of the status quo as defined by current policies.

The second is to quantify the expansion of higher education access that is needed to accomplish both a large expansion of the skilled workforce and a large reduction in wage inequality.

At the core of the model in Ferreyra, Garriga, and Manuelli (2016) is the aggregate production function of Card and Lemieux (2011), which can be used to study the long-run effects on skills, returns, and inequality of any given policy that raises the number of college graduates. Furthermore, these predictions can be made without solving for the full model, and require only a few pieces of readily available information.[26] The critical assumption of the model is that in a competitive equilibrium, workers are paid the value of their marginal productivity.

We use this production function to project the long-run effects of the status quo, and the long-run effects of raising the number of college graduates by 50 percent. In each case we calculate a stationary equilibrium in which the outflow of workers into retirement is equal to the inflow of workers into the workforce, and the skill composition of the population is constant. The economy may need many years before reaching this equilibrium.

Long-Run Effects of the Status Quo

Table 4.5 presents the educational attainment for individuals in age groups 24–35 and 36–60 in Colombia and Brazil, conditional on having graduated from high school. Individuals with incomplete higher education are counted as high school graduates (or unskilled workers), and individuals with postgraduate education are counted as college graduates (or skilled workers).

In both countries, young cohorts are different from old ones in two ways. First, young cohorts are larger as a result of the "demographic bonus" experienced by the two countries. In Colombia, each young cohort has an average of 419,000 individuals versus 200,000 in each old cohort; in Brazil, the corresponding figures are 1,800,000 and 970,000, respectively. Second, young cohorts are less skilled. In Colombia, the fraction of skilled workers in young cohorts is 24 percent relative to 29 percent in old cohorts; in Brazil, the corresponding figures are 21 percent and 29 percent, respectively.[27]

Table 4.5 Educational Attainment, by Age Group, Colombia and Brazil, 2012

	Colombia			*Brazil*		
	Ages 24–35 years	*Ages 36–60 years*	*Total ages 24–60 years*	*Ages 24–35 years*	*Ages 36–60 years*	*Total ages 24–60 years*
High school graduates (thousands)	3,795	3,555	7,350	17,864	17,251	35,115
College graduates (thousands)	1,231	1,450	2,681	4,852	6,958	11,811
Total (thousands)	5,026	5,005	10,031	22,717	24,209	46,926
College graduates (%)	24	29	27	21	29	25

Source: Ferreyra, Garriga, and Manuelli 2016, based on SEDLAC.
Note: The table shows the number of individuals by educational attainment, conditional on having finished at least high school. High school graduates include individuals with incomplete higher education. College graduates include individuals with postgraduate education.

Figure 4.15 Projected Share of Skilled Workers in the Labor Force in Colombia and Brazil, 2010–60

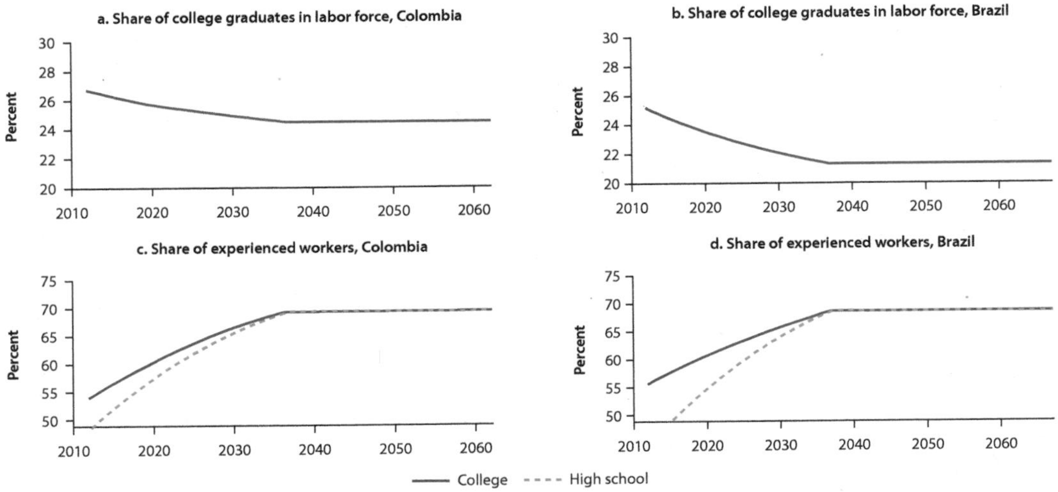

a. Share of college graduates in labor force, Colombia

b. Share of college graduates in labor force, Brazil

c. Share of experienced workers, Colombia

d. Share of experienced workers, Brazil

College ---- High school

Source: Ferreyra, Garriga, and Manuelli 2016.

In the new equilibrium, the old cohorts will be replaced by cohorts such as the young ones. Panels a and b in figure 4.15 depict the projected trajectory toward the new equilibrium. The adjustment toward the new equilibrium takes time because the young cohorts are different from the old ones in size and skill composition.

In Colombia, currently 27 percent of workers are skilled. Once all cohorts from the age group 36–60 years are replaced by cohorts such as those in the age group 24–35 years, the population will have only 24 percent of skilled workers. By a similar process, the percent of skilled workers in Brazil will fall from 25 percent to 21 percent, respectively.

As panels c and d of figure 4.15 show, the share of experienced workers is projected to rise for each skill level. For example, currently 54 percent of college graduates in Colombia belong to the age group 36–60 years. In the long run, this fraction will converge to approximately 68 percent, given that the 36–60-year old group accounts for approximately 68 percent of the whole population ages 24–60 years.[28]

As a result of the decline in the share of skilled workers in the labor force, the college premium rises in Colombia and Brazil (see figure 4.16, panels a and b), and so does inequality. The age premium falls both for college and high school graduates as experienced workers become a greater share of each skill level (see figure 4.16, panels c and d).

Thus, an important lesson emerges from the long-run projection of the status quo: absent other changes, the demographic bonus will not lead to an expansion in the share of skilled workers—or a reduction in inequality—unless young cohorts are more skilled than the old ones. As a consequence, failure to educate the young cohorts could have long-lasting, far-reaching consequences on these countries' inequality levels.

Figure 4.16 Projected College and Age Premium in Colombia and Brazil, 2010–60

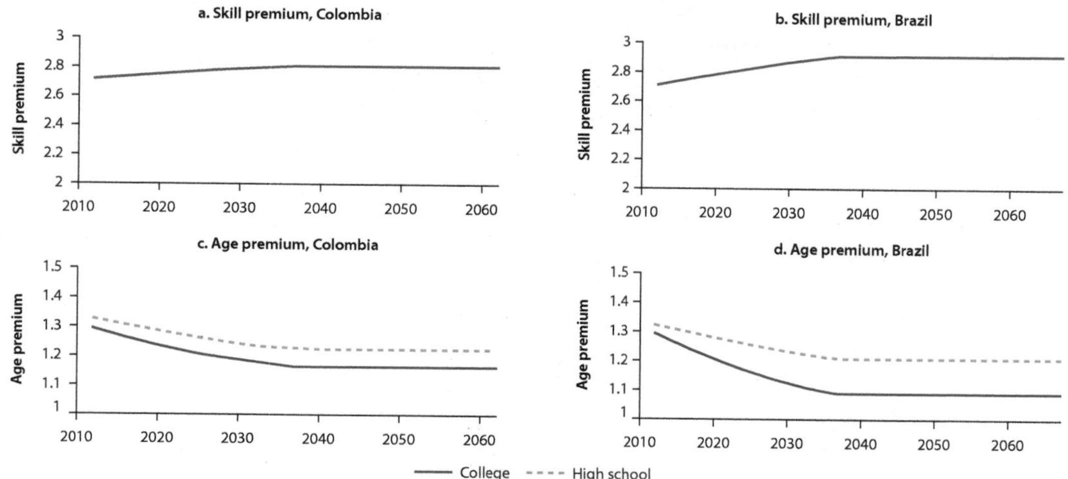

Source: Ferreyra, Garriga, and Manuelli 2016.

Long-Run Effects of Raising the Number of College Graduates by 50 Percent

Even if the policy maker attempted to exploit the demographic bonus by raising the share of college graduates among the young, the effects on the share of skilled workers and inequality might be disappointingly small and slow. Consider, for instance, a hypothetical policy that succeeds at raising the number of college graduates by 50 percent in all the young cohorts. To put this policy in perspective, given that dropout rates in the region are approximately equal to 50 percent, such a policy would entail the sizable endeavor of doubling higher education enrollment. For the sake of this discussion, which specific policy is implemented is not important as long as it raises the number of college graduates in young cohorts by 50 percent.

As figure 4.17, panels a and b, shows, this intervention would raise the share of skilled population from 27 percent to 35 percent in Colombia, and from 25 percent to 32 percent in Brazil. Consequently, the skill premium would fall, as shown in panels c and d, from approximately 2.7 to 2.4 in each country. These changes would not be fast: arriving at the new stationary equilibrium would take approximately 35 years as the new cohorts replace all the old ones.

The slowness of this adjustment is important. The very fact that the WAP comprises multiple cohorts—and only one retiring cohort is replaced by an entering cohort per year—means that each entering cohort has a small effect on the overall composition of the WAP. While broadening access to higher education might indeed expand the fraction of skilled population, effects on the WAP will be small and gradual.

Although seemingly a large intervention, raising the number of college graduates by 50 percent would have a small long-run impact in the labor market. The intervention would raise the share of skilled population to about one-third,

Figure 4.17 Simulated Effects of Raising the Number of College Graduates by 50 percent in Young Cohorts in Colombia and Brazil, 2010–60

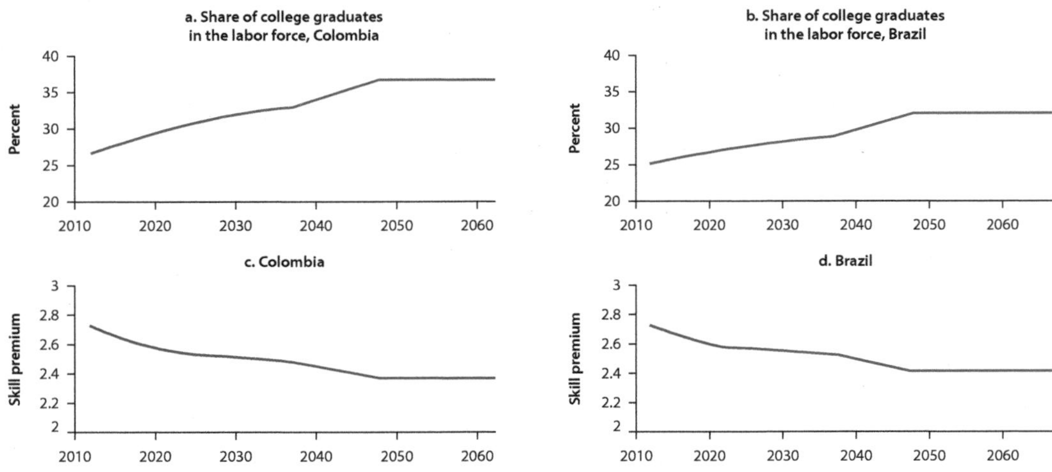

Source: Ferreyra, Garriga, and Manuelli 2016.

yet this share would still be much lower than in the United States (currently at 47 percent). And, while the college premium would fall to about 2.4, it would remain much higher than in the United States (where it equals 1.7). In other words, the equalizing role of a large higher education expansion would be limited. Furthermore, the effects would take many years to materialize in full.

Thus, a policy maker interested in large increases in the fraction of skilled workers—or large reductions in inequality—might need to resort to other policies besides merely expanding higher education access. One possible policy is the adoption of shorter and more streamlined college degrees to produce skilled workers faster. For example, the average statutory program length in the United States for a bachelor's program is four years, where it is closer to five in much of Latin America and the Caribbean. Another possibility is the improvement in academic readiness among high school graduates, since these constitute the pipeline of college students. A third possibility consists of easing immigration requirements for skilled workers.

To summarize, the high returns to college in Latin America and the Caribbean imply that expanding higher education is a profitable endeavor. However, not all funding mechanisms to expand access to higher education are created equal. Furthermore, such mechanisms have a number of effects beyond those on access; these can actually undermine the original intent of expanding access because of the characteristics of the individuals who benefit from the mechanisms and the incentives created by the mechanisms.

Only if the expansion raises the fraction of the skilled workforce does it have the potential of reducing wage inequality. Moreover, substantial reductions in wage inequality require very sizable interventions, not only in terms of financing access but also in terms of accelerating students' training and improving precollege abilities.

Conclusions

In this chapter we have examined demand-side determinants of access to higher education. Most countries in the region subsidize public education and ration access based on test scores. In recent years, many countries have made efforts to expand access to public and private education through credit or scholarships. Indeed, most countries in Latin America and the Caribbean have expanded access mostly by means of raising high school graduation rates. The countries that accomplished the largest access expansion also implemented policies aimed at raising college entry rates among high school graduates.

The expansion attracted new students into the system. To understand their characteristics and choices, we examined Colombia, where higher education enrollment almost doubled between 2000 and 2013. Since low-income and high-ability students account for much of the enrollment growth, the expansion was equity enhancing. As most of these students were admitted to high-end HEIs, the expansion did not merely give them access to higher education; it also gave them access to a quality higher education. In addition, low-income, low-ability students became more likely to attend college, either in short-cycle programs or in new bachelor's programs. Thus, variety in higher education was key to the equity gains experienced by these students.

While some of the Colombian expansion would have taken place merely because of changes in the number and characteristics of high school graduates, we found that less than half of the expansion can be attributed to these sources, and more than half to supply and policy changes. These policy changes include the very policies that raised access, such as capacity expansions on the part of public HEIs, and the expansion of loans and scholarships.

Besides affecting enrollment and sorting, large-scale funding changes can have other, unintended effects. For instance, both free tuition and credit can expand enrollment, but free tuition is likely to expand dropout rates. Furthermore, free tuition provides fewer incentives than loans for students to exert effort and graduate because students do not internalize their education cost. Thus, free tuition on a merit- or performance-based fashion is a more promising and efficient option.

Ultimately, if a country seeks to expand higher education to form skilled human capital and promote economic growth, it must focus squarely on policies that raise the fraction of skilled population: policies that will have the added benefit of lowering income inequality. The analysis here shows that even when funding policies are efficient at forming skilled human capital, large funding increases may be needed to expand human capital as desired in a short timeframe. Hence, other higher education reforms may be necessary, such as shortening the statutory duration of college programs, promoting short-cycle programs, and improving the academic readiness of the high school graduates who constitute the potential higher education students.

Annex 4A: Admission Mechanisms in Latin America and the Caribbean

Table 4A.1 Admission Mechanisms, Selected Latin American and Caribbean Countries

Country	*Is a standardized test used for admissions?*	*Admission mechanisms in public HEIs*	*Admission mechanisms in private HEIs*
Argentina	No	Unrestricted admission is the predominant mechanism, though some HEIs require approval of pre-university courses; for example, ciclo basico comun (common basic cycle) at the Universidad de Buenos Aires. Students older than 25 can enroll in HEI without a high school diploma provided they approve HEI-specific exams.	
Bolivia	No	Each HEI has its own admission system. Some HEIs give the Prueba de Suficiencia Academica (Academic Proficiency Test); the test is specific to each HEI.	
Brazil	Yes	Highly selective, based on entry tests (*vestibular*) that vary across HEIs, such as ENEM. Quota system: In federal HEIs, 50% of vacancies must be filled by high school graduates from public high schools.	Less selective than public HEIs; they may use their own admission tests.
Caribbean OECS countries	Yes - CAPE	Have general requirements based on CAPE or other tests, and additional requirements for specific programs. English test is sometimes required for students who are nonnative speakers.	n.a.
Chile	Yes – PSU	CRUCH universities and some private universities share the same highly selective admission process, which relies on PSU, high school grades and class rank. Other HEIs are less selective and have their own admission mechanisms, some of which use PSU as well.	
Colombia	Yes – Saber 11 (mandatory high school graduation exam).	Selective; rely on Saber 11 and/or their own exams.	Less selective than public HEIs on average. They may use their own admission tests, Saber 11 scores, and other elements such as interviews and essays.
Costa Rica	Yes	2 (out of 5) public HEIs use PAA; 2 use other exams; 1 does not use any exam. There are major-specific requirements as well; high school grades are also considered.	May have their own program-specific tests.
Dominican Republic	Yes	All students must take POMA to enroll in a HEI. Some HEIs use the POMA score as selection mechanism.	
Ecuador	Yes	The SNNA uses ENES, high school exit exams, and HEI-specific requirements to determine admissions.	May have their own admission mechanisms. Some may use ENES score.
El Salvador	No	There is only one public higher education institution. Admission relies on an admission exam, Prueba de Conocimientos Especificos. Students who do not pass the exam in the first round but obtain a sufficiently high score can take another exam.	Admission processes are varied; some private institutions have knowledge admission tests, while others combine these with vocational tests.

table continues next page

Table 4A.1 Admission Mechanisms, Selected Latin American and Caribbean Countries *(continued)*

Country	*Is a standardized test used for admissions?*	*Admission mechanisms in public HEIs*	*Admission mechanisms in private HEIs*
Guatemala	Yes	There is only one public HEI: Universidad San Carlos de Guatemala, which has an admission process where students take three subsequent tests: a vocational test, a general knowledge test, and a field-specific test. Students who do not pass the tests may be admitted provided they approve a 10-month course of five basic subjects.	Private HEIs usually have two admission tests: a vocational and an academic readiness test.
Haiti	No	Have their own admission tests.	No admission tests.
Honduras	No	Some have their own admission exams.	No admission tests in majority of HEIs.
Mexico	Yes	Each HEI has a different admission process, which may include an exam. Most public HEIs use EXANI-II. Some public HEIs (for example, UNAM) have open admission (*pase automatico*) for the highest GPA graduates from the high school associated with the HEI.	Elite private institutions have admission tests and a high school GPA requirement. Nonselective private institutions do not have admission tests.
Nicaragua	No	Have their own admission tests; admissions depend on these and high school grades.	No admission tests.
Panama	No	Have their admission tests.	No admission tests.
Paraguay	No	Have their own admission tests.	Do not have admission exams, but may require approval of entry courses.
Peru	No	Each HEI has its own admission exam. Other mechanisms, such as high school class rank, are also used. Some universities run "pre-university centers" that prepare students (for a fee) to take the higher education admission exam.	
		For admission to education programs, students must pass a national and a vocational exam.	
Uruguay	No	All HEIs have open admission, with the exception of some programs such as music, medicine, and nutrition.	
Venezuela, RB	No	In 2008, a law prohibited the use of admission exams.	
		The OPSU assigns students to programs through the SNIES, based on student socioeconomic conditions and high school grades.	Despite the 2008 law, some HEIs still have admission tests.

Sources: CINDA 2011; education ministries' web pages (accessed in May 2016).
Note: All countries, except Argentina, require graduation from secondary education to pursue higher education. CAPE = Caribbean Advanced Proficiency Exam; ENES = Examen Nacional para la Educacion Superior; EXANI-II = Examenes Nacionales de Ingreso; GPA = grade point average. HEI = higher education institution; n.a. = not applicable. OECS = Organization of Eastern Caribbean States; OPSU = Oficina de Planificacion del Sector Universitario; PAA = Prueba de Aptitud Academica; POMA = Prueba de Seleccion y Orientación academica; PSU = Prueba de Selección Universitaria; SNNA = Sistema Nacional de Nivelación y Admisión; SNIES = Sistema Nacional de Ingreso; n/a = not available.

Annex 4B: Student Funding Mechanisms in Latin America and the Caribbean

Table 4B.1 Student Funding Mechanisms, Selected Latin American and Caribbean Countries

Country	*Do public HEIs charge tuition?*	*Financial aid*		*Student loans*	
		For public HEIs	*For private HEIs*	*For public HEIs*	*For private HEIs*
Argentina	No	Two major merit- and need-based scholarship programs to cover nontuition expenses: PNBB and PNBU. Each program is targeted to specific fields.	HEIs have their own merit-and need-based scholarship programs, funded by own resources or external sponsors.	No	HEIs may run their own loan programs.
Bolivia	No	No	By law, each HEI must provide scholarships to 10% of its students.	No	FUNDADICEP is a private organization in charge of student loans. There are no government programs.
Brazil	No	Public HEIs generally offer reduced-price lunch or housing for high-need students.	A government program, ProUni, provides a partial or full tuition remission, depending on income.		HEIs may have their own loan programs. Some commercial banks offer students loans, which are not state-guaranteed. FIES is a government-run loan program for students whose per capita monthly family income is up to 2.5 times the minimum wage and whose ENEM score is 450 or higher. FIES covers up to 100% of tuition depending on income. It charges a subsidized interest rate and has favorable repayment terms. The loan is guaranteed by a private fund, FGEDUC, but students with a family income >1.5 minimum wage need a private guarantor.
Chile	Yes	Several government programs cover tuition expenses, such as: - *Gratuidad*: highly subsidized tuition for the bottom 50% of family income distribution, for students admitted to participating HEIs. - Merit-based scholarships programs such as Beca Bicentenario (for students with a PSU>500) or Beca Excelencia Academica (for top students in their high school cohort), among others.		FSCU is a student loan with favorable terms (2% interest rate, repayment period starts 2 years after graduation, repayment amount is at most 5% of previous year student's total income). Beneficiaries are students in traditional (CRUCH) universities with a PSU ≥ 475 and from the bottom 80% of the income distribution. CAE, administered by Ingresa, is a loan made by a commercial bank. Guarantee is provided by the government or by the HEI in case the student drops out during the first two years. Additional benefits include a repayment period starting 18 months after graduation, a subsidized interest rate, suspension of payment in case of unemployment, and a maximum repayment amount of 10% of student's income. Potential beneficiaries are students with a PSU ≥ 475.	

table continues next page

Table 4B.1 Student Funding Mechanisms, Selected Latin American and Caribbean Countries *(continued)*

Country	Do public HEIs charge tuition?	Financial aid		Student loans	
		For public HEIs	*For private HEIs*	*For public HEIs*	*For private HEIs*
Colombia	Yes	Public HEIs generally provide subsidized tuition and other expenses on need help for the lowest income students.	Private HEIs often have their own merit-based scholarship programs, and provide loans. Some private firms give scholarships.	Loans are given by a public institution, ICETEX, for studies at private and public HEIs. ICETEX loans mostly target low-income students with high SABER 11 scores (>=310). ICETEX condones 25% of the capital owed upon graduation and includes a subsidy for living expenses for low-income students. Students need a guarantor; there is a guarantee fund available to students who cannot have a private guarantor. A new, merit- and need-based credit line is Ser Pilo Paga, created in 2014. This loan does not need a guarantor, is 100% condonable upon graduation, and is restricted for studies in HEIs with high-quality accreditation.	
Costa Rica	Yes	Public HEIs count with several scholarships programs, which are often need-based. Some scholarships cover tuition, living expenses and other expenses (for example, books and transportation)	Government scholarships by FONABE	CONAPE is the public entity in charge of student loans for studies in public and private HEIs. Loans are need- and merit-based. The repayment period starts after graduation, and it charges a low interest rate. It covers up to 100% of tuition and may cover other expenses (for example, living expenses, equipment). Students need a guarantor.	
		A government institution, FONABE, also gives need-based scholarships for studies in public and private HEIs.	Private HEI have their own scholarships and loans programs that are need-based or merit-based.	Some commercial banks have student loan programs.	
Dominican Republic	Yes	The Education Ministry provides scholarships for studies in public and private HEIs to students with a high school GPA of 80 (out of 100). Not all degrees apply for the scholarships (law, psychology, accounting, marketing, and management are not covered).		FUNDAPEC, a nonprofit, provides student loans for tuition and other expenses for students with a GPA of 70 or higher. Students need one or two private guarantors (according to the loan magnitude). Interests have to be paid while studying, although payments on the principal can be delayed until graduation.	

table continues next page

Table 4B.1 Student Funding Mechanisms, Selected Latin American and Caribbean Countries *(continued)*

Country	Do public HEIs charge tuition?	Financial aid		Student loans	
		For public HEIs	*For private HEIs*	*For public HEIs*	*For private HEIs*
Ecuador	No	- Programa de Becas Nacionales provides scholarships for living, traveling, and moving expenses, targeted to different student groups (for example, high-performing students, high-level athletes, disabled students). All students must be admitted to a public or private HEI system through the national admission system. - By law, private institutions must give scholarships to 10% of their students in good standing.		- Banco del Pacifico provides student loans for studies in private and public HEIs. The credit is not state guaranteed; students need a private guarantor.	
El Salvador		Universidad de El Salvador gives free tuition to (a) high school graduates who graduate top of their class, (b) high-performing, low-income students with a GPA greater than 6.0. When multiple siblings are enrolled in the university, only one of them pays.	Private HEIs offer tuition discounts to low-income students. Private HEIs offer scholarships, with their own or external funding.	Both private and public HEIs offer credit to low-income students. These loans are not state guaranteed and are payable after graduation.	
Guatemala	Yes	The USAC offers financial aid to high-ability, low-income students. Maintaining the scholarship requires good academic performance.	Private HEIs generally offer scholarships to high-ability students to cover tuition and living expenses.	No	
Mexico	Yes	Programa de Nacional de Becas offers financial aid to low-income students in short-cycle and bachelor's programs in public HEIs. Aid consists of a monthly stipend. It is unconditional the first two years, but depends on academic performance afterward.	Some selective private HEIs provide merit-based scholarships.	No	Private HEIs offer student loans to be repaid after graduation. Nonelite institutions charge low tuition and offer flexible payment schemes.

table continues next page

Table 4B.1 Student Funding Mechanisms, Selected Latin American and Caribbean Countries *(continued)*

Country	Do public HEIs charge tuition?	Financial aid		Student loans	
		For public HEIs	*For private HEIs*	*For public HEIs*	*For private HEIs*
Honduras	Yes	There is no a centralized program or entity in charge of financial help for higher education. Each institution offers scholarships for low-income, high-ability students as well as loans.			
Paraguay	Yes	Scholarships to attend public or private HEISs are given by the Consejo Nacional de Becas. They cover tuition, living expenses, and transportation. They are need- and merit-based; their renewal requires good academic performance. Private HEIs have also their own scholarship system.		No	Some private HEIs have their own credit lines.
Peru	Yes	PRONABEC is the public entity in charge of scholarships and student loans. There are different scholarship programs, the largest being Beca 18, which supports students in poverty and extreme poverty.		PRONABEC provides student loans at a low interest rate. Students need a guarantor; loans are not state guaranteed.	
Uruguay	No	Need-based financial help for transportation and living expenses is given by the Fondo de Solidaridad, which receives contributions from higher education graduates.	Private HEIs give their own scholarships. Around 10% to 30% of the students in private HEI receive financial help in the form of scholarships. Normally, they cover tuition costs partially (around 30% to 80%). The scholarships are assigned based on high school students' performance and family income.	No	Private HEIs have their own credit lines.

Source: CINDA 2011; web pages of education ministries and various programs (accessed in May 2016).
Note: CONAPE = Comisional Nacional de Prestamos para Educacion; ENEM = Examen Nacional de Ensino Medio; FIES = Fundo de Financiamento Estudantil; FONABE = Fondo Nacional de Becas; HEI = higher education institution; ICETEX = Instituto Colombiano de Crédito Educativo y Estudios Técnicos en el Exterior; PNBB = Programa Nacional de Becas Bicentenario; PNBU = Programa Nacional de Becas Universitarias; PRONABEC = Programa Nacional de Becas y Crédito Educativo; ProUni = Programa Universidade para Todos; PSU = Prueba de Selección Universitaria; USAC = Universidad de San Carlos de Guatemala.

Annex 4C: Higher Education and Labor Market Statistics for the United States, Brazil, and Colombia

Table 4C.1 Higher Education and Labor Market Statistics for the United States, Brazil, and Colombia

	United States	*Brazil*	*Colombia*
1. Enrollment rate (%)			
Net enrollment rate	39.9	15.84	19.51
Conditional enrollment rate (conditional on high school graduation)	65.9	38	41.52
2. Dropout rate (from the system) (%)	23.6	56.5	37
3. Students enrolled in public HEIs (%)	72.37	27	47.7
4. Tuition			
Average annual tuition in private HEIs	US$25,696	R$7,236	Col$5,381,984
Average tuition in public HEIs	US$8,312	No tuition charged	Col$910,376
5. Financial aid and loans (%)			
Higher education students with loans	41.9	11.5	10.7
Higher education students with scholarships or grants	59.1	9.5	2.8
6. Time-to-degree			
Average statutory time-to-degree (years)	4	4.2	4.8
Average actual time-to-degree (years)	5.6	5.06	6.13
Time-to-degree (actual/statutory)	1.42	1.20	1.28
7. Work while in college			
Students who work while in college (%)	47	54	37
Students who work full time (≥40 hrs) (%)	13	32	19
Average number of hours worked (conditional on working)	25.5	35.51	33.32
8. WAP, by educational attainment (conditional on complete high school) (%)			
Complete high school	33.7	57.7	50.3
Incomplete higher education	19.4	16.3	22.5
Complete higher education (undergraduate)	34.7	24.4	20.5
Complete graduate	12.1	1.6	6.7
9. Wages			
Average wage of college graduates	US$1,137	R$27.64	Col $10,395
Average wage of workers with incomplete college	US$738	R$14.7	Col$5,072
Average wage of high school graduates	US$678	R$10	Col$3,825
10. College premium			
Complete college premium	1.677	2.764	2.718
Incomplete college premium	1.088	1.470	1.326
11. Age premium	1.27	1.61	1.3
Age premium for incomplete college workers	n/a	1.58	1.284
Age premium for college-educated workers	1.55	1.44	1.3

Sources: Ferreyra, Garriga, and Manuelli 2016; World Bank calculations based on multiple administrative sources.
Note: Data from circa 2012 (Colombia and Brazil) and the most recent year of available data (United States). Items 1, 2, 3 and 6 correspond exclusively to bachelor's programs. The conditional enrollment rate is the fraction of high school graduates that enrolls in college. The age premium of college-educated workers is the ratio between the average wage of college-educated workers ages 36–60 years and the average wage of those ages 24–35 years, and similarly for high school workers and incomplete college workers. Tuition is annual. Tuition data are in current prices for 2013–14 (United States), 2012 (Brazil), and 2014 (Colombia). Wage data are in current prices of 2015 (United States), 2012 (Brazil), and 2011 (Colombia). WAP = working-age population.

Notes

1. Ecuador fits the broad description in that it charges no tuition, and public HEIs have more than 50 percent market share. Nonetheless, Ecuador provides scholarships for students enrolled in private HEIs. In Mexico, public HEIs charge tuition, yet this tuition is extremely low.
2. We calculate the access rate as the total number of individuals ages 18–24 years who have ever been enrolled in higher education, divided by the total number of individuals ages 18–24 years. Individuals who have ever been enrolled in college include those who enrolled and have already graduated, those who are still enrolled and have not finished, and those who enrolled but dropped out.
3. We calculate the entry rate as the number of individuals ages 18–24 years who have ever enrolled in higher education, divided by the number of individuals ages 18–24 years who have graduated from secondary school.
4. This decomposition is similar to the one applied in chapter 2 to explain access gaps between different student groups. The decomposition in chapter 2 explains the gap among different student groups at one point in time; here we explain the change in access rate between two points in time.
5. For the United States, there is a vast literature documenting that financial aid can raise college enrollment (for example, Abraham and Clark 2006; Angrist, Hudson, and Pallais 2014; Castleman and Long 2016; Dynarski 2000, 2003, 2005; Kane 2003, 2007; Seftor and Turner 2002; van der Klaauw 2002). Dynarski and Scott-Clayton (2013) draw research-based lessons on financial aid. Although the research evidence on the effect of U.S. college loans on enrollment is limited, recent evidence from Chile (Rau and others 2013; Solis 2017) and Colombia (Barrera-Osorio and others 2011; Melguizo, Sanchez, and Velasco 2016) suggests positive enrollment effects from credit availability.
6. World Bank calculations based on 2013 program-level data from SNIES (Sistema Nacional de Información de la Educación Superior).
7. To make this classification, we calculate the average SABER 11 in 2000 at the HEI level and find the median of these HEI-level indicators. HEIs whose average SABER 11 is above (below) the median are considered "high end" ("low end"). For HEIs that did not exist in 2000, we use the average SABER 11 for students taking it in 2009.
8. Among students in the 2000 cohort who enter college, 71 percent do so in the 2001–05 window. It is perhaps surprising that only 38 percent enters college immediately after finishing high school.
9. SABER 11 is given twice a year, in each semester. It is not comparable over time. Hence, we standardize test scores (relative to all test takers) by semester, taking the average score of six subjects: math, physics, chemistry, biology, language, and philosophy.
10. Total number of students is not identical in table 4.2 and table 4.3 because some data are missing for the analyses based on table 4.3.
11. For instance, 59 percent (= 3.4 / 5.78 × 100) of students of the top income bracket in 2009 belong to the top-ability quintile, whereas only 9 percent (= 2.6 / 27.71 × 100) of students of the bottom income bracket belong to the top-ability quintile.
12. The increase is from 28 percent to 40 percent if we include all students in table 4.2.
13. Figures for Colombia in this section pertain to programs taught at HEIs and do not include SENA.

14. World Bank calculations based on Informes de Gestion from ICETEX.
15. The model predicts a dropout rate closer to the one in the United States (24 percent) than the one in Colombia (39 percent). Dropout rates might be higher in Colombia (and in Latin American and the Caribbean in general) because of rigidities in students' transfer across programs and the absence of a general education curriculum, features which are not captured by the model.
16. This is consistent with Rau, Rojas, and Urzúa (2013), who show that the introduction of state-guaranteed loans in Chile expanded enrollment probabilities and lowered dropout probabilities.
17. Privately provided Loans may have a fiscal cost is they entail a public subsidy or if they have state guarantee.
18. For example, Bianchi (2016) exploits a policy that eased admission requirements for science, technology, engineering, and mathematics (STEM) programs in Italy in the mid-1960s, as a result of which the student-faculty ratio rose and the peer ability of the student body fell. He finds evidence of lower learning among the affected cohorts because of overcrowded universities and negative peer effects. He also finds evidence of long-lasting negative on the returns to STEM degrees. Bound, Lovenheim, and Turner (2010) find that while enrollment rates in bachelor's programs have grown in the United States, completion rates have fallen. They conclude that most of the completion decline is attributable to the rise in student-faculty ratios because of the expansion, and to a greater tendency of students to begin their college career in non-selective public institutions or in short-cycle colleges. Bound, Lovenheim, and Turner (2012) reach a similar conclusion regarding the rise in TTD. For Colombia, Saavedra (2012) finds that with funding increases enacted over the past few decades have not compensated for enrollment growth, thus leading to lower per-student funding and academic outcomes.
19. See Dynarski and Scott-Clayton (2013) for a discussion on loan design informed by related literature. For a theoretical treatment of loan design, see Ionescu (2009).
20. See, for example, Bettinger (2004), DesJardins and McCall (2009), and Dynarski (2005).
21. For Colombia we focus on students who started their first bachelor's program in the first semester of 2006. World Bank source is SPADIES. A student is considered a dropout from the system if she is not enrolled in any program on the 14th or 15th semester since the beginning of the first program she started, and has not graduated from any previous program. For the United States, we focus on first-time higher education students from the 2003–04 cohort who started higher education at a four-year HEI, based on the 2003–04 Beginning Postsecondary Students Longitudinal Study, Second Follow-up (BSP: 04/09), conducted by the National Center for Education Statistics (NCES). See Skomsvold, Walton, and Berkner (2011).
22. The window is equal to 7.5 years in Colombia and 6 years in the United States, given that the average statutory duration of these programs is 4.8 years in Colombia and 4 years in the United States. Furthermore, the Ministry of Education in Colombia uses a similar time window to count on-time graduates.
23. There is a large literature documenting the role of precollege cognitive ability on college outcomes (for example, Arcidiacono and Koedel 2014; Belfield and Crosta 2012; Bound, Lovenheim, and Turner 2012; Deke and Haimson 2006).
24. Bordon and Fu (2015) consider the potential effects in Chile of switching from the current system, in which students choose both a HEI and a program upon enrollment,

to a system in which students choose a HEI first and a major after time in college. They estimate that the new system would yield better student–program matches, particularly for female, low-income or low-ability students.

25. A cautionary note is in order regarding this figure. Some students ages 25–29 years might no longer live with their parents, in which case we do not observe their family income. Hence, these calculations are based on students who still live with their parents, and family income is computed as the income of all household members except for the student herself. Completion rates are very similar between individuals who live with their parents, and those who do not.
26. The calculations require the estimation of the elasticity of substitution between skilled and unskilled workers, and between experienced and inexperienced workers. They also require the estimation of "efficiency parameters" for each skill and experience level. For Latin American and Caribbean countries, these parameters can be easily estimated using household survey data on workforce composition and wages.
27. Even if we do not condition on individuals with at least a high school diploma, young cohorts are still larger than old cohorts.
28. The share of experienced skilled workers rises because each exiting cohort is replaced with an entering cohort that has more workers in total, and a greater number (although not a greater proportion) of college graduates. The entry of young cohorts raises the total stock of skilled workers, yet as young cohorts become old, they raise the stock of experienced skilled workers at a higher rate. A similar reasoning applies to the share of experienced unskilled workers. Along the path in this figure, the share of experienced workers is larger among college than high school graduates because the fraction of college graduates is higher among experienced than inexperienced workers.

References

Abraham, K. G., and M. A. Clark. 2006. "Financial Aid and Students' College Decisions Evidence from the District of Columbia Tuition Assistance Grant Program." *Journal of Human Resources* 41 (3): 578–610.

Albrecht, D., and A. Ziderman. 1992. "Funding Mechanisms for Higher Education." World Bank Discussion Papers 153, World Bank, Washington, DC.

Angrist, J., S. Hudson, and A. Pallais. 2014. "Leveling Up: Early Results from a Randomized Evaluation of Post-Secondary Aid." NBER Working Paper 20800, National Bureau of Economic Research, Cambridge, MA.

Arcidiacono, P., and C. Koedel. 2014. "Race and College Success: Evidence from Missouri." *American Economic Journal: Applied Economics* 6 (3): 20–57.

Avery, C. and T. Kane. 2004. "Student Perceptions of College Opportunities. The Boston COACH Program." In *College Choices: The Economics of Where to Go, When to Go, and How to Pay For It*, edited by C. Hoxby, 355–94. Chicago, IL: University of Chicago Press.

Barrera-Osorio, F., M. Bertrand, L. L. Linden, and F. Perez-Calle. 2011. "Improving the Design of Conditional Transfer Programs: Evidence from a Randomized Education Experiment in Colombia." *American Economic Journal: Applied Economics* 3 (2): 167–95.

Belfield, C. R., and P. M. Crosta. 2012. "Predicting Success in College: The Importance of Placement Tests and High School Transcripts." CCRC Working Paper 42, Community College Research Center, New York, NY.

Bettinger, E. 2004. "How Financial Aid Affects Persistence." In *College Choices: The Economics of Where to Go When to Go, and How to Pay for It*, edited by C. Hoxby, 207–38. Chicago, IL: University of Chicago Press.

Bianchi, N. 2016. "The Indirect Effects of Educational Expansions: Evidence from a Large Enrollment Increase in STEM Majors." Working paper, Northwestern University, Chicago, IL.

Bordon, P., and C. Fu. 2015. "College-Major Choice to College-Then-Major Choice." *Review of Economic Studies* 82 (4): 1247–288.

Bound, J., M. F. Lovenheim, and S. Turner. 2010. "Why Have College Completion Rates Declined? An Analysis of Changing Student Preparation and Collegiate Resources." *American Economic Journal: Applied Economics* 2 (3): 129–57.

———. 2012. "Increasing Time to Baccalaureate Degree in the United States." *Education Finance and Policy* 7 (4): 375–424.

Brunner, J. J., and R. F. Hurtado. 2011. "Educación Superior en Iberoamérica—Informe 2011." Centro Interuniversitario de Desarrollo Providencia, Chile, October.

Card, D., and T. Lemieux. 2001. "Can Falling Supply Explain the Rising Return to College for Younger Men? A Cohort-Based Analysis." *Quarterly Journal of Economics* 116 (2): 705–46.

Carranza, J. E., and M. M. Ferreyra. 2016. "Increasing Higher Education Coverage: Students Sorting and Expansion and Supply Expansion in Colombia." Background paper for this report.

Castleman, B. L. 2013. "Prompts, Personalization, and Pay-Offs: Strategies to Improve the Design and Delivery of College and Financial Aid Information." Working paper, Center on Education Policy and Workforce Competitiveness, University of Virginia, Charlottesville.

Castleman, B. L., and B. T. Long. 2016. "Looking Beyond Enrollment: The Causal Effect of Need-Based Grants on College Access, Persistence, and Graduation." *Journal of Labor Economics* 34 (4): 1023–73.

de Fanelli, Ana García. 2008. "The Challenges of Funding Higher Education in Latin America." Manuscript presented at the seminar "Funding Higher Education: A Comparative Overview," Brasilia, Brazil, October 13.

Deke, J., and J. Haimson. 2006. "Valuing Student Competencies: Which Ones Predict Postsecondary Educational Attainment and Earnings, and for Whom? Final Report." Mathematica Policy Research, Washington, D.C.

DesJardins, S. L., and B. P. McCall. 2009. "The Impact of Washington State Achievers Scholarship on Student Outcomes." Working paper, University of Michigan.

Dynarski, S. M. 2000. "Hope for Whom? Financial Aid for the Middle Class and Its Impact on College Attendance." *National Tax Journal* 53 (3): 629–62.

———. 2003. "Does Aid Matter? Measuring the Effect of Student Aid on College Attendance and Completion." *American Economic Review* 93: 279–88.

———. 2005. "Finishing College: The Role of State Policy in Degree Attainment." Working paper, Harvard University, Kennedy School of Government, Cambridge, MA.

Dynarski, S. M., and J. E. Scott-Clayton. 2006. "The Cost of Complexity in Federal Student Aid: Lessons from Optimal Tax Theory and Behavioral Economics." *National Tax Journal* 59 (2): 319–56.

———. 2013. "Financial Aid Policy: Lessons from Research." *The Future of Children* 23 (1): 67–91.

Dynarski, S. M., and M. Wiederspan. 2012. "Student Aid Simplication: Looking Back and Looking Ahead." *National Tax Journal* 65 (1) 211–34.

Espinoza, R., and S. Urzúa. 2015. "On The Inappropriateness of Levying a Graduate Tax to Finance a Tuition-Free Higher Education." *Economía y Política* 2 (2): 77–106.

Ferreyra, M. M., C. Garriga, and R. Manuelli. 2016. "General Equilibrium Effects of Higher Education Funding: The Case of Colombia and Brazil." Background paper for this report.

Ionescu, F. 2009. "The Federal Student Loan Program: Quantitative Implications for College Enrollment and Default Rates." *Review of Economic Dynamics* 12 (1): 205–31.

Hastings, J., C. Neilson, A. Ramírez, and S. Zimmerman. 2016. "(Un)informed College and Major Choice: Evidence from Linked Survey and Administrative Data" Economics of Education Review 51: 136–151.

Horn, L., X. Chen, and C. Chapman. 2003. *Getting Ready to Pay for College: What Students and Their Parents Know about the Cost of College Tuition and What They Are Doing to Find Out.* Statistical Report, National Center for Education Statistics, Washington, DC.

Hoxby, C., and S. Turner. 2015. "What High-Achieving Low-Income Students Know About College" NBER Working Paper 20861, National Bureau of Economic Research, Cambridge, MA.

Kane, T. J. 2003. "A Quasi-Experimental Estimate of the Impact of Financial Aid on College-Going." NBER Working Paper 9703, National Bureau of Economic Research, Cambridge, MA.

———. 2007. "Evaluating the Impact of the DC Tuition Assistance Grant Program." *Journal of Human Resources* 42 (3): 555–82.

Melguizo, T., F. Sanchez, and T. Velasco. 2016. "Credit for Low-Income Students and Access to and Academic Performance in Higher Education in Colombia: A Regression Discontinuity Approach." *World Development* 80: 61–77.

Rau, T., E. Rojas, and S. Urzúa. 2013. "Loans for Higher Education: Does the Dream Come True?" NBER Working Paper 9138, National Bureau of Economic Research, Cambridge, MA.

Saavedra, J. E. "Resource Constraints and Educational Attainment in Developing Countries: Colombia 1945–2005." *Journal of Development Economics* 99 (1): 80–91.

Seftor, N. S., and S. E. Turner. 2002. "Back to School: Federal Student Aid Policy and Adult College Enrollment." *Journal of Human Resources* 37 (2): 336–52.

Skomsvold, P., A. Walton, and L. Berkner. 2011. "Web Tables: Six-Year Attainment, Persistence, Transfer, Retention, and Withdrawal Rates of Students Who Began Postsecondary Education in 2003–04." National Center for Education Statistics. Washington, DC.

Solis, A. 2017. "Credit Access and College Enrollment." *Journal of Political Economy*. (forthcoming).

Szekely, M. 2016. "Recent Trends in Higher Education in Latin America." Working Paper, Centro de Estudios Educativos y Sociales CEES.

Tornatzky, L. G., R. H. Cutler, and J. Lee. 2002. "College Knowledge: What Latino Parents Need to Know and Why They Don't Know It." Report, Tomás Rivera Policy Institute, Los Angeles, CA.

Van der Klaauw, W. 2002. "Estimating the Effect of Financial Aid Offers on College Enrollment: A Regression–Discontinuity Approach." *International Economic Review* 43 (4): 1249–87.

CHAPTER 5

The Supply Side of the Higher Education Expansion

María Marta Ferreyra

Abstract

Higher education supply in the region has experienced staggering growth since 2000 as new higher education institutions (HEIs) and programs have been opened. The private sector has expanded supply more than the public sector and has gained market share in the region. Variety has grown through greater participation of nonuniversity HEIs and new programs. Both private and public HEIs have now a greater share of "new" students. While public HEIs have mostly expanded existing programs, private HEIs have mostly created new ones, particularly to attract the "new" students. Selective programs expanded mostly by admitting high ability students, yet nonselective programs expanded by admitting lower ability students. HEIs are more likely to open new programs in fields in which they already have a presence. Other things being equal, business, law, and social science are new programs' most common fields. While highly selective programs are quite isolated from the competition of lower tier programs, competition for students is most intense among middle tier programs.

Introduction

The great expansion in access in the region took place because the system was able to absorb the increased demand. Hence, in this chapter we study the role of the supply in the recent expansion. "Supply Expansion in the Region" describes the expansion in the number of HEIs and programs, and examines changes in market share for various types of HEIs. We also examine whether the relative sorting between public and private HEI has changed as a result of the expansion.

"Expansion Strategies and Student Sorting in Colombia" analyzes the expansion strategies on the part of HEIs. To expand, an HEI can either enlarge its existing programs or open new programs. We investigate the use of each strategy by different HEI types and the factors related to the opening of new programs. Colombia serves as a case study.

"Expansion, 'Business Stealing,' and Ability Peer Effects in Chile" investigates competition among HEIs. We focus on whether quality improvements in one program (for example, through better faculty or facilities) can attract students away from other programs and adversely affect their peer ability. Chile serves as a case study. "Students Loans and Supply Expansion: Evidence from Chile" studies the effects that a loan-induced expansion has on the supply side, using Chile again as a case study. A final section concludes and summarizes lessons learned in the chapter.

It is important to note that the higher education market is segmented. Selective, high-quality HEIs are capacity constrained. While they might expand somewhat, they are generally not able to absorb the large enrollment increase such as the one witnessed by the region over the last 10 or 15 years. This role, instead, falls on less selective institutions, which are critical to understanding the supply-side of the expansion. Furthermore, if selective institutions or programs wish to remain so, the only new students they can absorb are those with high ability, leaving the remaining new students to the less selective institutions and programs.

Supply Expansion in the Region

Higher education supply has experienced a large expansion in the region. In this section we document that expansion and compare data, for each country, before and after the expansion. Although the specific before and after years vary across countries, or within countries depending on the variable being compared, in general *before* refers to the earliest year after 2000 with available data (hereafter, *circa 2000*), and *after* refers to the most recent year with available data (hereafter, *circa 2013*). We describe the supply expansion for the countries with available information. For the most part, the data come from each country's own administrative sources. Annex 5A, table 5A.1, presents further information on data sources.

Change in the Number of HEIs and Programs

As figure 5.1 shows, the number of HEIs rose in all countries except Peru, the Dominican Republic, and Chile. The increase was particularly large in Brazil, followed by Mexico and Argentina. These patterns remain even if we consider the number of HEIs per 10,000 people, ages 20–24 years, who constitute most of the potential demand for higher education.

The role of the public and private sector has varied across countries, yet most of the new institutions in the region are private. Figure 5.2 shows that although most of the new institutions are public in Argentina, Ecuador, and Peru, they are private in Bolivia, Brazil, Colombia, Costa Rica, Mexico, and Uruguay. In the countries with the largest increase in the number of HEIs, namely Brazil and Mexico, private growth has been particularly large. In contrast, the number of private HEIs has fallen in Chile and Peru, where many private nonuniversity HEIs closed during the expansion.

In Argentina and Brazil, most of the new HEIs are nonuniversity institutions. Furthermore, some countries allow the existence of for-profit private HEIs (Bolivia, Brazil, Chile, Haiti, Mexico, Panama, and Peru), whereas others do not. Box 5.1 discusses for-profit HEIs in Brazil.

Figure 5.1 Number of HEIs in Latin America and the Caribbean, circa 2000 and 2013

a. Argentina, Brazil, Mexico, and Peru

HEIs, number

3,500
3,000
2,500
2,000
1,500
1,000
500
0

Mexico
Brazil
Argentina
Peru

b. Bolivia, Chile, Colombia, Costa Rica, Dominican Republic, Ecuador, Guyana, and Uruguay

HEIs, number

350
300
250
200
150
100
50
0

Colombia
Chile
Bolivia
Ecuador
Costa Rica
Dominican Republic
Uruguay
Guyana

■ Circa 2000 ■ Circa 2013

Source: Countries' administrative information; see annex 5A for detailed information.
Note: Data pertain to the following years: Argentina (2000, 2013), Bolivia (2000, 2011), Brazil (2001, 2013), Chile (2000, 2010), Colombia (2000, 2013), Costa Rica (2000, 2014), the Dominican Republic (2006, 2011), Ecuador (2000, 2016), Guyana (2000, 2015), Mexico (2006, 2013), Peru (2005, 2013), Uruguay (2000, 2014). Country-specific notes on the counting of HEIs: Chile: new branches of existing HEIs are not counted as new HEIs for consistency with other countries. Colombia: SENA and institutions specialized in graduate education are not included. HEIs are identified by their SNIES code rather than by their name. Mexico: institutions specialized in graduate programs are included; exclusively online institutions are not. Bolivia and Ecuador: only universities are included. Costa Rica: five international HEIs are not included because of lack of enrollment data. HEI = higher education institution; SENA = Servicio Nacional de Aprendizaje; SNIES = Sistema Nacional de Información de la Educación Superior.

Figure 5.2 Change in the Number of Public and Private Institutions, Latin America and the Caribbean, circa 2000–13

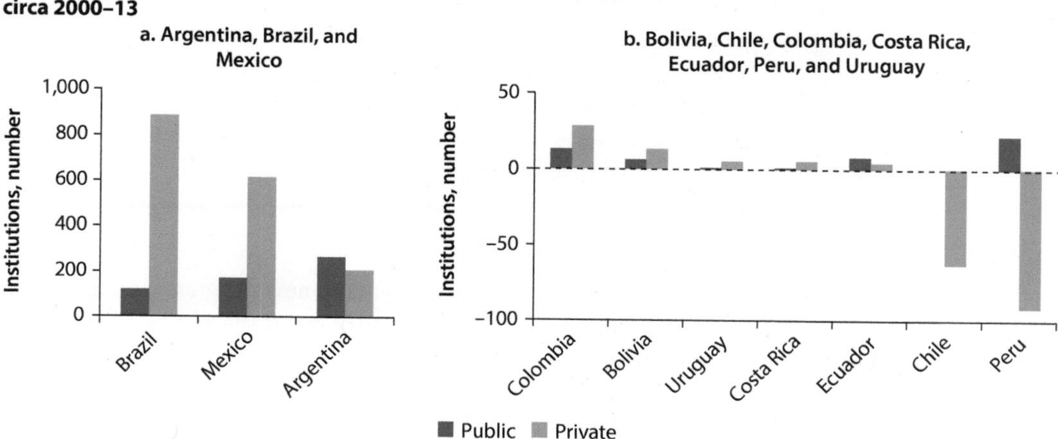

Source: Countries' administrative information; see annex 5A for detailed information.
Note: The figure depicts the change between circa 2000 and circa 2013 in the number of HEIs by public and private types. The large decrease in the number of private HEIs in Chile is mostly explained by the closing of technological institutes. In Peru, the negative change in the number of private HEIs is explained by the closing of teacher education institutions. Country-specific notes on the counting of HEIs: Chile: new branches of existing HEIs are not counted as new HEIs for consistency with other countries. Colombia: Servicio Nacional de Aprendizaje (SENA) and institutions specialized in graduate education are not included. HEIs are identified by Sistema Nacional de Información de la Educación Superior (SNIES) code rather than name. Mexico: institutions specialized in graduate programs are included; exclusively online institutions are not. Bolivia and Ecuador: only universities are included. Costa Rica: five international HEIs are not included because of lack of enrollment data. HEI = higher education institution.

Box 5.1 Unintended Consequences: Tuition Increases and For-Profit Institutions in Brazil

In a 1987 op-ed piece in the *New York Times*, then-U.S. Secretary of Education William Bennett conjectured that greater availability of financial aid would enable HEIs to raise tuition, since students would offset price increases with federal loans and aid. Cellini and Goldin (2014), Epple and others (2013), and Long (2004) have found support for the so-called "Bennett hypothesis" in the United States. Recently, De Mello and Duarte (2015) have found evidence of the effect in Brazil.

Pinho de Mello and Duarte show that the 2009 expansion of Brazil's student loan program—Fundo de Financiamento Estudantil (FIES, Student Finance Fund)—led to large tuition increases in private HEIs. While the loan expansion would raise demand and hence lead to a tuition increase in the absence of a perfectly elastic higher education supply, the authors document that an additional mechanism is at work in the case of Brazil, namely the reduction in the students' price elasticity of demand. In other words, greater loan availability has rendered students less responsive to price.

The authors conjecture that students may have become more price inelastic because they do not anticipate having to pay the debt in full, perhaps because the government cannot credibly commit to collecting it. By not internalizing the full cost of their higher education, students may overspend in it. Although higher education returns remain high in Brazil, the fact that returns are declining in the region and are most likely heterogeneous across programs (as they are in Chile and Peru, see chapter 3), gives reason for caution.

A further cautionary tale comes from the fact that about one-third of higher education students in Brazil are enrolled in for-profit institutions (Salto 2014). A number of U.S.-based for-profit companies operate in Brazil, such as Laureate, DeVry, and Apollo. The largest Brazilian for-profit conglomerate, Kroton, is the second-largest educational company in the world as measured by capitalization. In addition to a few large companies, there are numerous small ones (Pinho de Mello and Duarte 2015). In 2012 the 10 largest companies absorbed 32 percent of total higher education enrollment in São Paulo and Rio de Janeiro; 49 percent, Matto Grosso; and 61 percent, Rio Grande do Norte. This high concentration at the local level further increases for-profits' market power and their ability to raise prices in response to FIES.

In addition to new HEIs, the region also has many new programs. As figure 5.3 shows, the number of programs rose for all countries, and sharply in Brazil, Chile, Argentina, and Colombia. With the exception of programs in Argentina, the greatest increase in the number of programs took place in the private sector; the increase was particularly large in Brazil and Chile (see figure 5.4).

Enrollment Growth in Different HEI Types

As figure 5.5 shows, most of the enrollment growth corresponded to public HEIs in Mexico, Argentina, Uruguay, Bolivia, and Colombia, yet it corresponded to private HEIs in other countries. Brazil, Peru, and Chile experienced a particularly large enrollment growth in private HEIs.

Figure 5.3 Number of Programs in Latin America and the Caribbean, circa 2000 and 2013

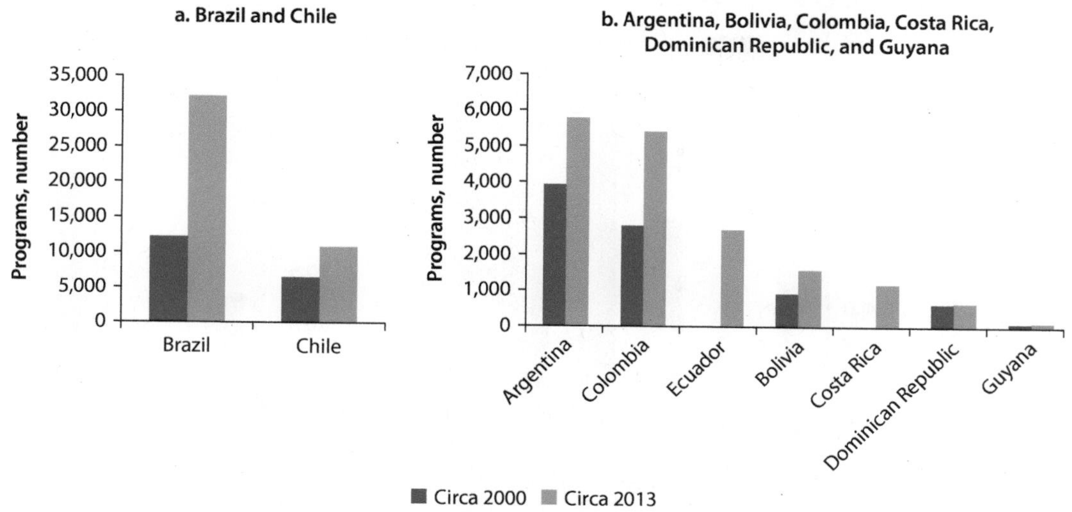

a. Brazil and Chile

Programs, number
35,000
30,000
25,000
20,000
15,000
10,000
5,000
0
Brazil
Chile

b. Argentina, Bolivia, Colombia, Costa Rica, Dominican Republic, and Guyana

Programs, number
7,000
6,000
5,000
4,000
3,000
2,000
1,000
0
Argentina
Colombia
Ecuador
Bolivia
Costa Rica
Dominican Republic
Guyana

■ Circa 2000 ■ Circa 2013

Source: Countries' administrative information; see annex 5A for detailed information.
Note: Data pertain to the following years: Argentina (2005, 2013), Bolivia (2000, 2011), Brazil (2001, 2013), Chile (2005, 2015), Colombia (2000, 2013), the Dominican Republic (2006, 2011), Guyana (2003, 2008). Country-specific notes on the counting of programs: Argentina: only programs offered by universities are included. Brazil: *cursos de graduacao* are reported, including online programs for 2013. There were 16 distance programs in 2001 (not included in the figure) and 1,258 in 2013 (included). Colombia: SENA programs are included. The Dominican Republic: includes graduate programs. Bolivia: only programs offered by universities are included. Guyana: refers only to University of Guyana programs. SENA = Servicio Nacional de Aprendizaje.

Figure 5.4 Change in the Number of Programs in Public and Private HEIs in Latin America and the Caribbean, circa 2013 Minus circa 2000

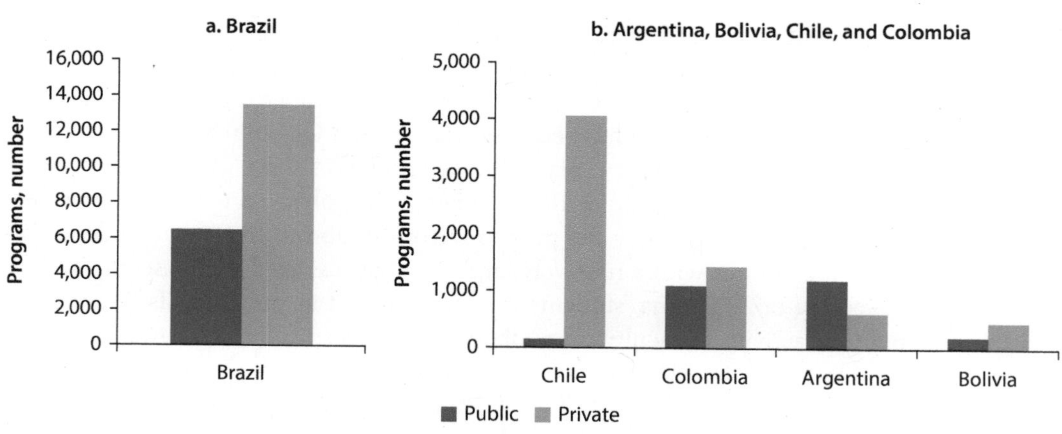

Source: Countries' administrative information; see annex 5A for detailed information.
Note: Data pertain to the following years: Argentina (2005, 2013), Bolivia (2000, 2011), Brazil (2001, 2013), Chile (2005, 2015), Colombia (2000, 2013).

Figure 5.5 Change in the Number of Students Enrolled in Public and Private HEIs in Latin America and the Caribbean, circa 2013 Minus circa 2000

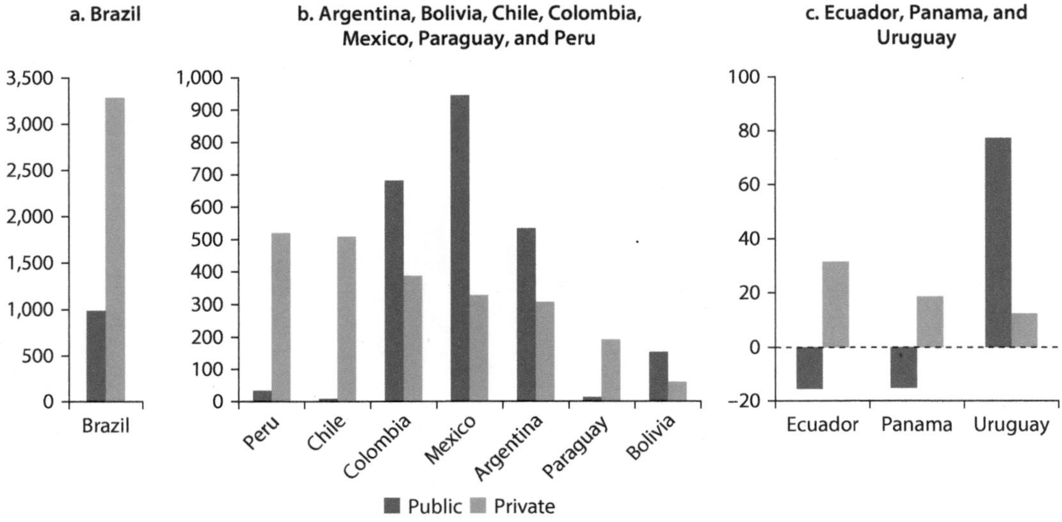

Source: Countries' administrative information; see annex 5A for detailed information.
Note: Data pertain to these years: Argentina (2000, 2013), Bolivia (2000, 2011), Brazil (2001, 2013), Chile (2005, 2015), Colombia (2000, 2013), Ecuador (2012, 2014), Guyana (2003, 2015), Mexico (2000, 2013), Peru (2005, 2013), Uruguay (2000, 2014). Enrollment in graduate programs is not included. Country-specific notes: Argentina: enrollment in *universidades provinciales* (state universities) is counted as public enrollment. Chile: enrollment in military institutions is not included. Colombia: enrollment in military institutions is not included; SENA is included. For a given year, enrollment corresponds to that reported in the first semester. Mexico: enrollment refers only to *servicios escolarizados* (school-based services). Ecuador, Bolivia, and Paraguay: only enrollment in the university sector is included. SENA = Servicio Nacional de Aprendizaje (national learning service).

The market share of public and private HEIs has changed (see figure 5.6). Currently, there is large variation in private HEIs' market share, ranging from 25 percent or less in Uruguay, Panama, Bolivia, and Argentina, to 70 percent or more in Brazil, Chile, and Paraguay. Overall, private HEIs gained market share during the expansion in all countries with available data except for Uruguay and Mexico, where the share has been quite stable, and Colombia.

Multiple factors might explain the recent market share gains for the private sector. In countries such as Brazil, where the public sector is selective and capacity-constrained, only the private sector can absorb the "new" students. Yet even in countries with a relatively large, highly subsidized public sector, such as Colombia or Argentina, students might not enroll in public HEIs because the political activity of faculty or students in these institutions (through strikes or protests) may lead to disruptions in the class or exam schedule, thus prolonging a student's time-to-degree (TTD). Private HEIs might also be more attuned to the needs of the marketplace and thus offer degrees with greater employability. In addition, they might have better connections with future employers through internships and career placement services, and might offer more flexible schedules for working students. Private HEIs might provide better student services such as office hours and access to faculty. They might have lower faculty-student ratios and hence offer more personalized attention. They might provide more

Figure 5.6 Enrollment Share of Public and Private HEIs in Latin America and the Caribbean, circa 2000 and 2013

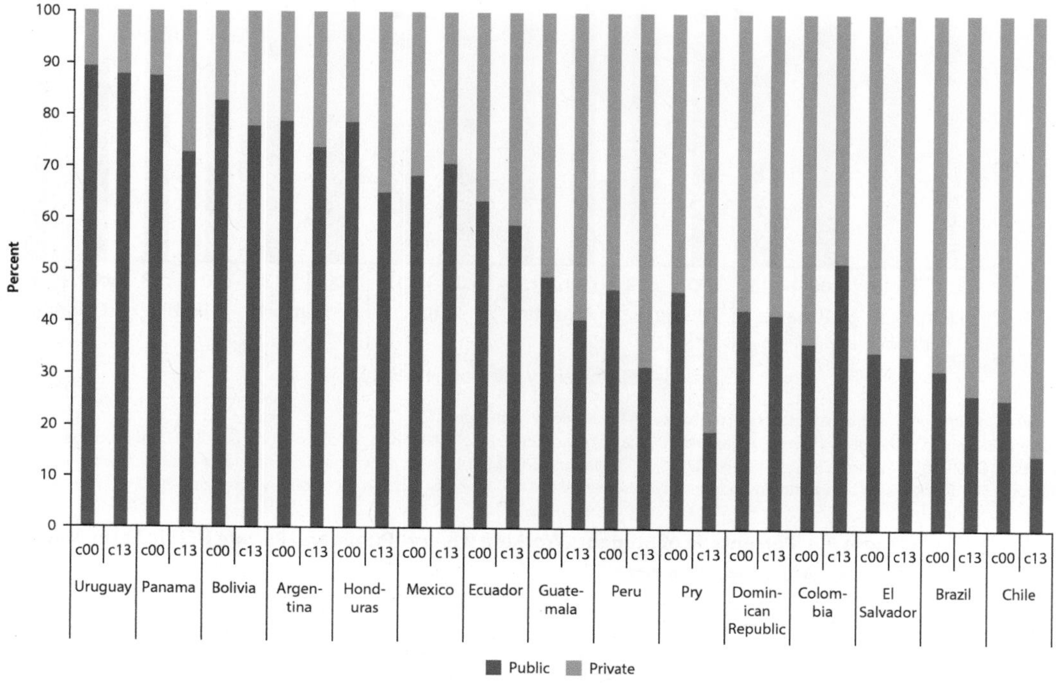

Source: Countries' administrative information and SEDLAC; see annex 5A for detailed information.
Note: Data pertain to these years: Argentina (2000, 2013), Bolivia (2000, 2011), Brazil (2001, 2013), Chile (2005, 2015), Colombia (2000, 2013), Ecuador (2012, 2014), Mexico (2000, 2013), Peru (2005, 2013), Uruguay (2000, 2014). Enrollment in graduate programs is not included. See country-specific notes of figure 5.5. We complement the administrative data with information provided from the household surveys, regarding the public and private sorting of students ages 18–24 years circa 2000 and 2013, for Honduras, Guatemala, the Dominican Republic, and El Salvador. c00 = s circa 2000; c13 = circa 2013.

academic advising and career counseling services, or simply be more effective at advertising their offerings.

Throughout the expansion, the market share of university and nonuniversity HEIs changed (see figure 5.7). Currently nonuniversity HEIs have less than a 15 percent share in the Dominican Republic, Panama, and Uruguay, but approximately 40 percent in Chile, Brazil, and Colombia. Nonuniversity HEIs gained market share in all countries except Peru (which closed a number of them).

Changes in Student Sorting Across Public and Private HEIs

Since public and private HEIs expanded at different rates in different countries, we now explore whether student sorting across public and private HEIs changed with the expansion. We focus on three student characteristics: (a) whether they work while attending higher education, (b) whether they live in an urban area, and (c) what level their family income is. For each characteristic we first show sorting patterns as of 2013, and then examine sorting changes between 2000 and 2013. This analysis gives us insight into the expansion strategies of public and private HEIs.

Figure 5.7 Enrollment Share of University and Nonuniversity HEIs in Latin America and the Caribbean, circa 2000 and 2013

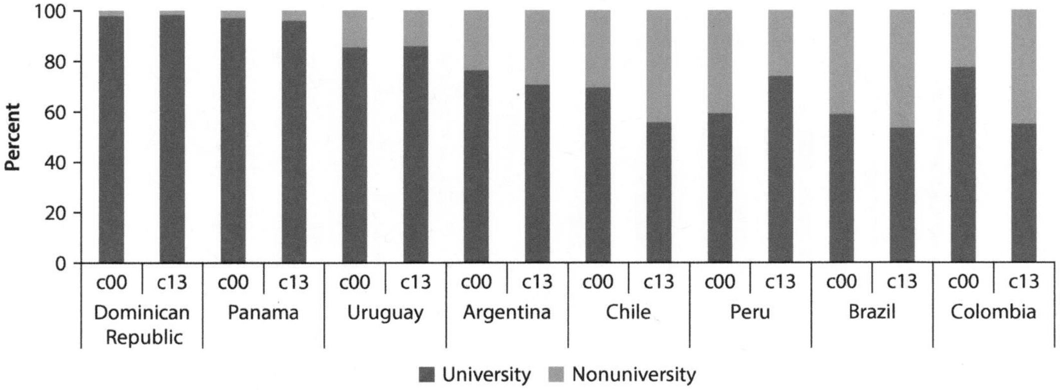

Source: Countries' administrative information; see annex 5A for detailed information.
Note: Data pertain to the following years: Argentina (2000, 2013), Brazil (2003, 2013), Chile (2005, 2015), Colombia (2000, 2013), the Dominican Republic (2006, 2011), Panama (2002, 2013), Peru (2005, 2013), Uruguay (2000, 2014). Enrollment in graduate programs is not included. See annex 5B, table 5B.1, for details on the institutions included in the university and nonuniversity sector in each country. c00 = circa 2000; c13 = circa 2013.

Figure 5.8 Percentage of Students Working while at Public and Private HEIs in Latin America and the Caribbean, circa 2013

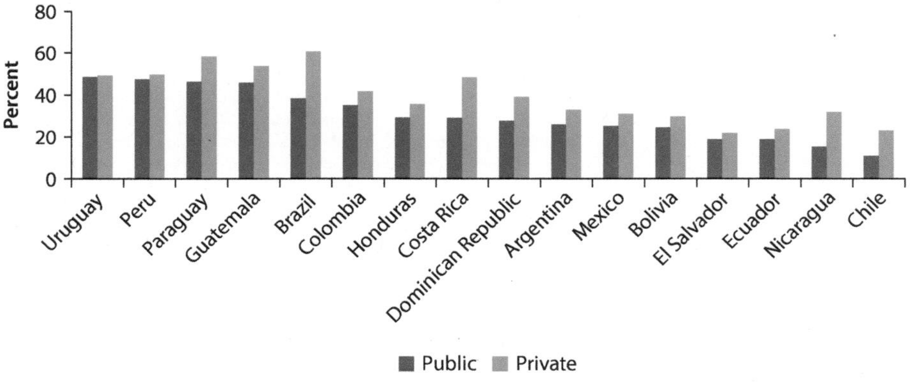

Source: World Bank calculations using SEDLAC.
Note: Because of change in survey coverage, we restricted the sample to 28 urban cities in Argentina, and Montevideo in Uruguay, which includes individuals ages 18–24 years who are currently enrolled in higher education. HEI = higher education institution.

Student Work Status

As figure 5.8 shows, students in private HEIs are more likely to work while attending college than those in public HEIs. One possible explanation is that private HEIs might provide more flexible, accommodating class schedules that allow a student to work while attending college. Another possible explanation is that private HEIs might provide more programs with direct applicability in students' current jobs, or might be better at establishing connections with firms. Yet another explanation might be that a greater number of students need to work to pay for tuition.

In Brazil, 60 percent of students enrolled at private HEIs report working; the percent is almost as high in Paraguay and Guatemala. It is lowest in Chile, at approximately 20 percent. With the exception of the Dominican Republic and Ecuador, working students from private HEIs work a higher number of hours than working students from public HEIs. While the percentage of full-time working students was already higher in private than public HEIs in 2000, the private-public gap has become larger in most countries (figure 5.9).

Student Geographic Location

In 2013, the percentage of students who live in urban areas is larger at private than public HEIs for half of the countries. As figure 5.10 shows, students in public HEIs became less likely to live in urban areas (and hence more likely to live outside urban areas) in 2013 than in 2000 in all countries, probably reflecting deliberate efforts on the part of those countries to expand public higher education to nonurban areas. Students in private HEIs also became more likely to reside outside urban areas in most countries. This, in turn, might reflect the decision, on the part of private HEIs, to pursue new markets.

Student Family Income

Figure 5.11 shows the income distribution of students in public and private HEIs by country in 2013. For each country and HEI type (public or private), the figure depicts the fraction of students who come from each income quintile. For a particular country, the fractions add up to 1 for public HEIs, and similarly for private HEIs.

Figure 5.9 Difference between Private and Public HEIs in Percentage of Students Working Full Time, Latin America and the Caribbean, circa 2000 and 2013

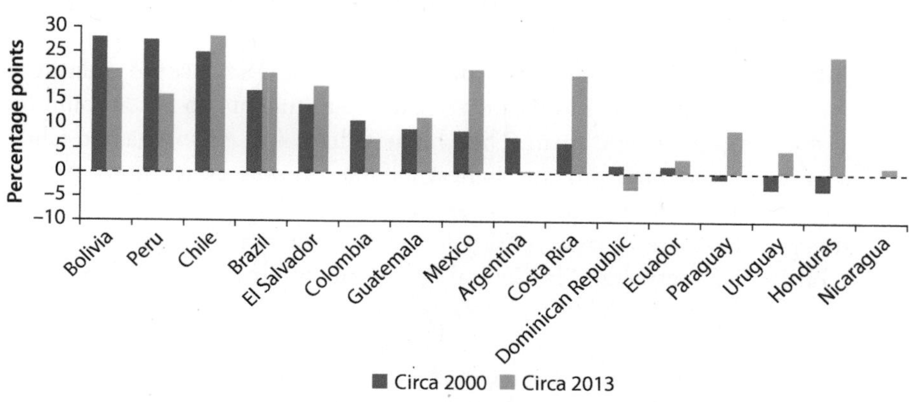

Source: World Bank calculations using SEDLAC.

Note: Difference is calculated as percent of private HEI students who work full time minus percent of public HEI students who work full time. Full-time work involves 40+ hours a week. Because of changes in survey coverage, the sample is restricted to 28 urban areas in Argentina and Montevideo in Uruguay. Calculations include only students ages 18–24 years who are currently enrolled in higher education. HEI = higher education institution.

Figure 5.10 Change in Share of Urban Students in Public and Private HEIs in Latin America and the Caribbean, 2000–13

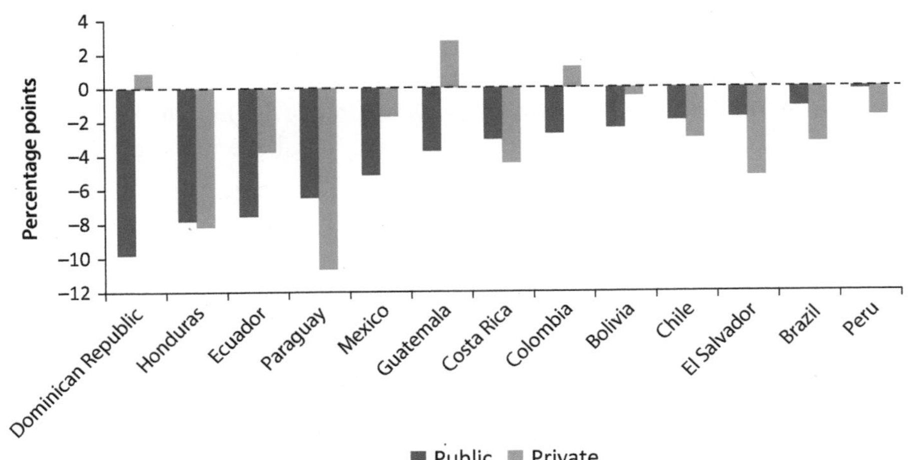

Source: World Bank calculations using SEDLAC.
Note: For public HEIs, change is calculated as the percent of public HEI students who live in urban areas in 2013 minus percent of public HEI students who live in urban areas in 2000. A similar calculation applies to private HEIs. Because of changes in survey coverage, the sample is restricted to 28 urban areas in Argentina and Montevideo in Uruguay. Calculations include only students ages 18–24 years who are currently enrolled in higher education. HEI = higher education institution.

Among students enrolled in private HEIs, students are most likely to come from the top two quintiles of the income distribution. The higher the income quintile, the higher the fraction of students who come from it. Only in Chile (and to some extent Argentina) are all quintiles represented rather equally.

In contrast, students enrolled in public HEIs are most likely to come from the second- and third-highest income quintiles. The exceptions are Honduras and Guatemala, where public HEIs' students have a high probability of coming from the top income quintile (they have an equally high probability of coming from that quintile in private HEIs).

While the percent of students coming from the lowest income quintile is higher in public than private HEIs, on average these students do not account for a large share of public enrollment. Their highest share is in Argentina and Chile.

On average, students from the highest income quintile constitute a greater share of the student body in private than public HEIs. However, they constitute a relatively large share of public HEIs' enrollment in Brazil and Chile, whose public HEIs are selective, and in Central American countries.

As figure 5.12 shows, the expansion has changed the income-based sorting in public and private HEIs. In general, the highest quintile has lost share both in public and private HEIs as lower income students have gained access to higher education. The second-highest quintile has lost share as well in public HEIs. In contrast, the bottom three quintiles have generally gained shares, with the greatest gains accruing to the second- or third-lowest quintile. The lowest quintile has gained the most in Chile, both in public and private HEIs.

Figure 5.11 Income Distribution of Students in Public and Private HEIs, Latin America and the Caribbean, circa 2013
Percent

	Public HEIs					Private HEIs				
	q1	q2	q3	q4	q5	q1	q2	q3	q4	q5
Argentina										
Bolivia										
Brazil										
Chile										
Colombia										
Costa Rica										
Dominican Republic										
Ecuador										
El Salvador										
Mexico										
Paraguay										
Peru										
Uruguay										

0–9 9–16 16–21 21–28 28–78

Source: World Bank calculations using SEDLAC.
Note: q1 denotes the lowest quintile of the income distribution; q2, second-lowest; and so forth. For public HEIs, the figure shows for each country the percent of students from each quintile of the income distribution, and similarly for private HEIs. Because of changes in survey coverage, the sample is restricted to 28 urban areas in Argentina and Montevideo in Uruguay. Calculations include only students ages 18–24 years who are currently enrolled in higher education. HEI = higher education institution.

As we saw in chapter 2, the existence of distance programs (including online programs) is another source of variety for students. Relative to total higher education enrollment, the market share of distance programs went from 0.18 percent to 16 percent in Brazil, from 8.5 percent to 14.2 percent in Colombia, and from 10.6 percent to 11.7 percent in Ecuador. Furthermore, distance programs currently capture 12.5 percent of students in Mexico.[1]

To summarize, Latin America and the Caribbean countries have experienced a large supply-side expansion in higher education, measured both by the number of HEIs and programs. The expansion increased the variety of program offerings and HEIs in the system and broadened the geographic scope of higher education. Although the role of public and private HEIs in the expansion varies across countries, overall private HEIs have gained market share, as have nonuniversity HEIs. Students in private HEIs were more likely to work than students in public HEIs before the expansion and became even more likely to do so, which might reflect the increased supply of flexible programs and schedules in the private sector. On average, students living outside urban areas now constitute a greater share of the student body both in public and private HEIs. This likely reflects

Figure 5.12 Change in Income Distribution of Students in Public and Private HEIs, Latin America and the Caribbean, circa 2000–13

Percentage points

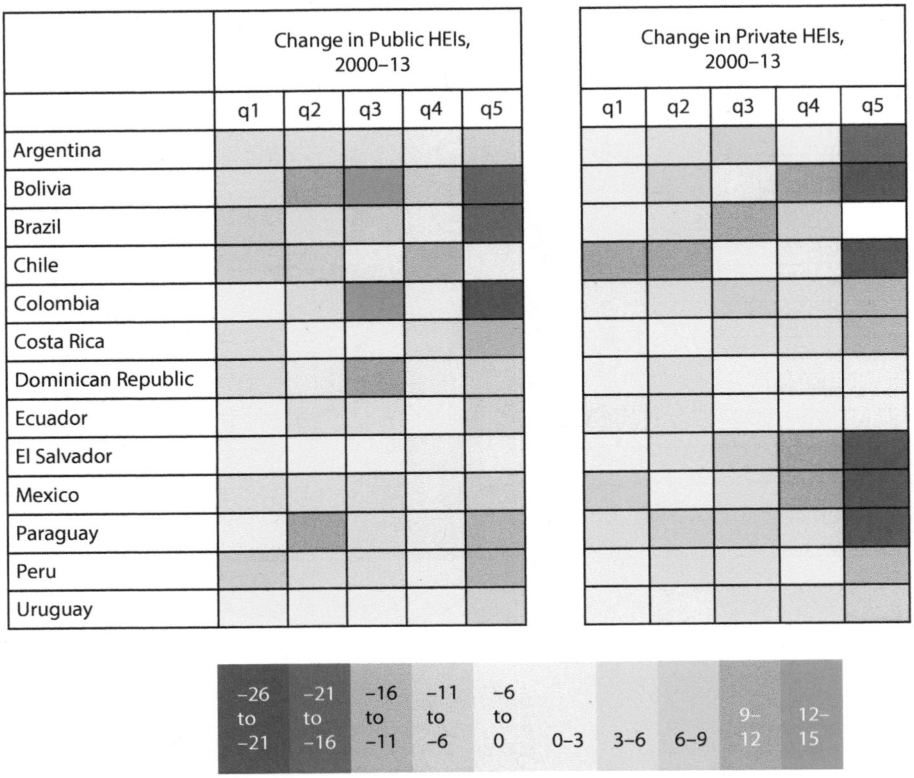

	Change in Public HEIs, 2000–13					Change in Private HEIs, 2000–13				
	q1	q2	q3	q4	q5	q1	q2	q3	q4	q5
Argentina										
Bolivia										
Brazil										
Chile										
Colombia										
Costa Rica										
Dominican Republic										
Ecuador										
El Salvador										
Mexico										
Paraguay										
Peru										
Uruguay										

−26 to −21	−21 to −16	−16 to −11	−11 to −6	−6 to 0	0–3	3–6	6–9	9–12	12–15

Source: World Bank calculations using SEDLAC.
Note: For public HEIs, the figure shows the change (in percentage points) in the fraction of students coming from each quintile (q) of the income distribution in each country. A similar calculation applies to private HEIs. Because of changes in survey coverage, the sample is restricted to 28 urban areas in Argentina and Montevideo in Uruguay. Only students ages 18–24 years and currently enrolled in higher education are included in the calculations. HEI = higher education institution.

public HEIs' deliberate efforts to reach students outside urban areas, and private HEIs' pursuit of new markets. While public HEIs tend to attract lower income students than private HEIs, both public and private HEIs now have larger shares of low-income students.

Expansion Strategies and Student Sorting in Colombia

This section discusses the supply strategies of higher education providers during the expansion. We seek to learn the extent to which HEIs relied on the expansion of existing programs relative to the opening of new ones; the type of students that benefitted most from the increase in the number of program offerings; and the factors behind the decision to open new programs. This section explores these aspects for Colombia. The section draws heavily on Carranza and Ferreyra (2017). Chapter 4 described Carranza and

Ferreyra's study setup. Since this section exploits student-level data, it does not include Servicio Nacional de Aprendizaje (SENA, National Learning Service) programs. Much of the material corresponds to a comparison of first-year students who took the high school exit exam SABER 11 in 2000 and 2009 (the "2000 cohort" and "2009 cohort," respectively).

Growth Strategies and New Programs

As figure 5.13 shows, enrollment grew both in existing and new programs between 2000 and 2013.[2] As of 2013, new programs account for 17 percent of total enrollment. Almost one-half and one-quarter of the total new program enrollment correspond to low-end and high-end private HEIs, respectively, while 15 percent and 16 percent correspond to low-end public and high-end public HEIs, respectively.

Enrollment grew in all HEI types between 2000 and 2013 (see table 5.1), but it grew the most in low-end private and high-end public HEIs. Although the private sector accounts for 51 percent of total growth, the average public HEIs have grown more than the average private HEIs, as public HEIs are fewer and larger than private HEIs.

Growth strategies have differed between public and private HEIs, and between high- and low-end HEIs. Between 40 percent and 50 percent of enrollment growth in private HEIs is due to the opening of new programs, relative to only 20 percent in that of public HEIs. At the same time, new programs have played a greater role in the growth of low-end than high-end HEIs, both public

Figure 5.13 Total Enrollment in New and Existing Bachelor's Programs in Colombia, 2000–13

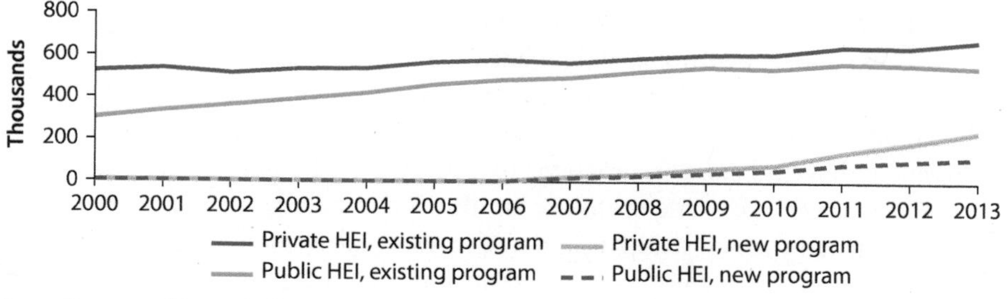

Source: Carranza and Ferreyra 2017.
Note: Total enrollment corresponds to each year's first semester. A program is classified as "new" when no first-year student enrolls in it each during 2000–05, but some do afterward. HEI = higher education institution.

Table 5.1 Enrollment Growth in Bachelor's Programs in Colombia, 2000–13

HEI type	*Overall growth*	*Percent of growth explained by new programs*	*Percent of growth explained by existing programs*
Low-end private	173,801	49.64	50.36
High-end private	127,362	43.84	56.16
Low-end public	123,057	25.24	74.76
High-end public	169,822	19.73	80.27

Source: Carranza and Ferreyra 2017.
Note: For the classification of HEIs, see chapter 4. HEI = higher education institution.

Figure 5.14 New Bachelor's Programs by New and Existing Fields and HEI Type in Colombia, 2006–13

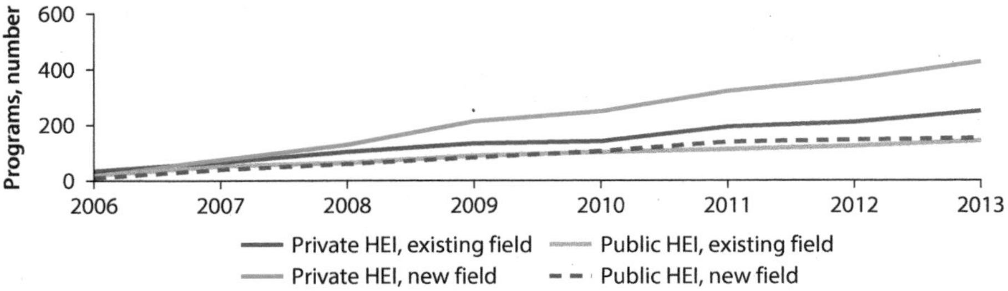

Source: Carranza and Ferreyra 2017.
Note: The figure depicts the number of programs with positive enrollment each year in either the first or second semester. Only new programs are included. We classify a program (or field) as new when its enrollment of first year students during 2000–05 is zero in all semesters. We use the classification of programs into fields established by the Ministry of Education in Colombia. HEI = higher education institution.

and private. Overall, new programs have played their greatest role explaining the expansion of low-end private HEIs.

Programs can be grouped into fields. For example, the business field might include programs such as business administration, international business, entrepreneurship, and business strategy. In Colombia, most new programs have corresponded to new fields opened by the HEIs (see figure 5.14).[3] This is particularly true for private HEIs, which are typically smaller than public HEIs and hence have fewer fields.

Market Segments and New Program Openings

As HEIs expand, they must decide what type of students to serve, and whether to serve them by expanding existing programs or opening new ones. Table 5.2 sheds light on this issue by showing the fraction of low-income and high-ability students in new and existing programs by HEI type. In low-end HEIs, students in new and existing programs are quite similar. Nonetheless, they are different in high-end HEIs, in which students in new programs have lower ability and income than students in existing programs. Furthermore, peer ability in existing programs in high-end HEIs has remained roughly constant, as indicated by their percent of high-ability students in 2000 and 2009.

Therefore, high-end HEIs serve two different kinds of students. Through their existing programs they continue to serve high-ability students, yet through their new programs they serve more disadvantaged students (the same ones served by low-end HEIs). Since students in high-end HEIs' new programs have higher ability and income than those in low-end HEIs, we can conclude that through their new programs, high-end HEIs serve the least disadvantaged among the disadvantaged students, all the while maintaining the selectivity of their existing programs.

While the number of programs has grown in the system, not all students have access to all programs. Thus, table 5.3 examines the *number of programs*

Table 5.2 Share of High-Ability and Low-Income Students in HEIs, by HEI Type and Bachelor's Program Status, Colombia, 2000 and 2009
Percent

	High-ability students		*Low-income students*	
	High-ability students, 2000	*High-ability students, 2009*	*Low-income students, 2000*	*Low-income students, 2009*
Low-end private HEIs, existing programs	18.73	18.85	46.23	57.95
Low-end private HEIs, new programs	n.a.	17.79	n.a.	63.67
High-end private HEIs, existing program	43.07	45.87	21.73	28.82
High-end private HEIs new programs	n.a.	31.37	n.a.	42.4
Low-end public HEIs, existing programs	17.23	19.88	64.22	72.62
Low-end public HEIs, new programs	n.a.	18.35	n.a.	72.59
High-end public HEIs, existing programs	51.2	50.58	53.82	62.73
High-end public HEIs, new programs	n.a.	31.69	n.a.	74.49

Source: Carranza and Ferreyra 2017.
Note: Data pertain to programs chosen by students in the 2000 and 2009 cohorts (that is, who took Saber 11 in those years). In each row, we report unweighted averages over programs. High-ability = top ability quintile; low-income = bottom two income brackets (<1 MW and 1–2 MW). HEI = higher education institution; MW = minimum wage. Since new programs were opened after 2000, data for them are not available for year 2000, hence the "n.a." (not available) marker.

by student type. It shows the total number of programs in which students from each type are enrolled in 2000 and 2009 (panels a and b). It also shows the absolute change over this period (panel c) and the change relative to 2000 (panel d).[4] While the number of programs reflects student preferences as revealed by their enrollment decisions, it also reflects HEIs' decisions regarding whom to serve or, to put it differently, where to locate their programs in the student type space.

Between 2000 and 2009, the total number of programs rose from about 1,900 to 2,700 (see table 5.3). It rose for all student types except those in the highest income bracket, who experience a slight decline.[5] The largest increases were experienced by students in the second-lowest income bracket and the second-highest ability level, who are, approximately, the ones that account for most of the enrollment expansion, as discussed in chapter 4.

Figure 5.15 disaggregates the change in the number of programs by HEI type and reveals three important facts. First, the number of programs has grown more at private than public HEIs. Second, when raising their program numbers, high-end HEIs have favored higher ability students than those favored by low-end HEIs. Third, when raising program numbers, private HEIs have favored higher income students than those favored by public HEIs.

Table 5.3 Bachelor's Programs by Student Type, Colombia, 2000 and 2009
ability quintile

Income bracket	*Number of programs in 2000*						*Number of programs in 2009*					
	1	*2*	*3*	*4*	*5*	*Total*	*1*	*2*	*3*	*4*	*5*	*Total*
5+ MW	16.4	24.0	40.3	67.8	176.8	325.3	11.0	19.9	29.9	60.3	167.9	289.0
3–5 MW	20.5	35.3	53.6	82.4	139.4	331.2	23.9	37.7	54.0	90.7	167.4	373.7
2–3 MW	41.7	55.3	75.1	109.7	150.6	432.4	49.0	72.5	108.1	159.6	207.6	596.7
1–2 MW	69.8	91.4	119.6	145.1	171.8	597.7	107.8	157.8	216.6	276.3	286.2	1,044.8
<1 MW	33.9	38.8	41.0	48.0	53.6	215.4	51.7	73.4	91.4	113.6	91.6	421.8
Total	**182.4**	**244.9**	**329.6**	**453.0**	**692.2**	**1,902.0**	**243.4**	**361.3**	**500.0**	**700.4**	**920.8**	**2,726.0**
Income bracket	*Change in number of programs between 2000 and 2009*						*Change in number of programs relative to 2000 (%)*					
	1	*2*	*3*	*4*	*5*	*Total*	*1*	*2*	*3*	*4*	*5*	*Total*
5+ MW	−5.4	−4.1	−10.4	−7.6	−8.8	−36.3	−33	−17	−26	−11	−5	−11
3–5 MW	3.3	2.4	0.4	8.3	28.0	42.5	16	7	1	10	20	13
2–3 MW	7.3	17.2	33.0	49.9	57.0	164.3	18	31	44	45	38	38
1–2 MW	38.0	66.4	97.1	131.2	114.4	447.1	54	73	81	90	67	75
<1 MW	17.8	34.6	50.4	65.6	38.0	206.4	53	89	123	137	71	96
Total	**61.1**	**116.4**	**170.4**	**247.5**	**228.6**	**824.0**	**33**	**48**	**52**	**55**	**33**	**43**

Source: Carranza and Ferreyra 2017.
Note: MW = minimum wage.

Figure 5.15 Change in Number of Bachelor's Programs by HEI Type, Colombia, 2000–09

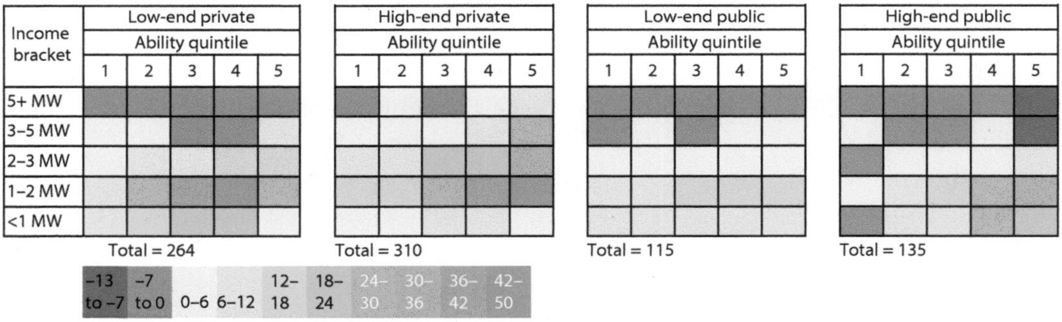

Source: Carranza and Ferreyra 2017.
Note: HEI = higher education institution; MW = minimum wage.

New program openings have favored low-income, high-ability students. Table 5.4 breaks down the change in the number of programs attended by each student type into the change in the number of existing programs (panel a), and the opening of new programs (panel b). Just as the increase in the number of programs is concentrated in the lower right triangle (namely, among the students who experienced the greatest enrollment growth, as described in chapter 4), new program openings are concentrated there as well.

Table 5.4 Change in Number of Existing and New Bachelor's Programs, Colombia, 2000–09

Income	*Change in number of existing programs, 2000–09*						*Number of new programs, 2009*						*Change in number of programs as a result of new programs (%)*					
bracket	*1*	*2*	*3*	*4*	*5*	*Total*	*1*	*2*	*3*	*4*	*5*	*Total*	*1*	*2*	*3*	*4*	*5*	*Total*
5+ MW	−8.3	−10.1	−16.7	−24.4	−36.2	−95.7	2.9	6.0	6.2	16.8	27.4	59.4	−54	−147	−60	−222	−310	−164
3–5 MW	−5.0	−10.6	−15.9	−16.3	−6.1	−53.8	8.4	13.0	16.3	24.6	34.1	96.3	250	538	4254	296	122	227
2–3 MW	−8.2	−6.2	−4.6	3.3	11.6	−4.2	15.5	23.4	37.6	46.6	45.3	168.4	213	136	114	93	80	103
1–2 MW	1.3	10.7	21.6	40.4	43.3	117.3	36.7	55.7	75.5	90.8	71.2	329.8	96	84	78	69	62	74
<1 MW	3.0	11.1	18.6	24.3	16.4	73.4	14.8	23.5	31.8	41.3	21.6	133.1	83	68	63	63	57	64
Total	−17.2	−5.2	3.0	27.3	29.0	37.0	78.3	121.6	167.4	220.2	199.5	787.0	128	104	98	89	87	96

Source: Carranza and Ferreyra 2017.

Note: The values depicted represent ability quintiles. There is an increase in the total number of *existing* programs (equal to 37) because there are 37 programs with two characteristics: they were not attended by members of the 2000 cohorts in the 2000–05 period, albeit they were attended by other students during that period based on SNIES; and they were attended by members of the 2009 cohort. MW = minimum wage; SNIES = Servicio de Información de Educación Superior.

New programs have played a critical role in the expansion of students' options. For every student type, program openings surpass the change in the number of existing programs. Furthermore, new programs have been particularly important for low-income, low-ability students, for whom they account for a relatively large share of their total program number growth (panel c).[6]

To summarize, as a result of the expansion, most student types have encountered an increase in the number of programs, most of which was due to new program openings. The largest increase, and the largest opening of new programs, were experienced by low-income, high-ability students, who are mostly served by high-end private and public HEIs. However, new program openings have contributed the most to expanding options for low-income, low-ability students, who are mostly served by low-end private HEIs.[7] These findings are consistent with the large role played by supply and policy in the expansion decompositions presented in chapter 4.

Decision to open a new program

Given the critical role of new programs in the expansion of options available to students, it is interesting to examine the factors associated with the decision to open a new program. Since most higher education students enroll in institutions located in their own state, the relevant geographic market for an HEI is the metropolitan area, or the state, where the HEI is located. In principle, HEIs can open new programs in any field, regardless of whether they already offer other programs in the field.

Regression analysis yields a number of insights into new program openings.[8] First, HEIs are more likely to open a new program when they already offer programs in that field. Since starting a new field entails a fixed cost, an HEI enjoys an advantage when it can exploit a field's existing infrastructure for a new program. We can expect that the higher the fixed cost of a particular field, the less likely it is that an HEI will start it anew. Since private HEIs were already less likely, before the expansion, to offer high fixed-cost fields (for example, science, technology, engineering, and mathematics [STEM] fields), they did not start many programs in those fields, either.

Second, low-end private HEIs prompt competitive responses on the part of other HEIs. In particular, high-end private HEIs and low-end public HEIs are more likely to open a program in a particular field when low-end private HEIs are already offering programs in that field. For example, consider the case of a low-end private HEI offering an accounting program in a particular city. In response, a high-end private HEI may decide to offer an accounting program to attract higher ability, higher income students than those attracted by low-end private HEIs. To compete for the same students as those attending the low-end private HEI program by charging lower tuition, a low-end public HEI may decide to open an accounting program in that city, too.[9] The fact that institutions are responsive to decisions made by low-end private HEIs suggests that competition is most intense in the market segment of nonselective programs.

Third, different HEI types open programs in different fields. Low-end private HEIs are most likely to open programs in business, economics, and accounting. High-end private HEIs are most likely to open programs in business, economics, design, and social communications. (Although both low-end and high-end private HEIs are most likely to open programs in business and economics, high-end private HEIs are twice as likely as low-end private HEIs to open programs in business and economics.) High-end public HEIs are most likely to open programs in business, education, and industrial engineering. Low-end public HEIs do not show a definitive pattern.

To summarize, enrollment growth in Colombia was almost equally split between public and private HEIs. Private HEIs have relied more on new program openings than in existing program expansion than public HEIs. In contrast, public HEIs have mostly relied on the expansion of existing programs and have increased program size more than private HEIs. Although new programs cater to students with lower ability and income than existing programs, new programs in high-end HEIs attract the most advantaged students from this group. It is important to note that high-end HEIs serve two different student populations: (a) high-ability students in existing programs, and (b) lower ability students in new programs. When opening new programs, business is a top choice for most HEI types, followed by economics in private HEIs and education in (high-end) public HEIs.

Expansion, "Business Stealing," and Ability Peer Effects in Chile

While the expansion of the higher education system increases the options available to students and improves access, it has a negative side effect on the enrollment and peer quality of some programs and HEIs. This effect happens because when expanding, an HEI does not consider its impact on other HEIs. Facing a decrease in student numbers as a result of the expansion of an HEI (which thus engages in "business stealing"), competing HEIs are forced to adopt strategies to curb student loss. One such strategy is to lower admission standards. While the strategy may curb the student loss, it may also lower the peer ability of the student body.[10] Furthermore, the decline in peer ability of the student body may lead to a student loss to the extent that students care about their peers' ability, thus undermining the intent of lowering admission the admission standards.

Hence, the opening of new programs and institutions may inflict enrollment and peer ability losses on others, which may face challenges covering fixed costs. From a social perspective, student gains from the existence of additional options may not suffice to counter the associated rise in fixed costs, and competition may lead to inefficiency and social waste. Therefore, in this section we explore competition, "business stealing," and ability peer effects in the Chilean higher education market. The section draws heavily on Bordon and others (2016), written for this report.

Higher Education in Chile

The Chilean higher education system is highly decentralized and competitive, and has experienced radical changes in the past few decades. In 1990 most Chilean universities were public and concentrated their activity in one region. Over the following 20 years, the private HEI share grew from 25 percent to 54 percent, and the fraction of high school graduates going onto college rose from about 25 percent in 1980 to 50 percent. Universities opened new campuses, and the average number of campuses grew from 1.6 to 2.6 for public HEIs and from 1.25 to 3.9 for private HEIs. The enrollment growth was associated with the implementation of policies that sought to expand access through scholarships and loans. For instance, a need-based loan program with a state guarantee was created in 2006, and grants were expanded in 2011 to include students up to the third income quintile.

As of 2012, the higher education landscape in Chile featured institutions of varied selectivity and curriculum specialization. The system consisted of 60 universities, 45 professional institutes, and 73 technical training centers. The 60 universities comprise the 25 "traditional" universities that existed before 1980 (members of the Consejo de Rectores de Universidades Chilenas [CRUCH]; 16 of these institutions are public and 9 are private), and 35 private universities created after 1980. The 25 CRUCH universities, plus 8 of the 35 non-CRUCH private universities, share a centralized admission system based on the test score in the Prueba de Selección Universitaria ([PSU], University Selection Test). PSU has several sections, and universities differ in the weight they assign to each PSU section. These 33 institutions are selective; the remaining institutions have mostly open admission.

This analysis focuses on the students who apply to the centralized system, whether they are admitted to one of the 33 participating universities or not. These 33 universities are classified into three groups: (a) elite CRUCH, which comprises public and private universities usually found in international rankings; (b) nonelite CRUCH, which comprises the remaining CRUCH universities; and (c) non-CRUCH private, which comprises the eight private, non-CRUCH universities that participate in the centralized admission system. Among the students who apply to the centralized system, about two-thirds are not admitted to any of the 33 universities and are said to choose the "outside option," consisting of attending a private, nonselective institution, a professional institute or technical center, or not attending higher education at all.

Sorting, Growth Strategies, and New Programs

As table 5.5 shows, there has been a large increase in the number of programs between 2005 and 2015. As in Colombia, the growth has been particularly large in private universities.

Another similarity with Colombia is the existence of clear student sorting patterns among HEIs. As table 5.6 shows, the highest ability students attend elite CRUCH universities, followed by non-CRUCH private universities. In terms of income and parental education, students in these two types of institutions are quite similar. In contrast, students in other CRUCH universities are less

Table 5.5 Increase in HEI Programs, Chile, 2005–15

Year	Number of majors	Majors per HEI	
		Private	*Traditional*
2005	1,634	59.3	66.9
2006	1,678	61.9	67.9
2007	1,643	60.7	66.6
2008	1,737	65.3	74.2
2009	1,796	71.7	73.2
2010	1,850	82.4	75.5
2011	1,946	95.2	78.1
2012	1,910	101.4	71.8
2013	2,051	105.8	76.8
2014	2,099	108.7	77.1
2015	2,148	109.1	79.3

Source: Bordon and others 2016.
Note: This table presents the number of undergraduate programs in total and the number of programs per HEI type for traditional (CRUCH) HEIs and (non-CRUCH) private HEIs. CRUCH = Consejo de Rectores de Universidades Chilenas; HEI = higher education institution.

Table 5.6 Average Student Characteristics across Types of Selective Institutions, Chile, 2012

	Elite CRUCH	*Other CRUCH*	*Private non-CRUCH*	*Outside option*
Average family income	8.99	5.42	9.98	4.58
Average mother's education	13.47	12.05	13.49	10.99
Average PSUs	646.53	573.78	596.36	467.43
Proportion of students with scholarship	0.45	0.45	0.22	0.16
Proportion of students with loans	0.25	0.39	0.36	0.23
Proportion of students from private school	0.31	0.10	0.38	0.12

Source: Bordon and others 2016.
Note: This table presents average characteristics of students attending each type of HEI. *Family income* represents annual income measured in millions of pesos. *Mother's education* is measured in years of education. The outside option includes a nonselective university, a nonuniversity HEI, or no higher education enrollment. CRUCH = Consejo de Rectores de Universidades Chilenas; HEI = higher education institution; PSU = Prueba de Selección Universitaria.

advantaged in income, ability, and parental education. Interestingly, sorting patterns have changed in recent years.

Non-CRUCH private institutions have led in terms of number of programs and enrollment (see table 5.7). They account for 48 percent of total growth, followed by elite CRUCH universities (which account for 36 percent of total growth) and nonelite CRUCH universities (16 percent). Since elite CRUCH institutions raised enrollment more than the number of programs, their average program size grew over time, as was the case for public HEIs in Colombia.

Each university type had its own growth strategy. Non-CRUCH private universities grew mostly through new program openings; elite CRUCH universities grew almost equally through new program openings and existing program expansions, and nonelite CRUCH universities grew through new program openings (while shrinking existing programs).

Table 5.7 Growth by Type of Selective Institution, Chile, 2005–15

	Total number of programs			*Total enrollment*		
	Elite CRUCH	*Other CRUCH*	*Private non-CRUCH*	*Elite CRUCH*	*Other CRUCH*	*Private non-CRUCH*
2005	435	918	281	21,152	38,289	15,888
2006	447	942	296	22,618	36,218	19,133
2007	426	932	292	24,221	33,522	19,024
2008	427	1,002	312	23,931	33,485	21,576
2009	447	1,015	343	24,134	34,144	22,903
2010	452	1,025	373	25,983	35,716	24,117
2011	453	1,074	419	26,584	35,708	25,125
2012	462	1,003	445	28,364	35,538	27,028
2013	489	1,091	471	28,345	39,093	28,488
2014	479	1,129	491	28,282	39,800	29,851
2015	488	1,163	497	30,174	42,209	28,829
Total growth (%)	1.20	2.48	5.94	3.67	1.1	6.32

Source: Bordon and others 2016.
Note: Columns 1–3 show the number of programs in each year by type of institution. CRUCH = Consejo de Rectores de Universidades Chilenas.

Table 5.8 Changes in Average University Student Ability, Chile, 2005–15

	Minimum PSU			*Average PSU*		
Year	*Elite CRUCH*	*Other CRUCH*	*Private non-CRUCH*	*Elite CRUCH*	*Other CRUCH*	*Private non-CRUCH*
2005	562.8	495.5	332.7	634.0	568.4	572.4
2006	567.6	497.9	339.9	634.7	561.9	573.5
2007	578.9	502.7	328	644.4	570.2	583.7
2008	575.2	500.9	328.6	643.6	566.6	585.8
2009	587.3	504.9	342.5	648.7	572.3	595.0
2010	582.2	505.9	563.6	649.5	573.5	611.1
2011	577.1	508.3	565.7	648.0	576.0	612.9
2012	572	496.9	518.6	643.4	569.2	595.8
2013	558.5	496.8	519	639.1	571.0	592.4
2014	548.4	491.5	514.7	637.4	567.5	589.0
2015	548.2	492.5	516.3	639.1	568.0	589.4

Source: Bordon and others 2016.
Note: Columns 1–3 show the average math and language score of the marginal (that is, lowest PSU) student admitted in each type of institution. CRUCH = Consejo de Rectores de Universidades Chilenas; PSU = Prueba de Selección Universitaria.

Table 5.8 shows that the expansion was accompanied by a change in the relative selectivity of the three university types. As indicated by the minimum PSU, both elite and nonelite CRUCH universities were more selective than non-CRUCH private universities until 2010, yet non-CRUCH private universities have been more selective than nonelite CRUCH universities since then. This is because non-CRUCH private universities experienced a sudden jump in applicant ability when they joined the centralized system.[11] While their PSU scores remain higher than in nonelite CRUCH universities, they have been falling since 2012. Their increase in average ability is all the more impressive considering their large growth in recent years. Further analysis indicates that this increase was attained mostly by raising average ability in existing programs.

Student Preferences over Higher Education Options and Program Attributes

To understand enrollment growth and changes in student sorting patterns, Bordon and others (2016) develop and estimate a structural model. In the model, a student chooses among the programs to which she is likely to be admitted, given her PSU score. She views a program as a *bundle* of characteristics and considers multiple factors when choosing a program, including (a) her ability relative to minimum and average ability in the program; (b) the weight placed by the program's admission rules on the PSU math section; (c) the location of the program relative to her home location; and (d) out-of-pocket price, which depends on tuition, financial aid, and loans. In addition, the model allows a student's choice to depend on gender, parental education, and per capita family income. It is important to note that the model captures the fact that a program's average ability depends on the students enrolled in the program and, thus, changes with the student body.

Estimates from the model yield important insights on students' preferences toward college programs. According to these estimates, a student prefers programs whose average student has a similar ability to hers. In other words, a student does not like to attend a program in which she is much more or less able than her average peer. In particular, she does not like to attend a program where the least qualified student is much less able than her. Furthermore, high-ability students are more sensitive to peer ability than low-ability students. These preferences regarding peer ability have important implications for "business stealing" and ability peer effects.[12]

In addition, model estimates show that female students are less likely than males to choose science programs even after considering their math scores. It is important to note that estimates show that students have a strong preference for geographically close options.

The estimates also show that when choosing a program, students trade off multiple attributes. If students cared only about a program's average ability, we would observe *perfect ability sorting:* the highest ability students going to the most selective schools until filling them up, the next highest ability students going to the next most selective schools, and so forth. However, the estimates indicate that students care about multiple program attributes, and they care about them differently depending on personal characteristics. This, for instance, might lead an extremely able student to turn down a very selective school in favor of a less selective one because the latter is closer to her home. In other words, student preferences are one factor behind the *imperfect ability sorting* observed in reality.

Competition, Business Stealing, and Ability Peer Effects

HEIs compete along multiple dimensions. Since students care about other attributes besides peer ability, HEIs have the opportunity to entice them by offering elements such as an attractive location or financial aid package, an appealing curriculum, state-of-the-art facilities, and nonacademic amenities. Thus, HEIs can compete for students not just by raising peer ability but also by offering other elements of interest.

The model is used to investigate the effects of improving a program's quality (generally understood as attractiveness) on the enrollment and peer ability of other programs. The quality improvement is not due to peer ability changes but to other elements, such as infrastructure and facilities. Thus, we refer to it as a "nonpeer quality improvement."

Students reallocate across programs in response to a program's quality improvement. Table 5.9 shows the effect of such reallocation. Programs are grouped into four tiers depending on their average peer ability.[13]

As table 5.9 shows, an improvement in a program's quality attracts students from *all* other institutions, including those previously choosing the "outside option." For instance, a quality improvement in the second-lowest tier draws the most able students from the lowest tier, the least able students from the highest and second-highest tier (by offering them some amenity of their interest), and students from programs in the same tier. In addition, it draws students from the outside option. Since, as we saw before, students wish to attend programs with other students of similar ability and do not wish to be much more able than the least able student, lower tier programs have limited capacity to attract students from top tier programs.

In contrast, when a top tier program improves, it can draw only those students who fulfill the admission requirements, namely other high-ability students. Most of these students already attend top tier programs, which explains why 61 percent of the students "stolen" by a top tier program come from other top tier programs.

Table 5.9 Business Substitutions When Nonpeer Quality Increases, Chile, 2012

		Rival peer ability			
Own peer ability	*Outside option*	$(\bar{a}_{min}, \bar{a}_{.25})$	$(\bar{a}_{.25}, \bar{a}_{.5})$	$(\bar{a}_{.5}, \bar{a}_{.75})$	$(\bar{a}_{.75}, \bar{a}_{1})$
$(\bar{a}_{min}, \bar{a}_{.25})$	0.55	0.14	0.18	0.10	0.03
$(\bar{a}_{.25}, \bar{a}_{.5})$	0.48	0.11	0.20	0.16	0.06
$(\bar{a}_{.5}, \bar{a}_{.75})$	0.36	0.06	0.16	0.24	0.18
$(\bar{a}_{.75}, \bar{a}_{1})$	0.20	0.01	0.05	0.13	0.61

Source: Bordon and others 2016.
Note: Programs are classified in four groups according to the average student ability. The first row corresponds to the lowest ability quartile; second row, second-lowest; and so on. Each cell shows the average fraction of new students coming from programs in the *column* tiers who switch to programs in a *row* tier in response to a marginal nonpeer quality improvement in the latter. For instance, when a program in the bottom tier improves quality, 14 percent of new students come from other programs in the same tier; 18 percent, second-lowest tier; and so on. *Outside option* represents nonselective institutions, nonuniversity HEIs, and not attending college.

The remaining 39 percent of stolen students are the most able students of lower tier programs or of the outside option.

Because of their selectivity, top tier programs mostly suffer "business stealing" at the hands of similar programs, thus remaining somewhat isolated from the rest of the market. Similarly, because of their *lack* of selectivity, the bottom tier programs mostly suffer business stealing at the hands of other bottom tier programs. Yet the middle tier programs suffer business stealing at the hands of both higher and lower tier programs, and thus face the strongest competitive pressure.[14] Hence, to the extent that there is inefficient entry or program opening in higher education, it is most likely to exist in the middle tier segment.

As a result of the student reallocation induced by improvements in a program's quality, peer ability changes in that program and others, as shown in table 5.10.

When they improve, programs in elite CRUCH institutions attract the highest ability students from other institutions. Table 5.10 shows that when the average program in elite CRUCH institutions improves, its peer ability rises at the expense of other programs because it attracts better-than-average students from these programs. Programs at non-CRUCH private institutions are hurt the most because they lose their most able students, who would have qualified to attend elite CRUCH institutions but chose non-CRUCH private institutions in response to a nonpeer amenity.

In contrast, a quality improvement in nonelite CRUCH or non-CRUCH private institutions attracts students from other programs. These students are less able than the average student in their programs of origin, but more able than the average student in the improving HEIs. As a result, peer ability rises *both* at the improving program and its rivals. This finding is consistent with the fact that, over the study period, peer ability in these programs rose mostly by the improvement of the existing programs.

To summarize, the expansion in Chile relied largely on non-CRUCH private universities—and to a lesser extent on elite universities. Furthermore, it relied mostly on new programs. Programs in the middle tier of peer ability are subject to the strongest competitive pressures. Top-tier programs are most isolated from business stealing pressure on the part of lower tier programs, yet they can inflict much damage on rivals' peer ability.

Table 5.10 Effect on Average Peer Ability When Nonpeer Quality Increases, Chile, 2012

		Rival peer ability		
Own quality	*Own peer ability*	*Elite CRUCH*	*Other CRUCH*	*Private non-CRUCH*
Elite CRUCH	1.984	−0.413	−0.152	−1.736
Other CRUCH	2.579	4.321	2.841	3.268
Private non-CRUCH	2.215	1.386	0.423	3.483

Source: Bordon and others 2016.
Note: Each cell shows the change in average peer ability (in PSU) in a *column* school when a *row* school marginally increases its nonpeer quality using the results from the estimation. A positive change denotes a peer ability improvement; a negative change denotes a peer ability decline. CRUCH = Consejo de Rectores de Universidades Chilenas; PSU = Prueba de Selección Universitaria.

Students Loans and Supply Expansion in Chile

In the previous section we examined the expansion of the 33 selective universities in Chile that participate in the centralized admission system. Yet the whole higher education sector experienced impressive growth in Chile, most of it coming from nonselective universities and from nonuniversity HEIs (that is, technical institutes and professional institutes), which in the previous section were folded into the "outside option" category. This staggering growth was associated with the implementation of state-guaranteed student loans in 2006.

In a paper written for this report, Neilson, Hastings, and Zimmerman (2016) document the growth of demand induced by loans and the supply-side response in terms of new programs. As figure 5.16 shows, the recent enrollment growth has been mostly due to private universities and, in particular, nonuniversity HEIs.

As in Colombia, not only has the expansion brought new students into the market in Chile but it has also altered student sorting across higher education options. Since loan eligibility requirements in each type of HEI depended on income and ability (PSU score), students became more likely to choose the options for which they could obtain loans. For instance, students who did not qualify for a loan to study at a university but did qualify for a loan to study at a technical institute became 30 percentage points more likely to choose the latter.

In response to this demand increase, the number of programs grew from about 7,000 in 2005 to about 11,000 in 2010. As in Colombia, the number of new programs grew the most for the "new" students, for whom the vertical distance between the blue and red lines (figure 5.17) is the greatest.

The Chilean expansion was fueled by greater credit availability. While successful at expanding access, credit availability can have negative unintended effects, as explored in box 5.1 with Brazil.

Figure 5.16 Evolution of Higher Education Enrollment in Chile, 1985–2013

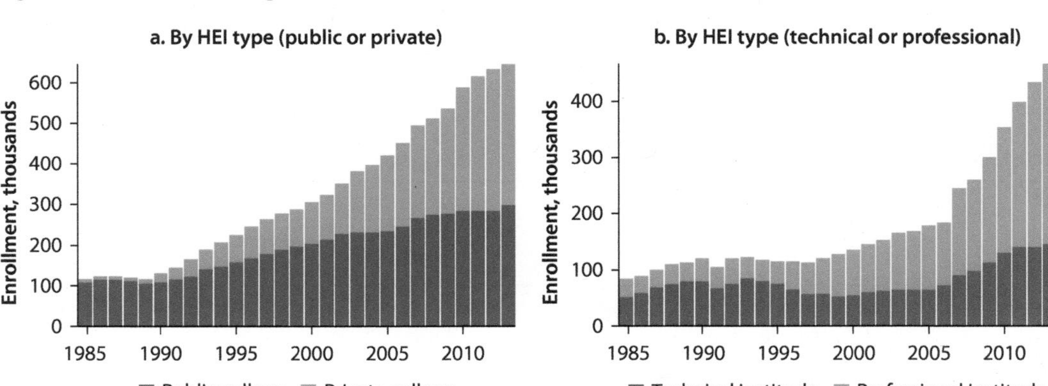

Source: Neilson, Hastings, and Zimmerman 2016.
Note: Panel a includes all types of HEIs; panel b includes only technical or professional institutes (excluding universities). HEI = higher education institution.

Figure 5.17 Evolution of the Number of Degrees in Chile, by PSU Score, 2007 and 2012

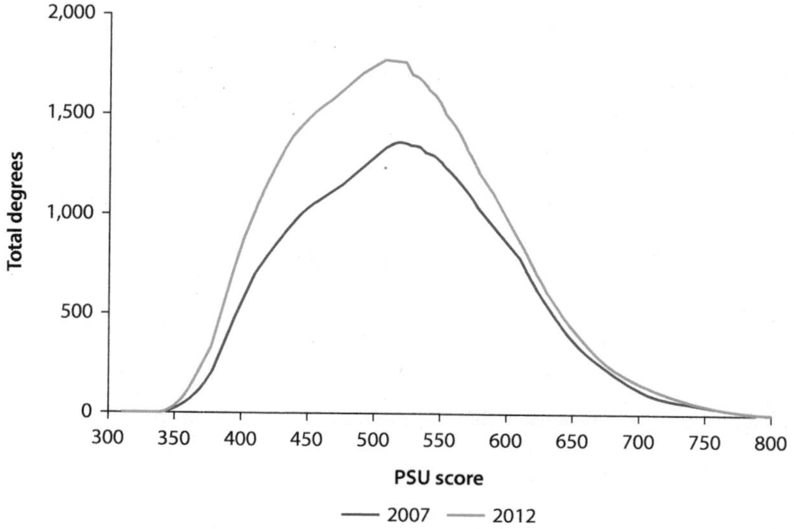

Source: Neilson, Hastings, and Zimmerman 2016.
Note: The PSU is the higher education entry exam. The figure shows the number of programs (degrees) available to students with a given PSU score in 2007 and 2012. PSU = Prueba de Selección Universitaria.

Conclusions

We have studied the role of supply in the recent higher education expansion in the region. Latin America and the Caribbean experienced a large supply-side expansion, measured both by the number of HEIs and programs. Although the role of public and private HEIs in the expansion varies across countries, overall private HEIs gained market share, as did nonuniversity HEIs. Students in private HEIs are more likely to work while attending higher education, and became even more likely to do so during the expansion. Furthermore, both public and private HEIs now reach a larger fraction of nonurban students. While public HEIs tend to attract lower income students than private HEIs, both public and private HEIs have now larger shares of low-income students.

Both in Chile and Colombia, the private sector has played an important role in higher education expansion, mostly through the creation of new programs. Nonselective HEIs, in turn, rely more on program creation than selective HEIs, which rely mostly on program expansion. In Colombia, new programs tend to attract lower ability, lower income students than existing programs. However, the most advantaged of these students enroll in the new programs offered by selective HEIs. Indeed, selective HEIs in Colombia serve mostly high-ability students with their existing programs, and lower ability students with their new programs. Evidence from Chile also shows that HEIs have opened new programs mostly to serve the "new" students.

Simulations suggest that competition is indeed associated with business stealing and negative ability peer effects in some programs in Chile. Because students choose programs based on multiple personal characteristics and program attributes, they have complex substitution patterns. Hence, a quality improvement in one program attracts students away from programs of various peer abilities. While improvements in middle tier and top tier HEIs affect mostly same tier schools, lower tier HEIs mostly attract students who are either not enrolled in higher education, or who are enrolled in lower quality programs. Competition, thus, is particularly fierce among middle tier programs.

Annex 5A: Sources of Administrative Information about Number of HEIs, Programs and Enrollment

Table 5A.1 Sources of Administrative Information about Number of HEIs, Programs, and Enrollment, Latin America and the Caribbean

Country		*Source*
Argentina	Statistical Yearbook, 1999–2000, 2013. National Center of Information and Education Quality Evaluation, Ministry of Education.	Anuario Estadístico 1999–2000, 2013 Dirección Nacional de Información y Evaluación de la Calidad Educativa Estadísticas Universitarias Argentinas Ministerio de Educación Secretaría de Políticas Universitarias
Bolivia	Guide to Universities of Bolivia, 2011. National Statistical Institute. Ministry of Education.	Guia de Universidades del Estado Plurinacional de Bolivia, 2011 Instituto Nacional de Estadística Ministerio de Educación
Brazil	DEED, Ministry of Education. Technical Overview of the Higher Education Census, 2002, 2010, 2013.	DEED Ministerio de Educação Resumo Técnico Censo da Educação Superior 2002, 2010, 2013
Chile	Center for Research, Ministry of Education. Higher Education, National Council of Education. Education Statistics Reports 2008, 2010.	Centro de Estudios, Ministerio de Educación Educación Superior, Consejo Nacional de Educación Informes Estadísticas de la Educación 2008, 2010
Colombia	National Information System of Higher Education, SNIES. Ministry of Education.	Ministerio de Educación Sistema Nacional de Información de la Educación Superior, SNIES
Costa Rica	State of Education 2005, 2015. State of the Nation Program.	Estado de la Educación 2005, 2015 Programa Estado de la Nación
Dominican Republic	General Statistical Reports of Higher Education, 2006/09, 2010–2011. Ministry of Education, Science and Technology.	Informe General sobre Estadísticas de Educación Superior, 2006/09, 2010–2011 Ministerio de Educación Superior, Ciencia y Tecnología
Ecuador	Data provided by the Office of Higher Education, Science, Technology and Innovation.	Data provided by the Secretaría de Educación Superior, Ciencia, Tecnología e Innovación Original Source: SNIESE del Ecuador
Guyana	Strategic Plan 2009–12 University of Guyana	Strategic Plan 2009–12 University of Guyana

table continues next page

Table 5A.1 Sources of Administrative Information about Number of HEIs, Programs, and Enrollment, Latin America and the Caribbean *(continued)*

Country		*Source*
Jamaica	Tertiary Education in Jamaica: Identifying barriers to the performance of the sector trough the assessment of finance and governance policies and practices. Kosaraju et al (2015)	Tertiary Education in Jamaica: Identifying barriers to the performance of the sector trough the assessment of finance and governance policies and practices. Kosaraju et al (2015)
Mexico	Public Education Secretary. Interactive System of Education Statistical Information.	Secretaría de Educación Pública Sistema Interactivo de Consulta de Estadística Educativa
Panama	Education Statistics 2002, 2013. National Institute of Statistics and Census.	Contraloría General de la República de Panamá Estadísticas Educativa 2002, 2013 Instituto Nacional de Estadística y Censo
Paraguay	Higher Education Statistics, 2nd Edition. Ministry of Education and Culture.	Datos sobre la Educación Superior, 2da Edición, Abril 2012 Ministerio de Educación y la Cultura
Peru	Statistics of Education Quality ESCALE. Ministry of Education. National Institute of Statistics and Information.	Estadística de la Calidad Educativa ESCALE, Ministerio de Educación Instituto Nacional de Estadística e Informática
Uruguay	Education Statistical Yearbook 2000, 2013. Ministry of Education and Culture.	Anuario Estadístico de la Educación 200, 2013 Ministerio de Educación y Cultura

Annex 5B: HEIs in the University and Nonuniversity Sectors

Table 5B.1 lists institutions that are considered "university" or "nonuniversity" HEIs in each country.

Table 5B.1 HEIs in the University and Nonuniversity Sectors, Latin America and the Caribbean, 2000–15

	University sector	*Nonuniversity sector*
Argentina	Universities	Teaching education institutions, technical-professional education institutions
Brazil	University institutes, universities	University centers, faculties, federal institutes, federal centers for technological education
Chile	Universities	Professional institutes, technical education centers
Colombia	Universities	Technical-professional education institutions, technological institutions, university institutions, technological schools, SENA.
Dominican Republic	Universities	Specialized higher education institutions, higher education technical institutes
Ecuador	Universities, politechnical schools	Technical and technological institutes
Paraguay	Universities	Higher institutes, technical higher institutes, and teaching education institutes
Peru	Universities	Teaching, technological, and artistic education institutes
Uruguay	Universities, university institutes	Teaching education institutes

Note: This table lists the type of institutions that constitute the university and nonuniversity sectors of higher education in each country. SENA = Servicio Nacional de Aprendizaje (National Learning Service).

Notes

1. The evidence of online learning on student outcomes in the US is mixed. For instance, Bowen and others (2014) find no effects, and Joyce and others (2014) find small, positive effects. Figlio and others (2013) find small and positive effects (albeit not statistically significant) for live instruction over online instruction, although the effect is significant (and positive) for Hispanics. When analyzing the relationship between online education and costs, Deming and others (2015) do not find evidence of lower prices for schools with higher shares of online students.
2. A program is considered "new" when its enrollment of first-year students is zero during 2000 and 2005, but positive afterward.
3. Sometimes new fields are an innovation for the system as a whole (as would be the case, for instance, of an institution creating the country's first set of human–computer interaction programs). Most of the time, however, the field is "new" just to the institution, which did not have it before, although other institutions did.
4. To illustrate our counting of programs, consider student type X enrolled in programs A and B. In program A, 30 percent of the students are of type X; in program B, 50 percent are of type X. Hence, student type X is enrolled in 0.8 (=0.3 + 0.5) programs in total.
5. Following the logic of the previous note, the decline is due to the fact that these student types represent a smaller share of the student body in any programs.
6. Real per-student funding in public HEIs fell by about 30 percent between 2006 and 2013 (World Bank calculations based on Ministry of Education's data).
7. Recall, from chapter 4, that these students have the greatest propensity of all student types to choose new programs.
8. These findings correspond to markets located in metropolitan areas. Small sample sizes preclude this analysis for nonmetropolitan area markets.
9. This competition between low-end private and public HEIs is similar to that between for-profit colleges and community colleges in the United States. Cellini (2009) provides evidence suggestive of the substitutability of these two institution types.
10. We define a program's "peer ability" as the average ability of the program's students.
11. To participate in the centralized system, an HEI must have a minimum PSU of at least 500. As a result, these institutions cannot avail themselves of the same strategy as high-end Colombian institutions (namely, to offer existing programs to high-ability students and new programs to low-ability ones). Although programs within an HEI can have different admission requirements, they must all comply with the minimum PSU requirement. Non-CRUCH private HEIs joined the centralized system before 2010.
12. Jacob and others (2013) analyzed college student preferences in the United States, and whether demand-side market pressures explain colleges' decisions to provide consumption amenities (for example, gyms, student lounges, and cafeterias) to students. They find heterogeneous preferences among students. Based on the authors' estimates, high-achieving students are willing to pay more for academic quality than their less academically oriented peers, and wealthy students are willing to pay more for consumption amenities. Hence, selective schools have a greater incentive to invest in academic quality, while less selective schools are more likely to invest in consumption amenities.
13. The simulations assume that programs do not adjust their admission threshold. Thus, they illustrate the effect of enrollment and peer ability if thresholds stay constant.

In equilibrium, however, thresholds would adjust, which would further aggravate the peer ability loss.

14. This is consistent with findings from the United States by Epple and others (2006), who conclude that low- and medium-quality colleges have little market power by virtue of their large number and substitutability. In contrast, high-quality colleges have more market power because they have fewer substitutes and their quality is substantially higher than those of less selective institutions. Hence, high-quality colleges can apply higher markups above marginal cost.

References

Bordon, P., C. Fu, S. Gazmurri, and J. F. Houde. 2016. "Competition and Cannibalization of College Quality." Background paper for this report.

Bowen, W., M., Chingos, K. Lack., and T. Nygren. 2014. "Interactive Learning Online at Public Universities: Evidence from a Six-Campus Randomized Trial." *Journal of Policy Analysis and Management* 33 (1): 94–111.

Carranza, J. E., and M. M. Ferreyra. 2017. "Increasing Higher Education Coverage: Supply Expansion and Student Sorting in Colombia" Background paper for this report.

Cellini, S. R. 2009. "Crowded Colleges and College Crowd-Out: The Impact of Public Subsidies on the Two-Year College Market." *American Economic Journal: Economic Policy* 1 (2): 1–30.

Cellini, S., and C. Goldin. 2014. "Does Federal Student Aid Raise Tuition? New evidence on For-Profit Colleges." *American Economic Journal: Economic Policy* 6 (4): 174–206.

De Mello, J., and I. F. Duarte. 2015. "The Effect of the Availability of Student Credit on Tuitions: Testing the Bennett Hypothesis Using Evidence from a Large-Scale Student Loan Program in Brazil." Working Paper, INSPER.

Deming, D., C. Golding, L. F. Katz, and N. Yuchtman. 2015. "Can Online Learning Bend the Higher Education Cost Curve?" NBER Working Paper 20890, National Bureau of Economic Research, Cambridge, MA.

Epple, D., R. Romano, S. Sarpça, and H. Sieg. 2013. "The US Market for Higher Education: A General Equilibrium Analysis of State and Private Colleges and Public Funding Policies." NBER Working Paper 19298, National Bureau of Economic Research, Cambridge, MA.

Epple, D., R. Romano, and H. Sieg. 2006. "Admission, Tuition, and Financial Aid Policies in the Market for Higher Education." *Econometrica* 74 (4): 885–928.

Figlio, D., M. Rush, and L. Yin. 2013. "Is It Live or Is It Internet? Experimental Estimates of the Effects of Online Instruction on Student Learning" *Journal of Labor Economics* 31 (4): 763–84.

Jacob, B., B. McCall, and K. M. Stange. 2013. "College as Country Club: Do Colleges Cater to Students' Preferences for Consumption?" NBER Working Paper 18745, National Bureau of Economic Research, Cambridge, MA.

Joyce, T., S. Crockett, D. Jaeger, O. Altindag and S. O'Connell. "Does Classroom Time Matter? A Randomized Field Experiment of Hybrid and Traditional Lecture Formats in Economics." NBER Working paper 20006, National Bureau of Economic Research, Cambridge, MA.

Long, B. T. 2004. "The Impact of Federal Tax Credits for Higher Education Expenses." In *The Economics of Where to Go, When to Go and How to Pay For It*. 355–94, edited by C. Hoxby. University of Chicago Press, Chicago, IL

Neilson, C., J. Hasting, S. Zimmerman. 2016. "Student Loan Policy and Higher Education Markets: Preliminary Evidence from Chile." Background paper for this report.

Salto, D. J. 2014. "Brazil: A For-Profit Giant." *International Higher Education* 74: 21–22.

Kosaraju, S., Marmolejo, F., and Nannyonjo, H. 2015. "Tertiary Education in Jamaica: Identifying Barriers to the Performance of the Sector through the Assessment of Finance and Governance Policies ans Practices." World Bank, Washington, DC.

CHAPTER 6

The Current Landscape of Policies and Institutions for Higher Education

Javier Botero Álvarez

Abstract

This chapter describes the landscape of institutional arrangements prevailing in higher education in the region. Governments have powerful instruments to steer the system through regulation, quality control, and assurance, and special financial instruments. The level of development of these instruments in the region is discussed. Three aspects of the governance of higher education systems are described for the region: distribution of authority, function allocation, and system coordination. A brief discussion follows of the comprehensive reforms undertaken in Ecuador and Peru. Most of the information in this chapter is based on a survey made by the World Bank to the higher education leading authorities (Box 6.1), presented in detail in annex 6, tables 6A.1, 6A.2, and 6A.3. The survey was answered by 25 out of 32 countries.

Vision for Higher Education

A vision of a higher education system serves as a guide for its steering. It summarizes the aspirational description of what a higher education system would like to achieve or accomplish in the long term (World Bank 2015). Developing this vision involves answering major questions, such as the following:

- What is higher education for?
- Who can be trusted to provide higher education, and how?
- What is the role, if any, of the private sector and the community?
- What are the principal goals that it should achieve?
- What targets should be set in terms of enrollment, retention, and graduation in higher education?
- How will these targets be achieved: by what form of institution, by what mode, and over what time?

Box 6.1 Survey to Higher Education Leading Authorities in Latin America and the Caribbean

A survey to leading governmental authorities in all countries of the region was conducted to gather cross-country data on aspects not normally captured in existing datasets (for example, household surveys and United Nations Educational, Scientific and Cultural Organization [UNESCO] EduStats), including, among others, governance arrangements. The survey was answered by 25 countries. No responses were received from Bolivia, Cuba, Panama, Honduras, and Nicaragua (see tables 6A.1, 6A.2, and 6A.3 in annex 6 for participation information).

The survey was conducted during May and September 2015, using a web-based platform. The more than 200 questions were organized around the following themes:

- Functions and structure of leading higher education authority
- Structure of the higher education system
- Legal framework of higher education
- Engagement with other levels of education and with other sectors
- Data collection, analysis, and dissemination
- Planning and vision of the higher education sector
- Quality assurance (QA) for higher education
- Financing of higher education
- Admissions processes in HEIs
- Autonomy of HEIs

Note that the survey was a snapshot with no time series of evolution of the variables. It presents the point of view of the higher education leading authority, not other stakeholders, and there was no fact-checking, other than—in some cases—sending it to government authorities for comment.

This vision is shaped primarily by a country's legal framework and, if existing, long-term strategy. Answers to the first three questions are usually found in the regulatory framework, either at the constitutional or legal levels. Answers to the last three questions are obtained through strategic planning, an important (but frequently cumbersome) consultative process commonly led by the leading higher education authority. However, historical reasons, mainly related to autonomy and academic freedom, may prevent leading authorities in higher education to lead these processes. Figure 6.1 indexes and visually represents the strength of planning and long-term vision for the countries in the region. This index is calculated based on a normalization of the answers to six question of the World Bank survey related to long term planning, participation, and follow up (see box 6.1 and tables in annex 6). It is worth noticing that in 9 countries of the region (Argentina, Costa Rica, Ecuador, Guyana, Suriname, Uruguay, Barbados, Grenada, Jamaica and St. Vincent and the Grenadines) the higher education leading authority does not participate in long term strategic planning or the process does not exist in the country.

Figure 6.1 Index of Strength of Planning and Long-Term Vision, Latin America and the Caribbean, May and September 2015

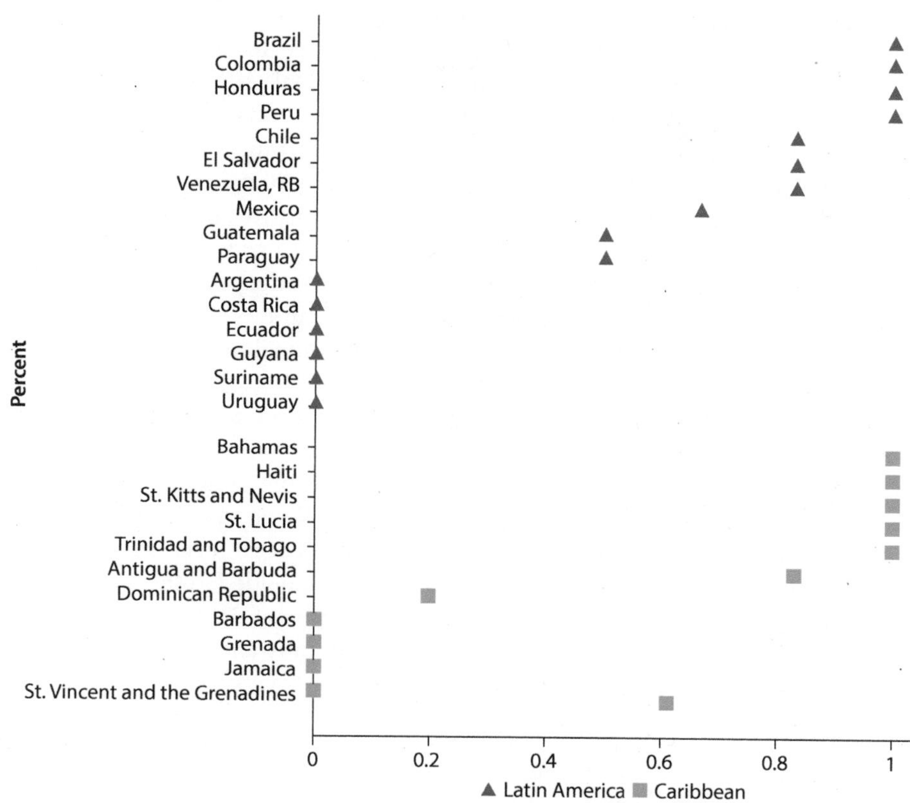

Source: World Bank 2015.
Note: World Bank survey was sent to countries' higher education authorities, May and September 2015. The index is calculated by normalizing the answers to the survey corresponding to the themes of planning and vision.

Governments have successfully managed to engage stakeholders outside of government in planning and decision making. Participation of higher education stakeholders in long-term strategic planning is important for long-term vision and planning to be adopted and implemented by the sector. Governments have been good at harnessing participation of various stakeholders in the higher education system. World Bank survey results show a high participation of nongovernment entities (92 percent) and stakeholders (85 percent) in long-term planning on higher education, especially university presidents (83 percent), students (58 percent), administrative personnel (58 percent), and professors (50 percent).

System Steering through Regulatory Framework and Special Financing Mechanisms

There are two ways commonly used by governments to steer a higher education system: (a) hard steering by establishing and enforcing a regulatory framework, and (b) soft steering by special financing mechanisms.

Role of Regulation: Hard Steering Instrument

The regulatory framework sets the rules in higher education policy making. A regulatory framework considers the set of constitutional and legal norms and organizational arrangements that a state has in place to assure an adequate provision of higher education in a country (World Bank 2015). The main purpose of the regulatory framework is to protect the interests of all higher education stakeholders, especially students and society, through the proper use of public funds and a guarantee of professional suitability of graduates. The overall regulatory framework defines the context in which institutions of higher education operate, stating eligibility of public and private providers for entrance into the higher education sector, certification, and other regulatory requirements for operations (Fielden 2008). Regulatory frameworks usually include elements of governance, financing, QA, and institutional arrangements within the government.

The framework's constitutional limitations and regulatory depth inversely shape the government's capacity to affect and reform the system. The level at which the regulatory framework is set up and the degree of detail that it establishes determine in most part the flexibility of the system. Very detailed regulation or much of the regulation at the constitutional or legal levels make it more difficult to reform. Some aspects that are commonly included in the constitution refer to higher education as a public good or fundamental right or as a public or social service (see figure 6.2) and the degree of autonomy and academic freedom of higher education institutions (see figure 6.3).

Figure 6.2 Number of Countries Where Higher Education Is Considered a Fundamental Right, a Public Service, or a Social Service, Latin America and the Caribbean, May and September 2015

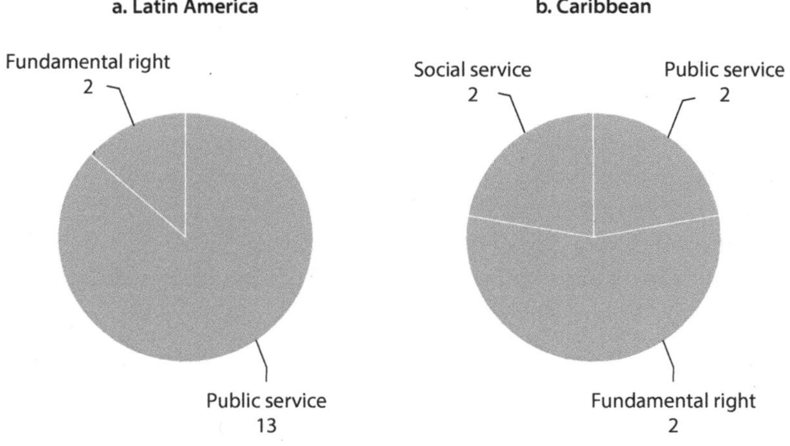

Source: World Bank 2015.
Note: World Bank survey was sent to countries' higher education authorities, May and September 2015. Data are from 15 countries in Latin American and 9 countries in the Caribbean.

Figure 6.3 Number of Countries Guaranteeing HEI Autonomy by the Constitution or by Law, Latin America and the Caribbean, May and September 2015

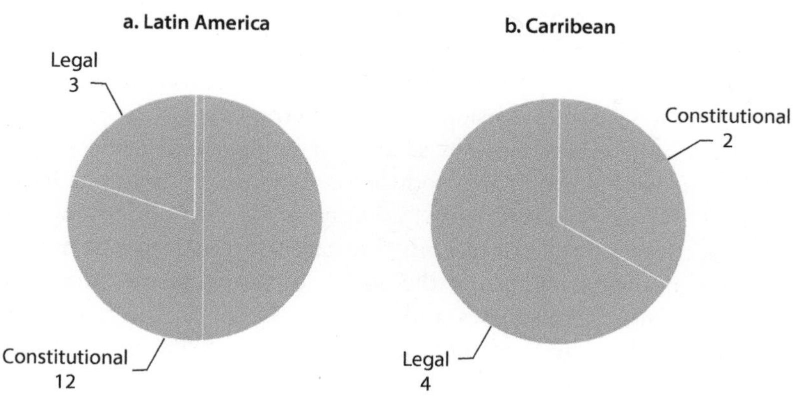

Source: World Bank 2015.
Note: World Bank survey was sent to countries' higher education authorities, May and September 2015. Data are from 15 countries in Latin American and 6 countries in the Caribbean. HEI = higher education institution.

Defining higher education as a fundamental right or a public good is widespread in Latin America but not in the Caribbean. The decision to declare higher education as a fundamental right has profound consequences. These consequences are far-reaching in terms of

- **Financing.** Public goods or fundamental rights may be considered free for all, at least in public institutions
- **Selectivity in admissions.** A public good or fundamental right may be considered a right for all, independent of academic merit or readiness
- **Permanence.** Independent of academic merit and advances
- **Time-to-degree (TTD).** Students may want to exercise their fundamental right as long as they want

Other common regulations refer to (a) the types of HEIs and requisites to create them; (b) program types and degrees (in some cases related to a qualifications framework); and (c) the types of HEIs that can offer different types of programs. Recent reforms in the region tend to increase regulation for both public and private HEIs. In addition, in most Latin American and Caribbean countries, the level and type of steering exercised by governments varies depending on the type of HEIs. For example, in most Central American countries, public universities are highly autonomous while private institutions are more regulated, sometimes even by the public universities. An example of the latter is Guatemala, where the main public university, Universidad de San Carlos, is the entity in charge of granting licenses to and overseeing private institutions.

Tensions between institutional autonomy and state regulation can influence government steering. Autonomy and academic freedom are understood as the principles stating that universities should be independent and exercise full control over their governance, management, budget, curriculum, and what and how they teach or research. These principles have been part of the region since the beginning of the 20th century. It is actually a constitutional right in many countries. This has created tensions when governments try to regulate, since academics ask how an autonomous sector can be regulated from outside. The answer that many countries have produced is that autonomy has its limits, and that it should be accompanied by (a) accountability, since universities manage public funds that they get either from the state or from students; and (b) the capacity of a government to assure the quality of the programs offered, for the sake of the students, the graduates, and society.

Accountability measures are not easy to implement. They aim at reducing the information asymmetry that exists in the sector by publicizing information related to HEIs on (a) inputs (for example, public and private funds received, disaggregated budgets, number and academic level of faculty, number of administrative staff, and infrastructure); (b) outputs (for example, number of graduates, research and innovation products, consultancies, and community engagements); and (c) outcomes (for example, level of competence and employability of graduates, applicability of research, and innovation results). Some countries in the region, such as Colombia, enforce public disclosure of information to all public HEIs. Some private HEIs follow the initiative, but only a few. In general, accountability of HEIs is very low in the region, and it is common to use autonomy and academic freedom as a shield to it. Accreditation systems point in the direction of more accountability by making public the degree of quality of an HEI or a program, but they are mainly centered on inputs and are voluntary in many countries.

Autonomy is common in the region but exercised in different ways. In some countries, especially in Central America, full autonomy is granted only to public universities, while private universities and other HEIs are regulated closely. In others, such as most South American countries, the level of autonomy is not dependent on whether an institution is public or private. It may depend, however, on whether the institution is a university (in which case it has full autonomy) or a nonuniversity HEI (in which case its autonomy is limited). In most countries nonuniversity institutions are not autonomous. Technical HEIs in most countries, for example, have their curricula determined by the state.

The participation of the private sector in education has continued to expand, mainly after 1970. Private higher education has a long history in the region. The first universities in the region were founded by the church as "private" universities that then were recognized by the king of Spain as "Real and Pontifical Universities." Such is the case of some of the oldest universities of the region, Lima's Univerisdad Real y Pontificia de San Marcos, and Mexico City's Universidad Real y Pontificia de Mexico, which after closings and reopening became in 1910 the well-known Universidad Nacional Autonoma de Mexico. During the 20th century, the number of universities and other HEIs grew dramatically, especially after 1970, with a large number of private institutions of all sorts being created (for example, universities, polytechnics, and technical and technological institutions). Between 2005 and 2010, more than 1,100 new institutions were created, most of them private, in Mexico, Bolivia, and Brazil, while in Argentina most were public (Brunner and Ferrada, 2011). In all Latin American and Caribbean countries, with the exception of Cuba and República Bolivariana de Venezuela, the number of private institutions is greater than the number of public institutions.[1]

This HEI large expansion was due to a combination of rapid growth in demand and the private sector's greater responsiveness and flexibility to adjust supply. Demand for higher education grew quickly during the last decades, mainly driven by the large increase of high school graduates and by industry demand for higher skilled workers. Private institutions in most countries were more responsive to the growth of the demand than public ones mainly because of two factors: (a) more flexibility to expand supply by creating new institutions or new programs in private institutions; and (b) financial restrictions in public institutions resulting from a scarcity of public funds.

Liberal policies toward private institutions in Chile and Peru led to especially rapid expansion in higher education. For example, in Chile almost 70 percent of students are in private institutions. Chile's regulation, under reform by President Bachelet's government, states that once created, an institution has up to 11 years to be granted full autonomy by Consejo Nacional de Educación (National Education Council, CNED). During this process, CNED closely supervises the institutions, but once they acquire full autonomy, they are free to open new programs and new campuses all over Chile. During 2000 and 2010 the number of branches of private universities increased from 55 to 148.[2] This situation permitted a large expansion but perhaps at the cost, in many cases, of lowering quality.

Peru has a similar situation to expansion as Chile. The number of private universities between 1995 and 2010 increased by 124 percent (in 2011 there were 94 private universities: 46 fully authorized, 29 provisionally authorized, and 19 under implementation), while the public ones increased only by 25 percent. This dramatic increase does not count the number of subsidiaries and decentralized campuses that universities could create without much government oversight. At the same time, the number of nonuniversity institutions—*instituciones de educación superior tecnológica* (higher education technological institutes); institutes of pedagogical higher education (higher education pedagogical institutes); and institutes of arts (art institutes)—grew exponentially to 1,133. Of these, 649 of them were private, with even less quality control.[3]

The region has a large variety of private HEIs. An important aspect that regulatory frames define are the types of private HEIs that may exist. The following are the most common types:

- Nonprofit private universities that receive public funds only indirectly through research grants, student loans, tax exemptions, or consultancy, and charge tuition to students. These exist in most countries in the region, with the exception of Cuba.
- Nonprofit private universities that receive public funds directly from the government and charge tuition. These universities also receive public funds indirectly. They have full autonomy. Examples of these are the so-called "traditional universities" in Chile and Ecuador.
- Nonprofit nonuniversity HEIs that receive public funds indirectly. They charge tuition and their autonomy is limited. The region has a large variety of these. Some examples are: *institutos profesionales* (professional institutes) and professional education centers in Chile; university institutions, technological institutions, and technical institutions in Colombia; technological institutions, pedagogical institutions, and institutes for the arts in Peru.
- For-profit private universities and nonuniversity institutions that receive public funds indirectly (for example, research grants and student loans) and don't pay corporate taxes. These exist in Peru, Paraguay, Panama, and Brazil.
- For-profit private universities and nonuniversity institutions that receive public funds indirectly (for example, research grants and student loans), but pay corporate taxes. (found in Mexico, Chile, Costa Rica, and Honduras)

Having a large number of private providers is not a problem by itself. It becomes a problem only when there is no effective regulation that guarantees the quality of the programs. Without proper regulation, some private providers, especially those that are for-profit and therefore have to respond to their stakeholders or owners, may tend to maximize profit at the cost of quality and relevance. This situation has made many countries take stricter measures and strengthen or create new quality assurance systems (QAS). Such is the case in Ecuador and Peru, which recently passed higher education laws; and in Chile and Colombia, which are in the process of reforming their QAS.

On the other side, excessively strict regulation may hinder the capacity of the system to respond to the needs of industry and society. Approval processes may become too complex and laborious with duplication of functions and inefficiencies in use of resources—increasing the risk of corruption. A sensible equilibrium between regulation and autonomy—accompanied by accountability and efficiency in the processes and use of information, and capacity building at the institutional level—may promote continuous improvement of higher education in the region.

Quality Systems

Quality systems (QS) seek to guarantee the quality and pertinence of the system. QS are established by governments to guarantee the quality of the higher education supply with mainly two related purposes. The first is to protect the students who are spending precious years of their youth preparing themselves for a productive life. The purpose of the QS is then to guarantee that students' time, effort, and other resources invested are fruitful. The second purpose is to guarantee employers—and society—competent graduates. QS therefore function as safeguards and consumer protection mechanisms, especially given the large increase of the number and type of providers.

QS may be set up in different ways. The most commonly used in the region are composed of two subsystems: quality control and QA.

Quality Control

Licensing processes, which establish minimum standards for operation, are almost ubiquitous in the region. Quality control systems in higher education have two main purposes: first, to guarantee minimum or basic quality standards of institutions and programs. To this end, countries have established a licensing process for higher education programs and institutions. A governmental entity, either within the Ministry of Education or independently, defines a set of standards—usually with the academic sector—that have to be complied by institutions or programs to operate. The licensing process mainly verifies inputs and processes, and in many countries is based only on documents.

All Latin American and Caribbean countries, with the exemption of Guatemala, St. Lucia, Grenada, the Bahamas, St. Kitts and Nevis, Guyana, and Haiti, have some sort of licensing process for programs or institutions. Duration of licenses vary in the region. In the region, 66 percent of the countries grant program licenses for a determined duration of time, while 34 percent do it permanently; for institutions, the proportions are 44 percent and 66 percent, respectively. In the Caribbean the duration of the licenses is usually shorter.

The second purpose of quality control systems is to oversee normative, financial (for example, nonprofit compliancy), and administrative aspects of higher education. The overseeing duties are usually accomplished by a division within the higher education authority or by an independent entity. These administrative units also take and process complaints and act as mediators in student or staff conflicts with the HEI when the case is not for the general judiciary system. In the last few years, several countries have created or strengthened superintendencies or similar entities that assume these responsibilities. For example, Peru and Ecuador have higher education superintendencies as a result of recent reforms, and Chile and Colombia are in the planning stages.

Quality Assurance

QA in higher education is necessary to assess, maintain or improve the quality of HEIs and programs. It differs from quality control in that the purpose of QA goes beyond the verification of basic or minimum standards and has to do more with assessing and improving quality. Sometimes "quality control" and "QA" are combined and called "QAS," analogous to what we called "quality systems." We prefer to separate quality control and QA to present the differences among countries more clearly.

Box 6.2 System Oversight: Superintendencies in Latin America

The following countries have provided the first examples in the region for autonomous bodies to oversee the higher education system.

Peru. The Superintendencia Nacional de Educación Superior Universitaria (University Higher Education National Superintendence, SUNEDU) was created within the major University Law (30220) of 2014. With technical, functional, fiscal, and administrative autonomy, it is still part of the Ministry of Education. Its main goals are the licensing of institutions and programs, auditing and oversight of the system's quality (with powers to determine and sanction irregularities). It is also responsible for a biannual report on the state of the system, with rankings of national universities. The confirmation of this body received especially vocal opposition from the university community and its authorities, many of which refused to comply with the new institution.

Colombia. The Superintendencia de Educación Superior was created through the Law 124 of 2014, but has not been implemented. Analogous with that of Peru, it will be in charge of inspection and oversight of the higher education system, but in this case the Ministry of Education is empowered to intervene in cases of malpractice or crisis. The Ministry can, for example, designate inspectors, suspend programs' legal licenses as preventative measures, or order the creation of budget-administering trusts to institutions failing to comply.

Countries in the region use a range of QA mechanisms. The first three discussed here are accreditation, learning outcomes assessment, and information provision.

Accreditation refers to a public recognition of a certain level of quality of a program or an institution based on a self-assessment and an external evaluation. Accreditation systems in the region began in the early 1990s, led by Chile, Argentina, and Colombia. Only a few countries in the region do not have some sort of higher education accreditation mechanisms, either national or regional.

Accreditation processes are led by independent agencies supported by the government. The number of years for which a program or an institution may be accredited depend on the country, varying between 2 and 10 years. This duration of the accreditation is generally used as a qualifier of the accredited program or institution: the greater the number of years the better is the institution or the program. In a few countries, accreditation of institutions and programs is permanent (Mexico and República Bolivariana de Venezuela), and in a few others, program accreditation is permanent (Uruguay, Honduras, the Bahamas, Paraguay, and Costa Rica). Only 20 percent of the countries use an additional accreditation qualifier, such as different levels of accreditation. For example, Ecuador has established four levels and other countries are following that direction.

Even though accreditation is voluntary in most countries for individual programs and institutions, in some countries, accreditation is compulsory for specific disciplines (for example, Chile and Colombia for teacher training programs). The number of programs and institutions that have been accredited varies widely in the region depending on (a) the incentives given to institutions to be accredited; (b) the degree of acceptance of the process; and (c) how rigorous the process is. In countries where accreditation is compulsory, all programs need to be accredited, of course; therefore, accreditation becomes a quality control mechanism similar to licensing.

Accreditation systems mainly evaluate inputs and processes but rarely outcomes. There is a tendency—influenced by some European countries—to include two additional elements in the QA process. The first concerns the importance of internal QA systems within HEIs, referring to the institutions as the main entity responsible for QA.[4] The QA process at the national level becomes then mainly an evaluation of the institutional QA system. The second element is the importance of evaluating outcomes, especially student learning outcomes. Latin America and the Caribbean should follow this path of incorporating outcomes evaluations if countries want to establish solid and sustainable QS.

Learning outcomes assessments are important inputs for QS. They refer to national or regional standardized student evaluations at different stages. In higher education, the assessment of student's learning outcomes has traditionally been an internal matter for HEIs. However, national assessments of graduates or final year students may be a good instrument for quality improvement and accountability, since they produce comparative learning outcomes measures that may inform policy and decision making for the improvement of education quality. They also may provide useful information for other stakeholders, such as high school graduates, their families, and employers. Assessment of Higher Education Learning Outcomes (AHELO), a recent international initiative led by the Organisation of Economic Co-operation and Development (OECD),[5] and assessments in the United States such as the College Learning Assessment (CLA) and the Graduate Skills Assessment (GSA), have shown the complexities and difficulties of designing learning outcomes assessments (Kim and Lalancette 2013).

The number, scope, and quality of exit- or outcome-based exams in the region continue to expand, even if entrance exams are used only in a few countries. Only Colombia and Brazil have national, compulsory student learning assessments for higher education students, while in Mexico, national, standardized students learning assessments are voluntary. In the Colombian case, students must take the Saber Pro test during their last year of study to graduate. Colombia has been applying the Saber Pro since 2003, but it has been compulsory only since 2009.[6] The test consists of three modules. The first (about 50 percent of the test) is common for all students and assesses general skills (critical reading, quantitative reasoning, written communication, citizenship, and English). The second assesses semispecific skills, meaning those that are common to a wide range of disciplines (for example, scientific enquiry or project management); while the third assesses specific skills of a discipline or reference group of programs (for example, engineering, administration, natural sciences, or economics). Results at the individual level (de-identified) are public. Even though all students are assessed with the same generic tests—and many with the same semispecific ones—comparisons are not made indistinctly among them. Comparisons are made within reference groups, which are groups of programs within which comparing results at the individual or program levels makes sense.

Colombia has had a higher education entrance exam since 1968. Saber 11 is a high school graduate assessment. It is a requirement for admission to any HEI in Colombia. Even though it is not designed as an admission test, many HEIs use it as such. In the last few years, there have been attempts at measuring the value added of higher education using the results of Saber 11 and Saber Pro (see Shavelson and others 2016).

Brazil has had the Exame Nacional de Desempenho de Estudantes (ENADE, National Assessment of Student Achievement), an assessment of undergraduate programs that consists of an exam administered to students who are finishing these courses in HEIs throughout Brazil. The programs are grouped in three representative areas, and each year one group is assessed, meaning that each program is assessed every three years. For the students graduating in those years, the test is compulsory. During this exam, students also answer a survey about the institution. The ENADE results are disclosed as a grade ranging from 1 to 5, which, together with other metrics, are used to calculate an index called "CPC," ranging from 1 to 5. The weighted average of CPC (according to the number of students) is the institutional quality index called "IGC."

In Mexico, the assessments are administered by Centro Nacional de Evaluación para la Educación Superior (CENEVAL, National Center for Evaluation of Higher Education), a private nonprofit organization that designs and implements assessment instruments of knowledge, skills, and competencies, as well as analysis and dissemination of results. For higher education, CENEVAL administers, among other assessments, (a) EXANI-II, an entrance exam for higher education; an intermediate examination for majors of basic science in engineering, which measures knowledge and intellectual skills in the basic sciences (physics and chemistry); (b) engineering mathematics, at the intermediate stage of degree, designed for students who have completed at least 50 percent of their studies; and (c) EGEL, a test of national coverage that assesses the level of knowledge and academic skills of the newly graduated from bachelor's degrees, identifies whether graduates of a given degree have the knowledge and skills needed to start effectively professional practice, and assesses the knowledge and skills in the areas and subareas of training of a given degree, agreed by the corresponding technical council.

The Caribbean Examinations Council is the major provider of exit exams in many countries of the Caribbean, but only for technical, nonuniversity programs (associate degrees).[7]

QAS in the region are still mostly weak, as shown in figure 6.4. The index was calculated normalizing the answers to the World Bank survey regarding the existence of quality control systems, such as licensing, the existence of an accreditation system, HEIs' international recognition, and the existence of learning outcomes assessment systems. Nine countries in the region—four in South America and five in the Caribbean—consider themselves still weak in QAS (with an index less than 0.5), while only seven—five in South America in two in the Caribbean—consider themselves strong in QAS (with an index greater than 0.8).

Figure 6.4 Strength of QAS, Latin America and the Caribbean, May and September 2015

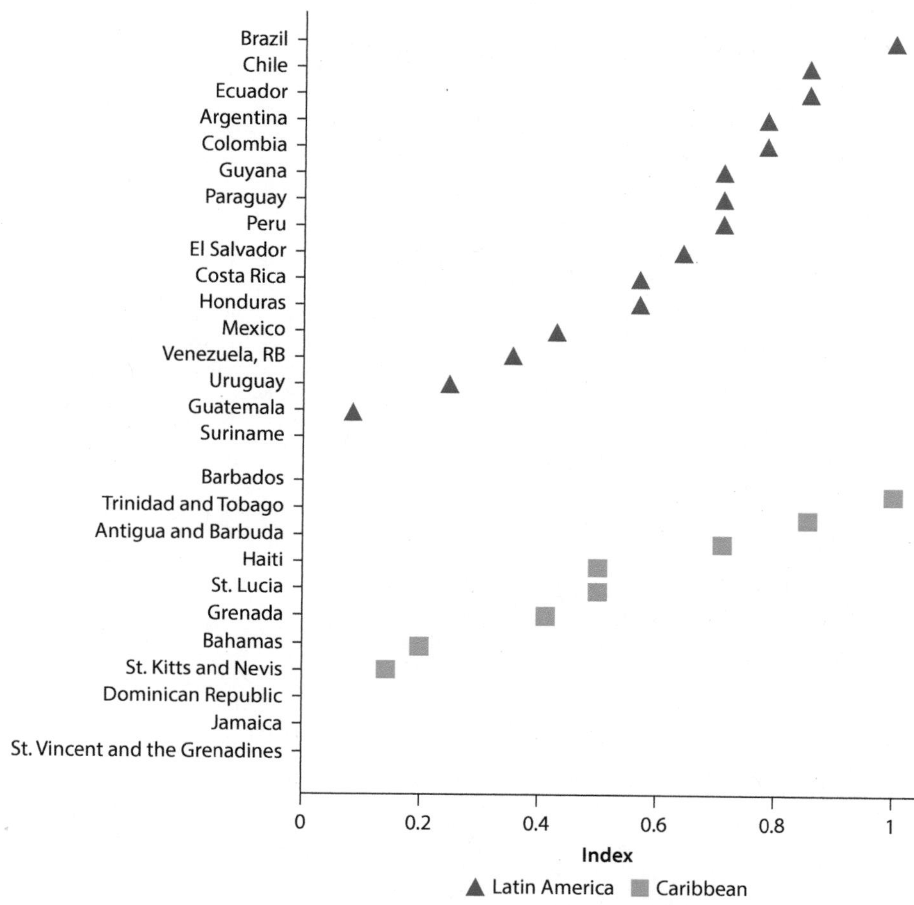

Source: World Bank 2015.
Note: World Bank survey was sent to countries' higher education authorities, May and September 2015. The index is calculated by normalizing survey answers to the theme of quality assurance. QAS = quality assurance systems.

An important aspect in a QAS is the availability of current, relevant information. Collecting, analyzing, systematizing, and disseminating higher education data (for example, the number of institutions and programs, student enrollment and graduation, and faculty members and their highest degrees) are essential for all stakeholders and policy designers to make appropriate decisions.

Latin American countries present strong collection and dissemination systems, while the Caribbean presents more heterogeneity. Figures 6.5 and 6.6 show the strength of information systems in the region regarding their collecting capacity and disseminating information, as self-reported in the World Bank survey. Most South American countries report high strength in both collecting and disseminating information, while the capacity in the Caribbean is far less. The indices were built normalizing the answers to the survey regarding collection and dissemination data

Figure 6.5 Strength of Data Collection Systems, Latin America and the Caribbean, May and September 2015

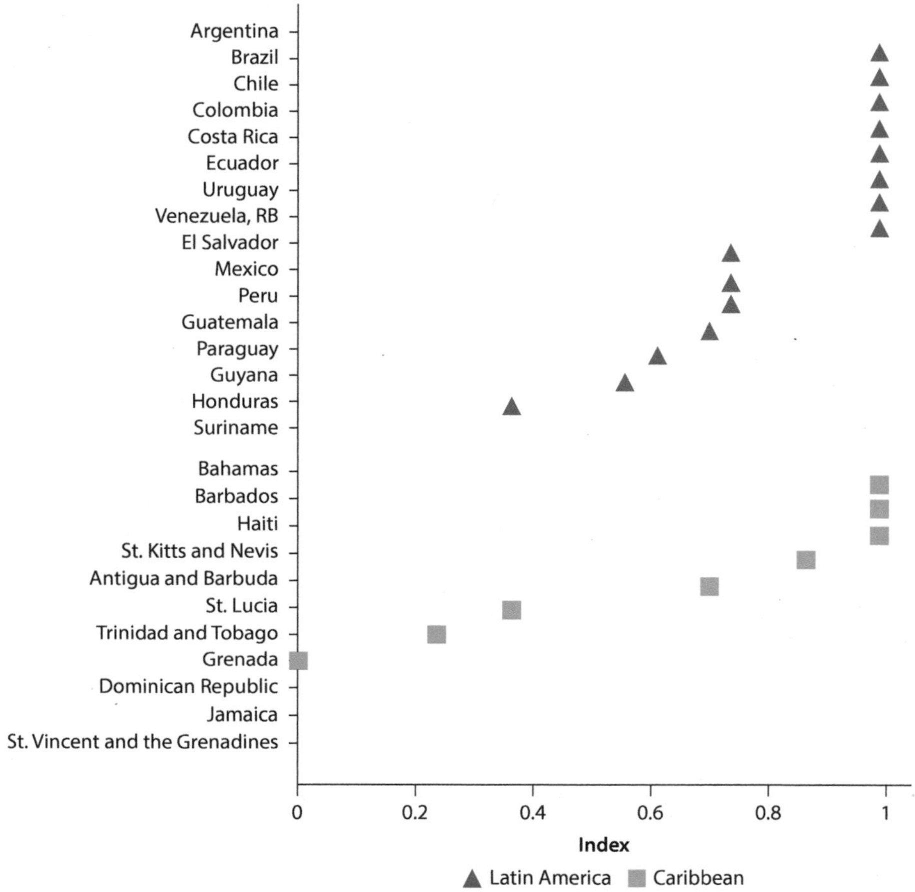

Argentina
Brazil
Chile
Colombia
Costa Rica
Ecuador
Uruguay
Venezuela, RB
El Salvador
Mexico
Peru
Guatemala
Paraguay
Guyana
Honduras
Suriname
Bahamas
Barbados
Haiti
St. Kitts and Nevis
Antigua and Barbuda
St. Lucia
Trinidad and Tobago
Grenada
Dominican Republic
Jamaica
St. Vincent and the Grenadines
0 0.2 0.4 0.6 0.8 1
Index
Latin America Caribbean

Source: World Bank 2015.
Note: World Bank survey was sent to countries' higher education authorities, May and September 2015. The index is calculated by normalizing survey answers corresponding to the theme of data collection.

on institutions, programs, students (admitted, matriculated, and dropouts), graduates, professors and their educational levels, and research and innovation results.

Graduate tracking systems help steer the relevance of higher education systems in the region, but few countries have such systems in place. Knowing the employability, salaries, and other qualitative variables of graduates help policy makers and others evaluate the quality and relevance of the programs. For example, Observatorio Laboral para la Educacion in Colombia and Mi Futuro in Chile have been tracking graduates for more than a decade; data have provided useful information for high school graduates and their families, higher education institutions directives, HE authorities and other decision makers.

Figure 6.6 Strength of Data Dissemination Systems, Latin America and the Caribbean, May and September 2015

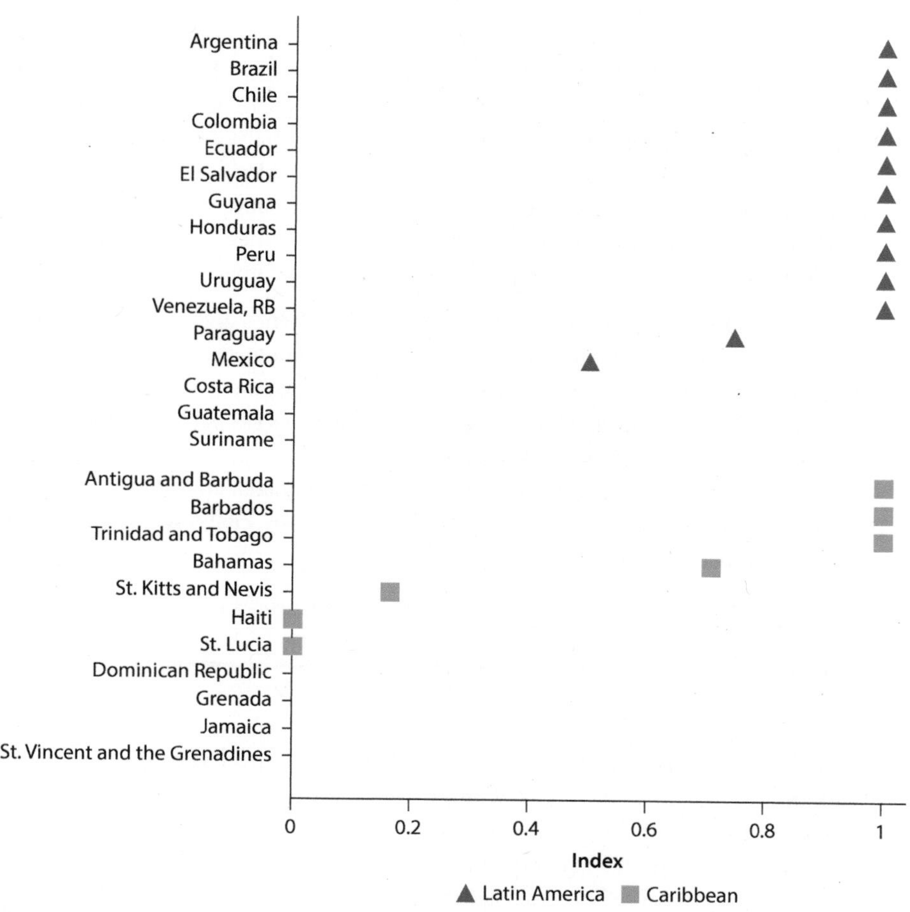

Source: World Bank 2015.
Note: World Bank survey was sent to countries' higher education authorities, May and September 2015. The index is calculated by normalizing survey answers corresponding to the theme of data dissemination.

Role of National Qualifications Framework

National qualifications frameworks (NQFs) establish learning outcomes and skills, increasing system articulation and flexibility. NQFs are set up to show what learners may be expected to know, understand, and be able to do on the basis of a given qualification (learning outcomes). They also indicate how qualifications within a system relate to each other, that is, how learners may move between qualifications in an education system. In a higher education system, NQFs help relate degrees and diplomas with qualifications and skills for institutions to align their curricula and for employers to differentiate among a wide range of degrees and higher education levels.

Box 6.3 Ranking Quality with Local Standards through Colombia's MIDE

Colombia's Modelo de Indicadores del Desempeño de la Educación (Model of Indicators of Education Performance, MIDE) is one of the first and most closely watched national rankings for HEIs in the region. Exclusively focused on Colombian institutions, it seeks to "generate a common language that facilitates the provision of information on the current state of higher education for students, parents and HEI."[a] Founded on four principles—relevance, objectivity, transparency, and replicability—it strives to differentiate its informative mission from any links to resource allocation, QA, or accreditation. Its methodology is meant to be revised; but for the moment, it weights different dimensions of quality based on indicators of the following:

- **Institutions (20 percent).** Attendance (10 percent: permanence and generation of own resources) and internationalization (10 percent: English and international coauthoring)
- **Students (40 percent).** Learning outcomes (25 percent: quantitative reasoning, critical reading, and specific competencies) and graduation outcomes (15 percent: employability, exit salaries, and postgraduate degree insertion)
- **Faculty (40 percent).** Teaching (20 percent: student–faculty relations, faculty with post-graduate degrees or PhDs) and research (20 percent: articles, citations, patents, artistic works, number of researchers)

a. Ministerio de Educación Nacional, Colombia, 2014, http://www.colombiaaprende.edu.co/html/micrositios/1752/w3-propertyname-3214.html

Development of NQFs in the region has been slow and led primarily by the vocational education sector. Even though Mexico does not have a proper QF, it is the country that has advanced most toward one through its Sistema Nacional de Competencias (SNC, the National System of Competences), led by Consejo Nacional de Normalización y Cretificación de Normas Laborales (CONOCER,[8] the National Council for the Normalization and Certification of Competences). Colombia established in 2010 the Sistema Nacional de Gestión del Capital Humano (SNGCH, National System for the Management of Human Capital).[9] One of SNGCH's duties is to conform the National System of Qualifications, which includes an NQF. Advances, however, have been limited. The Ministry of Education has established a comprehensive NQF to be completed by 2018 (it will include all education levels). Chile is also developing an NQF. It includes qualification frameworks for specific education sectors (for example, mining and energy) and for specific levels (for example, technical upper secondary and vocational). The current government's goal is to develop an NQF that includes higher education by 2018.

There have been some advances on regional initiatives. For example, the Caribbean Vocational Qualifications Framework for technical vocational and education training (TVET) established the Caribbean Vocational Qualifications on five levels. The qualifications are being used by Caribbean Community and Common Market (CARICOM) countries. Another regional example is the Marco de Cualificaciones Para la Educación Superior Centroamericana (Qualifications Framework for Higher Education in Central America), which uses as qualifications the existent higher education degrees.

Soft Steering through Special Financing Instruments

Discretionary, competitive, and performance financing are especially powerful tools to steer the system. Discretionary funds distributed wisely can be useful instruments for change within a higher education system or institution (Saint 2006). As flexible additions to normal operating budgets, usually distributed by block grants on a historical basis, discretionary funds offer rare opportunities for steering the system. This means that relatively small amounts of additional funds can be effective incentives for steering a system, an institution, or specific parts of it toward strategic goals. Examples of these are competitive funds and performance-based financing.

The region has a long history of using competitive and performance funds successfully, especially in research-oriented projects. A broader use of discretionary funds to steer higher education systems toward quality improvement have been used in Mexico (FOMES, PROFOCIES, PROMEP); Chile (MECESUP, Millennium Initiative); República Bolivariana de Venezuela (Millennium Initiative); Argentina (FOMEC, Progresar); Peru (PROCALIDAD); Brazil (Consortia Program); Ecuador (PROMETEO); and Colombia (CREE, Technical and Technological Improvement Fund).

There are three main benefits of *competitive funds* for higher education quality improvement. First, the competitive factor means that institutions have to prepare a proposal and therefore have more ownership of the project. Second, the competitive component makes the use of resources more effective than other traditional funding mechanisms. Last, there is more space for innovative ideas that otherwise would have been difficult to get funded and implemented (Saint 2006).

Performance-based financing is another way that governments can steer HEIs toward development goals. Universities receive part of state budgets as a flexible lump sum that links budgets with outcome-oriented performance measures (for example, course completion, credit attainment, and degree completion), instead of allocating funding based entirely on enrollment or other historical basis. Chile led the way regionally with performance-based agreements as part of MECESUP in 2006, and the agreements have been used within MECESUP for the Institutional Improvement Plans (Yutronic and others 2010). In Chile, these were the main advantages of performance-based financing:

- Generating a new form of dialogue between universities and the government: a dialogue about outcomes and strategies to achieve them
- Bringing performance and outcomes to the institutional discussion
- Leveraging its own institutional investments or investment from other sources toward achieving the proposed outcomes

Governance of the Higher Education System and Its Institutions

Importance of Governance

According to Aghion (2008) and Albach and Salmi (2011), effective governance is one of the key factors determining the performance of higher education systems. By *governance* we mean, "all those structures, processes and activities that are involved in the planning and direction of the institutions and people working in Higher Education" (Fielden 2008). From the government's perspective, governance includes the legal and regulatory frameworks and the policies and processes aimed at improving effectiveness of the system.

Measuring governance is difficult, but too important *not* to do. Systems Approach for Better Education Results (SABER) has developed a rubric based on a package of indicators on the main elements of governance related to articulation, institutional accountability, and institutional autonomy (World Bank 2015).

Dimensions of Governance

Three elements of analysis will be addressed to better understand and compare the higher education governance in the region: (a) governments' distribution of authority; (b) the function allocation; and (c) the capacity to coordinate and articulate the system.

Distribution of authority. A surprisingly high number of Latin American and Caribbean countries do not possess a high-level authority for higher education. Distribution of authority refers to the importance level and scope of the higher education leading authority, which is dependent on its position within the government and its functional range. The shape of the higher education system and the distribution of authority among its actors depend mainly on three factors. The first is the position and scope of the higher education leading authority. The higher education leading authority in the region is typically the Ministry of Education, which governs the sector through an undersecretariat, a directorate, a division, or several of these units. Table 6.1 gives the position of the higher education leading authority in the region.

The second factor on which the distribution of authority depends is the government system. In unitary governments (those in which most or all of the

Table 6.1 Position of the Higher Education Leading Authority, Latin America and the Caribbean, May and September 2015

Position within the government	*Countries*
Ministry	Brazil, Cuba, Ecuador, Mexico, Dominican Republic, Trinidad and Tobago, Venezuela, RB
Vice ministry or deputy ministry	Argentina, Bolivia, Colombia, Honduras, Paraguay
Directorship	Belize, Chile, Peru
Other or nonexistent	Antigua and Barbuda, The Bahamas, Costa Rica, Dominica, Grenada, Guatemala, Jamaica, St. Kitts and Nevis, St. Lucia, St. Vincent and Grenadines, Uruguay

Source: World Bank 2015.
Note: World Bank survey was sent to countries' higher education authorities, May and September 2015.

governing power resides in a centralized government, such as Argentina, Colombia, Peru, and Chile, among many others), the education leading authority is a national-level ministry. In these cases, as shown in table 6.1, the higher education leading authority is within this federal ministry. In federal countries such as Brazil and Mexico, while there is a federal ministry with a role in higher education, the state governments have distinctive attributions over their local higher education systems.

Lastly, the distribution of authority depends on the level of control of the government: from central control to institutional autonomy. The degree of direct control of the higher education leading authority over the HEIs is a continuum that varies depending on two factors: the decision-making system and the service-provision system. The decision-making system could impose direct control of the higher education leading authority on the HEI degrees, curriculum, admissions process, and personnel. In Brazil and Peru, for example, the technical HEIs have to follow prescribed curricula. In most countries public HEI staff salaries are determined by the central government. On the other hand, HEIs can be completely autonomous—as is the case for universities in most of the region—and multiple stakeholders can be involved in the decision-making process.

The balance between public and private HEIs influences the degree of government control. The range of possibilities goes from higher education fully delivered by public institutions to the full privatization of the higher education system. A higher education system comprised only of public HEIs offers greater opportunities of control to the higher education leading authority (Cuba is currently the only country in the region with such a system). For instance, in Uruguay and Argentina, most of the higher education services are delivered through public institutions. On the other hand, the introduction of market forces naturally limits the scope of the government's action, introduces competition, and places emphasis on outcomes, as is the case today in Chile, Brazil, Colombia, Mexico, Peru, and most other countries in Latin America.

Function allocation influences the steering capacity of the higher education leading authority but varies in the region. It refers to the scope of action of the higher education leading authority, the functions directly managed by this authority, and the way it relates to other institutions that are part of the system. Most leading authorities of higher education are accompanied by several public agencies. However, the number of agencies—as well as how their functions are allocated—varies among countries. There are six essential functions to all higher education systems:

- Defining the higher education sector policy and leadership
- Funding the system
- Establishing QA
- Maintaining accountability and control
- Establishing admission processes
- Supporting science and research

It is crucial to understand how each system addresses these functions. Table 6.2 shows the main functions allocated to the higher education authority throughout the region.

Over time, higher education authorities' duties have become more complex with a wider range of functions. We have seen in chapters 4 and 5 that institutional and student variety have grown dramatically over the past years. The same has happened on the governmental side. Education authorities' roles have been reformed to better integrate and be closer to higher education institutions, and new agencies have been created to manage quality control, QA, information systems, and qualifications frameworks, just to name a few. How the leading authority engages with these other sectors determines its governing capacity.

System coordination. Higher education authorities present robust articulation with institutions in charge of other education levels, labor policies, and science,

Table 6.2 Functions Allocated to the Higher Education Authority, Latin America and the Caribbean, 2015

Country	*Design national policies*	*Implement national policies*	*Planning*	*Implement QA policies*	*Implement dissemination policies*	*Regulate*
Antigua and Barbuda	Yes	Yes	Yes	Yes	Yes	Yes
Argentina	Yes	Yes	Yes	Yes	Yes	Yes
Barbados	Yes	Yes	Yes	Yes	Yes	Yes
Chile	Yes	Yes	Yes	No	Yes	Yes
Colombia	Yes	Yes	Yes	Yes	Yes	Yes
Dominican Republic	Yes	Yes	Yes	Yes	Yes	Yes
Ecuador	Yes	Yes	No	No	Yes	No
El Salvador	Yes	Yes	Yes	Yes	Yes	Yes
Grenada	Yes	No	Yes	No	Yes	Yes
Guatemala	No	No	No	No	No	No
Guyana	Yes	Yes	Yes	n.a.	Yes	Yes
Haiti	No	Yes	No	No	Yes	No
Honduras	Yes	Yes	Yes	Yes	Yes	Yes
Jamaica	Yes	Yes	Yes	Yes	Yes	n.a.
Mexico	Yes	Yes	Yes	Yes	Yes	Yes
Paraguay	Yes	Yes	No	Yes	Yes	No
Peru	Yes	Yes	Yes	Yes	Yes	No
Saint Lucia	Yes	No	Yes	No	Yes	Yes
St. Kitts and Nevis	Yes	Yes	Yes	Yes	Yes	No
St. Vincent and the Grenadines	Yes	Yes	Yes	Yes	Yes	Yes
Suriname	Yes	Yes	Yes	Yes	Yes	Yes
The Bahamas	No	No	No	No	Yes	Yes
Trinidad and Tobago	Yes	Yes	Yes	Yes	Yes	Yes
Uruguay	n.a.	Yes	n.a.	Yes	Yes	n.a.
Venezuela, RB	Yes	Yes	Yes	Yes	Yes	Yes

Source: World Bank 2015.
Note: World Bank survey was sent to countries' higher education authorities, May and September 2015. n.a. = not applicable (fields not filled in the survey); QA = quality assurance.

technology, and innovation (ST&I), but surprisingly weak articulation with higher education agencies at the subnational level. Higher education systems are complex and diverse. They are closely related to basic and secondary education because basic and secondary levels prepare students who come to higher education, and higher education prepares the teachers who teach in basic and secondary education. Higher education systems are also closely related to other sectors (for example, vocational training sector, labor, and ST&I): they share responsibilities, challenges, and outcomes with those sectors because higher education prepares the labor force. How the leading higher education authority coordinates and relates to other sectors and to other education levels becomes an important issue for the governance of the system.

Figure 6.7 shows the level of engagement of the leading higher education authority with different sectors. Notice the low engagement with subnational authorities (45 percent), even though subnational authorities have much to say in many countries, especially in those with a federal type of government.

The quality and coverage of previous levels of education frame and determine the potential of the higher education system, which in turn can powerfully influence other levels through teacher training. Higher education is part of a greater

Figure 6.7 Share of Engagement of Leading Higher Education Authority, Latin America and the Caribbean, May and September 2015

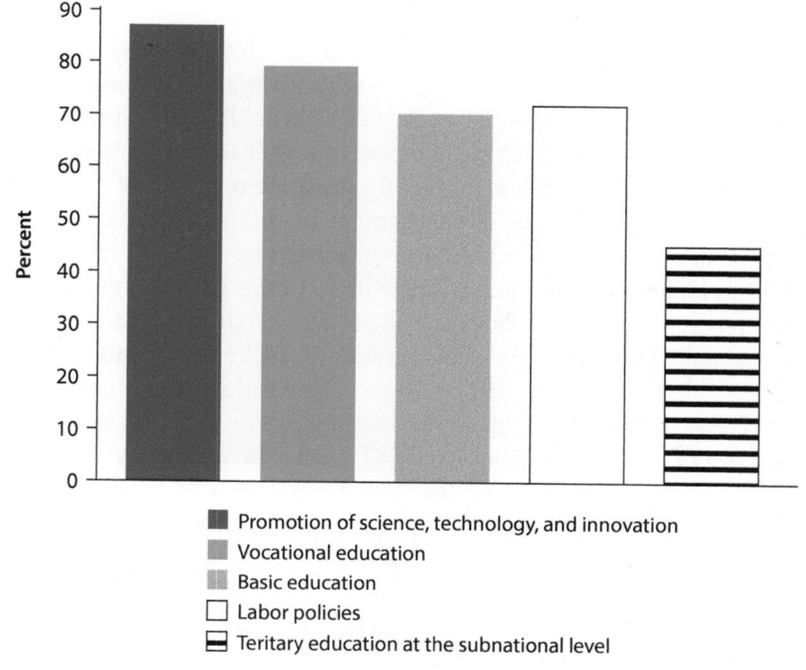

Source: World Bank 2015.
Note: World Bank survey was sent to countries' higher education authorities, May and September 2015. Survey respondents were asked: "Does your entity engage with another entity in charge of...?"

educational system, and it affects (and is affected by) the previous levels. Students come to higher education after 11 to 12 years of schooling, where most of the general competences should have been developed. Academic readiness is an essential factor for higher education success and an important factor for the high dropout rates in the region. Engagement of higher education authorities and HEIs with authorities of previous levels of education could contribute to improve the quality of basic and secondary education. An important element is teacher training. As shown in Bruns and Luque (2014), quality initial and in-service training of teachers is an essential element for the quality of teaching. In general, 70 percent of the leading higher education authorities claim in the World Bank survey to have a good engagement with previous levels of education (World Bank 2015).

Another type of engagement of higher education with secondary education is articulation: strategies to facilitate and increase the transition of students from secondary to tertiary education. One regional example is Chile's Programa de Acompañamiento y Acceso Efectivo a la Educación Superior[10] (PACE, Program for Tutoring and Effective Access to Higher Education), which is aimed at increasing equity and diversity in tertiary education by tutoring (academically and socioemotionally) vulnerable students during their last two years of high school and their first two years of tertiary education. Another is the articulation program in Colombia,[11] focused mainly on technical education at the secondary and tertiary levels.

Of similar importance is the level of engagement with vocational education and the labor sectors. For many high school graduates, vocational education is an alternative to higher education to continue their education and training. The region has a wide range of TVET systems with a variety of offerings reviewed elsewhere (for example, Aedo and Walker 2012 and Llisterri and others 2014). According to World Bank (2015), 79 percent of higher education leading authorities in the region claim to have a good engagement with the TVET sector. Figure 6.8 shows the strength of engagement of the higher education leading authority with other education level and the labor sector.

ST&I and higher education are strongly linked, especially because universities and their research centers are main suppliers of research products and advanced human capital. Therefore, the engagement of higher education authorities and HEIs with ST&I are of special relevance. The ST&I sector in Latin American and Caribbean countries is still underdeveloped. We show in figure 6.9 the participation of different regions in ST&I publications and its variation rate between 2008 and 2012. We see that the participation of Latin America and the Caribbean is low (4.2 percent) compared, for example, to Eastern Europe and Asia, and that its rate of variation is also lower than other regions (0.44 percent compared with 5.59 percent is Asia). Even though a high percentage of scientific production in the region comes from universities, the number of research universities in the region is low (depending on the definition of *research universities,* it ranges between 30 and 45), with about 60 percent of them

Figure 6.8 Strength of Engagement in Education- and Jobs-Related Sectors, Latin America and the Caribbean, May and September 2015

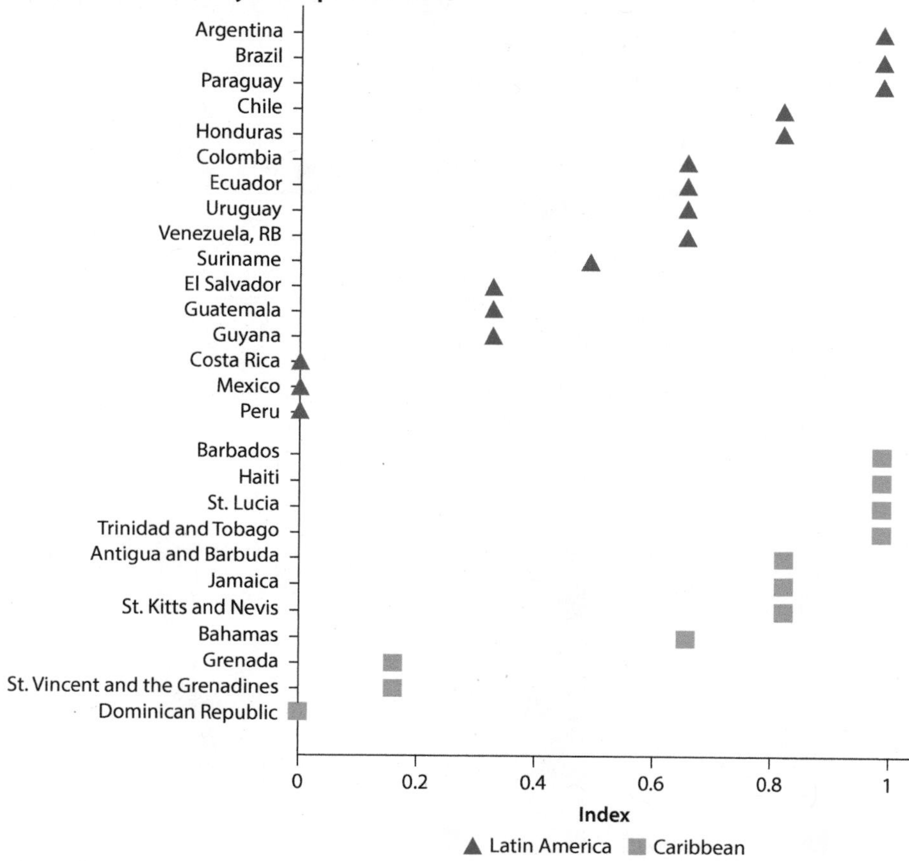

Source: World Bank 2015.
Note: World Bank survey was sent to countries' higher education authorities, May and September 2015. The index is calculated by normalizing survey answers corresponding to the themes of engagement of the higher education authority with the education and jobs sectors.

in Brazil (Altbach and Salmi 2011). However, engagement of higher education authorities in the region with ST&I systems appears generally insufficient, as shown in figure 6.10. Figure 6.11 shows the level of engagement with ST&I and other related sectors (ST&I, health, and other industry-related sectors).

Student mobility within countries—and especially within the region—lags behind other regions (Egron-Polak 2010). Coordination and articulation within the higher education system is also important, especially for student mobility, given the large variety of institutions and degrees, both at the national and regional level. At the national level, none of the countries of the region has a full academic credit accumulation scheme that could facilitate student mobility, especially between nonuniversity and university programs. Implementation of NQF could facilitate this mobility.

Figure 6.9 Scientific Production, by Geographic Region, 2008–12

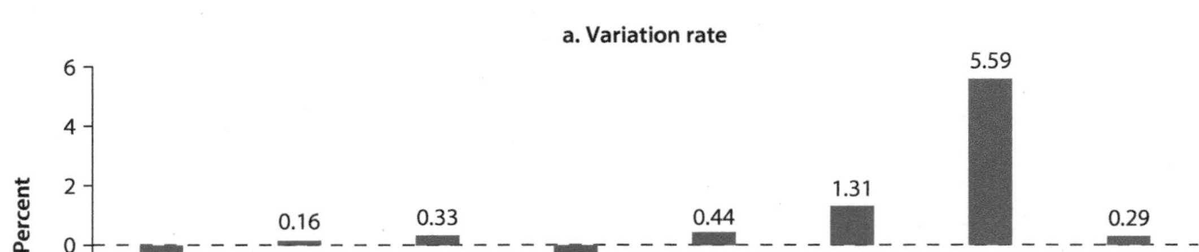

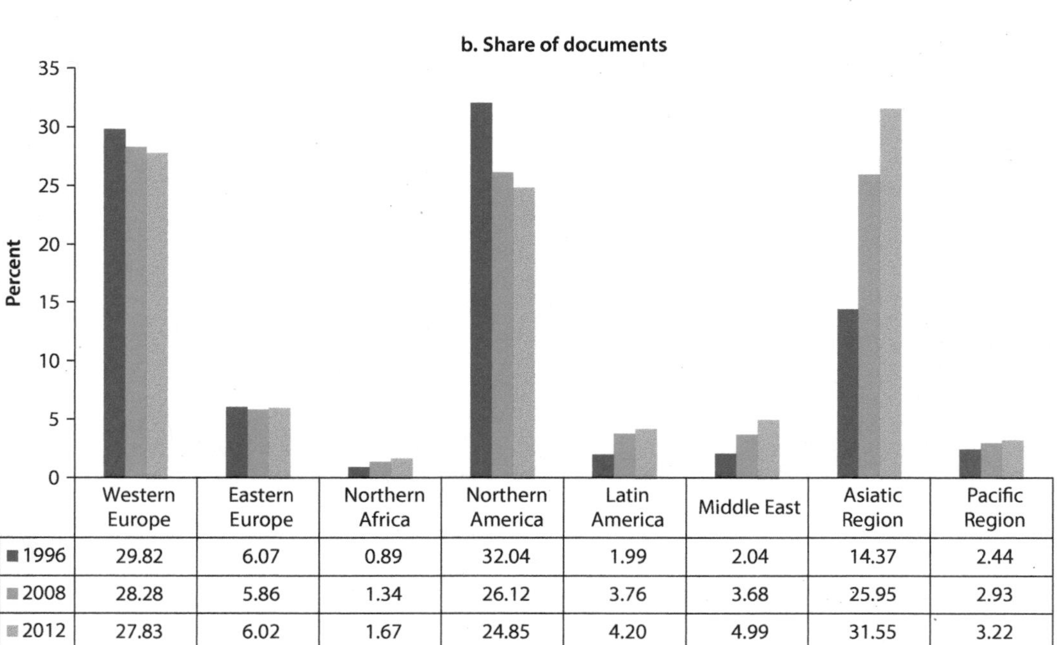

	Western Europe	Eastern Europe	Northern Africa	Northern America	Latin America	Middle East	Asiatic Region	Pacific Region
■ 1996	29.82	6.07	0.89	32.04	1.99	2.04	14.37	2.44
■ 2008	28.28	5.86	1.34	26.12	3.76	3.68	25.95	2.93
■ 2012	27.83	6.02	1.67	24.85	4.20	4.99	31.55	3.22

Source: Adapted from "Principales Indicadores Cienciométricos de la Actividad Científica Chilena, Informe 2014, http://www.informacioncientifica.cl/Informe_2014/" based on data from Scopus and Conicyt 2014.

Latin America and the Caribbean is more behind in the approval and implementation of UNESCO's degree recognition regional agreement compared with other regions (see figure 6.12 showing the results of UNESCO IESALC requesting the agreement). As shown in table 6.3, most of the countries in the region have opted for bilateral agreements for mutual degree recognition.

Figure 6.10 Number of Countries, by Level of Engagement with Entity Responsible for Promoting Science, Technology, and Innovation, Latin America and the Caribbean, May and September 2015

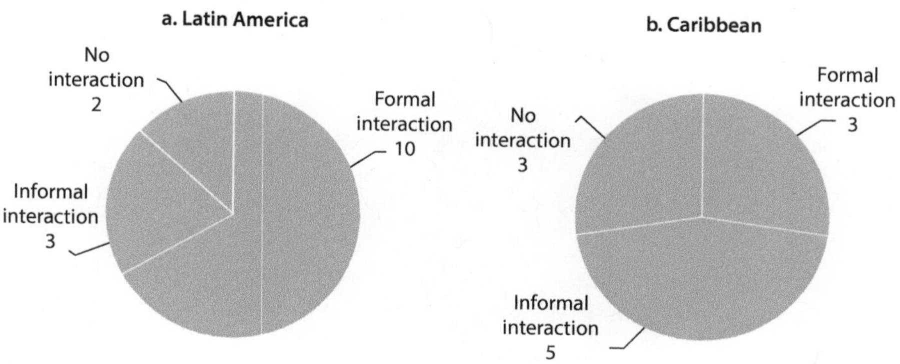

Source: World Bank 2015.
Note: World Bank survey was sent to countries' higher education authorities, May and September 2015. Data are from 15 countries in Latin American and 11 countries in the Caribbean.

Figure 6.11 Strength of Engagement in Sectors with HEI-Related Fields, Latin America and the Caribbean, May and September 2015

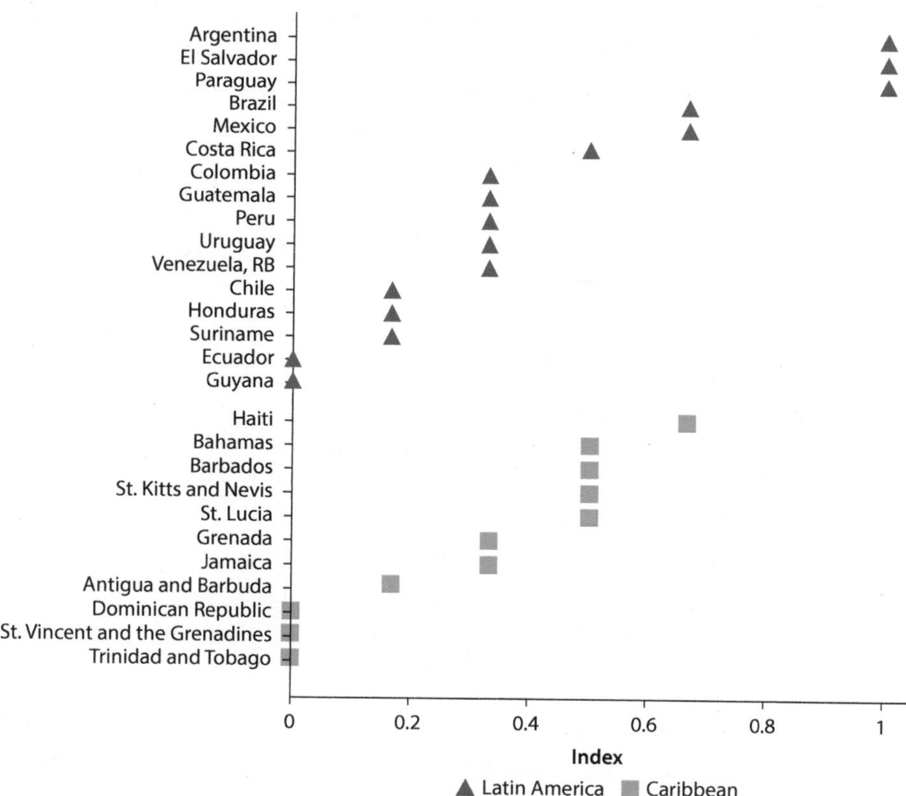

Source: World Bank 2015.
Note: World Bank survey was sent to countries' higher education authorities, May and September 2015. The index is calculated by normalizing survey answers corresponding to the theme of engagement with related sectors.

Figure 6.12 Results of Requests Sent to the Heads of Latin American and Caribbean Countries, May and September 2015

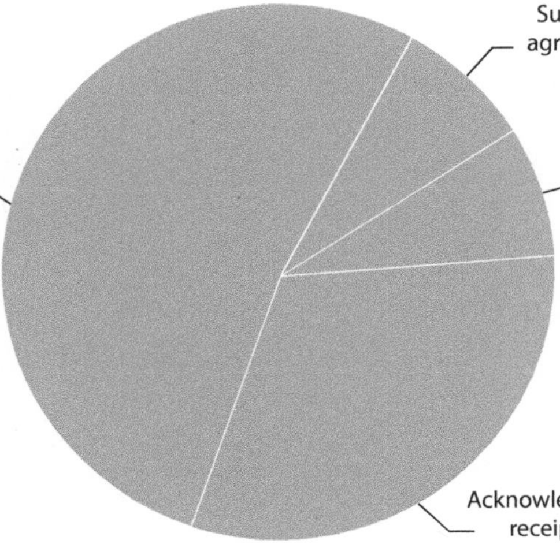

Sources: Private communication; UNESCO-IESALC.
Note: In the pie figure, each slice represents one Latin American or Caribbean country.

Table 6.3 Bilateral Agreements for Recognition of Degrees, Latin America and the Caribbean, 2015

Country	*Arg*	*Bol*	*Chl*	*Bra*	*Col*	*Cri*	*Dom*	*ES*	*Hon*	*Mex*	*Nic*	*Pan*	*Pry*	*Per*
Argentina		x	x		x	x				x				x
Bolivia	x		x		x								x	
Brazil			x							x				
Chile	x	x		x	x								x	x
Colombia	x	x	x							x			x	x
Costa Rica	x							x	x		x			
El Salvador						x			x		x			
Honduras						x		x			x			x
Mexico					x								x	
Nicaragua						x		x	x					
Panama							x						x	
Paraguay	x	x								x		x		
Peru		x			x				x	x				
Dominican Republic												x		

Sources: The information on this table was communicated privately by UNESCO IESALC.
Note: Each "x" in the Table represents a bilateral agreement between the country on the row and the corresponding country on the column while an empty cell represents that no agreement between the countries exist.

Recent Reforms

Reforms in higher education, even when highly necessary, are politically difficult to formulate, pass through the legislative process, and implement. The reasons span from the number and wide range—and often conflicting, interests of stakeholders usually involved (for example, students, faculty, staff, institution controllers, industry, and society in general)—to ideological opposition in some sectors of the population and student and faculty outcry. Colombia, Honduras, Paraguay, and—more recently—Chile have been trying to formulate and implement reforms during the past few years, without much success. In this section we present two comprehensive reforms to the higher education system in the past five years in Ecuador and Peru.

Ecuador

During the past five years, Ecuador has implemented one of the deepest higher education reforms in the region. It started in 2008 with the new Constitution, Plan Nacional del Buen Vivir (National Plan for Living Well), and the Organic Law on Higher Education of 2012. Prior to this, the Ecuadorian government had very little interference in higher education, and public funding was scarce. The system was led by the independent bodies Consejo Nacional De Educación Superior (CONESUP, National Council for Higher Education), which coordinated, regulated, and planned the higher education system, and Consejo Nacional de Evaluación y Acreditación (CONEA. Evaluation and Accreditation Council), in charge of QA, including the creation of new institutions. Between 1998 and 2000, 13 new private and two public universities were created after a mainly documental review process. Of the 71 universities that existed in Ecuador in 2013, 46 had been created after 1996.

The new Constitution establishes higher education as a system that responds to public interest, whose institutions should be not-for-profit, and gives the state the exclusive powers for action, control and regulation of teacher education.

Ecuador's Organic Law on Higher Education establishes a new framework for higher education based on the principles of (a) responsible autonomy, which means academic freedom with responsibility, accountability, and within the legal framework; (b) co-government, which means distributing institutional roles and responsibilities among all members of the university community (that is, faculty, staff, and students); and (c) equity, manifested in free education in all public institutions, conditional on student academic merit. These principles are reflected in private institutions in the sense that tuition is allowed, but should be differentiated based on family income and academic merit. Quality is expressed as the constant pursuit of excellence to achieve optimum production and transmission of knowledge through constant evaluation and improvement. Relevance means that higher education should respond to the expectations and needs of society. Articulation means that higher education is connected with the other levels of education (for example, Pacheco and Pacheco 2015). The Organic Law also guarantees that at least 5 percent of the public budget is dedicated to teacher education.

The Organic Law redefines institutional arrangements: it created a Coordinating Ministry for Human Talent and Knowledge, a State Secretary for Higher Education and Research, a new body for QA, and a new accreditation agency. After three years of implementation, it has had an effect on quality: 14 HEI were closed after they did not satisfy quality conditions. In that time, the government has also created four new public universities.

Peru

Peru has had a large expansion in higher education. In 1996 Peru opened the doors to for-profit HEIs. Since then, Peru experienced a rapid growth of the university sector. Between 1996 and 2012, 59 private and 11 public universities were created. During the same period, enrollment grew 2.5 times. However, this expansion occurred without proper planning and rigorous QA. Control and regulation of universities was under the Asociación Nacional de Rectores (ANR, National Rectors Association), and the Ministry of Education oversaw technical institutions.

With the purpose of better regulating the university sector, accelerating the process of QA and quality improvement, and giving the Ministry of Education a clear role and responsibility, the Government of Peru presented to Congress a law that was approved in June 2014 (Law 30220, 2014).

The new law has redefined institutional arrangements and governance, giving the Ministry of Education full responsibility for the entire higher education sector and creating a superintendent in charge of quality control. It has established standards for teaching and graduation; reformed the accreditation system (still to be finalized by a law for accreditation); and established universal suffrage for the designation of university authorities.

The law has strengthened research through the creation of funds whose disbursement is linked to performance and competitive. Furthermore, the law mandates the existence of at least one research institute in all public universities and encourages private universities to have one, considering it as a positive indicator for accreditation.

Conclusions

Governments have tools to steer higher education systems that, if used properly, can improve the systems' quality and equity. Our examples have shown how countries have used some of these tools—for example, establishing a vision and steering the system through regulation and special financing and governance—and how they are using them. We conclude that large heterogeneity exists on all aspects within the region and that no single solution applies everywhere. For instance, the government plays a leading role in higher education in some countries and is almost absent in others.

The capacity of governments to lead long-term strategy building or to have a common vision that serves as a guide for its development is one example of this absence. In several countries, the leading higher education governmental authority does not participate at all in this process, while in others the government leads it. The regulatory framework sets the rules of the game in higher education policy making. A regulatory framework considers the set of constitutional and legal norms and organizational arrangements that a state has in place to ensure an adequate provision for higher education. Among these, QS play an important role. They have advanced in most of the region, with some heterogeneity. According to the World Bank survey, most countries have set up quality control and QA: a top priority for many governments.

The governance of the higher education system—as one of the key factors of performance—is varied. Few countries (only seven out of the 25) have higher education at the highest level of a government ministry (or its equivalent), while 11 countries have explicit higher education authority, or it is low in the hierarchy. Given the diversity and complexity of the higher education system and the number of sectors with which they have to interact, the leading authorities have become more complex, with a variety of functions to play and a large number of agencies or other entities to coordinate.

A cross-cutting aspect is the importance of information systems. Some countries have strong systems to collect, analyze, and disseminate information, while many others have weak systems. In many cases, even if the leading authorities reported in the World Bank survey that their country had such a system, it is difficult to access it. As explained in chapter 7, information is a critical issue as higher education systems move forward.

Annex 6A: Participation in Survey among Higher Education Authorities, May and September 2015

Table 6A.1 Survey Participation, South America, May and September 2015

	Response level	*Functions and structure*	*Legal framework*	*Engagement and articulation*	*Data collection*	*Planning and vision*	*Quality assurance*	*Financing*	*Autonomy*
Argentina	High	X	X	X	X	X	X	X	X
Bolivia	None								
Brazil	High	X	X	X	X	X	X	X	X
Chile	High	X	X	X	X	X	X	X	X
Colombia	High	X	X	X	X	X	X	X	X
Ecuador	High	X	X	X	X	X	X	X	X
Guyana	Medium	X	X	X		X	X		X
Paraguay	Medium	X	X	X		X	X		X
Peru	High	X	X	X	X	X	X	X	X
Suriname	Low	X	X	X					
Uruguay	Medium	X	X	X		X	X		X
Venezuela, RB	High	X	X	X	X	X	X	X	X

Source: World Bank 2015.
Note: "x" reflects the sections answered by the higher education authority of each respective country.

Table 6A.2 World Bank Survey Participation, Central America and Mexico, May and September 2015

	Response level	*Function and structure*	*Legal framework*	*Engagement and articulation*	*Data collection*	*Planning and vision*	*Quality and assurance*	*Financ-ing*	*Autonomy*
Belize	None								
Costa Rica	Medium	X	X	X	X	X	X	X	X
El Salvador	High	X	X	X	X	X	X	X	X
Grenada	Medium	X	X	X			X	X	X
Guatemala	Medium	X	X	X		X	X		X
Honduras	Medium	X	X	X	X	X	X		X
Mexico	High	X	X	X	X	X	X	X	X
Nicaragua	None								
Panama	None								

Source: World Bank 2015.
Note: "x" reflects the sections answered by the higher education authority of each respective country.

Table 6A.3 World Bank Survey Participation, Caribbean, May and September 2015

	Response level	*Functions and structure*	*Legal framework*	*Engagements and articulation*	*Data collection*	*Planning and vision*	*Quality assurance*	*Financing*	*Autonomy*
Antigua and Barbuda	High	X	X	X	X	X	X		
Barbados	High	X	X	X		X	X	X	X
Cuba	None								
Dominica	None								
Grenada	Medium	X	X	X			X	X	X
Haiti	Medium	X	X	X		X	X	X	X
Jamaica	Low	X	X	X					
Dominican Republic	Low	X	X	X					
St. Kitts and Nevis	High	X	X	X	X	X	X	X	X
St. Lucia	High	X	X	X	X	X	X	X	X
St. Vincent and the Grenadines	Low	X							
The Bahamas	Medium	X	X	X		X	X		X
Trinidad and Tobago	Medium	X	X	X		X	X	X	X

Source: World Bank 2015.
Note: "x" reflects the sections answered by the higher education authority of each respective country.

Notes

1. World Bank calculations based on information on web pages.
2. Statistics from the Ministry of Education, Chile.
3. INEI 2014; see http://www.inei.gob.pe/estadisticas/indice-tematico/education.

4. See for example, "Standards and Guidelines for Quality Assurance in the European Higher Education Area (ESG)" by the European Association for Quality Assurance in Higher Education, the European Students' Union, the European University Association, the European Association of Institutions in Higher Education, the Education International, USINESS EUROPE and the European Quality Assurance Register for Higher Education.
5. See the OECD website, http://www.oecd.org/edu/skills-beyond-school/testingstudentand universityperformancegloballyoecdsahelo.htm.
6. See, for example, the websites of ICFES: http://www.icfes.gov.co/examenes/saber-pro/informacion-general/antecedentes and http://www.icfes.gov.co/examenes/saber-pro/informacion-general/historicos-estructura-general-del-examen
7. See the Caribbean Examinations Council's website, http://www.cxc.org/examinations/cxc-associate-degrees/.
8. See CONOCER's website, www.conocer.gob.mx, for details of the SNC.
9. Document of the *Consejo de Política Económica y Social* CONPES 2364, 2010.
10. See the PACE website, http://pace.mineduc.cl/.
11. See the Colombian government's website, http://www.mineducacion.gov.co/1759/w3-article-299165.html; see also for the specific case on Bogota shttp://www.redalyc.org/articulo.oa?id=26824854001.

References

Aedo, C., and I. Walker. 2012. "Skills for the 21st Century in Latin America and the Caribbean." World Bank, Washington, DC.

Aghion, P. 2008. "Higher Education and Innovation." *Perspektiven der Wirtschaftspolitik* 9 (s1): 28–45.

Altbach, P. G., and J. Salmi. 2011. *The Road to Academic Excellence: The Making of World-Class Research Universities*. New York, NY: World Bank.

Brunner, J. J., and R. Ferrada. 2011. *Educación superior en Iberoamerica: informe 2011*. CINDA, Santiago, Chile.

Bruns, B., and J. Luque. 2014. *Great Teachers. How to Raise Student Learning in Latin America and the Caribbean*. Washington, DC: World Bank.

Egron-Polak, E., R. Hudson, and J. Gacel-Avila. 2010. *Internationalization of Higher Education: Global Trends, Regional Perspectives*: IAU 3rd Global Survey Report. Paris: International Association of Universities.

Fielden, J. 2008. "Global Trends in University Governance." World Bank Education Working Papers Series 9, World Bank, Washington, DC.

Kim, H., and D. Lalancette. 2013. *Literature Review on the Value-Added Measurement in Higher Education*. Paris: Organisation for Economic Co-operation and Development.

Llisterri, J., N. Gligo, O. Homs, and D. Ruiz-Devesa, 2014. "Educacióntécnica y formación profesional en América Latina, El reto de la productividad." SeriePolíticas Públicas y TransformaciónProductiva Number 13. CAF, Banco de Desarrollo de América Latina, http://scioteca.caf.com/handle/123456789/378.

Pacheco, L., and R. Pacheco. 2015. "Evolución de la educación superior en el Ecuador. La Revolución Educativa de la Universidad Ecuatoriana." Pacarinadel Sur [revista digital http://www.pacarinadelsur.com/].

Saint, W. 2006. "Innovation Funds for Higher Education: A Users' Guide for World Bank Funded Projects." World Bank Education Working Papers Series 1, World Bank, Washington, DC.

Shavelson, R. J., B. W. Domingue, J. P. Mariño, A. Molina, A. Morales, and E. E. 2016. "On the Practices and Challenges of Measuring Higher Education Value Added: The Case of Colombia." *Assessment & Evaluation in Higher Education* 41 (5): 695–720.

World Bank. 2015. *SABER-Tertiary Education. Conceptual Framework and Policy Data Collection Rubric*. Report No: AUS9716, World Bank, Washington, DC.

Yutronic, J., R. Reich, D. López, E. Rodriguez, and J. P. Prieto. 2010. "Performance-Based Agreements and Their Contribution to Higher Education Funding in Chile." *RevistaEducación Superior y Sociedad UNESCO–ESAL*, 25.

CHAPTER 7

Going Forward

Abstract

Despite progress in access, equity, and some aspects of variety, quality (as measured by inputs and outcomes) is a source of concern for many students, higher education institutions (HEIs), and programs. To inform policies that might take the region past this crossroads, this chapter recalls the reasons for policy intervention in the higher education market and points to the perils and limitations of higher education policy. The chapter then discusses the trade-offs between access and completion as higher education systems expand. It describes the role of several elements that might prove helpful at this juncture, given our previous findings and fundamental economic theory. These elements are incentives to students and HEIs; competition, variety, and student choice; monitoring, accountability, and regulation; and information collection and dissemination. The chapter concludes with a discussion of the importance of the larger context of higher education, including secondary education and the labor market.

Introduction

Higher education in Latin American and the Caribbean countries is currently at a crossroads. The large, fast expansion experienced since the early 2000s has given rise to a new, complex landscape. Concerned with increasing access and social mobility, policy makers expanded the system at a time of economic growth, fiscal abundance, and a rising middle class. As a result, access grew for all students, but particularly those from the low- and middle-income segments. These "new" students, who were previously underrepresented in higher education, constitute a critical piece of the new landscape, as are the HEIs and programs serving them.

Next to the large equity gains experienced by the system are looming concerns over quality. The rapid expansion of the system, the characteristics of the "new" students, and perhaps the lax regulation of some higher education institutions (HEIs) and programs have led many to question the equity of a system in which not every student gains access to a quality option. Perhaps no better illustration for these tensions exists than the recent student protests in Chile, a country whose enrollment rate mirrors that of much richer countries and that accomplished a tremendous, equitable expansion in a very short time—and where social discontent is, nonetheless, very high.

Given the region's urgency to raise productivity in a low-growth, fiscally constrained environment, skilled human capital must be formed fast and efficiently. An efficient higher education system offers quality, variety, and equity to maximize students' potential given their innate ability, interests, motivation, and academic readiness at the end of high school. In such a system, a student gains access to a suitable option, finishes her course of study in a reasonable amount of time, and enters the labor market armed with relevant skills that make her productive. The evidence we have presented, as well as some existing incentives, suggests that higher education systems in Latin America and the Caribbean might have room for efficiency gains.

For instance, although higher education access has become more equitable, it might still be leaving out some academically ready high school graduates—due, for instance, to liquidity constraints—who are thus unable to realize their productive potential. Meanwhile, higher education systems may be giving access to high school graduates who lack the academic readiness, interest, or motivation necessary to complete their course of study. While a positive dropout rate may be efficient as some students realize that higher education is not a good match for them, the high dropout rates in Latin America and the Caribbean are suggestive of system inefficiencies.

Connecting higher education programs with the greater economic context and the labor market is another avenue for efficiency gains. Low-quality programs, or programs with poor employment prospects, absorb resources and effort that might be better spent elsewhere.

Back to the Drawing Board

At this point, it is useful to recall why the policy maker needs to intervene in higher education, and some fundamental principles that should guide her actions.

Left to its own devices, a higher education "market" will not achieve the social optimum of maximizing each person's potential and meeting the economy's skill needs because of the presence of externalities, liquidity constraints, information-related problems, and imperfect competition. Each of these distortions calls for a different set of policies. Broadly, externalities call for government subsidies for higher education; liquidity constraints call either for government subsidies or for enabling student credit markets; information-related problems call for information provision and consumer protection; and imperfect competition calls for enabling competition through student choice while also monitoring and regulating the sector.

Given the multiple distortions, multiple tools are needed. For instance, it is not enough for the policy maker to subsidize access to higher education; through her subsidies she must enable student choice among HEIs and programs.

The problem, of course, is that removing one distortion can aggravate another. For example, removing liquidity constraints through credit can indeed expand access, yet also invite the entry of low-quality HEIs and programs with considerable market power over a segment of uninformed students.

Sound policy, then, requires a delicate balance of multiple instruments. Not all tools are created equal, though. The ultimate success of higher education policies depends on the behavior of higher education's key agents, namely students (and their families) and HEIs. Thus, a useful criterion to choose among tools is the extent to which they incentivize the desired behaviors and discourage others. The larger the scale of the policy, the more critical this becomes to avoid the type of negative unintended effects studied in chapters 3 and 4.

Trade-Offs between Higher Education Access and Completion

Providing access to higher education is a critical step toward the formation of skilled human capital. We can broadly think of two main access paradigms: restricted access and open access. Restricted access rations access based on ability or financial means, whereas open access applies little or no rationing. Thus, restricted access systems may not grant access to students who are academically ready (for example, because of HEIs' capacity constraints or students' lack of financial means), whereas open access systems may grant access to students who are not academically ready.

When designing their higher education systems, societies typically lean toward one of these paradigms (particularly through their public HEIs). In reality, most higher education systems have some HEIs with restricted access and others with open access. What is critical, though, is that each paradigm gives rise to consequential trade-offs. While restricted access regimes may be viewed by some as less fair than open access regimes, they may have higher completion rates by admitting academically ready students who are more likely to complete their studies, and by devoting more resources to each student. Furthermore, financial aid to low-income, academically ready students can substantially enhance the equity of these regimes.

Open access regimes, in turn, are viewed by many as providing a "second chance." For instance, students who received a low-quality secondary education or who enrolled in higher education relatively late in life because of family responsibilities benefit from open access regimes. Yet precisely by enrolling a greater proportion of less-prepared students, open access regimes may have lower completion rates. Furthermore, because the HEIs attended by these students do not ration entry, enrollment may be too high relative to the HEIs' resources, thus leading to low per-student resources. The ensuing combination of students' low academic readiness and HEIs' inadequate per-student resources can lead to poor academic outcomes. Note that as they raise enrollment, these HEIs need to increase resources to accommodate for the student expansion so as to keep per-student resources approximately constant. In addition, they may need an even *greater* increase to compensate for the students' lack of academic readiness (for example, through the provision of remedial education).

Thus, when choosing an access paradigm as part of its strategy to form human capital, societies must be aware of the trade-offs between access and completion. It is instructive to examine the experience of the United States, where the fraction of high school graduates enrolled in college rose from 48 percent for the class of 1972 to 70 percent for the class of 1992, yet the fraction of college students who completed their studies declined from 50.5 percent to 45.9 percent, respectively (Bound and others 2010).

This outcome deterioration in the United States might have been due to students' declining academic readiness on the part of the students, or to collegiate characteristic factors such as HEIs' declining resources per student and the type of HEI first attended. The evidence indicates that most of the outcome deterioration can be attributed to a change in collegiate characteristics (Bound and others 2010, 2012). In other words, expanding enrollment without a concomitant increase in resources—mostly in open access HEIs (nonselective public HEIs and two-year HEIs)—has been the leading cause of the recent decline in completion rates in the United States.

Given the region's need to form skilled human capital quickly, for some countries there might be a role for the provision of additional support to students who are not academically ready, either through the provision of remedial education, or through other programs such as tutoring, mentoring, and advising. The important point is that—depending on the access paradigm embraced by a country—further access expansion may require additional resources (either from the public or the private sector), at least partly to compensate for the lower academic readiness of the "new" students. While societies may choose to devote such additional resources in higher education, they should remain aware of their opportunity cost—including the improvement of the primary and secondary education system that prepares the future higher education students.

Role of Incentives, Competition, Monitoring, and Information

The evidence we have presented—with incentives in some of these higher education systems—suggests that the systems might not be operating efficiently, and that there might be room for efficiency gains. In moving past the current crossroads, an important role arises for incentives, competition, choice, monitoring, and information.

Incentives to Students and HEIs

Students who receive public funding need incentives to graduate, and to do it on time. Unconditional tuition subsidies (especially when coupled with unrestricted admission) may not accomplish this goal, but subsidies based on academic performance are more likely to succeed.

Student loans may provide even stronger incentives for student performance. To be sure, designing a sound loan system requires decisions about a number of issues. These include financial issues such as loan guarantees, default penalties, income-contingent repayment, and loan limits (especially as related to program cost and prospective earnings). They may also include incentives to raise student performance, such as providing more favorable repayment terms to students who graduate on time, or connecting loan disbursements with a students' academic progress.

Institutions, as well, need incentives to contribute to student success: that is, "skin in the game." Such incentives are not present, for example, when public HEIs receive funding without any kind of accountability. They are not present either when private HEIs receive public funding (in the form of financial aid given to students) regardless of outcomes.

As discussed in chapter 4, higher education finance mechanisms have large-scale implications. Furthermore, each mechanism has distinct fiscal implications. Precisely because higher education finance is a powerful and consequential tool, the design of efficient, responsible, and equitable funding systems remains an important item in the higher education agenda for the region.

Incentives are critical to addressing the worrisome fact that only half of enrolled students in the region have completed their degree by the ages of 25–29 years, and that most dropouts leave their programs at the end of their first year. Of course, these issues cannot be attributed only to the higher education system, since many students enter higher education without being academically ready. These dropout rates may be partly explained by (a) the requirement that students choose a program immediately upon entering higher education (as opposed to taking a set of general classes that transfer easily across programs should the student switch); (b) the scarcity of remedial programs in higher education; and (c) the lack of mentoring, tutoring, and counseling programs. The fact that, in some countries, approximately 10 percent of students drop out after four years into higher education should also call into question the length and appropriateness of the programs. To alleviate these issues, policy makers may consider (a) shorter programs, (b) the awarding of degrees upon completion of a set of requirements (even if they do not complete all the requirements for the program of their original intent), and (c) more flexible programs.

Competition, Variety, and Student Choice

The growth in the share of students enrolled in private HEIs, in nonuniversity HEIs, and in short-cycle programs (documented in chapters 1, 2 and 5) suggests that students value HEI and program variety. Furthermore, chapter 5 documents that students value program attributes such as HEI location and peer composition, and that not all students value all attributes equally. At the same time, returns are heterogeneous across HEIs and programs, as indicated in chapter 3. Thus, promoting variety, and enabling competition among HEIs and programs, can provide students with further choices and help them to find their best-fitting option.

Students, however, need the means to exercise choice, and low-income students often lack such means. Most countries in the region subsidize only their public HEIs, and this practice does not always give students the means to exercise choice. For many students, this practice amounts to giving them only one choice, namely the local public HEI, which thus commands substantial market power. Moreover, most countries focus their funding on university rather than nonuniversity HEIs, which further restricts students' choices.

Expanding choice, variety, and competition brings forth another challenge, namely overseeing the full range of HEIs that may command market power. Of special concern are the HEIs serving low-income, low-ability students, who either pay for tuition on their own or through student loans (and often over-borrow relative to their earnings prospects). This segment clearly deserves special attention from a regulatory standpoint.

While variety and competition expand student choice and can discipline the market, they may not improve outcomes for students who lack the capacity to assess the quality of the various options. To work properly, competition requires monitoring, accountability and regulation, and information.

Monitoring, Accountability, and Regulation

As in other areas of economic life characterized by pervasive information asymmetries, the use of monitoring, accountability, and regulation can improve higher education outcomes. Monitoring on the part of students, parents, and the policy maker can induce greater effort and quality on the part of the HEIs. Nonetheless, monitoring may be more costly for some students than others. For instance, first-generation students and students from low-income backgrounds may lack access to the relevant information or may not know how to process it. Public monitoring on the part of the policy maker becomes crucial in such cases of costly private monitoring (Ferreyra and Liang 2012).

As discussed by Deming and Figlio (2016), it is easier to agree on the need and rationale for higher education monitoring, accountability, and regulation than on the specifics of how to conduct them. If nothing else, these activities should avert negative, undesirable outcomes. They should act as a consumer protection mechanism for students (and their future employers) that enforces minimum standards and that provides the public service of information collection and dissemination. For each HEI, this information should include program-level student characteristics such as (a) percent of low-income students, (b) academic outcomes such as past graduation rates and time-to-degree (TTD), and (c) postgraduation outcomes such as recent graduates' employment and salary. A critical function of public monitoring is to make the information readily available in a transparent, accessible fashion.

Public monitoring is particularly necessary in cases of costly private monitoring, and also when HEIs receive large amounts of public funding or function in a noncompetitive setting. Monitoring is most useful when accompanied by accountability that attaches consequences to outcomes. Yet higher education monitoring, accountability, and general regulation are harder than they seem, largely because not all students pursue the same goals in higher education, and not all HEIs offer the same programs or serve the same students. Moreover, the very design of accountability systems creates incentives for HEIs, the regulator, and the students that may lead to undesired consequences. One such consequence is that public monitoring may crowd out private monitoring, as students and parents who become reliant on public monitoring may no longer see the need to conduct their own monitoring (Ferreyra and Liang 2012).

Powerful monitoring alone cannot improve outcomes. Only when a student has the ability to choose is monitoring useful. Nonetheless, a key input to exercising both monitoring and choice is information.

Information

Generating and disseminating information on programs' outcomes regarding completion, employment, and graduate salaries is key in the new landscape, as is creating a culture in which students and families can expect to receive timely, accessible, and easy-to-process information. As described in chapters 3 and 6, Colombia, Chile, and Peru have already taken steps in this direction.

Even if high-quality information becomes available, some students may have cognitive biases that prevent them from acting upon this information. For instance, students often think that they will perform better than average in the labor market, which is why information about returns' distribution might not affect their decisions as expected. Similarly, when taking student loans, students may not understand the financial calculations of costs, benefits, and returns, or the implications of repayment terms.[1]

Institutions' reputation poses an interesting problem. The reputation of a HEI is often given by the "quality" of its students (for example, measured by their admission test scores) regardless of its value added (MacLeod and others 2015). Nonetheless, there might be institutions with low student "quality" yet high value added that should be known by students as an attractive option.

How can these HEIs signal their quality? In Colombia, for example, all students take a standardized exit exam when finishing their higher education; these scores are public and students can show them in the marketplace. In the United States, students in public-interest careers such as law, medicine, and nursing take licensing exams; a law student, for instance, cannot practice law unless she passes the bar exam.

In a market in which reputation depends on students' entry abilities, history matters. Incumbents have a clear advantage, and new, up-and-coming HEIs might face an uphill battle as they try to convey their quality. Exit and licensing exams can play an important role in this market. They contribute to efficiency by conveying information and to equity, since they inform about the human capital of graduates that otherwise would be presumed to be lower skilled than those of selective, more established incumbents. These exams, however, might face considerable resistance on the part of HEIs.

To summarize, market distortions justify policy intervention in higher education. Multiple tools are needed, yet preference should be given to those that create incentives for students and HEIs, enhance competition, enable student choice, rely on monitoring and accountability, and produce and disseminate information. Next we turn to the larger context of higher education, namely the labor market and the pre- and postcollege stages.

Higher Education and the Larger Context

As technological progress alters the structure of jobs and careers, individuals can expect to switch jobs more often throughout their lives, and even to switch careers altogether. Thus, some higher education programs in the region may need to become shorter, more streamlined, and more flexible, and professional requirements may need to change to facilitate individuals' transitions among fields later in life. Such changes, in turn, might imply challenges for the staff of HEIs. Furthermore, HEIs may need to strengthen their ties with the labor market and offer more options for lifelong learning.

An urgent concern is raising the academic readiness of high school graduates. While the region has made strides in the quantity of high school graduates, and this has been the main driver of higher education expansion, the region will not form skilled human capital at the desired rate unless it makes similar strides in the quality of high school graduates.

Higher education graduates will only be as productive as their environments enable them to be. Productivity, innovation, and entrepreneurship are the outcomes of an economic context and cannot be mandated from the outside. At this crossroads, then, the policy maker needs not only to zoom in to higher education but also to zoom out to the labor market, the pre- and postcollege stages, and the general economic context.

Note

1. For an excellent summary of these issues, see Castleman, Schwartz, and Baum 2015.

References

Castleman, B., S. Schwartz, and S. Baum. 2015. "Decision Making for Students Success: Behavioral Insights to Improve College Access and Persistence." Routledge. New York, NY.

Bound, J., M. Lovenheim, and S. Turner. 2010. "Why Have College Completion Rates Declined? An Analysis of Changing Student Preparation and Collegiate Resources". *American Economic Journal: Applied Economics* 2: 129–157.

Bound, J., M. Lovenheim, and S. Turner. 2012. "Increasing Time to Baccalaureate Degree in the United States." *Education Finance and Policy* 7 (4): 375–424.

Deming, D. J., and D. Figlio. 2016. "Accountability in U.S. Higher Education: Applying Lessons from K-12 Experience to Higher Education." *Journal of Economic Perspectives* 30 (93): 33–56.

Ferreyra, M. M., and P. Liang. 2012. "Information Asymmetry and Equilibrium Monitoring in Education." *Journal of Public Economics* 96 (1): 237–54.

MacLeod, B., E. Riehl, J. E. Saavedra and M. Urquiola. Forthcoming. "The Big Sort: College Reputation and Labor Market Outcomes. *American Economic Journal: Applied Economics.*

Glossary

Access rate. Proportion of the population ages 18–24 years ever enrolled in a higher education program (that is, those with incomplete or complete higher education degrees), expressed as a percentage of the total population ages 18–24 years.

Bachelor's program or degree. Identifies programs encompassed under the level 6 of the United Nations Educational, Scientific and Cultural Organization's (UNESCO's) International Standard Classification of Education (ISCED), but expands the definition to include the traditionally longer length of these programs in Latin America (three to six years of full-time study). Programs at this level are often designed to provide participants with intermediate academic or professional knowledge, skills, and competencies, leading to a first degree or equivalent qualification in higher education. They tend to be theoretically based, but may include practical components, and are informed by state-of-the-art research or best professional practice. They are traditionally offered by universities or equivalent institutions. These programs may also provide a pathway to second or further degree programs that are typically one to two years long, often professionally oriented and more specialized than the first degree. For further details, please consult UNESCO-UIS, *ISCED 2011* (2012).[1]

Completion rate (higher education). Proportion of the population ages 25–29 years with a complete higher education degree as a percentage of the population ages 25–29 years with at least some higher education (including those with incomplete and complete higher education degrees).

Completion rate (high school). Proportion of the population ages 18–24 years with a complete high school education degree as a percentage of the population ages 18–24 years.

Entry rate. Proportion of the population ages 18–24 years ever enrolled in a higher education program (that is, those with incomplete or complete higher education degrees), expressed as a percentage of the total population ages 18–24 years with complete high school degrees.

Gross enrollment rate. Total enrollment in higher education, regardless of age, expressed as a percentage of the total population ages 18–24 years.

Higher education. Identifies programs encompassed under the levels 5 and 6 of UNESCO's ISCED, which are labeled as short-cycle tertiary education, and bachelor's or equivalent level, respectively. Note that this definition of *higher education*, which includes undergraduate education only, is different from UNESCO's definition, which includes levels 5, 6, 7, and 8 (the latter two corresponding to master's or equivalent level, and doctoral or equivalent level, respectively),[2] because of this report's focus on higher education at the undergraduate level. Higher education follows and builds on high school education, providing learning activities in specialized fields of education, and aims at learning at a high level of complexity and specialization. Higher education includes what is commonly understood as academic education but also includes advanced vocational or professional education.

Net enrollment rate. Total enrollment in higher education of the population ages 18–24 years, expressed as a percentage of the total population ages 18–24 years.

Short-cycle program. Identifies programs encompassed under the level 5 of UNESCO's ISCED, but expands the definition to include the traditionally longer duration of these programs in Latin America (1.5 to 3.5 years of full-time study at the higher education level). This level captures the lowest level of higher education, and is best represented by postsecondary, practical, occupationally specific programs designed to provide participants with professional knowledge, skills, and competencies that prepare them to enter the labor market. These programs may also provide a pathway to other higher education programs. For further details, please consult UNESCO-UIS, ISCED 2011, 2012.

Notes

1. See the UNESCO website, http://www.uis.unesco.org/Education/Documents/isced-2011-en.pdf.
2. See the UNESCO website, http://www.uis.unesco.org/Education/Documents/isced-2011-en.pdf.

Environmental Benefits Statement

The World Bank Group is committed to reducing its environmental footprint. In support of this commitment, we leverage electronic publishing options and print-on-demand technology, which is located in regional hubs worldwide. Together, these initiatives enable print runs to be lowered and shipping distances decreased, resulting in reduced paper consumption, chemical use, greenhouse gas emissions, and waste.

We follow the recommended standards for paper use set by the Green Press Initiative. The majority of our books are printed on Forest Stewardship Council (FSC)–certified paper, with nearly all containing 50–100 percent recycled content. The recycled fiber in our book paper is either unbleached or bleached using totally chlorine-free (TCF), processed chlorine–free (PCF), or enhanced elemental chlorine–free (EECF) processes.

More information about the Bank's environmental philosophy can be found at http://www.worldbank.org/corporateresponsibility.